PART II

The Modes of Writing

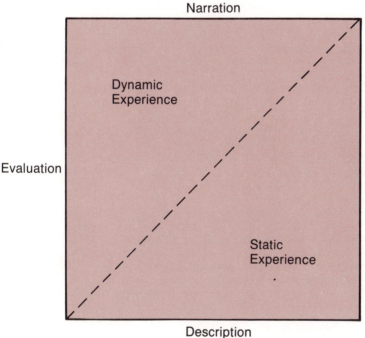

Writing in the Liberal Arts Tradition

WRITING IN THE LIBERAL ARTS TRADITION

A RHETORIC WITH READINGS

James L. Kinneavy
The University of Texas at Austin

William J. McCleary
Genesee Community College, New York

Neil Nakadate
Iowa State University

HARPER & ROW, PUBLISHERS, New York

*Cambridge, Philadelphia, San Francisco,
London, Mexico City, São Paulo, Singapore, Sydney*

Sponsoring Editor: Phillip Leininger
Project Editor: Ronni Strell
Text Design: Mina Greenstein
Cover Design: Abner Graboff
Text Art: Network Graphics
Production: Delia Tedoff
Compositor: Black Dot, Inc.
Printer and Binder: The Murray Printing Company

Library of Congress Cataloging in Publication Data

Kinneavy, James L., 1920-
   Writing in the liberal arts tradition.

   1. English language—Rhetoric.   2. College readers.
3. Humanities.   I. McCleary, William J.   II. Nakadate,
Neil.   III. Title.
PE1408.K6663   1985   808'.042   84-15838
ISBN 0-690-01522-4

85 86 87 88 9 8 7 6 5 4 3 2 1

Acknowledgments

CHAPTER 1

pp. 2–6, "Divorced Husband Demolishes House," "A Personal Letter," and "The Defense Attorney's Summary Plea to the Jury" are used with permission of Sara Liberta.

p. 7, "Divorced, Husband Demolishes House," by John Ciardi, from *In the Stoneworks,* published by Rutgers State University Press, 1961, New Brunswick, N.J. Reprinted with the permission of the author.

CHAPTER 2

pp. 23–27, "Once More to the Lake" - August 1941 - in *Essays of E. B. White,* by E. B. White, copyright 1941, 1969 by E. B. White. By permission of Harper & Row, Publishers, Inc.

pp. 27–29, "I Didn't Want to Move." Printed by permission of the author.

pp. 43–45, "Summer Beyond Wish," by Russell Baker. From *So This Is Depravity,* by Russell Baker. New York: Congdon & Weed, Inc. Copyright © 1980 by Russell Baker.

CHAPTER 3

pp. 48–50, Norman Cousins, "How to Make People Smaller Than They Are." Copyright 1978 by Saturday Review Magazine Corporation. Reprinted by permission of the author.

pp. 50–51, Bobbi Farrell, "Smoke." Printed by permission of the author.

p. 52, Delta Air Lines, "Delta is an airline run by more than 35,000 professionals." Untitled advertisement, 1982. Reprinted by permission of Delta Air Lines.

p. 70, U.S. Navy, "This Desk Can Reach Mach 2." Reprinted by permission.

pp. 71–72, John Robinson, "The Bambi Syndrome." Copyright © 1976 by *Harper's Magazine.* All rights reserved. Reprinted from the March 1976 issue by special permission.

pp. 73–77, Rachel Carson, "The Obligation to Endure." From *Silent Spring* by Rachel Carson. Copyright © 1962 by Rachel Carson. Reprinted by permission of Houghton Mifflin Company.

CHAPTER 4

pp. 84–87, "Gypsy Moth Control: A Divisive Question," by Shanya Panzer, April 8, 1979. © 1979 by the New York Times Company. Reprinted by permission.

pp. 88–91, Candee Douglass, "The Harp Seal: To Hunt or to Protect?" Printed by permission of the author.

CHAPTER 5

pp. 125–127, Reprinted by permission of the publisher from "Deceived Respondents: Once Bitten, Twice Shy," by Thomas Sheets, Allen Radlinski, James Kohne, G. Allen Brunner, *Public Opinion Quarterly,* col. 38, pp. 261–263. Copyright 1974 by the Trustees of Columbia University.

pp. 127–128, "Charges Weighed for Parents Who Let Baby Die Untreated," *New York Times,* UPI, April 16.

pp. 128–132, Ruth Goodhart, "Was It Ethical to Deny Baby Doe Medical Care?" Printed by permission of the author.

pp. 160–163, D. L. Rosenhan, "On Being Sane in Insane Places," *Science,* vol. 179, January 19, 1973, pp. 250–258. Copyright 1973 by the American Association for the Advancement of Science.

pp. 165–169, Bertrand Russell, "Committee of 100," from *A Matter of Life,* ed. by Clara Urquhart, copyright 1963 by Little Brown & Co., and Jonathan Cape Ltd. Reprinted by permission.

CHAPTER 6

pp. 174–180, Thor Heyerdahl, "A Theory," from *Kon-Tiki,* by Thor Heyerdahl. Copyright 1950 by Thor Heyerdahl. Published in the United States by Rand McNally & Company.

pp. 181–182, Andrew Eibl, "What Is Progress?" Printed by permission of the author.

pp. 202-204, Fred M. Hechinger, "SAT Scores: What Happened to the Best and the Brightest?" *Saturday Review/World,* Feb. 9, 1974. © 1974 Saturday Review Magazine Co. Reprinted by permission.

CHAPTER 7

p. 207, Robert Frost, "Design." From *The Poetry of Robert Frost*, edited by Edward Connery Lathem. Copyright 1936 by Robert Frost. Copyright © 1964 by Lesley Frost Ballantine. Copyright © 1969 by Holt, Rinehart and Winston. Reprinted by permission of Holt, Rinehart and Winston, Publishers.

p. 207, Stevie Smith, "Not Waving But Drowning." From Stevie Smith, *Selected Poems of Stevie Smith*. Copyright © 1964 by Stevie Smith. Reprinted by permission of New Directions Publishing Corporation, publishers and agents for the estate of Stevie Smith.

p. 208, Gary Snyder, "A Heifer Clambers Up." From Gary Snyder, *The Back Country*. Copyright © 1963 by Gary Snyder. Reprinted by permission of New Directions Publishing Corporation.

pp. 208–209, Susan Morrison, "The Diner." Copyright 1980 by Sketch Board. Reprinted by permission of Sketch Board and the author.

pp. 209–210, James Thurber, "The Unicorn in the Garden." Copyright © 1940 James Thurber. Copyright © 1968 Helen Thurber. From *Fables for Our Time*, published by Harper & Row. Reprinted by permission of Mrs. James Thurber.

pp. 210–211, W. S. Merwin, "The Dachau Shoe." In *The Miner's Pale Children*. Copyright © 1969, 1970, by W. S. Merwin. Reprinted with the permission of Atheneum Publishers.

pp. 211–217, Bruce Ouderkirk, "Together Again." Copyright 1978 by Sketch Board. Reprinted by permission of Sketch Board and the author.

pp. 230–235, Virginia Woolf, "The Legacy." From *A Haunted House and Other Stories*, by Virginia Woolf, copyright 1944, 1972 by Harcourt Brace Jovanovich, Inc. Reprinted by permission of the publisher. Reprinted by permission of the author's Literary Estate and The Hogarth Press.

p. 236, Jane Freese, "untitled." Copyright 1978 by Sketch Board. Reprinted by permission of Sketch Board and the author.

CHAPTER 8

p. 243, "The Goose That Laid the Golden Egg," from *Aesop's Fables*, edited by Elizabeth Stones, published by The Hyperion Press, copyright 1944.

p. 244, "Hipparchus' Classification of Stars According to Brightness," from *Astronomy Made Simple*, by Meir H. Degani. Copyright 1955 by Doubleday and Company, Inc.

pp. 244–245, Bernard DeVoto, "Who Is James K. Polk?" From *The Year of Decision: 1846*. Copyright 1943 by Houghton Mifflin Company.

pp. 245–246, William Glover, "Hawaii Musical a 'Drab Disaster'," *The Austin Statesman*, May 23, 1972, p. 16. Reprinted by permission of the Associated Press.

CHAPTER 9

pp. 255–263, Aleksandr I. Solzhenitsyn, "The Way of Life and Customs of the Natives" of *The Gulag Archipelago 1918–1956: An Experiment in Literary*

Investigation III-IV by Aleksandr I. Solzhenitsyn. Translated from the Russian by Thomas P. Whitney. Copyright © by Aleksandr I. Solzhenitsyn. English language translation copyright © 1975 by Harper & Row, Publishers, Inc. Reprinted by permission of Harper & Row, Publishers, Inc.

pp. 263–264, Maurice Algazi, "Description of a Mechanism: A Typewriter." Reprinted by permission of the author.

pp. 283–285, "Paris, France," *Illustrated World Encyclopedia,* One Volume Edition (Bobley Publishing Corporation, 1977). Published by permission of Bobley Publishing Corp.

CHAPTER 10

pp. 291–297, Bruno Bettelheim, "Joey: A 'Mechanical Boy.'" Copyright © 1959 by Scientific American, Inc. All rights reserved.

pp. 298–299, Diane Balmer, "Boris." Printed by permission of the author.

pp. 313, 316–317, Annie Dillard, "Learning to Stalk Muskrats." From pp. 190–192 in *Pilgrim at Tinker Creek,* by Annie Dillard. Copyright © 1974 by Annie Dillard. By permission of Harper & Row, Publishers, Inc.

pp. 314–315, Jerrold G. Simon, "How to Write a Resume." Copyright 1981 by International Paper Company. Reprinted by permission.

CHAPTER 11

pp. 321–324, Martin Luther King, Jr., "Pilgrimage to Nonviolence," from *Stride toward Freedom: The Montgomery Story,* by Martin Luther King, Jr. Copyright © 1958 by Martin Luther King, Jr. Reprinted by permission of Harper & Row, Publishers, Inc.

pp. 325–327, Robert Larry Ackridge, "Common Houseplants." Reprinted by courtesy of the author.

CHAPTER 12

pp. 351–363, Stephen Harrigan, "Life Behind Bars." Reprinted with permission from the February issue of *Texas Monthly.* Copyright 1981 by *Texas Monthly.*

pp. 363–364, "Spot Removers." Copyright 1979 by Consumers Union of United States, Inc., Mount Vernon, N.Y. 10553. Reprinted by permission from *Consumer Reports 1979 Buying Guide Issue.*

pp. 366–368, Danny Orange, "Salutatorian Speech, Johnston High School, 26 May 1981." Reprinted by permission of the author.

Contents

PART II: THE MODES OF WRITING

Preface

OUR ASSUMPTIONS AND ORGANIZATION

We believe that the study of the liberal arts has both a rich history and a vital place in contemporary life. Experience tells us that the result of a liberal education is the well-rounded person, one who has useful knowledge and basic skill in a number of fields.

The goal of learning to *write* "in the liberal arts tradition" is the well-rounded writer—a person with training and experience in a range of writing tasks, from term papers to poems and stories. We believe that well-rounded writing develops from knowledge and strategies that can be learned.

The main concern for a composition text, then, should be to teach a limited set of writing skills that is relevant and adaptable to many writing situations and tasks. Our solution to this concern is to teach the *thinking skills* that underlie the various types of writing; there are fewer categories of learnable thinking skills than of written forms. Our goal is to introduce all the basic kinds of writing in terms of the thought processes that support them and to give students practice in their use.

Our experience in teaching composition at three quite different institutions has convinced us that all developing writers benefit most from an understanding of (1) *why people write* and (2) *how successful writers look at or perceive* their subjects. The overall structure of this book, then, is based on *six major aims or purposes* of writing and *four major ways of perceiving and organizing* subject matter. Chapter 1 is an introduction to the text and to the aims or purposes of discourse discussed individually in the chapters that follow: self-expressing, persuading, informing, explaining and proving, exploring, and creating poems and stories. In each of these chapters we use representative readings to help explain the premises and processes behind specific types of writing tasks, whether the "logic" of this reasoning originates in the writer, the reader, the subject matter, or the creative potential of language itself. Chapter 8 is a brief introduction to what we call the "modes of writing," and it is followed by chapters on description, narration, defining and dividing, and evaluation. Each of these modes chapters also develops out of guided analyses of student and professional essays that reflect the relevant concerns of the topic in question.

In addressing ourselves to composition in terms of both the aims and the modes of writing, we have tried to provide students and instructors with a holistic overview and introduction. That is, our goal has been to provide a complete sense of the discipline of writing and to present the various types of writing both individually and as they relate to one another. It is customary, for example, for composition texts to include sections on persuasive discourse and on description; but often the important differences and connections between persuasion as *an aim* of writing and description as *a way of organizing* writing for any of the major purposes are ignored or obscured. Similarly, while most books discuss narrative writing, many fail to explain effectively the relationships between narration and the other possible ways of perceiving subjects—and thus the important distinctions and choices involved in organizing and developing them. Our two-part division of this book, and our systematic subdivision of the sections, is designed to promote an understanding of the distinctions and relationships among the purposes and strategies of writing that experienced writers understand but that developing writers are seldom shown.

This attempt to clarify the interrelationships among the aims and modes is carried through in individual chapters. For example, in our chapter on writing research papers (Chapter 4, Informing), we present research writing as one of three basic types of exposition, a kind of discourse related to yet different from explaining and proving (Chapter 5) and exploring (Chapter 6). In the chapter "Writing Poems and Stories" (Chapter 7), we reflect our awareness that while some composition courses involve creative units or assignments and many types of writing have creative components, the imaginative handling of language as one of the major aims of writing is not always addressed. (This is particularly ironic since composition is usually taught in English departments, where imaginative literature gets primary attention.) In part, Chapter 7 explains how what we often call "creative writing" relates to other purposes of writing and suggests that creativity in language is not limited to novelists and poets. Finally, the chapter on evaluation as a mode of organizing experience (Chapter 12) demonstrates that writing that compares and contrasts— description, definition, and division—is ultimately writing that helps us evaluate objects or entities by means of a value system, writing that assists us in making and revealing value judgments regarding what we compare and contrast. This is one of several instances in which we have tried to make clear the *productive application* of what might otherwise strike readers as merely academic distinctions and considerations.

OUR APPROACH TO TEACHING WRITING

All the major sections of the book—the six aims chapters and the four chapters on modes—develop from the simplest to the most complex and difficult. That is, they begin with assignments that are self-expressive or persuasive in aim or that involve the descriptive or narrative modes. By the same token, our chapters on research-based writing, on poems and stories, and on evaluative discourse are likely to strike both students and instructors as second-term or intermediate-level writing courses. With this in mind, a reasonable way to use this book would be sequentially, either by studying the aims first, by studying the modes first, or by following some kind of alternating sequence. At the same time, once both the aims and modes have been introduced into the course as working concepts (presumably, via Chapters 1 and 8), the individual aims and modes can be worked with in virtually any sequence determined by an instructor, course, or student audience.

Each chapter is organized according to the same basic pattern: the aim or mode is introduced in terms of a brief discussion of its importance; then, with the aid of student and professional essays, students are guided through prewriting, organizational, and stylistic considerations with an eye toward writing their own themes or papers. ("Prewriting" is a potentially misleading term; as the various chapters make clear, prewriting involves information gathering, topic selection and focus, on-paper brainstorming, and so on—a lot of preparatory writing even before the first real draft of a paper is begun.) Each subsection of a chapter contains exercises that contribute to understanding the principles and producing student essays.

We are aware that composition is concerned with both process and product. In the familiar controversy over "product versus process," the underlying question is whether an instructor or text should specify a certain type of writing—a product—and let students figure out the process of creating this product or whether students should be guided through a series of steps—a process—that if successfully completed would result in an appropriate product. This book combines the process and product approaches. We first show students examples of the type of product they will be asked to write and, by means of study questions, call attention to the key features that should appear in their own papers. This is the product emphasis. But we also take students step-by-step through the process of choosing an appropriate topic, inventing the material needed for the paper, and shaping and reshaping the material into the finished piece of writing.

We are convinced that in combining process and product in this way we gain the key advantages of both approaches—and follow the usual practice of most composition teachers, regardless of the textbook they use.

READING AND WRITING

Our decision to integrate readings with our explanations of the aims and modes of writing grew out of two basic considerations. First, we are aware of the proven usefulness in composition courses of reading material by both student and professional writers. A time-honored observation among teachers of writing is that perceptive reading ("decoding") and effective writing ("encoding") are complementary skills. Second, we wish to clarify not only the basic concepts but, more important, the *thinking processes* behind the aims and modes. We feel that analytical introductions, making use of representative concrete examples, are the most effective way to this. Our goal, then, is to provide readings illustrative of principles—but in such a way as to minimize the amount of classroom time required for the discussion of content and theme and, by contrast, to *stress rhetorical concepts and skills*. We feel that, when readings are used in a writing course, a student should understand, *as the reading of a given selection proceeds,* how this reading is related to the writing he or she will have to do.

Our inclusion of both professional and student writing in each chapter, as well as writing on a wide range of subjects, is meant to stress that despite variations in subject matter and complexity, the basic considerations in the writing of a given aim or more remain the same. At the same time, we make no claim to have included enough—or even the best—readings to satisfy all instructors. Some chapters contain supplementary readings, often connected with a final group of exercises and assignments, but from the beginning we have assumed that instructors may wish to supplement what we have provided with individual themes or professional essays of their own choosing.

The exercises we have provided at the end of each chapter and major section of a chapter are both instructive and suggestive. That is, a given set of exercises grows naturally out of the discussion of a particular section of the text, but at the same time these exercises are intended to provoke students and instructors into questions, suggestions, and variations on assignments. Some of the exercises provided are relatively short and are intended to help establish concepts, develop specific perceptions or skills, or contribute to the invention process. Other exercises are concerned with the ultimate need to coordinate and synthesize perceptions and skills in the writing of a complete theme or paper.

Users of this book will find that the exercises for Chapters 4, 5, and 6—on informing, explaining and proving, and exploring—guide students more systematically to the writing of their own papers than the exercises for the other chapters on the major purposes of writing. Since writing done for the expository aims is frequently longer and more evidence-oriented than other types, and since such writing tends toward set formats and patterns, we feel that students and instructors would welcome a suggested (though not ironclad) sequence of considerations and steps. Chapter 4, which includes our discussion of the gathering and presentation of research materials, is a relevant case in point. By contrast, Chapters 2, 3, and 7—on self-expression, persuasion, and the writing of poems and stories—contain exercises that are more free-wheeling and discrete. That is, the exercises in these chapters are less interdependent on one another and more spontaneous, as seems appropriate in writing that derives from the wide variety and numerous possibilities of writers, readers, and styles of language.

Because of features like those described here and others besides, many instructors and students will find this book significantly different from any textbook for writing they have used before. We hope this difference proves rewarding. We have been teaching composition in this way for many years because we find it both stabilizing and productive to be able to set out clear basic criteria for various types of papers and to apply those criteria in grading the papers. In the end, the result is a high percentage of successful writing, because students know where they are supposed to be going and some useful steps to take in getting there.

James L. Kinneavy
William J. McCleary
Neil Nakadate

THE AIMS
OF WRITING

PART I

Introduction to the Aims of Writing

AN AUDIENCE, A PURPOSE, AND SOMETHING TO SAY

The next time you find yourself talking to someone, ask yourself, "Why am I talking?" You will invariably find that you feel you have someone to talk to, something you want to say, and a specific purpose for saying it. Consider each of these factors of the basic communications situation—audience, purpose, subject matter. Do you use the same language when you talk to your friends as you do to a prospective employer? Do you write personal letters in the same style as lab reports for a biology class? Would you write up an account of a football game using language in the same way as for a history paper? It seems obvious that—by the complex nature of human experience—audience, purpose, and subject matter constantly change and interact to influence the ways we use language.

Yet it is precisely the writer's failure to pay attention to differences in audiences, purposes, and subject matters that lies at the root of most failures in composition. Consequently, it is well worth taking the time to consider some of these crucial differences.

A typical person's list of the uses of language might look like this:

to get someone to do something (e.g., loan you his or her car)
to amuse someone (e.g., tell a joke)
to exchange ideas or opinions
to explain something

to tell a story
to stimulate or inspire
to express beliefs (e.g., in a pledge, creed, or oath)
to influence behavior (e.g., in an ad or in a political speech)
to describe a scene
to express emotions or desires
to react to something that has happened
to give instructions
to convey knowledge
to prove something
to solve problems
to protest (e.g., a student or political demonstration)
to draw sympathy or attention to yourself
to enjoy yourself (e.g., go to a movie, read a novel)
to ask questions or pose problems
to get information (e.g., read the classified ads)
to get something off your chest
to test something (e.g., in an examination)

This list graphically demonstrates the complexity and the diversity of our communications life. Yet the *basic purposes* of language use are not infinite—in fact, they can be reduced to a manageable few. These basic purposes can be seen in the examples that follow, all different from one another, but all concerned with the same subject matter. Note that not only do the purposes of the respective selections differ, but so do the audiences and circumstances. The subject actually appeared first in a news item in a local newspaper. Then the poet, John Ciardi, created a poem from the news story. A teacher wrote the fictional versions of the wife's letter, the lawyer's defense, and the news story.

As you read each example, pay special attention to what you can learn from the text about the writer, the intended audience, the circumstances surrounding the writing, and the purpose of the message. Keep in mind while reading that one of the keys to good writing is recognizing such differences and adapting to the organizational patterns, conventions, and styles appropriate to various circumstances.

A NEWSPAPER ARTICLE

Divorced, Husband Demolishes House

1   Curtis Williams, 54, of Oak Manor Apartments, No. 126, hired a bulldozer and demolished his former home yesterday.

2   Williams went into action shortly after receiving his final divorce decree from his wife of twenty-seven years, Vera Williams, 52, of 1624 Springfield Road.

3   Mrs. Williams, who filed the petition for divorce, had requested that she be granted the family home in the division of their community property. Despite Williams' protests, the presiding judge awarded the house to Mrs. Williams.

4   Then Williams decided to take matters into his own hands.

5   When reached at her mother's home, Mrs. Williams said she is furious. She added that she is going to get her lawyer to file suit against Williams again tomorrow. She plans to charge her ex-husband with disturbing the peace, destroying her private property, and causing her severe mental anguish.

A PERSONAL LETTER

1   I just can't believe it! Of all the nerve! After all the years I worked and struggled to keep that house together. Now Curtis has gone and torn it down. He's really done it this time!

2   If it hadn't been for me, it would have fallen down years ago. Because he never would do anything to keep the house up. He was always going to do it, but he never got around to it unless I kept after him. I bet I had to nag him a week for every nail he ever put into the repair or the upkeep of that house.

3   He kept putting things off. Of course, if it was his boat or his camp, that had to be tended to on time. That was important! His boat had to be ready for summer fishing and his camp had to be ready for deer hunting in the winter. That was important! But the house didn't matter.

4   Besides, he always said I had everything I needed. He liked to point to all the appliances and say that I had all the gadgets on the market. What he didn't tell was that half of them didn't work most of the time.

5   Like the washing machine. Sure, I had all the modern appliances. But I was on my third washing machine—I had already worn out two—before I ever got any hot water to wash with. Right after World War II, when things were still hard to get, he had run a skinny little quarter-inch pipe to my washer connection. He claimed that was all he could get, and he promised to change it as soon as he could ever get some larger pipe. For all these years, whenever I turned the hot water on, all I got was a little dribble.

6   Then last summer I made a wedding dress for Susie, the girl across the street, and her daddy came and put in a decent-sized hot water pipe. And he installed the dishwasher Curtis had given me for Christmas six months before. As usual, Curtis was on a fishing trip.

7   You see, Curtis never would hire anybody to work on the house. He wouldn't hire a carpenter, or an electrician, or a plumber. And he wouldn't let me hire them either. He always said he could do that work himself and save the money. He could do the work.

9   But don't worry, he's not going to get away with this. I'll sue him for everything he's got. I'll get his boat, his horses, his camp! Oh no! He's not going to get away with this!

THE DEFENSE ATTORNEY'S SUMMARY PLEA TO THE JURY

1   Ladies and gentlemen of the jury, you are now charged with the grave responsibility of determining whether my client should be stripped of his few possessions to satisfy the demands of the woman who has freely confessed herself to be a perpetually nagging wife.

2   I ask you now to put yourselves in the place of poor Curtis Williams, the husband who painfully endured Vera Williams' complaints for over twenty-seven years. You have heard Williams' neighbors testify to his goodness—to his kindness and generosity. I ask you, ladies and gentlemen, is it any wonder that after all those years of frustrating endurance this kind and generous man was finally moved to an act of violence? Who better than he had the right to the house he had built with his own hands? And when he was denied that right, what could he do?

3   Surely we all agree with someone who said long ago that "A man's home is his castle."

4   Williams has testified under oath that his wife had never properly appreciated the home he had struggled so much to build for her in the early years of their marriage. This noble husband himself raised the ridge pole, shaped the walls—indeed, he built the entire house from foundation to roof. And all Vera Williams could do was complain because the water pipe was too small or the dishwasher wasn't installed quickly enough to suit her fancy.

5   You have heard an eminent psychiatrist testify that when the judge awarded the house to Mrs. Williams, Curtis Williams was in a state of extreme frustration. He felt a deep sense of loss. He could no longer communicate with his former wife. Indeed, he knew that she would continue to scorn his cozy little cottage and that she would endlessly berate him to their friends and neighbors every time some minor problem arose. In his own words, he "wanted to end all the fussing and nagging."

6   And so, denied the right to his castle, Williams determined that it should come down.

7   Now I am certain that you good ladies and gentlemen of the jury would not wish to cause further pain and suffering to this fine man who has already been through so much. And I have full confidence that you will see that justice is served in this case. You will deny Vera Williams' vain demands. You will leave Curtis Williams in full possession of his few pleasures, his horses, and his boat, and his humble little camp.

A POEM

A POEM

Divorced, Husband Demolishes House
News Item

It is time to break a house
What shall I say to you
but torn tin and the shriek
of nails pulled orange
from the ridge pole? Rip it
and throw it away. Beam
by beam. Sill, step, and lintel.
Crack it and knock it down.
Brick by brick. (I breathe
the dust of openings. My tongue
is thick with plaster. What can I
say to you? The sky has come
through our rafters. Our windows
are flung wide and the wind's
here. There are no doors
in or out.) Tug it
and let it crash. Haul it,
bulldoze it over. What can I say
to you except that nothing
must be left of the nothing
I cannot say to you? It's
done with. Let it come down.

John Ciardi

THE COMMUNICATION PROCESS AND THE AIMS OF WRITING

Let us pick out some important distinctions among the four examples by making some useful observations about the communication process.

WRITERS. One set of observations might be made about the writers of these various pieces. The writer of the news story is an unidentified reporter who is neutral toward the subject and does not intrude with personal views nor take sides, as do the other three writers. By contrast, Mrs. Williams is very involved in her letter, refers to herself explicitly 20 times, is emotional, excited, and obviously subjective and one-sided. The lawyer, although not as subjective and upset as Mrs. Williams, also intrudes and takes sides, as he should; he refers to himself six times, presumably to impress the jury. Finally, in the poem, John Ciardi provides the title and subtitle, but then in effect turns things over to the divorced husband. The husband then offers us a statement from a perspective unlike all the others.

AUDIENCES.   An even more important set of observations concerns the audiences of the four selections. One of the distinctive characteristics of the poem (and much other literature we read) is the assumption of more than one reader or hearer—that is, a complex audience. The actual readers of the poem are the subscribers to the magazine in which Ciardi's poem first appeared and those who purchase his subsequent books of poetry. The listener directly addressed by the husband within the poem is not identified, even though he (or she or they) is referred to as *you* three times and asked to help in the ripping, throwing, cracking, and knocking down. All of this makes for a fairly complex sense of audience in the poem. However, in each of the other three examples, the audience is fairly simple and quite distinct. The readers of the news story would ordinarily be local residents who subscribe to the local paper; they are assumed, but are neither mentioned nor identified in the story. The reader of the wife's letter is undoubtedly familiar with her family affairs, but this reader's influence is as unimportant as the influence of the newspaper reader. In fact, the recipient of the letter is just a sounding board for Mrs. Williams' reactions. In a sense the situation of the lawyer is the opposite, because to him the jury (his "readership") is all-important. As a matter of fact, the jury is mentioned directly 13 times, and the feelings, sense of fairness, prejudices, and basic humanity of its members are strongly appealed to and therefore "intrude into" the lawyer's speech.

It seems clear from this brief survey that writers "come across" and readers are addressed quite differently in different kinds of writing.

SITUATIONS OR CONTEXTS.   Note the situations or working contexts for the writers and readers of the selections. The reporter of the news story covers her territory and writes her story to meet a deadline in, what is for her, a routine manner; typical readers probably pick up their papers, sit down in comfortable settings, and start their own routine of "catching up on the news." The tone of the letter implies some sporadic correspondence between Mrs. Williams and her confidant, presumably a friend or relative who has been confided in before. In the four examples, this is probably the most informal of the situations. By contrast, the lawyer's summary defense is set in a very conventional situation in which years of tradition have established the basic relationships between speaker and listener. (Nevertheless, the lawyer does manage to inject into this solemn occasion a homely and friendly tone.)

But the situational contexts of the writer and reader of poetry are quite different from those of all the other selections. Unlike the first three sets of readers, readers of poetry who buy a magazine such as *Poetry* are a fairly small elite. The poet, sensitive to a tragic news story, decides to shape an aspect of the incident into a work of art. He writes in the conventions of much modern poetry (there is no rhyme, the rhythms do not follow those of traditional poetry, and so on), and many readers who can understand the other selections might well be puzzled at first by this kind of writing and its situation.

MEDIA.   Obviously the communications medium used in each case is significantly different and has a specific effect. The newspaper story employs the traditional journalistic format; Mrs. Williams discharges her feelings in a personal letter, a common vehicle for self-expression; the defense lawyer gives his summary argument in a speech; and Ciardi's small lyric poem is published in a magazine. These very different media are appropriate to the contrasting circumstances of communication in which the different writers and readers find themselves.

PURPOSES OR AIMS.   Finally, the most important feature separating these samples of writing is the clear difference of aim or purpose from one to the other. The news story is intended to convey information, and it does this accurately and concisely. The defense plea, by contrast, is much lower in information content, but is designed to persuade the jurors to allow Williams to retain his "few possessions." Mrs. Williams' letter does contain some information, but information really isn't the point; the key concern for her is that she give vent to her feelings. The poem is probably the least informative of all; its purpose is to delight the lover of poetry by conveying a human experience.

These four basically different purposes—to convey information, to persuade, to express the self, and to create literature—are given considerable attention in the rest of this book because all are fundamental aims of discourse; their respective strategies are very different from one another and require extended analysis and explanation. The strategies for informing are vastly different from those of persuading, and these in turn are quite different from those for self-expression; the strategies and skills for writing literature are equally specialized.

The four basic purposes or aims of discourse—self-expression, persuasion, exposition (which includes informing), and literature—can be remembered by means of a simple diagram. We can represent the key elements of the communication process by drawing a triangle on which the points and the center stand for the writer, the reader, the subject matter referred to by the writing, and the language structure of the writing itself (see Figure 1.1). As we have seen in analyzing the four examples, *self-expression* tends to focus on or emphasize the writer; *persuasion* concentrates the power of the communication on exerting an effect on the reader; *exposition* uses the power of communication to refer to subject matter as effectively as possible; and *literature* pays particular attention to

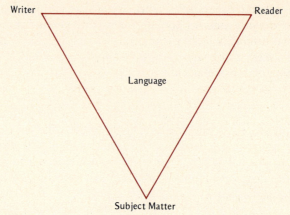

FIGURE 1.1. The major parts of the communication process.

such language characteristics as plot, characterization, rhythm, symbol, and dialogue.

Most writing does not attempt to achieve all of these aims at the same time. Most writings have a single dominant aim and subordinate the others, avoiding the conflicts and confusion that would result from one aim getting in the way of another. Figure 1.2, a variation on the basic communication triangle, illustrates the aims of writing and indicates the relationship between these basic purposes and each major element of the communication process.

In practice, of course, none of the writing purposes or aims is "pure": the aims sometimes overlap. As we have seen, the letter of self-expression contains considerable information. The lawyer's defense plea, persuasive in purpose, also contains a restricted but important amount of information.

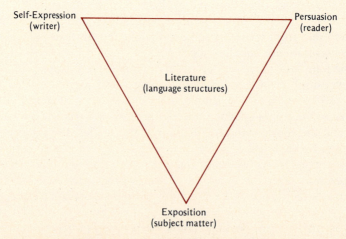

FIGURE 1.2. The major aims of writing.

Sometimes a given piece of writing can actually satisfy several interlocking aims. An example of this is *The Diary of a Young Girl*, by Anne Frank. This book was originally intended to be an instrument of self-expression in response to a frightening and oppressive situation. But it is also informative, or expository; it is extremely persuasive (it even precipitated anti-German riots in Holland when it first appeared); and finally, it is widely taught and read today as an example of literature. In placing Anne Frank's diary among the major aims of writing, we might better envision the aims as points on a pyramid rather than on a triangle. This is more sophisticated because the three-dimensional figure (see Figure 1.3) not only illustrates the basic aims, but also suggests the infinite overlap possibilities of dominant and subordinate aims. In the pyramid of Figure 1.3 Anne's diary is represented by the ball. This indicates an initial and perhaps dominant aim of self-expression; but, as the arrows indicate, self-expression is clearly linked to the other three purposes of writing—persuasion, exposition, and literature.

There are, of course, numerous variations of each aim or purpose. The list that follows categorizes some examples of each. Most people have encountered all of these in their personal or educational lives, and most could add many other examples to each list. Some are more commonly encountered in speaking than in writing, but all of them can be written.

You can see that the list under Exposition is subdivided into three large categories: Information, Exploration, and Explaining and Proving. The reasons for these subdivisions of expository writing will be explained in subsequent chapters. For now, it is enough to say that while the *overall aim* is similar, the *specific writing skills* used to inform are quite different from those of exploration, and both of these sets of skills differ in

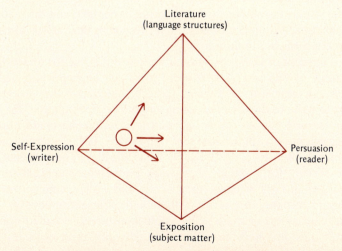

FIGURE 1.3.   The major aims of writing (II).

SOME COMMON EXAMPLES OF DIFFERENT AIMS OF LANGUAGE

Self-Expression	*Literature*	*Exposition*	*Persuasion*
Of Individuals	Short stories	Information	Advertising
Conversation	Jokes	News articles	Political
Journals	Ballads	Reports	speeches
Diaries	Folk songs	Textbooks	Religious
Gripe sessions	TV plays	Summaries	sermons
Prayer	Drama	Encyclopedia	Legal oratory
	Movies	articles	Editorials
Of Groups	Novels		
Protests	Poems	Exploration	
Myths	Epics	Dialogues	
Contracts		Seminars	
Religious credos		Discussions	
Declarations		Proposed	
Manifestos		solutions	
Utopia plans		to problems	
Laws		Diagnosis	
		Explaining and	
		Proving	
		Scientific reports	
		Research studies	
		Legal briefs	
		Mathematical	
		theorems	

important ways from those needed for explaining and proving. (Keep in mind that each aim of writing must be approached through an understanding of the writer, the audience, the situation or context, and the medium of communication. While not of equal importance in the various aims, each of these concerns is common to all.)

This concept of skill separation is an important one for understanding the strategy of this text. The concept has been an important one since Isocrates, an educator in ancient Greece, compared the processes of learning to write to those of becoming an athlete. For example, the novice wrestler learned various holds and positions before he could engage in actual competition with a variety of opponents. Today, learning to be a tennis player often involves the same basic strategy. The beginner might practice serving for a while, then work on her backhand, then try to improve her ground strokes, then serve and volley, and so on. In a match—and certainly in a series of them with different opponents and on different courts—all of these skills would eventually be called upon; but the player must first have developed the individual basic skills.

In composition, too, a person needs certain basic skills. Fundamental grammar and vocabulary skills, for example, are obviously necessary for effective writing. But there are also writing skills that have to do with planning different types of papers, with collecting information, with strategies of different kinds of proof and explanation, with techniques of adapting to different kinds of audiences, and so on. Student writers usually find it useful to single these skills out for special attention. As you advance through this book, you will develop a repertoire of skills that—as they accumulate—should make each new chapter easier to tackle.

In addition, you should be aware that the skills introduced in the following chapters are closely related to "real world" writing; these skills are far from academic abstractions. To cite one type of example, many professional writers and many middle-level executives in industry and government produce different types of what is here called informative writing. This writing includes different "assignments," such as news stories, financial reports, and medical records. But the broad group of writers suggested by these examples shares the basic obligation to convey accurate, factual information. The need to do informative writing is routinely, even frequently encountered in the real world by everyone from dogcatchers to doctors. The same is true of writing done for each aim of writing previously discussed and those to come in subsequent chapters.

Exercises on the Aims of Writing

1. Select what you would consider a typical day of the week for you, and keep a record of the different uses of language you engage in. Thus, reading news stories in the paper would be expository (informative), convincing a friend to let you use his or her car would be persuasive, watching a drama or a comedy on television would be literary, and griping about your instructor would be expressive.
2. Select a typical day of the week, and keep a record of what percentage of the communications you engage in during the day involve the act of writing, the act of reading (someone else's work), the act of listening, and the act of speaking.
3. Take a newspaper or a magazine and check the distribution of the aims of writing in it. If there is serious overlap of aims in a given text, give fractional credits. This exercise can be varied by comparing two newspapers or two magazines.
4. Select a radio or a television station and categorize the different programs and advertisements by dominant aim. You might vary this exercise by comparing several stations.
5. Try your hand at turning a short news story into a persuasive plea related to some aspect of the story, or an expressive piece on the part of one of the participants, or even a poem.

6. Change the direction of the previous exercise by taking a poem you like and rewriting the information it contains in the form of a news story or a piece of persuasion.
7. If you have listened to a sermon lately, extract the new information you learned from it, and write a short summary of this information. How much information does your sermon contain? If you haven't heard a sermon lately, try this exercise with a political speech.
8. Find a typical piece of persuasive writing (for example, an ad, a sermon, or a political speech) and attempt to determine its audience, the circumstances of its composition, whatever you can about the author, what his or her various general and particular purposes might be, the medium and whatever you can find about it as a medium (for example, the general political, religious, and other biases of the newspaper or magazine), and the typical readers of the medium.

WRITING AS A PROCESS

The first part of this chapter sets up goals for the written discourse you wish to produce: your writing should speak to a consciously intended audience, and it should express an attitude, persuade to a position, transmit information, prove some point(s), explore a subject, or use language to create literature. Each of these specific goals is examined systematically in one of the next six chapters.

But what about the important question of *how* to write? Knowing the *aims* of discourse or *why* to write partially determines the answer. (Just how, in specific situations, will become clear as you read through the following chapters.) But the goal does not totally determine the process; there are different ways of producing steel, candy, dresses—and writing. Some ways are more efficient than others.

A good deal of research in the past twenty years has revealed some insights about the composing process that can save you hours of unproductive writing. If the results of this research can be crystallized into a simple assertion, it is this: Good writing is the result of paying close attention to the *process* through which it is being developed. This statement requires an explanation.

To begin with, you should write with a concern for the process even more than the product of your work. That is, if you are interested in the final product of your efforts to the extent that you pay no particular attention to such matters as preliminary information gathering, outlines and strategies, trial drafts, and rewriting, then the resulting product will probably be disappointing. The production of a well-written paper should be like the production of a Broadway play, a movie, a good wine, or a good automobile: The *how* of the production is crucial, and there ought to be quality checks all along the way.

A second point concerning writing as a process is this: The notion that good writing can be dashed off in one impromptu burst of creative inspiration and energy is simply misleading, whether we're talking about a great poem, a piece of historical writing, a business report, or a dissertation in mathematics. Occasionally, it might seem as though such an inspired process actually takes place. But upon examination, such instances reveal that the writer had been thinking about the subject for months or years, had been investigating it for some time, or had written on the topic in other situations—or perhaps all of these. Journalists, writing on a daily basis, have to pound their beats—the police station, the football stadium and locker room, the legislature—and then write their stories. Authors and other professional writers comb libraries, interview celebrities, conduct computer searches, dig in archives, and in general, gather and assemble information before they write. A sustained and coherent procedure underlies virtually all successful compositions.

A given piece of writing may actually be the product of a long and trying process. Ernest Hemingway, for example, is said to have rewritten the last chapter of *A Farewell to Arms* 17 times. Another example is this textbook, which began as a syllabus for a college composition course and has gone through three complete series of reviews, each one followed by extensive discussion among the authors and editors and by several revisions of the manuscript.

If experienced writers of one kind or another have to research, solicit the opinions of others, write, listen to reviews and editors, then rewrite and write some more, what must the student writer do? Like all other writers, a student writer needs *to understand and to undertake writing as a process.*

The long tradition of the teaching and learning of writing identifies a stage of thinking and inventing, a stage of organizing and arranging these thoughts, and a stage of paying attention to the style through which the thoughts and arrangements can be expressed. Modern students and teachers of writing, taking advantage of recent research, stress terms such as *planning*, *producing text*, and *revising*. This text combines the traditional with the modern but tries to avoid a serious misinterpretation under which both of these views of process have suffered. Specifically, it is possible to view planning, producing text, and revising as stages moving in a one-way line, without any second-guessing or backtracking into previous stages, or any looking forward to later ones. But such a linear view erroneously assumes the process to be a series of rigidly sequential independent steps, with no inventing done in the organizing stage, no stylistic considerations made until the end, and so on.

This is an incorrect assumption. Recent research has shown that though one or another phase of the writing process might be emphasized at a given time, any of the other phases might come into consideration or reconsideration as well. For example, we know that not only do experienced writers revise more than inexperienced ones, but also that they revise at virtually all stages of the writing process, not just when taking a last look at style and mechanics. We know that, even as they approach the end of their work, experienced writers readjust their thoughts about major or minor points, make further decisions about style, reorganize their work into larger or smaller units, and so on.

Yet another writing-as-a-process principle that underlies each chapter of this book is that the smallest parts and the overall whole of a given piece of writing usually change and develop in relation to each other. Contrary to what many assume (and what some textbooks suggest), effective writing is not a simple process of beginning with the smallest parts and working up to the larger and more complex.

It might seem simplest to start writing with word, phrase, and sentence units, move on to paragraphs, and end with complete themes, in what we might call a part-to-whole approach. But in reality, successful writers don't work this way any more than builders start building by laying down individual bricks. A person who wishes to construct a building begins with a fairly definite notion of the kind of building needed, then considers such factors as the building's various purposes or uses, its size, its location, and its cost. Will it be a bank, a condominium, or a fire station? Will it be located downtown or in the suburbs? How many people will it serve or house? How will its presence affect surrounding buildings? and so on. The builder hires an architect to draw up a full set of plans before a single brick (or load of lumber or roll of wallpaper) is purchased; the builder also hires a consultant to do an environmental impact study; and so on until the project has been considered from all foreseeable perspectives.

However, the process of writing can be more demanding in its way than the work of the builder. Most of the time the builder, architect, impact consultant, and interior designer of a piece of prose are the same person—you, the writer. Although you must obviously begin with some general idea of what your final piece will do, you usually can't foresee every situation and concern; your plans are subject to continual changes as you work with the various aspects of your composition. The large whole you foresee is affected by your available materials or parts (ideas, information, vocabulary, and so on), and you modify that developing whole in order to account for and use these parts. Occasionally new material comes to light, or your conception of the whole shifts, with corresponding impact on the various parts. This back-and-forth play between parts and whole goes on until you feel justified in stopping.

THE ORGANIZATION AND STRATEGY OF THIS BOOK

Since the learning of writing is closely allied to the learning of reading, each chapter of this book begins with a careful reading and analysis of one or more samples of the kind of writing under consideration. You are asked

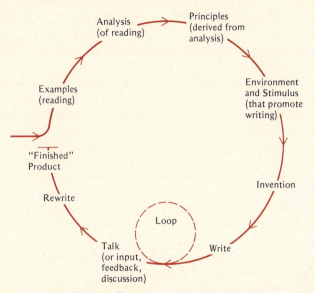

FIGURE 1.4.   One view of the writing process.

to read the samples with very specific questions in mind—questions regarding *how the selections are written*. In answering these questions, you will be analyzing the selection so as to discover some of the fundamental writing principles of concern in the chapter. In short, this book develops in terms of reading and analysis as the first stages in the writing process.

Figure 1.4 gives you an overview of this process. The large circle shows the general movement of the writing process, and the smaller dotted circle within the larger one represents the possibility of "looping back" at any time to a previous stage or even several stages. The smaller circle is looked upon as a ball that can roll freely back and forth inside the larger one.

After a few general observations on the importance of the skill being studied, the remainder of the chapter follows a circuit around the larger circle, but with occasional loopings back to the talk stage for feedback from peers or instructor and second-guessing by you. For example, reorganizing or rewriting may occur at almost any of the latter stages, and stylistic decisions can be made at any time. Exercises are usually provided at each major stage.

The general picture that should emerge from this view and introduction to the process of writing is that of continually drafting, rethinking, and improving any given paper. There is not just one reading or writing; there are several, and the paper will be much better than otherwise because of these multiple examinations and reworkings.

Exercises on Writing Practices and Processes

1. Interview a local writer about his or her writing practices. Ask how the writer learned how to write, warms up to tasks, conducts research, develops a routine for writing, revises, and so on. Report on this to your class.
2. Select one of the following writers and consult a biography regarding his or her writing practices: Virginia Woolf, Ernest Hemingway, Pearl Buck, John Henry Cardinal Newman, James Michener, Flannery O'Connor.
3. Interview one of the faculty members on your campus who writes for publication. Ask him or her questions like those suggested in exercise 1 above. If your writer does both academic and popular writing, ask him or her to compare and contrast any differences in habits in the writing process.
4. If you have available a specimen of your own writing from high school, reexamine it in the light of your knowledge of and attitude toward its topic now. Would you rewrite it if you had an occasion to? Would the rewrite improve it? If so, in what ways? Rewrite it and submit the earlier and the later versions to several of your fellow students, but with any identifying marks of the versions removed. What is their verdict about the two versions?
5. In light of what you have discovered about different purposes and audiences in writing, can you think of some examples of writing you have seen in the past that would have benefited from being oriented to a different purpose or a different audience? How is rewriting related to changes of purpose or audience?

Expressing Yourself

THE IMPORTANCE OF SELF-EXPRESSION

"Know thyself" comes down to us from the ancient writers as one of the most important prescriptions for a happy and successful life. And, whether we do it consciously or not, most of us expend much effort in pursuit of knowledge about ourselves. We keep diaries, we talk endlessly about ourselves to others, we sift the comments of our friends to discover what they think of us, and, occasionally, we engage in autobiographical writing.

Of course, we do not always write autobiographically in order to know ourselves, but when we do have that purpose, the writing is called expressive discourse, or self-expression. For many people, it is the most enjoyable and profitable writing they do, and the prevalence of autobiographical books on the best seller lists and of autobiographical essays in popular magazines gives evidence that many readers must also enjoy it.

Let us consider, then, why "knowing thyself" is so important. We are all familiar with people who seem prone to tragedy. They have auto accidents. They go from one unhappy marriage to another. They start projects and quit. Or there are the people who seek friendship and fail: they talk too much, they stab their friends in the back, they enlist their friends in unwise adventures. Finally, we see people engaged in hopeless struggle with the world around them—building houses in flood plains, planning to become engineers even though they fail at math, or concentrating all their efforts on a career in professional sports despite the odds against success. We see all of this daily, and we wonder why these people don't know themselves. Perhaps they don't engage in introspection, or perhaps they try and fail. Whatever the reason, we easily recognize the importance of self-expression (and self-knowledge) for our own happiness.

There are two general types of self-expression—personal and group. Personal self-expression is done by individuals who write about themselves in diaries, essays, and autobiographies. Group self-expression may also be written by individuals, but in this case the individuals write about a group they belong to, seeking to identify the character of the group and to work out relationships with other groups and with society at large. Examples of group self-expression include manifestos, declarations of independence, creeds, and pledges of allegiance.

In this chapter we shall concentrate just on personal self-expression, in particular the short autobiographical pieces often called *personal essays*. For this type of essay you will write about one of your experiences or a series of related experiences. The purpose will be to help you extract meaning—some sort of knowledge about yourself—from the experience. The topics of your essays need not be adventures, although adventures are not ruled out; any experience that you believe to have been important in your life makes a satisfactory topic for this assignment.

SOME EXAMPLES OF SELF-EXPRESSIVE ESSAYS

Let us examine two examples of self-expressive essays, one by a profession-al writer and the second by a student. You should first check through the prereading activities that follow (comments on vocabulary and some study questions), then read the two essays, and finally come back and work through the study questions carefully. The prereading activities deal only with the professionally written example; we will discuss the student example at the end of the chapter.

Prereading Activities for "Once More to the Lake," by E. B. White

VOCABULARY.   There aren't many difficult words in White's essay —if one is a fisherman and a New Englander. But since many readers are neither fishermen nor New Englanders, the following definitions may be helpful.

New Englanders use the word *camp* to refer to buildings that in other parts of the country are called *cabins* or *cottages*. These vacation homes range from one-room shacks to near-mansions with swimming pools and many rooms.

Several of the terms refer to *baits* used to catch fish. A *hellgramite* is the larva of a dobson fly; in other parts of the country the hellgramite is called a *dobson* or a *grampus*. *Plugs* and *spinners* are artificial baits, usually manufactured to resemble a minnow. Plugs are usually carved out of wood or plastic and actually look like minnows; spinners have slender bodies and feature large, flashy pieces of metal that revolve (spin) as they are pulled through the water. Fish think that spinners are minnows, but no one else would believe it.

Ordinarily, the sporting aspect of fishing is to *fight* the fish, but some fish don't fight and can simply be dragged into the boat. One of these is the mackerel, so when White says that they pulled in the bass like a mackerel, he means they didn't let the bass fight. The *bass* here are probably small-mouth black bass, fish that seldom grow very large but will put up a vigorous battle if allowed.

Boats may be powered either by *inboard* or *outboard* motors. Inboard motors resemble automobile engines and are permanently built into the stern of the boat. They are entirely enclosed and therefore fairly quiet. Outboard motors are detachable and are simply fastened onto the stern of a boat. This exposed position makes them rather noisy, but their relatively low cost has caused them to become the most popular power plant for fishing boats.

Finally, White refers to "the small steamboat that had a long rounded stern like the lip of a Ubangi." The *World Book Encyclopedia* says that "Ubangi is the nickname given to the women members of the Sara, an African Negro tribe living near the Ubangi River in the Central African Republic. Many of the women wear flat wooden disks in their pierced lips." (The name was bestowed on the Sara by Ringling Brothers and Barnum and Bailey Circus, which brought several of these women to the United States in the 1930s.)

ORGANIZATION. It is often helpful in reading and analyzing a piece of writing to be able to observe the sequence, or organization, that the author is following. This will not only show you one way to organize your own papers, but it will also help you see how the various parts relate to each other. As might be expected with any recital of an experience, the organization is chronological, beginning with the idea for the trip, and then proceeding through the trip to the lake, arrival, the first day, the rest of the week, and finally the grasping of the full meaning of the experience. This organization can easily be seen as follows (the numbers in parentheses are the paragraph numbers):

    I.   Introduction (1–3)
        A. Remembering the lake
        B. Deciding to revisit it
        C. Going to the lake
        D. Arriving
        E. Description of the cabin

II.   The first morning (4–6)
    A. Lying in bed
    B. The boy sneaks out
    C. The "strange feeling" begins
    D. Going fishing

III. The first afternoon (7–10)
    A. Going to dinner
    B. Generalizing about vacations
    C. Past arrivals at the lake
    D. Motors, past and present

IV.   The rest of the week (11–13)
    A. General activities
    B. The thunderstorm
    C. The boy goes swimming
    D. The "chill of death"

QUESTIONS.   Read the following list of questions. Keep them in mind while you read the essay, and then go back and try to answer them in some detail. The questions will help you understand the self-expressive nature of the essay.

1. What does the author of the essay tell us about himself? Consider such factors as his age, his powers of observation, and the experiences of his youth.
2. What other people are involved in the author's experience? List them.
3. What is the physical environment in which the experience takes place? Describe its main features.
4. In what ways has the physical environment changed since the author's youth and in what ways has it remained the same? Which are more significant, the changes or the similarities?
5. At what point does the author begin to sense that this visit to the lake will be a strange and important experience? What event first precipitates this feeling?
6. What is the nature of this strange feeling?
7. Here is a list of items from the story. How does each contribute to White's strange feeling?
    a. The inboard and outboard motors
    b. The hellgramite
    c. The road to the farmhouse
    d. The village store
    e. The dragonfly
    f. The tennis court
    g. The storm
8. State the central theme of the essay in your own words. What has White come to learn about himself as a result of this experience at the lake?
9. Why do the rest of us enjoy reading about experiences like this? What do we get out of such essays?

ONCE MORE TO THE LAKE

E. B. White

1 One summer, along about 1904, my father rented a camp on a lake in Maine and took us all there for the month of August. We all got ringworm from some kittens and had to rub Pond's Extract on our arms and legs night and morning, and my father rolled over in a canoe with all his clothes on; but outside of that the vacation was a success and from then on none of us ever thought there was any place in the world like that lake in Maine. We returned summer after summer—always on August 1 for one month. I have since become a salt-water man, but sometimes in summer there are days when the restlessness of the tides and the fearful cold of the sea water and the incessant wind which blows across the afternoon and into the evening make me wish for the placidity of a lake in the woods. A few weeks ago this feeling got so strong I bought myself a couple of bass hooks and a spinner and returned to the lake where we used to go, for a week's fishing and to revisit old haunts.

2 I took along my son, who had never had any fresh water up his nose and who had seen lily pads only from train windows. On the journey over to the lake I began to wonder what it would be like. I wondered how time would have marred this unique, this holy spot—the coves and streams, the hills that the sun set behind, the camps and the paths behind the camps. I was sure that the tarred road would have found it out and I wondered in what other ways it would be desolated. It is strange how much you can remember about places like that once you allow your mind to return into the grooves which lead back. You remember one thing, and that suddenly reminds you of another thing. I guess I remembered clearest of all the early mornings, when the lake was cool and motionless, remembered how the bedroom smelled of the lumber it was made of and of the wet woods whose scent entered through the screen. The partitions in the camp were thin and did not extend clear to the top of the rooms, and as I was always the first up I would dress softly so as not to wake the others, and sneak out into the sweet outdoors and start out in the canoe, keeping close along the shore in the long shadows of the pines. I remembered being very careful never to rub my paddle against the gunwale for fear of disturbing the stillness of the cathedral.

3 The lake had never been what you would call a wild lake. There were cottages sprinkled around the shores, and it was in farming country although the shores of the lake were quite heavily wooded. Some of the cottages were owned by nearby farmers, and you would live at the shore and eat your meals at the farmhouse. That's what our family did. But although it wasn't wild, it was a fairly large and undisturbed lake and there were places in it which, to a child at least, seemed infinitely remote and primeval.

4 I was right about the tar: it led to within half a mile of the shore. But when I got back there, with my boy, and we settled into a camp near a farmhouse and into the kind of summertime I had known, I could tell that it was going to be pretty much the same as it had been before—I knew it, lying

in bed the first morning, smelling the bedroom, and hearing the boy sneak quietly out and go off along the shore in a boat. I began to sustain the illusion that he was I, and therefore, by simple transposition, that I was my father. This sensation persisted, kept cropping up all the time we were there. It was not an entirely new feeling, but in this setting it grew much stronger. I seemed to be living a dual existence. I would be in the middle of some simple act, I would be picking up a bait box or laying down a table fork, or I would be saying something, and suddenly it would be not I but my father who was saying the words or making the gesture. It gave me a creepy sensation.

5   We went fishing the first morning. I felt the same damp moss covering the worms in the bait can, and saw the dragonfly alight on the tip of my rod as it hovered a few inches from the surface of the water. It was the arrival of this fly that convinced me beyond any doubt that everything was as it always had been, that the years were a mirage and that there had been no years. The small waves were the same, chucking the rowboat under the chin as we fished at anchor, and the boat was the same boat, the same color green and the ribs broken in the same places, and under the floor-boards the same fresh-water leavings and debris—the dead hellgramite, the wisps of moss, the rusty discarded fish-hook, the dried blood from yesterday's catch. We stared silently at the tips of our rods, at the dragonflies that came and went. I lowered the tip of mine into the water, tentatively, pensively dislodging the fly, which darted two feet away, poised, darted two feet back, and came to rest again little further up the rod. There had been no years between the ducking of this dragonfly and the other one—the one that was part of memory. I looked at the boy, who was silently watching his fly, and it was my hands that held his rod, my eyes watching. I felt dizzy and didn't know which rod I was at the end of.

6   We caught two bass, hauling them in briskly as though they were mackerel, pulling them over the side of the boat in a businesslike manner without any landing net, and stunning them with a blow on the back of the head. When we got back for a swim before lunch, the lake was exactly where we had left it, the same number of inches from the dock, and there was only the merest suggestion of a breeze. This seemed an utterly enchanted sea, this lake you could leave to its own devices for a few hours and come back to, and find that it had not stirred, this constant and trustworthy body of water. In the shallows, the dark, water-soaked sticks and twigs, smooth and old, were undulating in clusters on the bottom against the clean ribbed sand, and the track of the mussel was plain. A school of minnows swam by, each minnow with its small individual shadow, doubling the attendance, so clear and sharp in the sunlight. Some of the other campers were in swimming along the shore, one of them with a cake of soap, and the water felt thin and clear and unsubstantial. Over the years there had been this person with a cake of soap, this cultist, and here he was. There had been no years.

7   Up to the farmhouse to dinner through the teeming, dusty field, the road under our sneakers was only a two-track road. The middle track was missing, the one with the marks of the hooves and the splotches of dried, flaky manure. There had always been three tracks to choose from in choosing which track to walk in; now the choice was narrowed down to two. For a moment I missed terribly the middle alternative. But the way led past the

tennis court, and something about the way it lay there in the sun reassured me; the tape had loosened along the backline, the alleys were green with plantains and other weeds, and the net (installed in June and removed in September) sagged in the dry noon, and the whole place steamed with midday heat and hunger and emptiness. There was a choice of pie for dessert, and one was blueberry and one was apple, and the waitresses were still fifteen; their hair had been washed; that was the only difference—they had been to the movies and seen the pretty girls with the clean hair.

8   Summertime, oh summertime, pattern of life indelible, the fade-proof lake, the woods unshatterable, the pasture with the sweet-fern and the juniper forever and ever, summer without end; this was the background, and the life along the shore was the design, the cottages with their innocent and tranquil design, there against the white clouds in the blue sky, the little paths over the roots of the trees leading from camp to camp and the paths leading back to the outhouses and the can of lime for sprinkling, and at the souvenir counters at the store the miniature birchbark canoes and the post cards that showed things looking a little better than they looked. This was the American family at play, escaping the city heat, wondering whether the newcomers in the camp at the head of the cove were "common" or "nice," wondering whether it was true that the people who drove up for Sunday dinner at the farmhouse were turned away because there wasn't enough chicken.

9   It seemed to me, as I kept remembering all this, that those times and those summers had been infinitely precious and worth saving. There had been jollity and peace and goodness. The arriving (at the beginning of August) had been so big a business in itself, at the railway station the farm wagon drawn up, the first smell of the pine-laden air, the first glimpse of the smiling farmer, and the great importance of the trunks and your father's enormous authority in such matters, and the feel of the wagon under you for the long ten-mile haul, and at the top of the last long hill catching the first view of the lake after eleven months of not seeing this cherished body of water. The shouts and cries of the other campers when they saw you, and the trunks to be unpacked, to give up their rich burden. (Arriving was less exciting nowadays, when you sneaked up in your car and parked it under a tree near the camp and took out the bags and in five minutes it was all over, no fuss, no loud wonderful fuss about trunks.)

10   Peace and goodness and jollity. The only thing that was wrong now, really, was the sound of the place, an unfamiliar nervous sound of the outboard motors. This was the note that jarred, the one thing that would sometimes break the illusion and set the years moving. In those other summertimes all motors were inboard; and when they were at a little distance, the noise they made was a sedative, an ingredient of summer sleep. They were one-cylinder and two-cylinder engines, and some were make-and-break and some were jump-spark, but they all made a sleepy sound across the lake. The one-lungers throbbed and fluttered, and the twin-cylinder ones purred and purred, and that was a quiet sound too. But now the campers all had outboards. In the daytime, in the hot mornings, these motors made a petulant, irritable sound; at night, in the still evening when the afterglow lit the water, they whined about one's ears like mosquitoes. My boy loved our rented outboard, and his great desire was to achieve singlehanded mastery

over it, and authority, and he soon learned the trick of choking it a little (but not too much), and the adjustment of the needle valve. Watching him I would remember the things you could do with the old one-cylinder engine with the heavy flywheel, how you could have it eating out of your hand if you got really close to it spiritually. Motor boats in those days didn't have clutches, and you would make a landing by shutting off the motor at the proper time and coasting in with a dead rudder. But there was a way of reversing them, if you learned the trick, by shutting the switch and putting it on again exactly on the final dying revolution of the flywheel, so that it would kick back against compression and begin reversing. Approaching the dock in a strong following breeze, it was difficult to slow up sufficiently by the ordinary coasting method, and if a boy felt he had complete mastery over his motor, he was tempted to keep it running beyond its time and then reverse it a few feet from the dock. It took a cool nerve, because if you threw the switch a twentieth of a second too soon you would catch the flywheel when it still had speed enough to go up past center, and the boat would leap ahead, charging bull-fashion at the dock.

11   We had a good week at the camp. The bass were biting well and the sun shone endlessly, day after day. We would be tired at night and lie down in the accumulated heat of the little bedrooms after the long hot day and the breeze would stir almost imperceptibly outside and the smell of the swamp drift in through the rusty screens. Sleep would come easily and in the morning the red squirrel would be on the roof, tapping out his gay routine. I kept remembering everything, lying in bed in the mornings—the small steamboat that had a long rounded stern like the lip of a Ubangi, and how quietly she ran on the moonlight sails, when the older boys played their mandolins and the girls sang and we ate doughnuts dipped in sugar, and how sweet the music was on the water in the shining night, and what it had felt like to think about girls then. After breakfast we would go up to the store and the things were in the same place—the minnows in a bottle, the plugs and spinners disarranged and pawed over by the youngsters from the boys' camp, the fig newtons and the Beeman's gum. Outside the road was tarred and cars stood in front of the store. Inside, all was just as it had always been, except there was more Coca Cola and not so much Moxie and root beer and birch beer and sarsaparilla. We would walk out with a bottle of pop apiece and sometimes the pop would backfire up our noses and hurt. We explored the streams, quietly, where the turtles slid off the sunny logs and dug their way into the soft bottom; and we lay on the town wharf and fed worms to the tame bass. Everywhere we went I had trouble making out which was I, the one walking at my side, the one walking in my pants.

12   One afternoon while we were there at that lake a thunderstorm came up. It was like the revival of an old melodrama that I had seen long ago with childish awe. The second-act climax of the drama of the electrical disturbance over a lake in America had not changed in any important respect. This was the big scene, still the big scene. The whole thing was so familiar, the first feeling of oppression and heat and a general air around camp of not wanting to go very far away. In midafternoon (it was all the same) a curious darkening of the sky, and a lull in everything that had made life tick; and then the way the boats suddenly swung the other way at their moorings with the

coming of a breeze out of the new quarter and the premonitory rumble. Then the kettle drum, then the snare, then the bass drum and cymbals, then crackling light against the dark, and the gods grinning and licking their chops in the hills. Afterward the calm, the rain steadily rustling in the calm lake, the return of light and hope and spirits, and the campers running out in joy and relief to go swimming in the rain, their bright cries perpetuating the deathless joke about how they were getting simply drenched, and the children screaming with delight at the new sensation of bathing in the rain, and the joke about getting drenched linking the generations in a strong indestructible chain. And the comedian who waded in carrying an umbrella.

13   When the others went swimming, my son said he was going in, too. He pulled his dripping trunks from the line where they had hung all through the shower and wrung them out. Languidly, and with no thought of going in, I watched him, his hard little body, skinny and bare, saw him wince slightly as he pulled up around his vitals the small, soggy, icy garment. As he buckled the swollen belt, suddenly my groin felt the chill of death.

The Student Essay

The following essay, by a student, was written according to much the same pattern as the essay by E. B. White. That is, it covers a single incident in the writer's life, the incident is divided into several phases, and the paper's purpose is to help the writer understand the importance of the incident. Since this essay will be discussed in some detail only at the end of the chapter, no study questions are provided. However, if you wish to analyze the essay to some extent, you can use approximately the same questions provided for White's essay.

I DIDN'T WANT TO MOVE

1   When my parents decided to buy a siding business and move over 100 miles away from home, I was a shy 14-year-old, with a boyfriend who seemed to be slipping away from me. My world was concerned with showing others in my school a happy, confident image of myself and with struggling to keep the love of a boyfriend that I thought the world of. Moving 100 miles away simply did not fit into my world.

2   When I first met Mr. Smith, the owner of the business, I had no idea of the ordeal I was about to go through, yet even then I felt threatened by this silver-tongued, enigmatic salesman. Even while I sat in his office and listened to my parents and him discuss the high points of the business he was selling, I still didn't grasp the possibility that we would move if we bought the business. The reality never sank in until after the deal was closed and my father moved into an office in a more run-down part of _____.

3   The first weekend that my parents and I planned to stay at the office, my father threw his back out. My parents were lifting a couch onto the truck to

furnish the office with when my father's back went. Severe pain accompanied my father throughout his ownership of the business.

4   After that we set a pattern down. My dad lived in the office all week long and my mom and I visited every weekend. We planned to continue this until the business was established and we moved to _____.

5   I remembered my first impression of the office. Shock. The office was filthy, neglected, and in a shambles. I couldn't understand why we were moving into this hole. After all, both my parents had good jobs, we had a beautiful house, and certainly my father was no high pressure, greedy salesman like Mr. Smith, whom I had taken an instantaneous dislike to.

6   Mr. Smith liked to project a "Mr. Nice Guy" image. He saw himself as a helpful and good-hearted person, but I saw him as a heartless, corrupt salesman. In truth he was a persuasive phenomenon. For example, while he was helping my father get the business on its feet, he felt my father didn't quote one married couple a high enough price for the job and so before they signed the contract he gave them a quick speech about increased costs and so on, set the price $1,000 higher, and sealed the contract.

7   Often I mentioned to my parents how false and how greedy I felt Mr. Smith was. He was a salesman. I associated those characteristics with the fact that he was a salesman, and I didn't feel that my father had the right characteristics to be a salesman. I felt that salesmen were a different breed. The mere mention of Mr. Smith's name brought a disparaging remark from me.

8   During the first few weekends, we (mom, dad, Mr. Smith and I) all scrubbed and cleaned and furnished the office. The difference was like night and day. The full-length, crystal-clear windows at the front of the office offered an unobstructed vision of the modest front area which contained a desk and was separated from the back by a thin wall of paneling that didn't reach the ceiling. Sometimes I helped my father set up the siding samples in the display windows. Before Christmas I decorated them with lights, tinsel, and ornaments. Through a door in the separating panel was the living area. To the right, a couch rested against this side of the paneling. The white-washed wall on the right contained a large painting of beach and sky. Below that was a desk facing outward on which rested a phone and plenty of paperwork. My father tried to get me to answer the phone, but I never would. I was too scared. At night the couch unfolded into a bed for my parents. The cushions were then arranged on the floor and a sleeping bag placed on top for me to sleep in. Used to my own quiet neighborhood, I was kept awake at night by the street noises. Sometimes it seemed like an unreal adventure.

9   When my father first tried his hand at selling, he was apprehensive and slightly unnerved at the thought. For a while, selling was a difficult and not very successful task, so the business limped along with the help of Mr. Smith. I felt relief and a covert joy at this outcome, but my relief was smattered with guilt. My dad's bad back also hindered his potential at selling. This wasn't my fault and yet I felt an uneasy guilt when I thought about it. Was I such a bad person that I wanted my father in pain so he would have to sell the business?

10   I was unhappy about moving. I was apprehensive, no, scared to death, of meeting people and making new friends. I didn't have the confidence that I

could do it. My mom also was rather reluctant to move. She was averse to leaving her job at Kodak and the house she and my dad had put so much into. I didn't hesitate to let her know how unhappy I was to be leaving my school and my boyfriend behind. Maybe I didn't have the influence on whether we moved, but my mother did.

11   One weekend, after I had gone to a concert with a friend from home, I particularly resented the idea of leaving home. I moped around the whole weekend, saying and doing little. Most of the time I sat around on the couch and spoke only when necessary. A few weekends later I overhead my father say to my mother how depressed I had seemed that weekend and that he hadn't realized how deeply this bothered me. For some reason, I felt apprehension at his words.

12   Another weekend, after my father sealed a contract for a big job, my parents and I celebrated by having dinner at a luxurious restaurant. We had a good meal, and I enjoyed the occasion very much. We toasted to the success of his deal.

13   My dad's selling skills improved and his confidence increased, but somehow we had gotten into a rut. We had owned the business some nine months. We had tried to go halfway but it just couldn't work halfway. My father had grown in his selling ability and had become more a part of the business, but my mom and I still lived at home, and those same fears of moving still gnawed at me. I hadn't grown. Soon, the attachment to home and security won out. The business was sold. Instead of starting anew, I won the right to continue struggling for a confident image in a school where I had always been shy.

14   My father went back to his job as a construction superintendent. One day after my father came home from work, I walked into the room to see him standing in the hallway, soaking wet from the cold rain that had poured all day on his job. In a voice that had always been humorous to me in the past, he was imitating the roaring and angry voice of his unreasonable boss. Only this time it wasn't funny to me. This time a part of me died inside.

PREWRITING

Choosing a Topic

The two expressive essays that you have just read demonstrate several aspects of the personal essay. First, they show that such essays need not be concerned with extraordinary adventures or unique feelings. The family that moves away from home is not unique, and the father who takes his son fishing is not likely to have an adventure. Few of us will ever do anything extraordinary, and in fact it is more useful to the reader if we find important themes in commonplace experiences that many people share. Readers do not come to expressive essays seeking thrills and excitement; they come hoping to identify with the author and to learn something about themselves.

Thus the necessity of finding meaning is the second characteristic of the personal essay. The writer does not simply recount events; the essay is not worth writing unless one probes the events for an underlying theme. That is why, incidentally, those inevitable high school essays about "What I Did Last Summer" or "My Most Embarrassing Moment" are seldom worth reading. Your embarrassing moments sometimes can be mildly amusing, but unless you get behind the moment, to discover something about yourself, there is little point to writing the essay.

Personal essays may, it is true, be painfully embarrassing, but this is not because writers deliberately look for an embarrassing moment to write about. It is because the third characteristic of good self-expression is that it be totally honest. By writing an expressive essay, you are trying to learn something about yourself, and you will not learn unless you are honest with yourself. Though you naturally hope to write an essay that other readers will find useful (your instructor will probably require this), the primary audience is yourself.

The best topic for your personal essay will probably not be an earthshaking event. The topic should simply be one that "feels important" to you even though you may not immediately understand what the importance is. An argument with your parents, the breakdown of your car, moving into your first apartment—all of these commonplace experiences may have something to tell you about yourself. And because these events happen to nearly everyone, you may be able to help your readers understand themselves a little better, too.

For this first assignment, then, choose as your topic an experience that "seemed important" at the time and one that you remember vividly. Your task is to tell about the experience and to figure out what that experience reveals about yourself. The following exercises may help you.

Exercises on Choosing a Topic

1. List two or three experiences that you have had that seemed important to you at the time.
2. Try to identify one aspect of each experience that made the experience seem important (such as White's feeling that he was his father and the son was White himself). Do this in writing.
3. You are looking for a topic that you strongly feel was important in forming or revealing some aspect of the "real you." At the same time, the exact nature of this importance remains a mystery to you. From the list of possible topics you made above, choose the one with the best combination of these two characteristics.
4. Show your choice to your instructor. Also, if your topic is not too embarrassing to you, check it with some classmates. Try to find out whether others would be interested in hearing more about your experience and if so, why.

Main Issues in Writing

When you sit down to write something, facing a blank piece of paper, it is seldom possible to start right off writing an essay, article, or whatever. You need to mull over what you are going to say, and you will probably find it helpful to jot down some ideas as they come to you. There is something comforting about having written something; you can look at what you have done, and your jottings may suggest other ideas.

At the same time, it may also be helpful to have a systematic way to proceed, some method to ensure that you have "touched all the bases" in your thinking. The method used in this book is to have you consider three "issues" connected to the type of writing you are trying to do. One issue will always have to do with yourself, the writer; another has to do with your intended readers; and the third has to do with some reality outside of both yourself and the readers. We will call these, respectively, the *writer issue*, the *reader issue*, and the *subject matter issue*.

The issues give you three distinctly different types, or areas, of things to think about, and they also vary according to the aim and mode you are working on. The issues can be placed on the communications triangle that was introduced in Chapter 1. At this point the triangle will simply help you remember what the issues are, but as you gain more experience with the triangle it will come to mean more to you than a simple memory device. It's difficult to explain this deeper meaning in words, so we won't try as yet.

For an expressive essay, the three issues to think about are the *self* (the writer issue), *others* (the reader issue), and the *world* (the subject matter issue). The communications triangle thus appears as in Figure 2.1.

These three issues are the three aspects of your experience, which we will be examining in more detail. They may be thought of as sources of

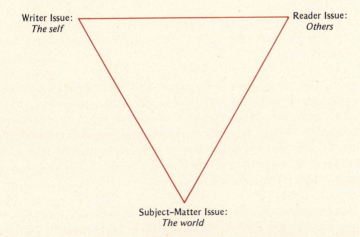

Writer Issue:
The self

Reader Issue:
Others

Subject–Matter Issue:
The world

FIGURE 2.1   **The three issues in self-expression.**

material for your essay, showing you what to think about and how to think about it. Exercises are also provided to guide you through the thinking process. These exercises should not be thought of as a means for developing a formal plan for the essay, such as an outline of some sort, but rather to get you thinking along appropriate lines and to help you generate written notes to be used later when you write the essay.

THE WRITER ISSUE: THE SELF. Consider first the kind of person you were when the experience occurred. You were many things, of course, not all of them relevant to the experience. Try to isolate those aspects that were relevant—age, sex, maturity, intelligence, skills, size, or whatever. You are looking for those aspects that caused you to get involved in the experience, that made you behave as you did, and that affected your feelings about the event. Some experiences, of course, happen by accident, but even in these cases our reactions to them are not accidental.

For instance, we can see that the causes of E. B. White's experience were not accidental and that many of these causes lay within White himself. His age was certainly a factor, since the recognition of oncoming death often occurs at the onset of middle age. Likewise, other important factors were that he was a father, that he had not returned to the lake for many years, and that he was male. Take away a single one of these factors and the experience could not have happened, at least not in the same way. True, he would probably have had a similar experience eventually, since recognition of our mortality happens to most people sooner or later, but then the essay would have been very different. Successful essays come from remembering vividly what did happen; without this, we tend to speak in unconvincing generalities.

Exercises on Remembering the Self

These exercises do not constitute a linear set of steps. Feel free to go back and forth between exercises, adding notes or crossing out notes that no longer seem relevant.

1. **Thinking back to the time of the experience, list those characteristics of yourself that might in any way be relevant to the experience (your sex, your age at the time, your mental state, and so on).**
2. **From the list, identify any characteristics that caused you to get into the experience. Jot down a brief note to remind yourself of this. (As you think about the causes of the experience, you may remember additional characteristics of yourself, which are not on your original list. If so, add them to the list.)**
3. **An experience occurs over a span of time, and to some extent what we do during the experience affects the course of the event. Identify on your list**

any personal characteristics that affected what happened. (Again, re-membering what happened may lead you to think of other characteristics to add to the list.)

4. Sometimes one or more of our personal characteristics may be changed by the experience. Identify any characteristics in your original list that were changed, and briefly describe the nature of the change.

5. Even though you may not yet have changed because of the experience, you may have resolved to try to change. If you made any such resolution, identify the characteristic that you hope to change.

THE READER ISSUE: OTHERS. One set of "others" that you must worry about in an expressive essay is the group of people who will be reading the essay. You want to recreate the experience for your readers in such detail and with such power that they feel as if they were there with you. You want them to experience the event vicariously so that they will learn from it what you have learned. However, it is too early in the writing process to worry overmuch about your readers. This kind of concern, at such an early date, often just gets in the way of your thinking.

For now, concentrate first on the others who were involved in the experience, both those who were physically present and those who, though not present, nevertheless exerted an influence on the experience.

Others are important, first, because we can see ourselves in them. In other words, when we learn something about other people, we may also learn something about ourselves. For example, this perspective was vital to E. B. White's experience. He saw himself in his son, and he saw his father in himself, to the point that the three people almost seemed to merge. It was this perspective that led him to his theme: that just as his father had died and then White had become the father, so he would die and his son would take his place. This recognition led in turn to the realization of his own mortality.

A second way that we learn from others is to discover how others see us. Our friends and acquaintances *know* us; they believe that they know what kind of people we are. (Their views may not be accurate, but then our own views of ourselves are not completely accurate, either. We all have a marvelous capacity for self-deception.) By discovering what other people think of us, we get a larger picture of the self.

Of course, discovering what other people think of us is difficult. Not only do we try to hide our true natures from others, but others may also be too polite to say anything. We have to watch for subtle clues. Do they ask our opinions? Do they confide in us? Do they laugh at our jokes? Do they trust our word? As you remember your experience, try to remember some of these clues.

Finally, we need to remember others because what they did may have had some influence on the experience itself. They may have caused the event to occur, their actions may have affected the course of the event, and they may still have an influence in our lives as a result of what happened.

Exercises on Remembering Others

1. Make a list of the *others* who were involved in the experience. Include both those who were physically present and those who, though not present, may have had some influence. Also include those who, like the man with the soap, might at first seem to have little relationship to the event. (Remember that, as you go through subsequent exercises, it's all right to add more people to this list if you think of them later.)
2. Identify anyone on the list who seemed to reflect some aspect of yourself. These are people who led you to wonder whether you look like that, or whether you act like that. Make a note of what you learned about yourself in this manner.
3. Identify those who gave you a clue as to what others think of you. Write down the nature of these clues.
4. Identify those who had some influence on the course of the event and what has happened to you since the event. Also, were any of these people influential in causing the event in the first place?

THE SUBJECT-MATTER ISSUE: THE WORLD.   The third aspect to consider as you think about your experience is *the world*. Here we include the physical environment—the place and time in which the experience occurred—as well as those human aspects such as institutions, society, the community, and so on. The world, then, is the whole context in which the experience occurred. Of course, it is again necessary to identify those features of the world which were relevant to the experience.

The first way to identify the relevant is again to *look for causes*. What was there in the world that caused the experience to occur and you to behave as you did? For E. B. White's essay, the world was probably the major cause of his experience. In his case the world consisted of the physical environment—the lake, the cabin, the dragonflies and fish, the store and farmhouse—plus that human institution, the vacation. White saw that the lake environment had not changed, and then he recognized that neither had the American summertime vacation. True, there were minor changes, but underneath was a sameness, a continual return to the lake as it was and always would be. Even the people did not really change; as one boy became a father and then died, so his place would be taken by another boy to whom the same process would occur.

A second aspect of the world is that it provides a set of *instruments* for accomplishing things. A lake, for example, which was once an instrument for obtaining food, is now for most of us a means of recreation, of resting and refreshing ourselves to return to the school, office, or factory. The institution of the vacation was developed for the same purpose. Thus as you examine the world in which your experience occurred, you will be looking not only for ways that the world caused certain events but also for the instruments that the world provided and what you did with those instruments. Did you make use of the opportunities provided you, or did you overlook them?

Exercises on Examining the World

1. **Write a brief description of the physical setting in which the experience occurred. Then add to it a list of as many details as you can remember. Be as concrete as possible.**
2. **Make a list of the human aspects of the world of your experience—political, cultural, social, and institutional. Again, be concrete in your description of each aspect.**
3. **Try to identify those aspects of the world that were causes of the experience and of the way in which the experience proceeded. Add brief notes to each item so identified, explaining how you think it was a cause.**
4. **Identify those aspects of the world that you were using as instruments for accomplishing something. Also identify aspects that you now wish you had used in a different manner.**
5. **If you are now using the instruments of the world in a manner different from the way you used them before the experience began, identify those instruments, too.**

TIME ORIENTATION: A FOURTH CONSIDERATION. As you may have observed from the exercises, there is a time aspect to self-expression. There is a *past*, before the experience began, which may have caused the experience to occur. Next comes the *present*, the time during the experience itself. And there there is the future, both what you are now as a result of the expeirence and what you will become.

The future is important because self-expression is often oriented toward goals. We examine our past to see how it led to the present and what the future will be if things go on as they are. And if the future does not look promising, we set goals for a different future.

Goals, then, are central to self-expression, perhaps the main purpose of probing the self. But they must be the right goals, chosen freely and with intelligence. Without accurate knowledge of the self and an understanding of the place of the self in the midst of others and the world, the setting of proper goals is difficult.

Exercises on Identifying and Setting Goals

1. **As you remember what you did during the experience, can you identify any goals that you were working toward? List several of your actions that**

**seem to have been goal-oriented, and write a brief explanation of what
was going on.**

2. **Examine each of the actions listed above. Does it seem now, in
   retrospect, that you were working toward a worthwhile goal?**
3. **Identify any goals you now have that seem to have resulted from the
   experience. Write a brief note of explanation for each.**

ORGANIZATION OF SELF-EXPRESSION

It is difficult to generalize about the organization of self-expression because
there are so many types of it. However, it is probably safe to say that the
personal essay about an event is usually organized in chronological order,
roughly following the pattern of White's essay. It would begin with the
background of the event—what you were doing before the event began,
and what there was within yourself, the others, and the world that
precipitated the event. Then the experience itself would begin, focused
particularly on the moment when you began to feel that there was
something special about the experience. Next you would continue with the
series of happenings, in the order in which they actually occurred, but
would return again and again to the growing recognition of the central
theme. Finally, you could end with the full statement of the theme or go
beyond that to tell about the impact of the event on your present and
future. The main variation on this pattern is that some writers prefer to
announce the theme first, in the introduction, so that the reader will know
where the essay is going.

The chronological pattern has two main advantages. First, it's a
"natural" pattern, growing out of the reality being pictured; you do not
have to reshuffle the events to make them fit into a preset pattern such as
is required for some of the other types of writing studied in this book.
Second, it is one that allows your readers to go through the experience with
you, to feel what you felt, and to see what you saw. This gives the readers
the best chance of learning about themselves what you learned about
yourself.

Within the main, chronological pattern, you may want to select a
specific internal pattern for organizing "chunks" of the essay. In expressive
writing, this is often a repetitive pattern that keeps recurring throughout
the essay. E. B. White's essay uses such a repetitive pattern. He mentions
an event in the present, which triggers a memory from the past, and this in
each case leads to a statement about the "strange feeling." For example, a
dragonfly alights on the fishing rod. White remembers dragonflies from the
past, and then the present and past merge; he can't tell which is the real
dragonfly and which exists in his memory.

Of course, at this point in your writing process, it may be too early to
give much attention to organization. You may not yet have figured out just

OUTLINE OF EXPRESSIVE CONSIDERATIONS

	PAST	PRESENT	FUTURE	
			If You Don't Plan	Your Plan or Goals
You and the *self*	What were your inherited characteristics and how have they been shaped over the years?	What you are like now, in terms of your emotional self, your rational self, and your physical abilities.	What you will probably be like in the future if you keep going in the present way.	Your goals for improving yourself, and how you plan to get there (based on a realistic assessment of what you are capable of becoming).
You and *others*	Your past position in relation to others with whom you have come in contact. How you stood with them, how you were regarded.	How you stand in relation to the people around you. What they think of you.	How you will stand with others if you continue in the present way.	Your goals for your future standing with others, and how you plan to get there (based on a realistic assessment of your chances).
You and the *world*	The physical, social, and political environments in which you have existed, and how they have affected you.	Your standing now in your society and your physical environments. How they are helping or hindering you.	How you will stand in relation to the society and your physical environment if you continue in the present way.	Your goals for using the physical, social, and political worlds to your best advantage, and your plan for getting there (based on a realistic view of the world).

why the experience seemed to be so important to you, and it's most unlikely that you have settled on a theme for the essay. What you need to do right now is to try writing a first draft of the essay, starting at the beginning of the experience and following it through. You can, to some extent, use your notes from the prewriting exercises as a guide to what to include and omit. In this way you can let the writing itself lead you to the theme. In fact, that's one of the advantages of writing; it forces us to give form and arrangement to what otherwise is a kaleidoscope of details.

Exercises on the Essay

1. Write the first draft of the essay, all the way through. Begin with what you were doing before the experience began and then proceed through the experience itself. If you do not come up with anything better, end with a retrospective: as you look back on the experience, what do you think of it now?
2. If no theme emerges during the first writing, show your essay to your instructor and some classmates. Perhaps they can suggest what the experience means, and then you can adapt one of their ideas for your own theme. .
3. Once you have figured out an approriate theme, give some thought as to whether you need to put it into words for the reader. If you think it's necessary to do so, try writing it out in a single sentence.
4. Give some thought as to where in the essay the reader needs to be told the theme. If the experience itself is interesting enough to keep the reader going to the end, the theme can be given at the end. If not, then you might need a standard introductory paragraph with the theme given in the introduction. If you decide on such an introduction, try writing it.
5. Identify the parts of the essay that contribute most strongly to the theme. On a second draft, try emphasizing these parts and omitting or de-emphasizing the rest.
6. Write a second complete draft of the essay.

THE STYLE OF SELF-EXPRESSION

Just as there are few conventional organizing patterns for personal essays, so there is no required style. Each writer is permitted to write in his or her natural, personal language, which will differ in some ways from the personal language of every other individual.

It is, of course, easy to say what expressive style is not; it is not the dry, pokerfaced style of the scientist, nor is it the brassy, self-confident style of the propagandist. Beyond this, we will have to confine our description of the style to a few general comments that seem to apply to most self-expression.

Expressive style is, first, intended to convey emotions, and the writer therefore tends to lean toward exclamations and superlatives. For example, White described the lake this way: "This seemed an utterly enchanted sea . . . this constant and trustworthy body." Words like *utterly*, *constant*, and *trustworthy* are superlatives; they leave no room for the lake to be less than enchanted or sometimes inconstant and treacherous. Or take White's description of the whole summertime scene: "pattern of life indelible, the fadeproof lake, the woods unshatterable, the pasture with sweetfern and the juniper forever and ever, summer without end." Again the list of superlatives: *indelible, fadeproof, unshatterable, forever and ever, without end.*

Such language also strongly evokes a mood, appealing to our senses and feelings, conveying more than simple information about the scene. "Sweet outdoors," "long shadows of the pines," "clean ribbed sand," "cherished body of water"—such phrases convey the emotions the author felt, his attitudes toward the scene. They also help the reader have the same feelings.

The mood is reinforced by various literary devices that give the essay an almost poetic sound at times. Prominent among these devices are repetitions of words, phrases, and rhythms: "Summertime, oh summertime, pattern of life indelible. . . ." There are also plenty of metaphors and similes: the quiet lake has the "stillness of the cathedral"; the steamboat has a "rounded stern like the lip of a Ubangi." Literary devices are so common in good self-expression that many classify such pieces as literature.

Finally, self-expression is marked by frequent use of first-person pronouns—*I, me, we,* and *us.* Students are often warned against using the first person in other kinds of writing, but for expressive essays such pronouns are unavoidable.

ANALYZING AND EVALUATING SELF-EXPRESSION

The principles we have discussed for planning and writing a self-expressive essay can also be used to analyze and evaluate essays such as "I Didn't Want to Move." You may want to reread the essay before reading the analysis that follows.

The Three Issues

We can see, first of all, how the three issues of self, others, and the world are handled in this essay.

The *self* in this case was a teenaged girl at the time of the experience. Like every person, she must have had many characteristics, yet the author chooses to concentrate on just a few: her boyfriend, her shyness, her concern for appearances at school, her comfortable middle-class life-style, and her opinions about salespeople. Given the experience, such a limited description of the self seems appropriate because these characteristics do seem to be the main reasons for her negative reactions to moving to another city. It may be that her negative opinions about salespeople are more a rationalization (i.e., a respectable reason to be against the move) than a true motivation, but the girl seems aware of this possibility. However, we can conclude that the writer has correctly identified the characteristics of the self that were most relevant to the theme of the essay.

Next, let us look at the *others* in the essay. The key one, of course, is the writer's father. He is the person who caused the experience and who eventually brings out the theme. On the one hand, we might have wished for the writer to say more about him: Why did he want to buy his own business? Did he come to enjoy being a salesman? On the other hand, one could argue that the writer's neglect of her father is part of the theme: her unawareness of *his* needs and motivations serves to emphasize her self-centeredness. The remaining key others, the mother and Mr. Smith, are also a bit puzzling. Why is there so much emphasis on Mr. Smith and so little on the mother? It is natural that Mr. Smith, being so foreign to the writer's experience, should have fascinated her. But we also would have liked to know what the mother thought of the move and how much she influenced the final decision to abandon the business. The writer will end up feeling very guilty about causing her father to quit, yet perhaps the mother bears more responsibility. Finally, the others include both the boyfriend and the writer's friends at school. We learn very little about these people, but they could have been a part of the theme. We can very well come to feel embarrassed, in later years, about the foolish importance that popularity assumes for teenagers.

The *world* is also very much present in the essay, and here the writer has done a very good job. There are three worlds involved—school, home, and office—but the key one is the office. This is described in plenty of detail so that we can know why the writer reacted so negatively. Some readers might have wished her to describe her home more completely, to point up the contrast between home and office, but most readers can supply the details easily from the hints that are dropped.

Organization

Like "Once More to the Lake," this essay is organized chronological-ly, but that is not the only similarity. The other similarity is that the essay hints at the theme very early, in the introduction, and then gradually builds toward a full recognition of it at the end. Perhaps you can see how this works if you first examine the following outline. (The numbers in parentheses are paragraph numbers.)

   I. Introduction (1)
     A. The decision to buy the business
     B. The author's *self* at the time of the decision
     C. The author's opposition to the move

  II. Initial experiences with the business
     A. Reactions to Mr. Smith (2)
     B. Father throws back out (3)
     C. Intended pattern of life (4)

 III. Learning to operate the business
     A. First impressions of the office (5)
     B. More about Mr. Smith (6–7)
     C. Cleaning up the office (8)
     D. The father's early experiences with selling (9)

 IV. Opposition to the move
     A. Attempts to influence the mother (10)
     B. The writer showing her opposition (11)

  V. Success and failure
     A. Success on a big deal (12)
     B. Father's improved ability to sell (13a)
     C. End of the experiment (13b)

 VI. Conclusion, recognition of the theme (14)

If you compare the outline to the essay, you will see that in every section but one there is some contribution to the theme. A section will begin with some narrative material about the experience and then will end with a comment related to the theme: "Was I such a bad person that I wanted my father in pain so that he would have to sell the business?" (paragraph 9). The only section where this was not done is Part II, and perhaps this is a weakness. It would have been quite simple to add one more sentence to paragraph 4 that would have helped the theme along.

On the whole, however, we can see that the main purpose of an organization—to construct *parts* that contribute to a *whole*—has been accomplished. A few improvements could have been made within each section of the essay, but discussing the organization further would require too much space. We should keep in mind, though, that for this type of essay making parts fit the whole is not often done with an outline or a first draft. You write a complete essay first, to figure out what the whole is, and then you redesign the parts to fit.

Style

The essay bears two of the distinct marks of self-expression: numerous first-person pronouns and much emotional language. The emotions are especially strong when the writer describes the office ("filthy, neglected, and in a shambles") and Mr. Smith ("a heartless, corrupt salesman"). However, there is little of the literary flavor of "Once More to the Lake," so the style is, overall, fairly plain.

How vital is a literary flavor? Well, we cannot expect anyone to match E. B. White, one of America's finest writers. But we can observe some places where the student has used clichés for metaphors and recommend that those would be places for improvement. For example, she says that the office was a "hole" and that, after cleaning, the difference was like "night and day" and the windows were "crystal-clear." Even the last sentence of the essay, which expresses the main theme, is a cliché. ("This time a part of me died inside.") While these clichés are appropriate language for the self-centered 14-year-old being described in the essay, they are not appropriate for the more mature person actually doing the writing. We can recommend that they be changed to language that is fresher and more precise.

Conclusion

Comments like those above demonstrate that the directions for prewriting in this chapter can also be guides to further revision. In addition, your instructor will be using them as criteria for grading your essay. Some instructors are reluctant to grade expressive essays for fear of being seen as denigrating deeply held feelings of students. But you can now see that such essays have fairly clear goals and means of reaching the goals. If the instructor concentrates on goals and means, there should be no problem.

Finally, you can use the criteria for a richer understanding of the published self-expression that you read. With practice, you will be able to separate "good" self-expressions from the bad. Good ones enlighten the authors about themselves and, because people share many characteristics, they enlighten the readers as well. Weak self-expression is an exercise in self-deception or pathos. The authors deceive themselves and may also deceive the unwary reader. Such "sob stories" may achieve a momentary popularity, but their falseness contributes to their eventually being for gotten

Exercises on Working for Greater Knowledge of the Self

1. Working together as a class, make a list of the types of facts that you believe every person ought to know about himself or herself. Your list should include such categories as age, sex, ethnic group, educational background, and so on. If you run out of ideas, examine some application forms, survey sheets, and similar data sheets to see what kinds of facts are called for by these instruments.
2. Working with the list of questions compiled by your class, supply the facts requested. If there is anything you cannot answer, seek help from your parents and other relatives or from school records.
3. Compile a dossier of "personal papers" that are or have been important in your life. Include such items as your birth certificate, your family tree, school transcripts, diplomas, and other documents.
4. Make a list of others who have been influential in your life. When possible, list them by name, but don't overlook those whom you know only by role (for example, "the kids laughed when I had to give a speech in class"). Then briefly describe what type of influence each person had and whether it was helpful or harmful.
5. Put your name at the top of a sheet of paper and pass it around the class. Ask each student to write something positive about you, or at least something neutral. (For your own peace of mind, request that they avoid the negative. Most of us already have more negative opinions about ourselves than we need.)
6. Make a list of your goals in life. Concentrate especially on the goals you hope to achieve by going to college. (If it appears that you have no goals, make a projection of where your present course of study is likely to take you. Consider whether you really want to go there.)

The following essay will give you another look at self-expression and another opportunity to examine those elements that make up a successful essay. Read the essay and then answer the questions that follow.

SUMMER BEYOND WISH

Russell Baker

1   A long time ago I lived in a crossroads village of northern Virginia and during its summer enjoyed innocence and never knew boredom, although nothing of consequence happened there.

2   Seven houses of varying lack of distinction constituted the community. A dirt road meandered off toward the mountain where a bootleg still supplied whiskey to the men of the countryside, and another dirt road ran

down to the creek. My cousin Kenneth and I would sit on the bank and fish with earthworms. One day we killed a copperhead, which was basking on a rock nearby. That was unusual.

3   The heat of summer was mellow and produced sweet scents which lay in the air so damp and rich you could almost taste them. Mornings smelled of purple wisteria, afternoons of the wild roses, which tumbled over stone fences and evenings of honeysuckle.

4   Even by standards of that time it was a primitive place. There was no electricity. Roads were unpaved. In our house there was no plumbing. The routine of summer days was shaped by these deficiencies. Lacking electric lights, one went early to bed and rose while the dew was still in the grass. Kerosene lamps were cleaned and polished in an early-morning hubbub of women, and children were sent to the spring for fresh water.

5   This afforded a chance to see whether the crayfish population had multiplied. Later, a trip to the outhouse would afford a chance to daydream in the Sears Roebuck catalog, mostly about shotguns and bicycles.

6   With no electricity, radio was not available for pacifying the young. One or two people did have radios that operated on mail-order batteries about the size of a present-day car battery, but these were not for children, though occasionally you might be invited in to hear "Amos 'n' Andy."

7   All I remember about "Amos 'n' Andy" at that time is that it was strange hearing voices come out of furniture. Much later I was advised that listening to "Amos 'n' Andy" was racist and was grateful that I hadn't heard much.

8   In the summer no pleasures were to be had indoors. Everything of delight occurred in the world outside. In the flowers there were humming-birds to be seen, tiny wings fluttering so fast that the birds seemed to have no wings at all.

9   In the heat of midafternoon the women would draw the blinds, spread blankets on the floor for coolness and nap, while in the fields the cattle herded together in the shade of spreading trees to escape the sun. Afternoons were absolutely still, yet filled with sounds.

10   Bees buzzed in the clover. Far away over the fields the chug of an ancient steam-powered threshing machine could be faintly heard. Birds rustled under the tin of the porch roof.

11   Rising dust along the road from the mountains signaled an approaching event. A car was coming. "Car's coming," someone would say. People emerged from houses. The approaching dust was studied. Guesses were hazarded about whom it might contain.

12   Then—a big moment in the day—the car would cruise past.

13   "Who was it?"

14   "I didn't get a good look."

15   "It looked like Packy Painter to me."

16   "Couldn't have been Packy. Wasn't his car."

17   The stillness resettled itself as gently as the dust, and you could wander past the henhouse and watch a hen settle herself to perform the mystery of laying an egg. For livelier adventure there was the field that contained the bull. There, one could test his courage by seeing how far he dared venture before running back through the fence.

18   The men drifted back with the falling sun, steaming with heat and

fatigue, and washed in tin basins with water hauled in buckets from the spring. I knew a few of their secrets, such as who kept his whiskey hidden in a Mason jar behind the lime barrel, and what they were really doing when they excused themselves from the kitchen and stepped out into the orchard and stayed out there laughing too hard.

19   I also knew what the women felt about it, though not what they thought. Even then I could see that matters between women and men could become very difficult and, sometimes, so difficult that they spoiled the air of summer.

20   At sunset people sat on the porches. As dusk deepened, the lightning bugs came out to be caught and bottled. As twilight edged into night, a bat swooped across the road. I was not afraid of bats then, although I feared ghosts, which made the approach of bedtime in a room where even the kerosene lamp would quickly be doused seem terrifying.

21   I was even more afraid of toads and specifically of the toad which lived under the porch steps and which everyone assured me would, if touched, give me warts. One night I was allowed to stay up until the stars were in full command of the sky. A woman of great age was dying in the village and it was considered fit to let the children stay abroad into the night.

22   As four of us sat there we saw a shooting star and someone said, "Make a wish."

23   I did not know what that meant. I didn't know anything to wish for.

Exercises on Reading and Analyzing Self-Expression

1. List the characteristics of the *self* that Russell Baker mentions. To what extent did any of these characteristics cause the experience or affect what happened?
2. List the *others* who were involved in the experience. To what extent did these others cause the experience or affect what happened? What did the author learn about himself as a result of observing others?
3. List the characteristics of the *world* in which the experience took place. Which parts are physical and which are social or cultural?
4. A brief essay like this cannot develop completely all three aspects of self-expression. Which of the three aspects—self, others, world—is the main subject of the essay?
5. What is the theme of the essay? How does this theme relate to your answer to Question 4? Were you adequately prepared for the theme?
6. Try to figure out the organization of the essay. To what extent is it chronological?
7. Pick out some words and phrases that seem especially pleasing to you. Consider why they seem so effective.
8. Note the short paragraphs, much shorter than most of those in "Once More to the Lake." What causes the difference in length?

Persuading

3

THE IMPORTANCE OF PERSUASION

Persuasion is the art of convincing an audience to agree with you on a given subject and, in many instances, to act on that agreement. Persuasion is the aim behind politicians and their speeches (they want your vote), sellers and advertisements (they want your money), novelists and their stories (they want your attention and belief). Persuasion is seen in courtship, lawsuits, and teaching; it is the aim of job applications and interviews, sermons, television commercials, and requests for contributions. Persuasion is pervasive in our society, and even when we are not aware of using or being affected by it, persuasion influences our lives.

For example, in the course of watching a movie on television, we are bombarded by dozens of appeals from various sources. In the movie itself we are asked to sympathize (even identify) with certain characters and to be hostile toward others; we are asked to understand all of the characters and events and to come to terms with what the makers of the movie are saying through them. During commercial breaks we are asked to buy toothpaste, cars, deodorant, and hamburgers; we are urged to call friends or relatives long distance or to get on a plane and visit them in person. We are asked to conserve energy, keep America beautiful, and stay tuned for the late news to follow. Some of these appeals are quite obvious and aggressive, as when the hero in the movie wears a white hat and is nice to children and animals. Other appeals are more subtle and "soft-sell" in their approach; for example, the "housewife" who endorses a particular laundry detergent projects her sincerity, and the "old-fashioned" cooking promoted by that restaurant chain is "just like grandma's."

The frequency and intensity with which we use or are confronted by persuasion is easily explained. First, people are mutually dependent upon each other. In relationships among individuals and between individuals and groups, approval, assent, and cooperative action are necessary in daily life. In a sense, the need for communication and cooperation is the need for persuasion. Second, both individuals and groups are only human, and human beings can be successfully appealed to in a variety of ways—not only in terms of reason, but also through emotional means, in terms of the personality of the persuader, or even through control of the style of the appeal itself. In short, our relationships (male and female, family and friends, seller and consumer, and so on) constantly require that we persuade or be persuaded, that we ask for or give others our attention, affection, loyalty, money, or time. And, barring legal or moral restrictions (for example, to deceptive advertising or to brutal physical or psychological tactics) these numerous relationships lead us to use whatever persuasive approach or combination of approaches works on a given audience and in a given situation.

SOME EXAMPLES OF PERSUASION

Many types of persuasion are common in our experience, so several examples are provided here. The first is an article from a general interest magazine, the second a student essay, and the third an ad from a weekly news magazine. All three samples exemplify the major components of persuasive discourse.

Norman Cousins wrote "How to Make People Smaller Than They Are" near the end of his long term as editor of *Saturday Review* and in response to a trend among college students toward a "practical" or vocational emphasis in the choice of courses and careers. In reading the article, you should attempt to answer the following questions:

1. What is the author's specific purpose here? That is, of what is he trying to persuade the reader?
2. What is the context of the article, the situation that prompts Cousins to write about his subject in the first place? How does Cousins try to give the reader a sense of this context?
3. To what beliefs, loyalties, or emotions in the audience does Cousins appeal here? If you had to pick, would you characterize his appeal as one *against* "vocationalization" or *for* the liberal arts?
4. In what ways does Cousins try to convince us that he is informed on the subject and capable of sound judgment? In what ways does Cousins convince us that he is to be trusted? How are we convinced that Cousins cares about college students and the society of which they are a part?
5. What useful information does Cousins bring into the essay? How does Cousins use this information to prove his point?

6. How would you describe the organization of "How to Make People Smaller Than They Are"? Into what major sections might Cousins' article be broken? How would you characterize the author's style?
7. How is the title of the article effective in helping Cousins make his point?

HOW TO MAKE PEOPLE SMALLER THAN THEY ARE

Norman Cousins

1   One of the biggest problems confronting American education today is the increasing vocationalization of our colleges and universities. Throughout the country, schools are under pressure to become job-training centers and employment agencies.

2   The pressure comes mainly from two sources. One is the growing determination of many citizens to reduce taxes—understandable and even commendable in itself, but irrational and irresponsible when connected to the reduction or dismantling of vital public services. The second source of pressure comes from parents and students who tend to scorn courses of study that do not teach people how to become attractive to employers in a rapidly tightening job market.

3   It is absurd to believe that the development of skills does not also require the systematic development of the human mind. Education is being measured more by the size of the benefits the individual can extract from society than by the extent to which the individual can come into possession of his or her full powers. The result is that the life-giving juices are in danger of being drained out of education.

4   Emphasis on "practicalities" is being characterized by the subordination of words to numbers. History is seen not as essential experience to be transmitted to new generations, but as abstractions that carry dank odors. Art is regarded as something that calls for indulgence or patronage and that has no place among the practical realities. Political science is viewed more as a specialized subject for people who want to go into politics than as an opportunity for citizens to develop a knowledgeable relationship with the systems by which human societies are governed. Finally, literature and philosophy are assigned the role of add-ons—intellectual adornments that have nothing to do with "genuine" education.

5   Instead of trying to shrink the liberal arts, the American people ought to be putting pressure on colleges and universities to increase the ratio of the humanities to the sciences. Most serious studies of medical-school curricula in recent years have called attention to the stark gaps in the liberal education of medical students. The experts agree that the schools shouldn't leave it up to students to close those gaps.

6   We must not make it appear, however, that nothing is being done. In the past decade, the National Endowment for the Humanities has been a prime mover in infusing the liberal arts into medical education and other special-ized schools. During this past year alone, NEH has given 108 grants to medical schools and research organizations in the areas of ethics and human

values. Some medical schools, like the one at Pennsylvania State University, have led the way in both the number and the depth of courses offered in the humanities. Penn State has been especially innovative in weaving literature and philosophy into the full medical course of study. It is ironical that the pressure against the humanities should be manifesting itself at precisely the times when so many medical schools are at long last moving in this direction.

7   The irony of the emphasis being placed on careers is that nothing is more valuable for anyone who has had a professional or vocational education than to be able to deal with abstractions or complexities, or to feel comfortable with subtleties of thought or language, or to think sequentially. The doctor who knows only disease is at a disadvantage alongside the doctor who knows at least as much about people as he does about pathological organisms. The lawyer who argues in court from a narrow legal base is no match for the lawyer who can connect legal precedents to historical experience and who employs wide-ranging intellectual resources. The business executive whose competence in general management is bolstered by an artistic ability to deal with people is of prime value to his company. For the technologist, the engineering of consent can be just as important as the engineering of moving parts. In all these respects, the liberal arts have much to offer. Just in terms of career preparation, therefore, a student is short-changing himself by shortcutting the humanities.

8   But even if it could be demonstrated that the humanities contribute nothing directly to a job, they would still be an essential part of the educational equipment of any person who wants to come to terms with life. The humanities would be expendable only if human beings didn't have to make decisions that affect their lives and the lives of others; if the human past never existed or had nothing to tell us about the present; if thought processes were irrelevant to the achievement of purpose; if creativity was beyond the human mind and had nothing to do with the joy of living; if human relationships were random aspects of life; if human beings never had to cope with panic or pain, or if they never had to anticipate the connection between cause and effect; if all the mysteries of mind and nature were fully plumbed; and if no special demands arose from the accident of being born a human being instead of a hen or a hog.

9   Finally, there would be good reason to eliminate the humanities if a free society were not absolutely dependent on a functioning citizenry. If the main purpose of a university is job training, then the underlying philosophy of our government has little meaning. The debates that went into the making of American society concerned not just institutions or governing principles but the capacity of humans to sustain those institutions. Whatever the disagreements were over other issues at the American Constitutional Convention, the fundamental question sensed by everyone, a question that lay over the entire assembly, was whether the people themselves would understand what it meant to hold the ultimate power of society, and whether they had enough of a sense of history and destiny to know where they had been and where they ought to be going.

10   Jefferson was prouder of having been the founder of the University of Virginia than of having been President of the United States. He knew that the

educated and developed mind was the best assurance that a political system could be made to work—a system based on the informed consent of the governed. If this idea fails, then all the saved tax dollars in the world will not be enough to prevent the nation from turning on itself.

In "How to Make People Smaller Than They Are," Cousins' primary goal is to convince his audience. In rereading and analyzing this and the following selections, ask yourself *how* the authors appeal to a significant range of general readers.

The second sample of persuasive writing is a student essay. The subject is different, but the key underlying principles of persuasive discourse are also evident in Bobbi Farrell's piece. As with the first selection, read the essay and answer the questions concerning thesis, context, author credibility, information provided, intended audience, and the style of the essay. In addition, pay particular attention to the kind and amount of evidence provided to convince us of the author's point.

SMOKE

Bobbi Farrell

1   I don't remember my father. But I can remember the day when my mother came home from the hospital, crying. She stood in the cellar doorway wearing her gray hat with the red feather and her beige winter coat. She twisted a pair of cloth gloves in her hands as she announced that he was dead. When my three-year-old sister began crying and climbed onto her lap, I vied for attention by showing how brave I was: I didn't cry. But how much can a four-year-old understand?

2   It was years later when I learned of their futile fight against his lung cancer—the seizures, the trips to Rochester, the bills. I know the memory can't be right. My father died in July, so why would my mother be wearing a beige winter coat with a gray hat? I probably only recognized that she was dressed up; both the gray hat and the beige coat were among her wardrobe of good clothes. I realize now that knowledge I acquired later became meshed with the real memory. This memory was all I knew about my father's death; I added to it as I learned more about what happened.

3   I was a little older when my grandfather died, so my picture of him is more accurate. He sat on his white recliner and held me in his lap. A gold spittoon waited for him on one side of the chair, a standing ashtray on the other. I picture him sitting there and smiling; I'm glad I didn't see him just before he died. I guess the throat cancer ate a hole all the way through his neck. I wouldn't want to remember him like that.

4   My aunt Petty had blond hair and a nose just like my mother's. She helped us wallpaper the upstairs bedrooms. Already that paper is brown and peeling. She moved to California about fifteen years ago. Fortunately. In California she was close to Mexico, and the Laetrile she smuggled in kept her alive for more than a year after her doctors gave up hope.

5   My uncle Ray was a chain smoker, and he never got cancer. Yet I hated to
be around him if I had to listen to him or had to try to talk to him. He had a
raspy voice and couldn't finish a sentence without going into a coughing
spasm. He couldn't even do his own work; my cousins took care of his farm,
and he sat in the house with my aunt. The emphysema finally killed him last
year.

6   I'm sure that, like the memory of my father, the pictures I have of these
people were developed over a long period of time and many experiences.
The facts of one loss, added to the facts of another, and yet another,
gradually led me to equate cigarettes with death.

7   I've always hated people who badger other people about smoking
because it isn't good for them. I do many things that aren't good for me, so
I'm not in any position to preach. And I know smokers have probably heard
all the warnings about the dangers of tobacco. Yet it is difficult for me to hold
comments back. I find the sickly smell of that lethal smoke repulsive. The
crumbly gray ashes in an ashtray, or worse, on a table or floor are dirty and
disgusting. I walk away if I can, but there are always situations where I am
required to stay and where people insist on smoking, insist on unconsciously
blowing the gray haze in my face, reminding me that, as much as I hate them,
I will never get away from cigarettes.

8   I have a cousin in Detroit who has finally thrown his cigarettes away, but
it's probably too late. He's waiting for the test results, but the doctors are
fairly sure of what they'll say. I'm glad I never knew him.

        The third example of persuasive writing is the accompanying adver-
tisement for Delta Air Lines. In reading this ad, account for the difference
in subject matter, but ask yourself the same basic questions regarding
persuasion as listed for the other two readings. In addition, answer the
following questions:

1. How would you describe the difference between the actual author(s) of the ad
    and the personality projected by it? How would you account for this difference?
2. What is repeated in this ad and what is the effect of this repetition?

PREWRITING

Recall that persuasion is the art of influencing others to accept the ideas or
to perform the actions you want. Ideally, this means getting others to
accept your *informed opinion*, an opinion for which you can offer logical as
well as emotional arguments and information as well as feeling. In the best
sense of the term, when you persuade you create, in a responsible manner
and for beneficial ends, an equation between yourself as writer of language
and your audience as reader. You attempt to cause the reader to identify
with your position or point of view. This aim is what all three of the
selections you have just read have in common.

Delta is an airline run by more than
35,000 professionals. Like Senior Customer
Services Agent Rod Hill, a man who takes
on loads of work every day.

Rod's been with Delta 10 years. Eight of them
have been in baggage service. With that much
experience he can tell you it takes far more than
muscle to load Delta's sophisticated jets. It takes precise
planning. Meticulous attention to detail. Plenty of hustle.
And a special kind of "can do" attitude.

You may not notice Rod on the job. On the ramp. On
the cargo tug. On the go. But you can pick up his
sense of dedication every time you pick up
your bag, on time, at your destination.

Delta is ready when you are.®

*This is Delta's Wide-Ride Lockheed
L-1011 TriStar. You fly in quiet luxury.*

Choosing a Topic

Virtually any subject of potential interest to an audience can be the focus or topic of persuasion. Student housing, athletic tickets, and course/instructor evaluations are familiar subjects on college campuses. The *quality* and *cost* of student housing, the *price* or *availability* of football or basketball tickets, and the *administration* and *use* of course/instructor evaluations might all be focuses of legitimate topics for persuasive discourse. For example, students might try to persuade the college administration not to demolish cheap, low-quality housing in order to build high-quality housing with a correspondingly high price tag. Similarly, instructors might contend that since course/instructor evaluations are administered in a variety of ways and are not uniformly required, the results of these evaluations are of limited value.

The crucial question in choosing a topic is whether the writer understands a given topic and recognizes *how it is or can be made relevant* to a particular audience. That is, the writer must understand from the beginning how addressing a given topic can help the audience answer a question or resolve a dilemma, deal with an issue or make a decision, confront a prejudice or allay anxiety, or otherwise satisfy the kinds of physical, emotional, economic, social, and intellectual needs people face every day. If, for example, students want low fees and ticket prices, and car buyers want safety, high quality, and good mileage, then it only makes sense for college administrators and auto manufacturers to keep these concerns in mind. If an observer sees a problematical trend toward vocational training, the deep personal effects of smoking, or customers' concerns related to air travel (as in the three preceding samples), then these issues can be made the focus of persuasive discourse. At its best, persuasion is the art of addressing and solving a human problem—a topic defined and spoken to with regard to a specific audience and its concerns—in a responsible and productive manner.

Exercises on Choosing a Topic for Persuasion

1. Identify, in your own experience, a conflict of needs or values that defines a situation calling for persuasion. Consider areas or concerns in your life such as money, privacy, (in)dependence, expectations, and recreation. Consider relationships such as those with friends, family, relatives, teachers, roommate(s), and employer. Explain the conflict and how persuasion might usefully be applied to it.
2. Identify, in general or public experience, a conflict of needs or values (an issue) that defines a situation calling for persuasion. Explain the conflict and how persuasion might usefully be applied to it.

3. **Establish a specific topic, appropriate for a persuasive essay, for each of the following general subjects:**
   a. **Off-campus housing**
   b. **Textbook pricing and buy-back policies**
   c. **The drinking age in your state**
   d. **Cable television**

Understanding Audience

Whether arguing in favor of the liberal arts, encouraging readers to travel on Delta Air Lines, or speaking against smoking, the authors of the preceding selections would have been foolish to try to deceive an educated and potentially skeptical audience, one that typically requires a minimum of relevant evidence to be persuaded of a point. It is the authors' understanding of and respect for their audience—the audience's assumptions, intelligence, and basic knowledge of the subject—that lies behind each of the selections. An understanding of audience must underlie any successful attempt at persuasive writing.

In the Norman Cousins essay an understanding of audience begins with the author's assumption that most readers of *Saturday Review* are themselves college-educated and have some interest in the relationship between a liberal arts education and the various vocations and professions. Cousins reflects his assumption by referring to both vocations and professions and by mentioning specifically not only medical schools and doctors, but also training in law, business, and technology.

In a more general sense Cousins shows his understanding of audience in paragraph 8, when he argues on behalf of the humanities in terms of the basic needs, values, and experiences of most people—people who want to "come to terms with life" by making decisions, understanding the past, grasping cause and effect relationships, being creative, and so on. Cousins knows his audience and what makes it tick, and this knowledge is reflected in the way he writes his essay.

In "Smoke" Bobbi Farrell shows her understanding of audience through her consistent appeal to our basic human need to have close personal relationships and to resent anything that causes them to end prematurely. Her assumption is that almost all readers have experienced or needed relationships with a father, grandfather, aunt, uncle, or cousin and will relate to the kinds of losses she describes.

In the Delta Air Lines ad the basic audience is anyone who might at some time need to travel by air (not, for example, just the "professional traveler"). But more specifically, this ad is aimed at people—most of us, presumably—who believe that experience and dedication in an airline can make air travel pleasant for its customers. According to the ad, Delta is "run by more than 35,000 professionals"—all presumably like Rod Hill, who not only "takes on loads of work every day," but also exemplifies the company's "precise planning," "attention to detail," "hustle," and " 'can do' attitude." In short, this ad attempts to persuade the reader to fly on Delta by claiming that Delta will fulfill the customer's needs for speed, dependability, and good service generally.

In doing persuasive writing of your own, note that persuasion is sometimes aimed at audiences even more specifically defined than those just discussed. For example, religious or political affiliation is often the key characteristic of the audience, as when a member of the clergy addresses a congregation or your representative in Congress solicits your financial support. Other significant characteristics often crucial when accounting for audience in persuasion are financial status, sex, age, educational level, ethnic background, and occupation or job status. Any one or a combination of these audience characteristics might determine the statement and shape of a given piece of persuasion.

Exercises on Understanding Audience

1. Identify a potential audience for one of the topics developed in one of the exercises above on "Choosing a Topic." Describe the audience's relationship to you as a potential writer and to the topic itself.
2. Write out a list of characteristics that describe a potential (that is, relevant) audience for one of the topics developed in one of the preceding exercises in this chapter; identify the audience's needs, expectations, knowledge, assumptions, beliefs, prejudices, fears, and so on. Which of these characteristics would you consider the dominant one, and why?

Understanding Cultural and Situational Context

In writing or analyzing persuasive discourse, you should be aware that the discourse makes sense only to the extent that it accounts for the cultural and situational contexts of the message and the intended audience. The *cultural context* of a given piece of persuasion includes the basic knowledge and underlying assumptions and beliefs with which the audience identifies. Cultural context includes the political, religious, and philosophical convictions that members of a given society often take for granted: convictions summarized in key terms such as capitalism, youth, Christianity, communism, progress, free enterprise, humanitarianism, and democracy.

Note that the combination of information and belief that we call cultural context is often summarized in a brief slogan or statement relevant to one or more aspects of the audience's collective experience:

Youth will be served.

The sun never sets on the British Empire.

America is the land of opportunity.

Our team is part of a long and glorious tradition.

We are entering an era of high technology.

Assertions like these, which often become powerful enough to dominate a particular time and place, have always been effective in persuading audiences.

Note also that contexts vary with culture. Claims or promises of "freedom of choice" in the context of politics or shopping are obviously comforting to the American public, but might only be taken as crude ironies by a person faced with a single candidate on a ballot or a single brand of a given product in the store. Similarly, an advertisement for dog food based on the assumption that dogs are finicky eaters might make sense to some American pet owners, but little sense in a culture in which pets are a luxury.

Finally, observe that persuasion does not always make *explicit* use of cultural beliefs; often the belief is an *implicit* working assumption on the part of both the persuader and the audience. For example, we are familiar with ads for everything from cosmetics to cars that only *imply* that in America "it's good to look, feel, or be young" or that it's patriotic to buy an American-made product. Similarly, while it's more likely that persuasion will make use of a positive cultural belief ("Prosperity is just around the corner") than a negative one ("We're in a depression"), in either case the belief itself need not be directly expressed at all to have an effect on the audience.

Situational context is the immediate situation in which the persuasion takes place—a 50-minute exam, a legislative debate, a sermon, a party, a bull session, a courtroom proceeding, the reading of a magazine, watching TV. Successful persuaders always select the best possible situations for their messages and (when this isn't possible) adapt their discourse to a given context. For example, aspirants for public office invariably select friendly hometown audiences (that is, situations) before which to make major announcements, and TV advertisers shape their commercial messages to 20- or 30-second time slots that will be brief but (presumably) tolerable interruptions in some type of entertainment. Similarly, the controlled conditions of an essay examination have a significant effect on what, how much, and how well the student writes and the actual product the instructor expects. That is, what is possible, preferable, and expected in any piece of persuasive discourse is affected by the conditions under which the writer or speaker works and the audience responds. As a writer of persuasion, try to create advantageous situational contexts when possible and to adapt productively to undesirable ones when necessary.

Exercises on Understanding Cultural and Situational Context

1. Describe the *cultural* context of each of the following:
   a. An increase in tuition at your college
   b. An ad for detergent on television
   c. An ad for a ten-day "miracle diet"
   d. An increase in insurance rates for drivers under 25
2. Describe two likely *immediate* or *situational* contexts for any two of the topics listed in the preceding exercise. For example, describe the most likely contexts—in terms of audience, timing, and placement—for a detergent ad.

Understanding Persuasive Appeals

Persuasion is carried out through the use of four basic appeals, commonly referred to as emotional, ethical, logical, and stylistic or esthetic. The first three of these are discussed in the sections that immediately follow; stylistic appeal is discussed in the section that corresponds to the sections on style in the other chapters of this book.

THE ROLE OF EMOTIONAL APPEAL. Emotional appeal in persuasion is essentially any appeal to *the emotional needs of the audience* that might help the writer make a point. Such basic human needs as those for love, security, flattery, self-assertion, companionship, attention, and sex are commonly appealed to in persuasive discourse. For example, lawyers, addressing judges and juries on behalf of their clients, make impassioned appeals for understanding and sympathy. Biologists and space scientists care deeply that others accept their work, and often argue emotionally on its behalf—particularly when immediately practical applications of projects or experiments are not apparent. Advertisers of everything from soft drinks to cars try to get us to see sexual implications in the purchase of their products.

In creating its advertisement, Delta Air Lines was obviously aware of and wished to avoid mentioning the most negative aspects of its product—aspects that evoke negative emotions and include everything from intentional overbooking to potential midair collisions. After all, the goal of the ad is to make the prospective customer think warmly of its product and to pay for it. So the company makes a positive emotional appeal (we want to believe we'll be taken care of) by greeting us with a smile and the assertion that "Delta is ready when you are."

In "How to Make People Smaller Than They Are," Norman Cousins is also essentially positive in his appeal. That is, his article is, in emphasis and tone, less an argument against "vocationalization" than one in favor of the liberal arts. Since it would do him little good to criticize people's concern with practicality and the job market (an emotional concern as well as a logical one), he explains why a solid background in the humanities can ultimately be an asset in our lives. The effect of paragraphs 8 and 9 in particular is to show us that the humanities not only help us make practical decisions and understand the past, but also help tie us to creativity, human relationships, "the joy of living," and the "free society" of Thomas Jefferson and the U.S. Constitution.

It is usually easier and more effective to appeal to audiences in positive rather than negative emotional terms. When this is impossible, good writers make clear why being negative is the only choice. "Smoke" is a good example of an essay cast in negative terms, beginning with the facts that smoking is an established cultural habit and Bobbi Farrell is against it. Her essay is necessarily negative, but it is successful because we as readers are made to see *not* smoking as a desirable choice and to identify with her and the deep emotions she has felt toward those who have died.

The emotional part of your audience's personality is potentially one of the most important to the success of your persuasion. Remember that no matter how logical people are or wish to be, they are capable of emotional responses to matters that concern them.

THE ROLE OF ETHICAL APPEAL. An *ethical appeal* in persuasion is an appeal based on the *ethos or character of the speaker or writer* of a given piece of discourse. The ethical appeal in persuasion is also often referred to as the *appeal of authority*, since it is an appeal in terms of the presumed authority of the speaker on the subject under discussion.

The Delta Air Lines ad offers an excellent example of an ethical appeal. Note that the ad literally projects to us an image of the airline, specifically the image of Rod Hill. While the actual text of the ad stresses the experience and dedication of Delta's many employees, the ad is dominated by the personality projected by the picture of a specific person. Rod Hill is meant to represent or characterize Delta Air Lines. We know, of course, that Delta Air Lines is actually a large corporation. We can also assume that, in the long run, a customer services agent has little say in the company as a whole. But Delta wishes to avoid striking the public as a faceless institution that might be unwilling or unable to respond effectively to the individual needs of customers.

Rod Hill—and by association, Delta Air Lines—projects to the reader of the ad three key personality traits that usually prove crucial in persuading audiences. Hill and Delta are seen as having good sense regarding the product, good will toward the reader-consumer, and good moral character. Once we recall how most of us tend (or at least want) to believe in those who possess knowledge and good judgment, express good intentions toward us, and project sincerity and responsibility, we can see why Delta chose Rod Hill to make its ethical appeal in this ad and how, in basic terms, the ethical appeal works.

"Smoke" too is heavily dependent on the ethical appeal. Bobbi Farrell wishes to convince us of how destructive smoking can be, and she accomplishes her purpose through the creation of a compelling first-person account. We consistently see the effects of smoking in personal terms, in terms of the "I" with whom the essay begins and ends. We are persuaded of Farrell's point because of the direct personal experience (hence knowledge and authority) of the narrator—the daughter, granddaughter, niece, and cousin of the smokers who died.

The Norman Cousins article makes much less use of the ethical appeal than either "Smoke" or the airline ad. In fact, Cousins tries to keep his personality out of the essay and to persuade by making effective use of what is called the *logical appeal*.

THE ROLE OF LOGICAL APPEAL. The logical appeal in persuasion is based on the writer's use (or apparent use) of *rational methods* for convincing the audience. Since the use of ethical or emotional appeal alone is often insufficient to convince an audience, the writer must frequently combine either or both of these appeals with the logical appeal, with *specific evidence handled in a way that makes sense*.

In "How to Make People Smaller Than They Are," Cousins creates a logical appeal by examining the evidence relevant to his subject and presenting specific examples of that evidence to the reader. To persuade us that the trend toward vocationalization does exist, Cousins provides examples of two sources of pressure, the determination to reduce taxes and the need to be attractive to employers (paragraph 2). In addition, Cousins gives as examples the way history, art, political science, literature, and philosophy are perceived and treated by many people today (paragraph 4). To persuade us that a liberal arts education can enable people to develop and function to their fullest human capacity, Cousins follows a three-part strategy. First, he cites as examples doctors, business executives, and others whose work can be enhanced by a liberal arts education (paragraph 9). Second, Cousins lists ways in which the humanities should be important to "any person who wants to come to terms with life" in making decisions, coping with pain, and so on (paragraph 8). He gives examples of the importance of humanistic knowledge in terms of basic human needs. Third, Cousins argues, using the example of American democracy, that education in the humanities is particularly important in a free society, a society "absolutely dependent on a functioning citizenry" (paragraphs 9–10).

As already mentioned, the Cousins essay is not without its emotional appeal, in terms of specific needs and convictions on the part of the audience (for example, responses to love and pain and basic patriotism). However, Cousins mainly leads us logically to his conclusions through the use of effective examples.

Bobbi Farrell's essay makes a logical appeal in basically the same way. For example, she knows of smokers who have *not* died of cancer, but that is not her point. Thus she selects and presents several examples of people who did die and, in addition, uses only examples of which she has direct knowledge. Note that the fact that she is able to cite so many cases in connection with one family adds strength to her persuasion and that her personal involvement makes her case both more convincing than it might otherwise be and difficult to dismiss as "too abstract and general."

In strictly formal usage—as in proving a thesis or in conducting scientific research—a logical argument requires that all of the available evidence be reported. But a writer seeking to *persuade* an audience—that is, to convince rather than to prove—is not obliged to follow strict "scientific" procedure. The persuasive writer might use as evidence one or any number of relevant examples, and not necessarily all those available. The persuasive writer will often select carefully from among a large number of examples and present to the reader only the best ones for the purpose: the kind and amount of evidence necessary to convince. (The use of one or more examples to make a general point is basic to what is more formally called *inductive proof*; see Chapter 5.)

You may find Figure 3.1 helpful in remembering the persuasive appeals explained here so far (as well as stylistic appeal, which follows). Note that each part of the triangle corresponds to a part of the basic rhetorical triangle (p. 10) and the major aims of writing (pp. 10, 11). This

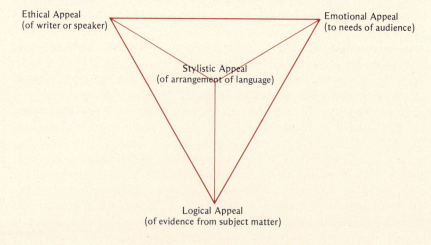

FIGURE 3.1 The persuasive appeals.

should clarify that persuasion involves all parts of the rhetorical process and all of the aims indirectly.

Exercises on Understanding Persuasive Appeals

1. Bring to class a particularly striking and presumably effective magazine ad for each of the following: a beverage, a cosmetic product, and an automobile. Discuss and group the ads submitted by the class in terms of their primary appeals: logical, emotional, and ethical. When an ad is dominated by color, picture, or design (its artistic appeal), categorize it in terms of the appeal you consider to be the next most important to its success.
2. What does the grouping of the ads in exercise 1 suggest about the dominant appeals in American advertising today? What does the grouping of these ads tell you about the nature and method of magazine advertising in particular?
3. Select one of the ads that works predominantly in terms of emotional appeal and describe as precisely and completely as possible the reader for whom it was intended.
4. Assuming a student audience, what appeal or appeals would Governor X use in persuading them to accept each of the following? Give reasons for your answers.
   a. A one-third reduction in state-sponsored student loans
   b. Building a new faculty club rather than a new intramural facility
   c. Starting an ROTC unit on the campus
5. Assuming an audience of business executives, what appeal or appeals would Governor X use in persuading them to accept each of the following? Provide reasons for your answers.
   a. Raising corporate taxes and increasing the amount of state funding available for student loans
   b. Providing inexpensive day-care facilities for use by student families at each state-supported university
6. Write a one-page analysis of how the primary persuasive appeal works in one of the ads used in exercise 1.
7. Write a 500 to 750 word speech for Governor X on any one of the topics mentioned in exercises 4 and 5.

WRITING PERSUASION: ORGANIZATION

Tradition tells us that the basic organization of persuasive writing is as follows: (1) the introduction, (2) background information necessary for an understanding of the subject, (3) the explicit statement of the writer's position or thesis, (4) an outline or list of points to be proven, (5) the proofs of these points, (6) the refutation of opposing positions, and (7) the conclusion. However, this pattern of organization is usually modified depending on specific subjects, audiences, and situational contexts. Certain basic units of organization are part of most persuasion, but which of these are necessary and the sequence in which they are used varies with the individual case.

Let's briefly examine "How to Make People Smaller Than They Are." An organizational outline of the article looks like this:

1. Introduction: title and paragraph 1; last sentence of paragraph 3
2. Background Information or Account of Circumstances: paragraphs 2–4, 6
3. Writer's Position: paragraph 5
4. Points to be Proven: first sentences of paragraphs 7–9
5. Proofs: paragraphs 7–10
6. Refutation: implicit only; never explicitly addressed
7. Conclusion: paragraph 10

Note that Cousins' article reflects the first three points of the traditional outline. His introduction presents his subject (paragraph 1) and grabs the reader's attention (title). His account of the circumstances behind the article (paragraphs 2–4) gives the reader basic information concerning American education today—information that serves as the logical basis or point of reference for the rest of the article and suggests that Cousins himself is informed enough to be able to tell us what's going on. Cousins' statement of position (paragraph 5) is quite direct and helps explain his title: surely no one would want to "shrink the liberal arts" if that also means "making people smaller than they are." This leads to the transition sentence: "The experts agree that the schools shouldn't leave it up to students to close those gaps."

After this, however, Cousins' essay illustrates how a given piece of persuasion can vary from the basic pattern. He never provides a separate list of points to be proven. These points are simply identified in the first sentences of the actual paragraphs (7–9) in which he provides his evidence and proof. As for refutation of the opposing view, Cousins never really provides one. He may feel that the prevailing trend in favor of vocationalization need not be confronted here, or that he lacks the space to do it.

The conclusion of the article (paragraph 10) is not so much an overall summary or statement of emphasis as a conclusion of the final example and proof (paragraph 9); that is, Cousins does not end by reviewing the essay as a whole but by stressing his final point.

Variations on the traditional pattern of organization can also be seen in the airline ad and Bobbi Farrell's "Smoke." For example, note that Delta does not offer a systematic refutation of its competitors' claims that *they* offer the best customer service. Note also that the airline ad lets us assume that the points discussed are the only ones relevant to such a discussion, and that there's no explicit list of what *is* being proven in the ad.

In "Smoke," note that it is not until late in her essay (paragraph 7), *after* she has provided almost all her evidence, that Farrell states her position explicitly, and that since this statement comes so near the end she needs no formal conclusion.

These examples show that neither the basic units of organization nor their sequence must be determined according to a rigid formula or pattern. In fact, many writers would reduce the list of seven basic units of organization to four: (1) introduction, (2) basic information on background or circumstances, (3) evidence or proof, and (4) conclusion. In such cases the writer will often incorporate a thesis statement or a list of points to be proven, or both, in the introductory paragraph. Still others would reduce the necessary units to two: (1) statement of the writer's position and (2) evidence or proof. Persuasive writing may actually do without formal introductions and conclusions, and any of the other traditional units may appear (when they do appear) almost anywhere in the essay they will be effective.

Exercises on Organizing Persuasion

1. Using the seven-point format described at the beginning of this section, write an outline for a persuasive theme for or against one of the topics developed in an exercise in the prewriting section of this chapter or on one of the following:
   a. A proposal to double the fee for student parking on campus
   b. A proposal to curtail library hours so your college or university can save on energy costs
   c. The suggestion that there be a fifty percent increase in social dues for your sorority, fraternity, or dormitory house
   d. A proposed city ordinance forbidding cats, as well as dogs, from being unleased except when under direct control of their owners
2. Reduce the seven-point outline of the preceding exercise to a simpler, four-point outline. Briefly explain—in terms of subject matter, audience, situational context, or other factors—why the points you eliminated might be dispensable.

WRITING PERSUASION: STYLE

Since the purpose of persuasion is to convey a strong message to a specific audience in order to establish belief and promote action, the persuasive writer can actually spend more time thinking about tactics for presenting a given subject than dealing with the subject itself. Style, a key persuasive appeal in its own right, can in some instances dominate a given piece of discourse.

Basic to effective style in persuasion is conscious attention to the following: (1) the topic, the audience, the primary persuasive appeal(s) to be used, and the cultural and situational contexts of the message, as discussed in the preceding sections of this chapter; (2) the communications medium being used; and (3) such specific writing concerns as format, length, repetition, diction, grammar, symbol, and rhythm.

The effects of topic, audience, persuasive appeals, and cultural and situational context on persuasive style will be reviewed by means of the examples following the discussion of communications media.

Communications Media

The style of persuasion is strongly affected by the medium used to convey the message. Advertisements, editorials, speeches, solicitation letters, lectures, and all other forms of persuasive discourse are strongly affected in strategy and style by the media in which they appear. As a general rule, the electronic media, and television in particular, tend to encourage short, quick-hitting statements that appeal to us in terms of color, sound, and action. As viewers, we are often bombarded with unsupported assertions that are carried along by minidramas, animation, and music. By contrast, the print media—including newspapers, maga-zines, professional journals, and books—often try to take advantage of the audience's opportunity to examine and reexamine material, and they frequently attempt to provide evidence and explanations. For example, note that a movie might be reviewed in a two-minute segment (including a selected clip or two) on a TV program, in a nontechnical one-column article in a popular magazine, or in an in-depth five-page article in a journal devoted to film.

Two further examples, those of a televised presidential press confer-ence and an in-class essay examination, will help illustrate how all the factors discussed so far can affect persuasive style.

A press conference typically involves some prepared remarks by the president on the preannounced topic (for example, the economy), fol-lowed by a question-and-answer session with the journalists. But this basic format is enhanced by a number of stylistic factors, beginning with the president's entrance and introduction to the audience. Further, the president is obviously groomed to make the best possible impression, looks serious when making key points, and often tries to smile even when responding to hostile questions, since his medium is a visual one. Beyond these points, though, the speech is inevitably general in nature (the audience isn't made up of economists), positive in tone (things will either stay good or get better, depending on the current economic context), and forceful with regard to the administration's role in the economic process and its relationship to the public (the president tries to project strong eithical appeal). Finally, observe that there is a style to the delivery of the speech itself, with emphasis on key words and phrases and strategic pauses for the applause that inevitably (and emotionally) follows references to such concepts (cultural context) as democracy, low unemployment, American know-how, and the free-enterprise system.

Now consider an in-class essay examination. Both the student (writer) and the instructor (reader) are aware that by necessity (situational context) the writing produced will be somewhat limited in scope and depth, and, since it will be handwritten in a booklet or on notepaper (medium), it won't be as polished as a paper might be. In addition, both writer and reader are aware that the student's job is to convince the instructor that he or she has a solid grasp of the course material, or some specific aspect of it, without having to present information on or prove an understanding of everything in the course. Obviously the general assumption (cultural context) is that the student is responsible for all the relevant reading and lecture material and thus should be able to make judicious, representative choices of information and examples with which to write a convincing (logically appealing) answer that both reflects overall understanding and offers some specific detail.

In short, the style of persuasive discourses as different as a press conference and an essay exam are affected at every level by an awareness of topic, audience, persuasive appeal, context, and medium of presentation.

Other Stylistic Considerations

BREVITY.   Since boredom and difficulty in understanding are two responses persuaders wish to avoid in their audiences, much persuasive discourse is relatively short in length; it is presented in terms of short sentences, paragraphs, and words. For example, note the impact of the first and last sentences of "Smoke" and that all of the "sentences" in the Delta Air Lines ad are short. Only when speakers have captive audiences, or when they badly misjudge the interest, expectations, or attention-span of those audiences, do they indulge in lengthy presentations.

REPETITION.   Since the goal of persuasion is usually to get the audience both to believe and to act on that belief, persuasive discourse is often characterized by repetition of words, names, figures, numbers, and sentence and paragraph structures. In the airline ad, for example, note the repetition of the name *Delta* and the repeated sentence pattern of "on the job. On the ramp. On the cargo tug. On the go," and, of course, "on time." In watching ads on TV, note how many times the name of a product is repeated in the span of a few seconds in order to make it stick in our minds. In reading essays, note less dependence on literal repetition and more on repetition of sentence and paragraph structures.

EVERYDAY SPEECH.   Most audiences respond positively to persuasion addressed to them in familiar terms. *Familiar* here means what a given audience considers the *ordinary style* of everyday discourse. Note that while the Norman Cousins essay is not written in the same informal idiom as the airline ad, it is written in language far from that of a formal or technical report. Bobbi Farrell's essay is even more conversational than Cousins', and, in comparison, the airline ad is almost chatty; but all three are clearly more conversational than a formal report or logical proof. A successful writer of persuasion makes the audience comfortable and receptive by communicating in a diction and tone the audience identifies with and understands.

FLEXIBILITY IN GRAMMAR AND SPELLING.   The language of everyday communication, particularly of everyday speech, is not only familiar but flexible. For example, most advertising makes liberal use of contractions because it wants to project a friendly, conversational tone; the avoidance of contractions, however right for formal prose, would undermine the personal appeal. In the same way, though in a different spirit, Bobbi Farrell's use of contractions sustains the conversational, almost intimate tone of "Smoke."

However, grammatical flexibility goes beyond this. In order to have the strongest impact on the audience, persuasion often manipulates language in ways that are technically incorrect but appropriate to a specific persuasive situation and goal. For example, consider the use of nonstandard diction and ungrammatical phrasing in television ads based on ethical appeal. Consider the frequent deletion of standard punctuation in many magazine ads. Consider the frequent appearance of sentence fragments, especially in naming a product, stating a belief, or emphasizing a particular point: "Quality. Just what you'd expect from us." "The Anacin difference." "Gaines Puppy Choice. With higher quality protein than dry puppy food."

Successful persuasion might also make use of questions and exclamations. Many persuasive questions are merely rhetorical ones, such as "Wouldn't you like to get better mileage from your car?" and "Don't you deserve the best there is?" But any pointed question that addresses the target audience's concerns—"Shouldn't students get more money back when they resell their books?"—immediately draws that audience into the subject of the writing. Exclamatory statements also seem to demand our attention: "America's turning 7-Up!" "Uncle Sam wants YOU!" And even "VEGAS!"

As for spelling, we need only recall that much persuasion—and particularly persuasion in advertising—makes frequent use not only of contractions (Dunkin' Donuts) and abbreviations (T. G. I. F., 4–6 P.M.), but of purposely misspelled, colloquial, or newly created words, such as U-Haul, Renuzit, "deelishious," Kool-Whip, "broasted" chicken, "Ladies' Nite!" and "Gotcha!"

PICTURES AND SYMBOLS, NAMES AND NUMBERS. You will recall that Delta wants us to accept Rod Hill as a representative of the company. In other words, for the purpose of the ad, he symbolizes the airline itself. In the same way, persuasive discourse makes constant use of pictures and symbols to make names and concepts stick in the public mind. Ronald McDonald is a symbol, as are Colonel Sanders, Mr. Clean, and the Blue-Bonnet girl. Santa Claus, Uncle Sam, and Smokey the Bear are also symbols that sell ideas. In American culture cowboys, athletes, models, and movie stars are also symbols for concepts such as independence, strength, skill, beauty, and practical experience of one kind or another. They are frequently used to promote products for which association with such concepts is important or seems relevant: cigarettes, politicians, beverages, charitable organizations, beauty products, and so on.

In persuasion, symbols are shortcut devices that help announce products or invoke concepts or major cultural beliefs without the use of words. In the same way, names and numbers often become important stylistic devices in the service of persuasive discourse. The same people who created the golden arches to help us locate hamburgers also remind us that "billions and billions" have already been sold. Politicians create such symbolic names as the New Deal and the New Frontier; books, records, and athletic teams are promoted as important if they are among the top ten; and many products are identified by catchy, memorable numbers, whether or not these numbers have logical connections with what they label: Ten-O-Six, 409, Colt 45, Seven-Eleven, and so on.

JINGLES AND RHYTHM. Much persuasion is made effective through emphasis on the rhythm of presentation. The most common manipulation of rhythm for persuasive purposes appears in television advertising, which invariably ties messages to catchy jingles composed specifically for that purpose. "You deserve a break today," the song assures us, while another jingle urges us to "Reach out and touch someone." They make it sound simple, easy, and right, like becoming a Pepper: "All you gotta do is taste!" Jingles like these—along with their skipping clowns, dancing cats, and pseudo-Broadway production numbers —set the pace for the selling of everything from pet food to soft drinks to stockings.

But rhythm is used in effective persuasion of any kind. Here is Winston Churchill, announcing Britain's defiance of Nazi aggression early in World War II:

We shall go on to the end. We shall fight in France, we shall fight on the seas and on the oceans, we shall fight with growing confidence and

growing strength in the air, we shall defend our island, whatever the
cost may be. We shall fight on the beaches, we shall fight on the landing
grounds, we shall fight in the fields and in the streets, we shall fight in
the hills; we shall never surrender.

Churchill's style is obviously, but effectively, repetitive; he creates a
rhythm that complements his meaning and in this way creates persuasion
that inspires a response and sticks in our minds.

Persuasive style ranges from the relatively detailed and semiformal
essay approach of Norman Cousins to the highly informal and almost
wordless approach of an advertisement based on a single picture or symbol
("Come to Marlboro Country"). Persuasive style ranges from words,
sentences, and paragraphs systematically arranged in an essay or speech to
words (old and new), nonsentences, symbols, and rhythm manipulated in
advertisements on TV ("Coke is it!"). In persuasion, style is a function of
topic, audience, persuasive appeal(s), context, and medium. Persuasive
style is, once these are accounted for, anything that works.

Exercises on Style in Persuasion

1. **Using the list of stylistic concepts discussed in this section, analyze one of
    the following:**
    a. **A magazine ad for a health care or beauty product**
    b. **A magazine ad for an automobile or motorcycle**
    c. **A television ad for a fast-food chain**
    d. **A letter soliciting donations for a political candidate or a charitable
        organization**
2. **Assume that you have been assigned to write copy for the following ads,
    but have been instructed to use no more than three of the stylistic devices
    previously discussed. For two of these products, determine which
    stylistic devices you would use and write the copy. Be ready to explain
    why you would eliminate the other devices.**
    a. **A magazine ad for an encyclopedia**
    b. **A television ad for a hospital or health care facility**
    c. **A newspaper ad for a minor-league professional athletic team**
    d. **An open letter ad, to be signed by other students, objecting to
        legislative efforts to raise the legal drinking age in your state**

Additional Exercises on Persuasion

1. **Write a 500-word "typical reader" profile for a special interest publica-
    tion of your choice based on your analysis of the articles and ads it
    contains. Consider publications such as those associated with sports,
    motor vehicles, electronic equipment, men (or boys) only, women (or
    girls) only, farming, and various professions. Your profile should reflect**

your understanding of the particular reader as not just interested in a particular subject or life-style (this would be obvious), but interested because of certain social, economic, political, and philosophical assumptions and needs.

2. Write a 1 to 2 paragraph objective account of an auto accident in which vehicle A "rear-ends" vehicle B—vehicle B having failed to signal for a left turn; that is, write a "neutral" description as might be filed by a police officer with his or her report of the accident. Then, write a separate 2 to 3 paragraph account of the same accident from the point of view of one of the following:
   a. Driver of vehicle A, Jane Doe, a high school senior
   b. Driver of vehicle B, John Roe, a retired bus driver
   In a class discussion, you might wish to compare the accounts of the same accident by the two drivers.

3. Write a letter in which you try to persuade your parent(s) that you should be able to do one of the following:
   a. Pledge (or not pledge) a sorority or fraternity
   b. Live in an apartment off campus
   c. Change roommates
   d. Quit the _____ team or organization
   e. Quit school and get a job
   Be sure to account in your letter for the reservations or objections your reader(s) might raise.

4. Write a refutation, either personal or general in reference, of Norman Cousins' argument in "How to Make People Smaller Than They Are."

5. Write a refutation, either personal or general in reference, of the argument set forth in one of the additional persuasive readings that follow.

FURTHER READING AND DISCUSSION

Below are three examples of persuasion—one advertisement and two essays. Also included are discussion questions for each example. Read the examples and answer the questions. Be prepared to discuss your answers in class.

QUESTIONS ON U.S. NAVY AD

1. What is a "desk job," and what are the connotations of this term? What kind of a "desk" does this ad describe? What is "Mach 2"?
2. To whom is this ad addressed? To whom is it not addressed?
3. To what needs in the intended audience does this ad speak?
4. What "product" is being sold here? What is the "cost" of the product to the "consumer"?
5. How is this ad organized? What are its basic units?

wheat than on one in which wheat is intermingled with other crops to which the insect is not adapted.

16   The same thing happens in other situations. A generation or more ago, the towns of large areas of the United States lined their streets with the noble elm tree. Now the beauty they hopefully created is threatened with complete destruction as disease sweeps through the elms, carried by a beetle that would have only limited chance to build up large populations and to spread from tree to tree if the elms were only occasional trees in a richly diversified planting.

17   Another factor in the modern insect problem is one that must be viewed against a background of geologic and human history: the spreading of thousands of different kinds of organisms from their native homes to invade new territories. This worldwide migration has been studied and graphically described by the British ecologist Charles Elton in his recent book *The Ecology of Invasions*. During the Cretaceous Period, some hundred million years ago, flooding seas cut many land bridges between continents and living things found themselves confined in what Elton calls "colossal separate nature reserves." There, isolated from others of their kind, they developed many new species. When some of the land masses were joined again, about 15 million years go, these species began to move out into new territories—a movement that is not only still in progress but is now receiving considerable assistance from man.

18   The importation of plants is the primary agent in the modern spread of species, for animals have almost invariably gone along with the plants, quarantine being a comparatively recent and not completely effective innovation. The United States Office of Plant Introduction alone has introduced almost 200,000 species and varieties of plants from all over the world. Nearly half of the 180 or so major insect enemies of plants in the United States are accidental imports from abroad, and most of them have come as hitchhikers on plants.

19   In new territory, out of reach of the restraining hand of the natural enemies that kept down its numbers in its native land, an invading plant or animal is able to become enormously abundant. Thus it is no accident that our most troublesome insects are introduced species.

20   These invasions, both the naturally occurring and those dependent on human assistance, are likely to continue indefinitely. Quarantine and massive chemical campaigns are only extremely expensive ways of buying time. We are faced, according to Dr. Elton, "with a life-and-death need not just to find new technological means of suppressing this plant or that animal"; instead we need the basic knowledge of animal populations and their relations to their surroundings that will "promote an even balance and damp down the explosive power of outbreaks and new invasions."

21   Much of the necessary knowledge is now available but we do not use it. We train ecologists in our universities and even employ them in our government agencies but we seldom take their advice. We allow the chemical death rain to fall as though there were no alternative, whereas in fact there are many, and our ingenuity could soon discover many more if given opportunity.

22   Have we fallen into a mesmerized state that makes us accept as

inevitable that which is inferior or detrimental, as though having lost the will or the vision to demand that which is good? Such thinking, in the words of the ecologist Paul Shepard, "idealizes life with only its head out of water, inches above the limits of toleration of the corruption of its own environment. . . . Why should we tolerate a diet of weak poisons, a home in insipid surroundings, a circle of acquaintances who are not quite our enemies, the noise of motors with just enough relief to prevent insanity? Who would want to live in a world which is just not quite fatal?"

23   Yet such a world is pressed upon us. The crusade to create a chemically sterile, insect-free world seems to have engendered a fanatic zeal on the part of many specialists and most of the so-called control agencies. On every hand there is evidence that those engaged in spraying operations exercise a ruthless power. "The regulatory entomologists . . . function as prosecutor, judge and jury, tax assessor and collector and sheriff to enforce their own orders," said Connecticut entomologist Neely Turner. The most flagrant abuses go unchecked in both state and federal agencies.

24   It is not my contention that chemical insecticides must never be used. I do contend that we have put poisonous and biologically potent chemicals indiscriminately into the hands of persons largely or wholly ignorant of their potentials for harm. We have subjected enormous numbers of people to contact with these poisons, without their consent and often without their knowledge. If the Bill of Rights contains no guarantee that a citizen shall be secure against lethal poisons distributed either by private individuals or by public officials, it is surely only because our forefathers, despite their considerable wisdom and foresight, could conceive of no such problem.

25   I contend, furthermore, that we have allowed these chemicals to be used with little or no advance investigation of their effect on soil, water, wildlife, and man himself. Future generations are unlikely to condone our lack of prudent concern for the integrity of the natural world that supports all life.

26   There is still very limited awareness of the nature of the threat. This is an era of specialists, each of whom sees his own problem and is unaware of or intolerant of the larger frame into which it fits. It is also an era dominated by industry, in which the right to make a dollar at whatever cost is seldom challenged. When the public protests, confronted with some obvious evidence of damaging results of pesticide applications, it is fed little tranquilizing pills of half truth. We urgently need an end to these false assurances, to the sugar coating of unpalatable facts. It is the public that is being asked to assume the risks that the insect controllers calculate. The public must decide whether it wishes to continue on the present road, and it can do so only when in full possession of the facts. In the words of Jean Rostand, "The obligation to endure gives us the right to know."

QUESTIONS ON "THE OBLIGATION TO ENDURE"

1. What is the "chain of evil" of which Carson writes? Is her term for this phenomenon justified? How?

2. Of what is Carson trying to persuade us in this essay?
3. According to Carson, in what basic ways are man and nature in conflict?
4. What kind of evidence does Carson offer to support her key assertions, and where in the writing is this evidence located?
5. Where in her writing does Carson account for the objections of those who wish to control insects?
6. What terms does Carson use to identify those whose actions she describes? What terms does she use to identify the problem she describes? Which of these terms are objective or denotative? Which are subjective or connotative?
7. Which words or phrases in paragraph 7 create a strong emotional appeal?
8. Carson wrote "The Obligation to Endure" two decades ago. How are her observations of value today?

Exercises Combining Persuasion and the Modes of Discourse

1. **Persuasion and description: Write a 150-word description, either appealing or unappealing, of one of the subjects that follows. That is, account for the various persuasive appeals in writing a description calculated to either attract or repel your reader.**
   a. **A room or apartment after a party**
   b. **A laboratory you have worked in**
   c. **A relative, neighbor, or co-worker**
   d. **The atmosphere of a bowling alley**
   e. **The typical atmosphere of a commuter car pool**
2. **Persuasion and classification/definition: Assume you have been assigned to write a 250 to 300 word editorial for your campus newspaper in support of student-paid subsidies for one of the following: on-campus day-care facilities for married students, a campus-based alcohol abuse program, or a campus literary magazine. Write your editorial, basing your argument on the type of project to be funded and its similarity to others already being subsidized (whether by students specifically or society in general).**
3. **Persuasion and narration: Assume you are assigned to create a television commercial for one of the following products: a newly developed disposable diaper, an established basketball or running shoe, or a newly developed cosmetic product by an established company. Write the scenario for a 30-second narrative commercial for one of these products (be as specific as possible) in which using the product leads to a happy ending. Begin by asking yourself what endings seem to be "inevitably" associated with a given product and why.**

4. Persuasion and evaluation: Write a short review in which you persuade fellow students to accept your judgment on one of the following:
   a. A specific course or instructor you have had
   b. A local restaurant
   c. A textbook you have used
   d. A campus organization or living group

Informing

THE IMPORTANCE OF INFORMATION

All of us need information frequently—a telephone number, how to repair a faucet, today's date, the rules of poker, the correct spelling of a word. For this reason thousands of people are involved in what is often called the *information business*, finding and supplying the information that others require. News reporters are the most glamorous of our information suppliers, but they comprise only a small part of a vast work force, which includes cataloguers, indexers, photographers, editors, data processors, and many other occupations.

In the first place, we need information just to run our daily lives. We need maps to tell us how to get from Cleveland to Chicago, airline schedules to tell us when planes leave and arrive, and operating instructions for new appliances. We could figure out most of these things for ourselves by trial and error; but in a complex society like ours, with so many things to learn and an enormous variety of tasks to perform, we find it far more efficient to rely on printed instructions.

In the second place, we need (or should need) information as a basis for opinions. For example, take the question, "What is causing inflation, and what should we do about it?" To answer this question requires information on prices, wages, supplies of raw materials, inventories of manufactured goods, and a host of other data. Only then will our opinions about inflation be *informed* opinions—based on facts, not just on wishes or hunches. It is true that two people can examine the same collection of facts and, sometimes, draw different conclusions from them; but an adequate collection of data gives the best opportunity for intelligent opinions.

Facts, then, are the main components of information. What is a fact? Various definitions have been given, but for our purposes the well-known commonsense definition is most useful: A *fact* is a report of something the writer has personally witnessed or a statement that authorities agree to be true beyond question. For example, if you witness an automobile accident, you can report, "The car went off the road and hit a tree." Readers assume, then, that you personally saw this happen. However, if you are a reporter taking the information over the telephone, you must write something like this: "Police say that the car went off the road and hit a tree."

Of course, the process of collecting and reporting facts is seldom as simple as this. The writer must find the facts, sort the relevant from the irrelevant, and organize the facts for presentation to a reader. These are skills that we will take up in this chapter.

SOME EXAMPLES OF INFORMATION

We will begin our study of informative writing by reading two examples. The first was written by a professional writer and the second by a student.

Although the two are obviously very different (one is a news story, and the other, a term paper), it is important for our future discussions to note *how* the two are different. The most noticeable differences lie in their methods of what is variously called *citing references, documenting,* or *giving sources.* The term paper carefully identifies the source of every fact except those that the author considers to be common knowledge, using a system of notes in the text and a bibliography (a modern version of documentation that eliminates the need for reference footnotes). The newspaper article, by contrast, does not list the exact source of each fact. Except for material that apparently came from letters or personal interviews, the reader has no way of knowing from where many of the facts came.

These are different approaches to documentation. The term paper uses the *scholarly* method, while the newspaper article uses an *informal* method appropriate for popular audiences. The scholarly method is used in academic writing on the grounds that many academic readers may want to follow up on the paper and read the original sources of information for themselves. The full documentation, therefore, provides exact data about where the information may be found. Popular audiences are not expected to do this kind of follow-up reading.

A term paper serves two purposes in a student's education. Writing the paper teaches students how to find information, sort it, and organize it. At the same time, students are learning the mechanics of scholarly writing, especially the skill of documentation. The extent to which college students become scholars is, of course, debatable; however, it is less debatable that all students ought to be able to perform as scholars if the need arises.

Be aware that by the time you read this, both the newspaper article and the term paper may contain information that is outdated. By *outdated*, we not only mean that the events happened some time ago but that some of the issues (such as the danger of certain pesticides) may have been settled. This is unavoidable because we intend to deal primarily with informative writing designed to "hook" a reader's interest (as opposed to the kind that sits in a reference book until a reader needs it), and the usual hook is to connect the information to a current event. Current events are no longer current by the time a book is published. However, we are studying the examples for their informative techniques and not for the information they contain.

Prereading Activities for "Gypsy Moth Control: A Divisive Question," by Shanya Panzer

VOCABULARY.   Like persuasion, information is usually written for a specific audience, and its vocabulary is thus pitched toward the reading level of that audience. When forced to use words that might be unfamiliar to the readers, the writer defines such words in the text.

This article was published in the *New York Times*, so its vocabulary is intended for the well-educated reader. As a college student, you are included in this group of readers and should therefore have no trouble with the vocabulary. The following terms are the only ones that might cause trouble for a few readers. (The numbers in parentheses indicate the paragraphs in which the terms are used.)

> **cacophony** (1)—sound that is jarring and out of tune; harsh sound
> **defoliated** (4)—to be without leaves (as in a "defoliated tree")
> **entomologist** (13)—an expert in the study of insects

ORGANIZATION.   An informative article consists of a collection of facts, and the writer must decide in what order to place the facts. Sometimes, as in the report of an event, there is a *natural* method that can be used, one that comes from the subject itself; for example, we often use chronological order in reporting events. But in covering a general topic, which is neither an object nor an event, the writer must impose an appropriate method of organization.

The writer of the article on gypsy moth control has chosen a fairly common type of imposed organization. The main outline of the facts is as follows (the numbers in parentheses are the paragraph numbers):

    I.   Introduction (1–2)

   II. General information about gypsy moths (3–8)
       A. How introduced to the U.S. (4)

STUDY QUESTIONS

1. Compare the outline of the article to the title and introduction. Which part of the article is most relevant to the title?
2. Which parts of the article seem less relevant to the title? Why has this less-relevant information been included?
3. Go through the article and see if you can determine the source of each piece of information. Make a list of the sources the author seems to have used.
4. The following sentences are quoted from the article. Why are sources given for the information in sentences d, e, and f but not for a, b, and c?
  a. The caterpillar emerges from its egg in May and eats a square foot of leaves—preferably oak—every 24 hours.
  b. But Sevin kills many beneficial insects, including bees, in addition to its target.
  c. Since Sevin is known to harm freshwater aquatic life, it is not sprayed on lakes and rivers.
  d. Mr. Kegg estimates that he spends 80 percent of his time on the spraying program.
  e. "The use of this material in an aerial spraying program in residential areas should be subject to the closest scrutiny," Mr. Conroy wrote.
  f. Although she [Dr. Ehrenfeld] could not be reached for additional comment, a check with the Library of Medicine at the National Institutes of Health

showed that there were at least that many on record (mostly of animals, but some of humans).

5. All of the sentences above would be considered facts. Why? How do you define *fact*?

6. Consider the language of the article (except for the direct quotations). Is it mainly connotative or denotative? How much figurative language is present? How often are first person pronouns used?

7. We have noted that some types of writing are organized around a central theme, or a *thesis*. Does this article have a thesis? Why or why not?

GYPSY MOTH CONTROL: A DIVISIVE QUESTION

Shanya Panzer

1 Along with the sleigh-bell choruses of peepers and the songs of nesting birds, spring in New Jersey also brings the cacophony of controversy over the gypsy moth.

2 On one side, the state's Department of Agriculture, which carries out an aerial spraying program to control the moth; on the other are conservationists, who say that spraying does more harm than good and is potentially dangerous to humans.

3 The gypsy moth is a prime example of a conservationist dictum: Don't fool around with Mother Nature.

4 A native European pest, it was introduced into the United States in 1869 by Leopold Trouvelot, a French naturalist who hoped to produce hardier silkworms by crossing them with gypsy moths. Some escaped into the woods near his home in Medford, Mass. By 1889 they had defoliated trees in a 360-square-mile area.

5 The caterpillar emerges from its egg in May and eats a square foot of leaves—preferably oak—every 24 hours. Healthy defoliated trees generally survive; trees that have been defoliated before, have endured drought or are growing in poor sites may succumb.

6 When the gypsy moth population grows beyond the available food supply, it is attacked by a virus and "crashes." Many die, and the cycle of buildup begins anew.

7 Although some birds eat the pest, its most effective natural enemies, or "biological controls," are certain wasps and flies that lay eggs in gypsy moth egg masses and destroy them.

8 Some of these wasps and flies have been introduced into New Jersey specifically to keep down the gypsy moth. They help, but do not do the whole job.

9 The homeowner who sees the hairy, yellow egg masses on his favorite old oak can hire someone to spray the tree with Sevin (carbaryl), a pesticide that, unlike DDT, breaks down into its chemical components within two weeks and is thus deactivated. But Sevin kills many beneficial insects, including bees, in addition to its target.

10 The homeowner also can ask a tree surgeon to spray with Bacillus

thuringiensis (B.t.), a bacterium that kills only gypsy moths and some other moths and butterflies, but so far has been found harmless to anything else. It is less effective than Sevin, and more expensive, for it requires two carefully timed applications.

11   He can put Tanglefoot (a sticky substance), creosote or burlap around the bottom of the tree, and daily pick off the moths that become trapped there as they wander up and down the trunk.

12   Or he can ask that his town participate in the state-operated aerial Sevin-spraying program.

13   John Kegg, an entomologist with the Agriculture Department, runs the spraying program, for which the Federal Government pays half the cost (the other half is borne equally by the state and participating towns). New Jersey has allocated $70,000 for its share this year, up $10,000 from 1978.

14   Mr. Kegg estimates that he spends 80 percent of his time on the spraying program. He gives priority to residential wooded areas with at least 20 homes per 100 acres and to "high use" recreation sectors.

15   Other areas must not be sprayed because Sevin kills the parasitic wasps and flies, and these have to survive to keep the moths down in succeeding years.

16   This combination of chemical pesticides and biological control is called "Integrated Pest Control."

17   Mr. Kegg begins by making an aerial survey in the summer to map defoliated areas. His inspectors follow up with an egg-mass count in the fall. Maps of areas that he believes will need spraying are sent to the affected towns as proposals.

18   Mr. Kegg then holds regional individual town meetings to describe the spraying program. At these sessions, he shows color slides of defoliated forests.

19   "Sevin," Mr. Kegg tells the townspeople and officials, "is safe and effective, widely used in agriculture and freely available, without licensing, to anyone."

20   "Human exposure to Sevin with our program is almost nonexistent," he asserts, explaining that the spraying takes place in the early morning (when people are indoors), that most of the pesticide is intercepted by the crowns of trees, and that the amount used—about three-quarters of a pound per acre—is small.

21   Since Sevin is known to harm freshwater aquatic life, it is not sprayed on lakes and rivers.

22   "The birth-defect issue is brought up at almost every meeting," Mr. Kegg said. "It is based on a 1969 Food and Drug Administration study of beagles in which beagle fetuses were injected with Sevin daily until birth. You can't go by results in a test like that."

23   Mendham, Chester and Randolph Townships, all near Morristown National Historic Park, have rejected the program, largely on the basis of conservationist testimony about the human and ecological dangers. Bernardsville, also in the area, is still undecided, although Mr. Kegg calls the situation there "the worst I've seen in the state."

24   The Bernardsville Environmental Commission has recommended par-

ticipation. Its chairman, James Fenimore, a high-school biology teacher, declared:

25   "The infestation problem here has been going up geometrically. Chemicals are a last resort as a means of insect control. But if the state doesn't use Sevin properly, any Tom, Dick, or Harry can go out and buy it and use it improperly, without control on amounts, wind conditions or anything else."

26   Mayor Richard Vetter of Mendham, in a statement explaining why he voted against spraying (although many residents requested it), wrote in part:

27   "Each pesticide that has been removed from the market was originally declared safe and nontoxic. We simply do not know whether or not Sevin is harmful, but there is a growing chorus of voices raising serious questions. I would rather err on the side of overcaution."

28   As one conservationist put it, Mr. Kegg "comes around with his scare pictures and says that Sevin is safe, based on his information, which he gets from Union Carbide (the manufacturer of Sevin)."

29   "He says that the Federal Government's Environmental Protection Agency has certified it as safe," the conservationist added, "which it has not."

30   Conservationists cite a letter from A. E. Conroy, director of pesticides and toxic substances for the E.P.A., to the Massachusetts Department of Forests. In it, Mr. Conroy states that Sevin is under review as being possibly unsafe, with studies indicating that it causes birth defects in dogs and swine and may cause them in humans.

31   "The use of this material in an aerial spraying program in residential areas should be subject to the closest scrutiny," Mr. Conroy wrote.

32   In support of its position against aerial spraying, the New Jersey Audubon Society offers a report by Dr. Joan Ehrenfeld, its Director of Research and a professor at Rutgers University. In 1977, she was hired by the National Park Service to investigate the long-term effects of the major gypsy moth infestation of Morristown National Historic Park in 1967–69. It killed 10,000 oak trees.

33   No chemical insecticides were used in the 1,500-acre park and reliance was placed on biological controls. Officials were resigned to some tree losses.

34   "By 1970, the moth population had crashed and has remained at low levels since that time," Dr. Ehrenfeld wrote. "The gaps in the forest were rapidly closed with other trees. The mortality was greatest among trees growing in shallow, waterlogged soil."

35   The Audubon Society side said that spraying was "likely to affect the introduced enemies of the gypsy moth," necessitating more future spraying.

36   Dr. Ehrenfeld also mentioned "300 cases of carbaryl Sevin poisoning." Although she could not be reached for additional comment, a check with the Library of Medicine at the National Institute of Health showed that there were at least that many on record (mostly of animals, but some of humans).

37   Mr. Kegg predicts a "severe infestation of gypsy moths and severe defoliation" of the Morristown park this year. But James Holcomb, the chief park ranger, who plans no spraying, disagrees.

38 "The forest is now made up of different trees—fewer oaks—so fewer will be affected," he said. "The forest will look and remain green this summer. The public will not notice any defoliation."

39 The Association of New Jersey Environmental Commissions, which advises individual municipal environmental commissions, many of which must prepare recommendations for dealing with gypsy moth problems, said in a recently published bulletin:

40 "The track record for pesticides has not been good, and common sense would dictate that, the less we release into the environment, the better."

The Student Essay

Although we are postponing a complete discussion of the student paper until later, read the paper now. If your instructor is requiring you to write a term paper, you can observe many of the features that your final draft will have to contain.

THE HARP SEAL: TO HUNT OR TO PROTECT?

I. Introduction
   A. Why the seals are so named
   B. Physical characteristics of the adult harp seal
   C. Facts about the pups
   D. Migration
      1. Breeding ground
      2. Birth of the pups
      3. Migration north
      4. The yearlings

II. The hunt
   A. Where it takes place
   B. Reasons for the hunt
   C. Facts and quotas on the hunt
   D. What the seals are used for

III. Protests and protection
   A. Why people protest the hunt
   B. Protests from around the world
      1. Switzerland
      2. Brian Davies, director of the International Fund for Animal Welfare
      3. Canada
      4. United States
   C. Ratification for the Convention of Antarctic Seals
   D. David M. Lavigne

IV. Summary of the issue for both sides

A typical title page for a student term paper.

THE HARP SEAL: TO HUNT OR TO PROTECT?

Candee Douglas

1   This year the annual harp seal hunt began on March 15, 1977, off the coast of Newfoundland. The hunt continued a tradition by which each year, for two weeks, Norwegian and Canadian hunters come to this area for the precious white furs of the harp seal pups. However, the traditional hunt has also become an issue of controversy, and protests were once again staged against the hunt this year.

2   The object of both hunt and protest is *Pagophilus groenlandicus,* "icelover from Greenland," known as the harp seal or saddleback because of the black band on its back. Greyish-white with a black head, the male harp seal weighs between 400 and 600 pounds. Females are lighter in color, with the black band less prominent, and weigh less than the male (Hall and Kelson 922).

3   Born on the ice floes in the spring, the harp seal pups weigh about 15 pounds at birth but grow rapidly to a weight of 100 pounds in three weeks' time. Their white coats are not for camouflage as some scientists have

thought, according to David M. Lavigne, a Canadian zoologist writing for *National Geographic*. It would make little difference since the pups cry almost constantly the entire time they are on the ice, which would attract any predator. Lavigne says that scientists have discovered that the white coats are for warmth, as the coat attracts the heat from the sun. Since the pups aren't born with the blubber necessary to keep them warm in their Arctic habitat, the white coat, nearly transparent, absorbs the ultraviolet rays from the sun (129). After about two weeks the pups will begin the molting process, when they will shed their coats. They then attain a light greyish coat with black dots which will eventually become the coat of an adult (Walker 1306).

4   In the winter, the seals migrate south from the Arctic to the gulf of the St. Lawrence and the ice off Labrador. Some have been seen as far south as Virginia. This is also their breeding ground and where the pups are born. Mating takes place in the water with certain rituals and mating calls. The births take place on the ice floes. Very rarely are twins born; it is most always a single birth (Hall 922).

5   Pups are weaned at two weeks old, and the cow then joins the herd, leaving her pup to fend for itself. The herds will then move north, out into open water for the summer. Yearling saddlebacks will remain in the Arctic the following winter. They will not migrate south with the herd until they are nearly two years old (Walker 1306).

6   The hunt for the pups takes place in the seals' breeding ground, off the coast of Newfoundland and Labrador each year. Lavigne says that the reasons for the hunt are the tradition and livelihood of the hunters. That is, not only is the hunt a long-established activity for the hunters, but many of them also depend heavily upon it for part of their yearly income. In Labrador and Newfoundland, especially, residents have a hard time making a living (139).

7   Lavigne has also summarized the present law in regard to sealing. Canadian and Norwegian sealing fleets are permitted, by law, to kill 120,000 seal pups. "Landsmen," or the residents of the St. Lawrence coast to northern Labrador, are allowed 30,000 seal pups during the two-week hunt. This is the result of the Committee on Seals and Sealing, set up by the Canadian Minister of Fisheries in 1971. The committee examined all points of the issue and banned large sealing vessels from the Gulf of St. Lawrence and reduced quotas (130).

8   Establishment of quotas is relatively recent. In the 1830s, there were no quotas, and some 700,000 pelts were taken. In 1929, 200,000 were taken during the seal hunt. Canada began restrictions in the late 1960s, beginning with the size of the club and how it should be used (Lavigne 141).

9   Although the adult harp seal is hunted in great numbers, primarily for blubber, pelts, and meat (Lavigne 129), the pups are hunted only for their white pelts. One newspaper, the *Buffalo Courier Express*, reported that these pelts are used for novelty fur, leather items, and stuffed toy seal dolls ("Slaughter" B4). Lavigne adds that the baby seals are skinned on the ice and the carcasses left behind. He says that the living seals that remain will not inhabit ground where a killing has taken place (139).

10   In addition to the claims of tradition and need for income, Lavigne reports several other arguments in favor of this killing. Sealers claim the hunt is necessary to preserve the fishing industry because of the voracious

appetites of the seals. They insist the seals must be controlled because of the great amounts of fish they feed on. The hunters also maintain that the use of the club is painless and the most humane way to hunt the seals (142).

11   However, many humans and environmental groups disagree with the hunt and have protested it this year and in years past. Their main objection, according to Lavigne, is that the clubbing of the defenseless pups is cruel and inhuman (129). In 1972, the hunt was banned altogether in the Gulf of St. Lawrence, because pressure from the protesters became too great ("Slaughter").

12   This year protests from all over the world were held in one form or another. A hotel in Switzerland, for example, turned down Canadian guests because of the hunt. The *Buffalo Evening News* quoted the hotel director as explaining his reasoning this way:

> As long as the majority of the Canadian nation is too cowardly or indifferent to attain an immediate end to this unworthy slaughter of defenseless animals, we will, in protest, no longer house Canadian guests or buy Canadian goods. A visit to your country cannot even be mentioned ("Snubbed" 1).

13   Brian Davies, director of the International Fund for Animal Welfare, is on the ice every year during the hunt. The *Buffalo Evening News* referred to him as an avid defender of the harp seal for many years and reports that, in 1976, he was arrested by Canadian officials for violation of the Seal Protection Act. Davies was charged with landing his helicopter too close to the seals during the hunt. The defense for Davies was successful and all charges were dismissed when the court ruled that Davies did not land in waters under Canadian jurisdiction ("Slaughter").

14   A similar incident happened again this year to Davies, when he was again charged with violating the Seal Protection Act. The *Buffalo Courier Express* quoted Davies as saying, "It is ironic. I was arrested for flying too close to the seals while they were being slaughtered" ("Weather" 4).

15   Others who have protested the harp seal hunt are members of the Greenpeace Foundation, a Canadian environmental group. They were on the ice, this year, during the hunt with their lawyers and newsmen. No incidents took place, but the newspaper says it was obvious why they were there ("Greenpeace" A7).

16   In other incidents this year, on March 19, 1977, sixty people marched on the Canadian consulate in New York City, protesting the hunt ("Hit" 3). And actress Brigitte Bardot attempted several times to reach the ice where the hunt took place, but due to bad weather conditions she was unable to do so ("More" 8).

17   In December, 1976, President Ford signed a ratification for the Convention of Antarctic Seals. This does not protect the seals, but the hope is to rectify the situation as it stands now. Its basic purpose is to prevent the seals' survival from becoming threatened (State Department 135).

18   Lavigne suggests that strict regulations should be set. He observes that the hunters cannot continue to harvest the seals from large factory ships. Perhaps the landsmen, under strict rules, can continue the seasonal hunts. He has studied the harp seal over a period of several years and concludes the seal is in danger of extinction unless something is done (142).

19 Now it is up to the people to decide. The hunters depend on the harp seal for their livelihood. They say the clubbing of a seal is humane and painless. Their arguments are strong, but are they strong enough?

20 The protestors, on the other hand, have a good case, too. Is the harp in danger of extinction? They insist the clubbing of the pups is cruel and inhuman.

21 More facts and figures must be provided for both sides, in order to come to a definite conclusion. In essence, the harp seal's survival or extinction may depend upon human reason and awareness.

Works Cited

"Baby Seal Slaughter." *Buffalo Courier Express* 20 Mar. 1977: B4.

"Canadians Snubbed Over Seal Hunt." *Buffalo Evening News* 18 Mar. 1977: 1.

"Greenpeace Protests Hunt." *New York Times* 16 Mar. 1977: A7.

Hall, E. Raymond, and Keith R. Kelson. *Mammals of North America*. New York: Ronald Press, 1959.

"Hit Seal Hunt." *Buffalo Courier Express* 22 Mar. 1977: 3.

Lavigne, David M. "Life or Death for the Harp Seal." *National Geographic* Jan. 1976: 129–38.

"More Seal Pups Killed." *Buffalo Evening News* 17 Mar. 1977: 8.

U.S. State Department. *Convention of Antarctic Seals*. Bulletin 76. Washington: GPO, 1977.

Walker, Ernest P. *Mammals of the World*. Baltimore: Johns Hopkins Press, 1968.

"Weather Halts Protest." *Buffalo Courier Express* 17 Mar. 1977: 4.

PREWRITING

In answering the questions, you should have noted most of the principal characteristics of information. These are characteristics you must consider as you write your own informative paper.

First, you probably noted that the article has no central theme or thesis. It is not an argument for a point of view; it simply covers a topic.

Second, you may have noted that there are three basic issues, having to do with the *subject matter*, the *intended audience*, and the *writer*. The subject-matter issue is that there is a topic, and it must be covered thoroughly; this is called the *principle of comprehensiveness*. The audience issue suggests that information is written for a specific group of people who need or want to know something. A good writer, therefore, concentrates on telling the anticipated readers what they need to know, either omitting what is already known or just briefly sketching in the known information. This is the principle of *surprise value*. Finally, the writer issue requires that the author report only what is known from personal observation, whether the observed material was actual events or published materials. This is the principle of *factuality*. These principles are represented in Figure 4.1, the communications triangle. We will consider comprehensiveness, surprise value, and factuality as we go through the prewriting process.

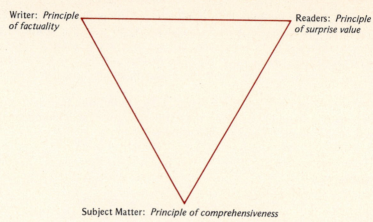

FIGURE 4.1.   The three issues in information.

Choosing a Topic

There are several common types of informative writing, ranging from news stories to term papers. But since most students are at some point required to write term papers, and since the writing of longer informative papers still requires the application of basic informative principles, much of the following discussion concerns how to write a longer informative piece that could become a term paper if your instructor so desires.

Consider, therefore, that you will be writing a report on a topic and that the information about the topic will be gathered mostly from books, magazines, and other publications that you will find in the library. We will examine at some length how to use the library and what to do with the published information when you find it. In fact, *prewriting for information involves discovering what there is to say about a topic and how much of it to say*.

Keep in mind that choosing a topic for a term paper can be difficult, since you don't know in advance whether you will be able to find the information you need. However, the three principles previously cited can be used to help identify some possible topics. For example, the principle of factuality implies that you should choose topics that you already know something about. This is not always possible, but certainly for the present assignment it is worth considering. That way, your personal interest in the topic will help to get you going.

The principle of surprise value suggests that you should have in mind a specific audience that might want or need the facts you are going to provide. In other words, it helps to have an occasion or purpose for writing, beyond the fact that you are trying to fulfill an assignment. We will have more to say about surprise value later.

Finally, the principle of comprehensiveness suggests that the topic should be one for which you can do a thorough job. All writers are limited in the amount of space they are allowed to fill, and you should choose a topic that can be covered thoroughly within the required limits your instructor sets. For a 1,000-word paper, the topic must be small and well defined; but if the limit is 30 pages, the topic can be fairly large. Also worth considering is the size of your library. A large university or city library should be adequate for nearly any topic. But access to a smaller library might well limit the range of topics you can choose.

In any case, you should have several topics in mind as you begin the prewriting process. As your preliminary work progresses, you can choose the topic that proves to be most appropriate for you, your readers, your resources, and your assignment.

Exercises on Choosing a Topic

1. Develop a list of five topics that you might like to write about. After each item on the list, briefly explain why that topic interests you.
2. For each topic try to think of some audiences that might also be interested in knowing about it. Briefly note who these people are and why they might need or want information on the topic.
3. Introduce yourself to a librarian. Ask which of your topics are most likely to be covered well by your library. (The librarian might not know for sure, but sometimes he or she can help you rule out topics that definitely are not covered in your library.)
4. Rank your topics from one to five. Base your rankings on your interests, the possibility of someone else's being interested, and the library resources available.
5. Choose your top-ranked topic as the tentative topic for your paper and check it with your instructor. Keep in mind that you might still have to narrow this topic or even abandon it if it doesn't work out.
6. If your library offers a tour or slide-tape program on using the library, schedule yourself to participate.
7. If your instructor has handed out an assignment sheet giving additional requirements beyond those in this chapter, carefully examine it.
8. Acquire a pack of 3″ × 5″ index cards, and another pack of larger cards, either 4″ × 6″ or 5″ × 8″.

The Three Principles Applied

COMPREHENSIVENESS. To be comprehensive is to be complete, so the principle of comprehensiveness requires thorough coverage of your topic. One way to think of this is to consider that each topic is made up of several subtopics, and to be comprehensive you must identify all of the subtopics and then cover them in your paper. In actual practice it is not always possible or necessary to be truly comprehensive, but this early in the prewriting process you must at least decide on subtopics.

Your first step in prewriting is to do some general reading about your topic so as to identify the subtopics. The best place to start is usually with an encyclopedia, which often will list the subtopics in the index or in boldface type in the main article about your topic. (Many instructors prohibit the use of information from an encyclopedia in a term paper, but encyclopedias still make good starting points.) For example, suppose that you were Shanya Panzer, getting ready to write an article on gypsy moths. Some preliminary reading on the topic of gypsy moths might turn up the following list of subtopics:

1. How gypsy moths were introduced to the U.S.
2. Genus, species, and other biological data
3. How gypsy moths spread
4. The damage caused by gypsy moths
5. Where gypsy moths can be found
6. Methods a homeowner can use to control gypsy moths
7. Natural enemies of gypsy moths
8. The history of efforts to control gypsy moths
9. Government-sponsored methods of controlling gypsy moths
10. Entomological research in new methods of control
11. Controversy over use of pesticides to control gypsy moths
12. Problems in each state with gypsy moths

Additional reading, later in the research process, may turn up more subtopics, but this beginning list reveals something about the size of the topic. We can see that, like most initial topics, this one about gypsy moths in general is much too big for a brief article, be it a newspaper feature or a term paper. If Panzer had tried to cover every topic comprehensively, she would have ended up with a small book. The solution is to "narrow" the topic by choosing just one subtopic to emphasize. (Here is a place to apply the principle of surprise value, which we will consider shortly.)

If you discover that your topic is far too big, you may immediately see a subtopic that you would like to convert into your new main topic. Then you would proceed to do more reading, seeking to identify the subtopics in this new topic. However, it may be too early to narrow your topic. You may want to wait and, for the moment, concentrate just on discovering all of the subtopics within your initial topic.

Exercises on Discovering the Size of Your Topic

1. **Look up your topic in an encyclopedia. Use the index to find all of the places in the encyclopedia where the topic is discussed. Make a list of all**

the subtopics the encyclopedia covers. For some topics, the subtopics will be listed in the index or set off in boldface type. For others, you will have to figure out the subtopics for yourself.

2. Make a preliminary judgment about narrowing your topic. If it seems that your topic must be narrowed, identify four or five subtopics that might, in themselves, make good main topics.

3. If you doubt that you have located all or most of the subtopics, check the card catalogue for other reference books that might cover your topic. Such cards have the abbreviation REF at the top. (For example, the reference section might well have several books, similar to encyclopedias, that cover just moths and butterflies.)

4. A comprehensive view of any topic cannot come just from encyclopedias and other reference books. Check the card catalogue, the *Readers Guide to Periodical Literature*, the *New York Times Index*, the vertical file, and any other indexes which seem appropriate. Put each source that you find on a separate 3" × 5" index card. (You are collecting a *bibliography*, and this first batch of 3" × 5" cards is called your *preliminary bibliography*.) Some examples of bibliography cards listing sources about gypsy moths are illustrated.

Warren Balgooyin, "Gypsy
Moth Readying '80
Assault,"
New York Times, Mar. 22,
Section 22, p.16, Col. 3. 1980

Frank E. Lutz,
Field Book of Insects,
3rd. edition
N.Y.; G.P. Putnam's
Sons, 1948

Lucy W. Clausen,
Insect Fact and
Folklore.
N.Y. Macmillan Co.,
1954

E. Alan Cameron and others
"Disruption of Gypsy Moth
Mating with Microencapsulated
Disparlure," Science
Vol. 183, March 8, 1974
pp. 972-73.

5. Using the library to find the sources of information you need is a skill that takes some time to develop. If you're new at this, give yourself plenty of time to just "mess around" in the library, seeing what it has to offer. Start your paper early and arrange your schedule so that you have three-or four-hour blocks of time several days in a row for this get-acquainted process.

6. **Give some additional thought as to whether your school library has enough information on your topic. Be prepared to abandon the topic if you discover that it's not appropriate, but don't give up too soon. If you haven't yet found many sources on the topic, it may be that you're just not looking in the right places.**
7. **Check your preliminary bibliography with your instructor.**

SURPRISE VALUE. Let us assume that you have located all or most of the subtopics within your original topic or, perhaps, have chosen a subtopic as your new main topic and have identified the subtopics within that. Your topic is probably still too big to be covered comprehensively, so you need to decide on an additional way to limit the task. This is the job of the principle of surprise value, which requires you to emphasize the subtopics that are most interesting to the reader and de-emphasize those the reader is already familiar with.

To see how such decisions are made, let us examine the subtopics once again in "Gypsy Moth Control: A Divisive Question," this time paying attention to the amount of space devoted to each one. Here is the list of subtopics again with the number of paragraphs devoted to each. (Because the article is from a newspaper, the paragraphs are much shorter than you may be accustomed to. However, the principle of space allotment is the same.)

1. General information on gypsy moths (6).
2. Basic control methods (4)
3. How the state-operated system of spraying with Sevin works (9)
4. The controversy over state-operated spraying (19)

As you can see, the last subtopic has received the most space, nearly half of the article. This is the subtopic that deals with the controversy in New Jersey over the government-sponsored spraying of Sevin. The other subtopics are given much less space, even though all three could easily be expanded into full-length articles.

What has happened here is that the author has chosen to feature the subtopic that she considers the most interesting and "newsy" for her readers. (Section 21 of the *New York Times* is a special section for New Jersey readers.) The other subtopics receive sketchy coverage because they have been covered by the *Times* in the past. We would say, therefore, that the last subtopic is the actual main topic of the article, and the other three serve mainly as background for the main topic. Of course, the title and introduction of the article also indicate what the main topic is.

Since you, too, want to limit your writing task, you can do it in a similar manner. However, you have a special problem when you write a term paper because your primary audience is your instructor, and your primary purpose is to demonstrate that you can write a satisfactory paper. Your instructor might well be satisfied if you teach yourself something new by writing the paper; it might not be necessary to tell the instructor something new. But writing for an audience of one who is willing to be bored by your paper is rather strange for a writer and not typical of situations outside of school. For this reason, attempt to provide surprise value even in this term paper. With a little effort, you *can* locate some information that will be surprising to your instructor.

Another alternative, which many instructors encourage, is to write for a different audience. For example, some of the best term papers are written to be published eventually as pamphlets for customers or clients. Nursing students, for instance, often find that patients have an appalling lack of information about their own diseases, so a student may set out to write a pamphlet about a particular disease. Accounting students may write about a particular tax problem, computer science students about the virtues and limitations of a new computer, and so on. Usually, the student must remove the footnotes and other scholarly apparatus before publishing the pamphlet, but as long as you write the paper to be read by a real audience it will be useful with or without the scholarly parts.

Exercises on Finding the Surprise Value

1. **Think first of your topic as if it were to be a newspaper feature article to be published in your local paper. Reexamine the list of subtopics to see if any of them are connected to matters of local interest. Also look for something that may be related to national current events.**
2. **Try another approach. Which subtopics would be familiar to nearly everyone, and which would be unfamiliar to some groups? Identify the groups of people who would find certain subtopics new to them.**
3. **Consider your topic as the subject of a pamphlet. What would be the occasion for distributing such a pamphlet, and who would receive it? Which subtopics would be of most concern to the recipients?**
4. **Suppose no one would read your paper except your instructor. Given what you know about your instructor, are there any subtopics that would be unfamiliar to him or her?**
5. **Make a preliminary decision about surprise value. Write a note to your instructor explaining the subtopic you have chosen to feature, the intended readers for the paper, and the form in which the paper might ultimately be "published."**
6. **Show your note to your instructor and classmates for their comments.**

FACTUALITY. The principle of factuality now requires you to do two primary tasks: (1) establish what is known about your topic, and (2) preserve this information in a form that will reveal its source. The two main skills involved for a term paper are using library sources to find the information and taking adequate notes. Let us take up these skills one at a time.

To establish what is known about the topic, you need to begin reading the books, magazine articles, and so on that you have listed on your bibliography cards. You can just skim the shorter pieces, looking for the information you need. For books, use the index to find where your topic is discussed. You are looking for detailed information on the subtopic that you have tentatively decided to feature in your paper, but of course you need to know something about the other subtopics as well, since a few of them will have to be used as background information.

Keep an open mind about your topic. If it becomes evident that your initial choice of a featured subtopic is not working out (perhaps there isn't enough information about it), be ready to switch to something else. Also be alert for other sources of information; books and articles from technical magazines often have bibliographies that list other sources that you can add to your own bibliography.

It is inevitable that many of the sources will turn out not to be useful. They will contain nothing on your topic, or they will repeat information that you already have; this is to be expected, so you can just set aside the bibliography cards for these sources. (This is one of the reasons for keeping your bibliography on cards rather than on a sheet of paper.)

As you read these sources, take notes on information that looks useful for your paper. (Use the larger index cards for your notes.) There are, in general, three ways to take notes: (1) you may copy the information exactly; (2) you may paraphrase the information (i.e., put it in your own words); or (3) you may photocopy the page. You may also do a combination of these things. It is probably safe to say that most students copy too much material; however, knowing when to copy and when to paraphrase is a skill that comes only with experience. The following are some general guidelines for notetaking.

1. Paraphrase (put in your own words) facts that you expect to use as background information.
2. Copy laws, opinions, and statements of doubtful truthfulness.
3. Paraphrase nearly everything else.
4. When you paraphrase, condense the original material as much as you can. Do not just make word-for-word substitutions of an author's sentence. After all, the main purpose of paraphrasing is to save time.

Whatever you do, be sure to keep an accurate record of whether the material is copied or paraphrased by putting quotation marks around quoted material. Also make an accurate record of from where the information came. Finally, many writers like to put a label on each card to indicate the subtopic covered by the notes on that card. In any case, you should put only a limited amount of information on each card and on one side only.

The accompanying illustrations are examples of note cards about gypsy moths. In this case the writer is hoping to make disparlure, a newly developed control method, the featured subtopic of the paper.

Natural Enemies

A carabid beetle, Calosoma sycophanta, is one of the natural enemies of the gypsy moth. Was brought from Europe (the natural home of the moths). Can eat up to 500 caterpillars before it dies.

from p. 106 of The Insects, by Url Lanham (NY: Columbia Univ. Press, 1954)

How Gypsy Moths Spread

Female moths can't fly, so everyone wondered how gypsy moths spread so fast. What happens is that very young caterpillars are small and light and have long hair. The wind picks them up and blows them around.

from p. 73 of Insects: Their Secret World, by Evelyn Cheesman. (N.Y.: William Sloane Associates, (1975)

Disparlure

"Our results suggest that 15 g of disparlure per hectare may be capable of disrupting incipient populations of the gypsy moth efficiently enough that population increase might be precluded.... The effective longevity of the lure against higher population densities, as well as the ability of disparlure to disrupt mating in

Source of the note

> *Disparlure*
> *residual populations after insecticides*
> *or pathogen treatments, or after*
> *population reduction through*
> *natural causes, remains to be*
> *determined,"*
> *from p.973 of "Disruption of Gypsy*
>   *Moth Mating with Microencap-*
> *sulated Disparlure", by E. Cameron*
> *and others.*
> *Science, 183, Mar. 8, 1974.*

Exercises on Taking Notes

1. Reexamine "Gypsy Moth Control: A Divisive Question" to see which facts have been quoted (directly or indirectly) and which are paraphrased. For each sentence be prepared to discuss why it is paraphrased, quoted directly, or quoted indirectly.
2. Note which subtopics contain the most quotations. Why is this?
3. There are more quotations in this newspaper article than one would ordinarily expect to find in a term paper. Why?
4. Take notes for your own paper, using the larger index cards that you acquired earlier. Check them with your instructor at least once to make certain that you are doing them correctly.
5. When you have taken all the notes you need for the paper, arrange them by putting together all the cards dealing with the same subtopic. Turn in the whole batch of note cards to your instructor for a final check.

Summary of Prewriting Principles

You have now seen the three principles involved in exploring a topic and the skills required to carry out those principles before writing a term paper. Let us briefly summarize them.

The principle of *comprehensiveness* requires you to say everything that is known about a topic. Because this is impractical for many topics, you may first have to "narrow" the topic by choosing just one aspect of it. Then you choose one subtopic of the narrowed topic to become the featured aspect of the paper. The remaining subtopics will be covered only as necessary to provide background information for the featured aspect.

You choose the featured subtopic according to the principle of *surprise*

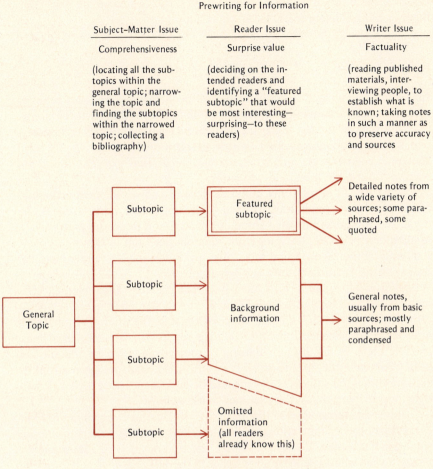

Prewriting for Information

Subject–Matter Issue	Reader Issue	Writer Issue
Comprehensiveness	Surprise value	Factuality
(locating all the subtopics within the general topic; narrowing the topic and finding the subtopics within the narrowed topic; collecting a bibliography)	(deciding on the intended readers and identifying a "featured subtopic" that would be most interesting—surprising—to these readers)	(reading published materials, interviewing people, to establish what is known; taking notes in such a manner as to preserve accuracy and sources

General Topic

Subtopic → Featured subtopic → Detailed notes from a wide variety of sources; some paraphrased, some quoted

Subtopic →
Subtopic → Background information → General notes, usually from basic sources; mostly paraphrased and condensed

Subtopic → Omitted information (all readers already know this)

FIGURE 4.2. **Prewriting for information.**

value. This means that you will choose an audience for the paper and then give that audience information on the subtopic that it knows the least about, trying also to choose an aspect your readers would find interesting and relevant. The audience may be the instructor for a course or someone else.

Finally, you will read the published sources on the topic and take notes on information that seems to be useful for the paper. Because of the principle of *factuality*, you will not only take accurate notes but will record the source of each note. When possible, condense the material in your own words, but in other cases copy the author's words exactly, using quotation marks to remind yourself that quoting has been done.

These three principles and their allied skills are outlined on the accompanying chart. Of course, all three principles will come up again when the time comes to write the paper. We will, therefore, be discussing them in the following sections on organization and style.

ORGANIZATION OF INFORMATION

Information is written in order to be useful to readers, and this requirement for usefulness affects the organizational patterns that writers employ. You will remember that there are, in general, two main types of informative writing: *reference articles*, which sit on a shelf in the library until someone needs them, and what we call *occasional articles*, which are written for specific users and occasions.

The patterns of reference material are well known. Readers ordinarily come to reference materials looking for a single fact, so references are organized to permit this use. Some of the common reference patterns are in alphabetical order (encyclopedias, dictionaries, and telephone books), sequential order (television schedules and cookbooks), and numerical order (Social Security rosters and law summaries.)

Occasional material also must be organized for the convenience of readers, but in this case readers are expected to examine the entire article rather than just look for a single fact. The organization therefore must be a little more sophisticated in order to help readers make sense of a large mass of facts. Sometimes a "natural" order is suggested by the subject itself. For example, if the subject is historical, chronological order is appropriate; if the subject is an object to be described, spatial order (left to right, top to bottom, and so on) may work well.

However, topics such as that of gypsy moth control, which are neither events nor objects large enough to be described, require writers to impose some kind of order. Let us reexamine the organization of the article by Panzer to see what type of order is imposed there. Look back at the outline on pp. 82–83 to refresh your memory.

Notice again, as you did earlier in the chapter, that the most surprising and relevant material comes last in the article (surprising and relevant, that is, in terms of the intended audience). This is the controversial issue of government-operated spraying of Sevin, also the featured subtopic of the article. The next most surprising and relevant material is the third item: how the spraying of Sevin is done in New Jersey. This subtopic is necessary in order to make the featured subtopic understandable.

We can see without going much further that the subtopics are arranged in order of surprise value, from least surprising to most surprising. This is called the *pyramid of surprise*, because the subtopics are arranged not only in order of surprise value but also in approximate order of the amount of space devoted to each one. The pattern of the pyramid of surprise may be diagramed as in Figure 4.3.

The pyramid of surprise is a fairly common pattern because it suits the

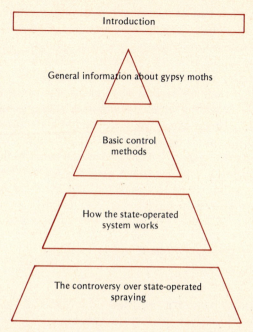

FIGURE 4.3. The pyramid of surprise organizational pattern.

convenience of readers very well. The introduction lays out the purpose of the article, and this is followed by background information. The background information gives basic facts to those readers who may need to learn them. Then the article works up to the featured topic, in this case the controversy about Sevin.

If at all possible, consider using the pyramid of surprise; it not only suits the convenience of the reader, but it is also easy to use in developing your paper. If you use any other pattern, you will need to figure out what to do with the background information: whether to group it all at the beginning as with the pyramid of surprise or to "drop it in" at appropriate places within your discussion of the featured subtopic. The most difficult part of using the pyramid of surprise is making transitions from one subtopic to the next. We will discuss several methods of doing this when we consider the student term paper.

Exercises on Organization

1. You should have already grouped your note cards by subtopic. First reexamine your subtopics and the notes for them to see if there are any subtopics that can be eliminated. Set those cards aside.
2. Pick out all the cards for your featured subtopic and set those aside

temporarily. Now look at the remaining subtopics and try to figure out a logical order for them. Try arranging them according to the amount of notes (least to most). If that doesn't seem suitable, rearrange them to closely approximate least relevant to most relevant.

3. Write a tentative outline. Make each of your subtopics a Roman numeral in the outline, then try several ways of arranging the material within each subtopic. (Material within a subtopic is usually arranged like one of the *modes of writing*. Since you may not yet have studied the modes, you will just have to do the best you can. This is only a tentative outline; when you write the paper, your intuitions will help you improve the logic of the organization, and you can rewrite the outline then.)

4. Show your outline to your instructor and your classmates for their comments.

WRITING INTRODUCTIONS AND CONCLUSIONS

If you are writing a paper with surprise value, the best rule for writing an introduction is to introduce the surprise value (i.e., the featured subtopic) immediately. This will tell the readers why the topic is interesting and let them know where you're going. The introduction, together with the title, also specifies the limits of the paper. Let us reexamine Panzer's introduction.

GYPSY MOTH CONTROL: A DIVISIVE QUESTION

Along with the sleigh-bell choruses of peepers and the songs of nesting birds, spring in New Jersey also brings the cacophony of controversy over the gypsy moth.

On one side, the state's Department of Agriculture, which carries out an aerial spraying program to control the moth; on the other are conservationists, who say that spraying does more harm than good and is potentially dangerous to humans.

As you can see, the introduction and title indicate the limits of the paper.

Topic: gypsy moths
Narrowed topic: gypsy moth control
Featured subtopic: a divisive question in New Jersey in spring between the state's Department of Agriculture and conservationists

While indicating the limits, Panzer has also made certain readers know that the article is local (New Jersey) and timely (spring); and she has written all of this in an imaginative way. While you may not be able to figure out an imaginative way to begin, at least let the readers know where the article is going.

The article does not have a clear-cut conclusion, although the last two paragraphs try to sum up the controversy. The best advice for writing a conclusion is either to write a similar summary or to remind the readers why the information is useful to them. The general principle involved is to tie the ending of the paper to the introduction.

THE STYLE OF INFORMATION

Most of the characteristics of informative style derive from the writer's attempt to preserve factuality. Therefore, a basic rule is to keep the language neutral and unbiased. For example, Shanya Panzer could have written that "John Kegg, a government bureaucrat, runs the spraying program . . . " but she didn't, because *bureaucrat* is a term with negative connotations. Instead, she wrote, "John Kegg, an entomologist with the Agriculture Department, runs the spraying program. . . ." This version is not only more factual (negative connotations are not facts) but also more precise.

The most troublesome rule to follow, however, is that *the sources of all facts, except common knowledge, must be given in the article.* This means that phrases like "Mr. Kegg estimates" and "Mr. Kegg said" are common stylistic features of informative writing. Such phrases are often called *attributions* and are used to meet the principle of factuality. For example, suppose the author had written, "Mr. Kegg spends 80 percent of his time on the spraying program." This is not a fact from the standpoint of the author, Shanya Panzer. You will remember that a fact is a statement about something an author has observed first-hand, and the statement above implies that Panzer observed Mr. Kegg spending 80 percent of his time in the manner designated. It's most unlikely, however, that Panzer observed any such thing. More likely, Kegg *told* Panzer the figure, and therefore what Panzer "observed" was Kegg's statement and nothing more. That's why she actually wrote, "*Mr. Kegg estimates* that he spends 80 percent of his time on the spraying program." (The italicized portion is the attribution.)

You, too, must use attributions, but your task for a term paper is complicated by the fact that scholarly documentation (bibliography plus references in the text) may also be seen as attributions. Students often wonder about matters such as whether the documentation can substitute for an attribution and whether either documentation or attributions are necessary for background information. These are matters about which experts sometimes differ. Here is some basic advice:

1. *Seldom* use an attribution for background information (especially if it's common knowledge). Technically, you don't need scholarly documentation either, but most students use it anyway to be on the safe side.
2. *Always* use both an attribution and documentation for a direct quotation. Nothing jars a reader more than a direct quotation in the middle of a paragraph with no internal sign of who is being quoted.
3. *Always* use an attribution and documentation for an opinion or disputed fact.
4. *Usually* use an attribution for a fact that is new to the reader. Some authors use the documentation alone to carry the attribution, but this practice isn't recommended. (The problem is that if you eliminate the documentation in order to publish the term paper as a newspaper article or pamphlet, you also lose the attribution. And if you lose the attribution, you lose factuality.)

This brings us to another matter of style that bothers some students: What is the proper form for documentation? The basic answer is that there are several widely accepted forms, and the proper one is the one your instructor specifies. The form exemplified in this chapter is an adaptation of the latest style recommended by the Modern Language Association. If no specific format is required, you can use the form given at the end of this chapter.

In addition to these rules having to do with factuality, there are several aspects of style related to the readers' needs. One is that technical terms, if you must use them, ought to be defined. Note, for example, how Panzer defines the word *Sevin* in two ways, first with its generic chemical name and then with a more common term: "The homeowner . . . can hire someone to spray the tree with Sevin *(carbaryl), a pesticide that . . .* "

Another practice to help readers is to use a visual aid such as a diagram, table, graph, or picture in cases where explaining in words doesn't work very well. For example, although Panzer does not use visuals, many other articles on gypsy moths include pictures of the moth, caterpillar, and egg masses. It would be difficult to describe these things completely enough in words to allow anyone to recognize them, so when the purpose of the article is to help homeowners assess the seriousness of local infestations, pictures are necessary.

Finally, it's traditional in most types of informative writing to avoid first-person pronouns (I, me, we, us, and so on) whenever possible. Panzer did this, as the following sentence shows:

> Although she [Dr. Ehrenfeld] could not be reached for additional comment, a check with the Library of Medicine at the National Institute of Health showed that there were at least that many on record. . . .

Had Panzer not been trying to avoid first-person pronouns, the sentence might have read as follows:

> Although I could not reach Dr. Ehrenfeld for additional comment, I checked with the Library of Medicine at the National Institute of Health and found that there were at least that many on record. . . .

The usual reason for avoiding the first person in informative writing is to avoid reminding the reader that a particular individual—potentially a biased and subjective one—is doing the writing. That is, the use of first person might seem to detract from a sense of objectivity and factuality in the writing.

Exercises on Practicing Informative Style and Writing the First Draft

1. The following is a news story. Identify each sentence as a fact (F) or a nonfact (NF). If you're not sure, mark it as questionable (Q). Be prepared to explain your answers.
   a. More than 300 Groveland residents attended a public hearing last night concerning the Groveland City School budget.
   b. At the opening of the meeting, Superintendent James Mackin presented a budget calling for expenditures of $2,350,000 for the coming school year.
   c. The proposed budget is seven percent higher than last year's.
   d. In making his presentation, Groveland's pugnacious superintendent claimed that the higher budget would not mean higher property taxes.
   e. "Rising property values will easily provide increased monies to meet this new budget," Mackin said.
   f. However, Mackin admitted under questioning that final tax rates will not be known until shortly before the first tax bills are sent out next month.
   g. But he again asserted stoutly that tax rates would not rise.
   h. Mackin's announcement was opposed by Clarence Graslin, a city resident.
   i. Mackin, Graslin said, was "grossly overestimating" growth of property values.
   j. "It's just another example of the way the school district hoodwinks us taxpayers every year," Graslin charged.
   k. Another city resident, John Assen, asked Mackin why cuts could not be made in the school budget.
   l. Losing his temper, Superintendent Mackin pounded the rostrum angrily and ruled the speakers out of order.
   m. "I'll not have anyone impugning the reputation of this school administration," Mackin snarled.
   n. In closing the meeting, Mackin cited figures, which he said "proved conclusively" that the school district was already underfinanced.
   o. Whether the taxpayers really do get a break for a change will be seen next month.
2. For the same news story, list the attributions.
3. If you believe that you need some practice in writing sentences with

attributions, try the following exercise. Assume that a bank robbery occurred this morning at the First National Bank of Groveland. You are a reporter for the city's afternoon newspaper and have been assigned to write a news story about the robbery. You obtained the following statements over the telephone. You may quote any of the sources. Use as much of this information as would normally be included in this type of story.

Unless your instructor tells you otherwise, do not worry much about paragraphing or organization. (News writers have specific rules for paragraphing and organization, which they must follow.) When you are finished, show your paper to your classmates and your instructor for their comments.

"At about 10:30 this morning two male caucasians held up the First National Bank. The teller pushed the silent alarm and two patrolmen responded. The patrolmen were Thomas Jepson and Joseph Anderson. They arrived at the bank just as the robbers were leaving and a shootout ensued. One robber was killed and the other was wounded. Patrolman Anderson was also wounded. Both wounded men were taken to the hospital and I have heard no reports on their condition as yet."

(Police Chief Roger Dawson)

"Patrolman Anderson and I were on patrol near the bank when we received the call at 10:28. We immediately drove to the bank, and the robbers were backing out of the door when we got there. We shouted for them to drop their guns, but they turned around and started shooting. Joe was hit right away but he returned their fire and so did I. We hit one subject and the other took off running east on Main Street. Then he got hit. I called for ambulances but the first subject to be hit was already dead. Joe and the other subject were taken to the hospital. I don't think Joe was hurt bad. He just got shot in the left arm as far as I could tell. The money was lying on the street and I recovered it."

(Patrolman Thomas Jepson)

"It was a slow morning and my window was the only one open for business. These two men came in and yelled that it was a holdup and nobody should move. Both had pistols. One man covered the other employees and the other one gave me a gym bag and told me to fill it up. While I was putting in the money, I stepped on the alarm button. I don't know how much money I gave them, but it was a lot.

Then they told us all to get down on the floor and not move for five minutes and they left. Both of them were pretty young, in their early twenties I would guess."

(Anita Shumberg, bank teller)

"I was in my office when the robbery occurred so I didn't see anything. As far as I can tell, the robbers got about $15,000 and the police recovered all of it. I won't know for sure until we finish our audit. That Miss Shumberg is one brave gal, I'll tell you. The other employees tell me she was cool as a cucumber during the whole thing."

(Arnold Sampson, bank president)

"Patrolman Anderson received a flesh wound in the upper portion of his left arm. He will probably be released later today. The men whom the police say robbed the bank were also brought here. One of them was shot in the neck. The bullet has been removed, and the man is in the Intensive Care Unit. He is in critical condition. The other man was dead on arrival. The medical examiner has not conducted an autopsy yet, but preliminary indications are that he was shot twice, once in the chest and the other in the face near his right eye. We still have not identified either man, but the police just came and took their fingerprints to send to the F.B.I."

(Spokesperson for Groveland Municipal Hospital)

"I was the only customer in the bank when the robbers came in. I was just standing there at the desk filling out a deposit slip, and one of them hollered for everybody to stay still. Believe me, I stood still. After the teller gave them the money, they told us all to lie down and then they backed out. I heard the cops yell at them to drop their guns, and that's when the shooting started. So I just stayed on the floor till the whole thing was over. One strange thing was that neither man wore a mask. Don't they know that banks have cameras these days?"

(Stephan Marcantis, bank customer)

4. **Look through the notes for your paper to see if there is some aspect of your topic that would benefit from a visual aid. Supply the required visual, either by making your own or copying it from one of your sources.**

(If you copy, keep a record of the source. Visuals, like everything else in term papers, need documentation.)

5. Write a first draft of your paper. Do not at this time worry about the proper form for documentation; just keep an ongoing record of where the facts came from. To ensure that the paper is your work and not copied from your sources, follow this procedure: Write the paper one section at a time, trying to follow your tentative outline. Look over your notes for a section, put them aside, and write the section without looking at the notes. Then check your notes for the accuracy of facts and quotations and to record the source of each fact. Finally, go on to the next section.

ANALYZING AND EVALUATING INFORMATION

Having studied the characteristics of information, you should now find it useful to gain further practice with these ideas by analyzing and evaluating an informative paper. For this purpose we will use the student term paper by Candee Douglas given earlier in the chapter. You may wish to reread the paper before we begin. (The student's assignment was to write a short, informative term paper of at least 1,000 words on a topic of her choice. The course was for first-semester freshmen.)

Comprehensiveness

In order to evaluate the comprehensiveness or completeness of coverage, we first need to figure out what the writer was trying to do. The guides to the writer's purpose ought to be in the title and introduction, where we should be told the general topic of the paper and the particular subtopic(s) to be featured. These indicate clearly that the general topic is "the harp seal," but there is a slight problem with the featured subtopics. The subtitle ("To hunt or to protect?") suggests that the writer will mainly discuss the arguments for and against hunting the harp seal, while the introduction repeats that subtopic ("the traditional hunt has also become an issue of controversy") and adds another possibility: "protests were once again staged against the hunt this year." Thus there are two possible subtopics to be featured: the pro and con arguments and this year's protests. Since the subtopics about the arguments are listed twice, we might expect those to be given the most substantial treatment. In any case, though, we expect that both subtopics will be covered comprehensively in the paper.

Next, we must consider the background information, which should be covered in order for the reader to understand the featured subtopics. Since the seal hunt has been widely covered in the news media, with gruesome pictures of the hunters clubbing and skinning the baby seals, the writer can expect her readers to know some background information before they read the paper. We know, or should know, how seals are killed, where the hunt takes place, and, to some extent, who does the killing and why. However, many of us probably do not know exactly what a harp seal is, its life cycle, how many of them exist, why the pups instead of the adults are hunted, and other such matters that a television news program would not have time to cover. The writer thus had a great variety of subtopics to choose from when she decided which ones to give us as background for the main story.

With these expectations in mind, let us look at an outline of the paper to see what the writer actually did. The following outline is only slightly changed from the one that the writer herself provided. (Numbers in parentheses are paragraph numbers.)

I.   Introduction (1)

II.   Background about the harp seal
A. Description and classification (2)
B. Description of the pups (3)
C. Migration (4)
D. Weaning and maturation of the pups (5)

III.   The hunting of the pups
A. Where and why (6)
B. History of the hunt
1. Quotas on various types of hunting (7)
2. Hunting before quotas (8)
C. Uses of harp seals—adults and pups (9)
D. Killing of the pups (10)

IV.   Controversy over the hunt
A. Arguments on both sides
1. Hunters' arguments (11)
2. Opposition arguments (12)
B. Protests of the hunt
1. Swiss opposition (12)
2. Internation Fund for Animal Welfare (13–14)
3. Greenpeace Foundation (15)
4. An example from the U.S. (16)
5. Brigitte Bardot (16)
C. International Convention of Antarctic Seals (17)
D. Lavigne's suggestions for new rules (18)

    V. Conclusion
        A. Summary of arguments for the hunt (19)
        B. Summary of arguments against (20)
        C. Need for more information (21)

We can see from the outline that the writer has done about what we expected. She has two sections of background information, one giving biological information and one discussing the hunt. Both seem adequate, although the history of the hunt (IIIB) and the killing of the pups (IIID) are rather sketchy, especially if you read the actual paragraphs in the paper and see how little is said. Probably this sketchiness can be justified in regard to the killing, since we have seen this on TV, but the historical section should be stronger.

When we get to the featured subtopics, we see a greater problem: the pro and con arguments are given in only two brief paragraphs, hardly enough for us to know why the issue is so controversial. The subtopic of this year's protests turns out to be the only one covered in some depth, and even here we seem to have more a list of examples of protests than a thorough coverage. We may also be puzzled about the Convention of Antarctic Seals. How, one wonders, can an agreement about *antarctic* seals protect harp seals living in the *arctic*?

Surprise Value

We can see from the outline that the author has used surprise value in several ways. For one thing, she has used it as the organizing principle, beginning with information least relevant to her main subtopic and gradually building up to the real topic of the paper. Second, her space allotments are also related to surprise value. The background subtopics were allotted four and five paragraphs, respectively, while the featured subtopic, if we include both possible subtopics within the last section, are given 10 paragraphs. Finally, she devoted the largest portion of the space to what happened in 1977, the year she wrote the paper, so she has the principle of timeliness.

However, timeliness alone may not be enough to interest a reader. Also, we are not certain who the intended readers are or why they should be interested in a summary of the protests. It would have been helpful, then, if the author had explained more clearly in the introduction and/or the conclusion for whom she was writing and why. Perhaps she could have added a sentence like this: "Now that the hunt and the consequent protests are over for 1977, it may be useful for the American reader to learn more about the harp seal and how large the protest movement has become." Of course, it is usually not possible to be so specific in the first or second draft of a paper, when it is normal for any writer to be unsure of his or her intentions; but once the body of the paper has been settled on, it would be worth taking time to rewrite the introduction to make one's intentions clear.

Factuality

Since we cannot assess the actual truth or falsity of the statements in a paper like this, for our discussion of factuality we will concentrate on attributions: those phrases within a sentence that tell us the sources of the information. This seems reasonable because the student herself probably does not know the truth of what she has written. As is usual with term papers, she has simply read certain material and is telling us what she read. We hope that she has chosen reliable sources (and we can check her documentation about this), but beyond that we only require that she use attributions to indicate that her information does not come from first-hand observations.

Most paragraphs on the first two pages contain no attributions, relying only on the documentation at the end of a paragraph (e.g., Hall and Kelson 922) to show readers that this is not first-hand knowledge. This approach seems reasonable for the first two pages since nearly all the information seems to be common knowledge, the kind of material available in any standard reference book. Whenever the material is less factual, as in reference to the purpose of the white coat on baby seals and the reasons for the seal hunt, an attribution has been used ("according to David M. Lavigne, a naturalist who . . . " and "Lavigne says").

This pattern continues for the rest of the paper. Of course, as the paper goes on, more and more attributions appear because the information is more current. In fact, the student seems to be using the "rule of thumb" that anything from a book is common knowledge and needs no attribution, while anything from a periodical (magazine or newspaper) does require an attribution. This rule of thumb seems to work in this case, but it's doubtful whether a writer should depend on it.

Another aspect of factuality concerns the accuracy of sources, and here again, one might find something to quibble about. Many of the sources for the paper are newspapers from Buffalo, New York, and it seems doubtful that a newspaper in Buffalo would have reporters in all the places where events concerning the harp seal took place. More likely, these stories came from a wire service such as the Associated Press; if so, it would be more accurate, for factuality's sake, to name the wire service both in the attribution and in the bibliography.

Finally, there are some problems with factuality in the concluding three paragraphs, since at least one sentence in each paragraph is clearly the writer's own opinion. While the opinions are balanced and noncontroversial, some readers might object.

Style

Attributions, one of the main aspects of informative style, were covered in the preceding section. However, there are several other aspects also worth discussing.

LANGUAGE. We expect the language of information to be objective, and, in most respects, the paper meets this criterion. However, it is worth noting that the verbs in the attributions are occasionally a bit biased. For example, the sealers "claim" but the opposing groups "disagree" and "protested." The writer thus has shown some possible doubt about the sealers' position but none about the opponents'. You have to be careful about word choices in attributions, for they are the most obvious places for biases to show up.

QUOTATIONS AND PARAPHRASING. Although direct quotations are in one sense more factual than indirect quotations or paraphrasing, it is probably safe to say that most students use too many of them, thus producing papers that sound choppy and pieced together. The writer of the term paper appears to have taken this warning to heart, since she has used only one direct quotation. However, she may have gone too far. One place where direct quotations might be useful is in the paragraph about the sealers' arguments. Why not let the sealers speak for themselves? Another place would be in reference to the "convention." Since this convention is a quasi-legal document and since legal language is easy to oversimplify, it might have been useful to quote some of the relevant portions.

FORMAT. There are many details in which the format of this paper differs from specifications given in one or another term-paper manual. Although we assume that the student has followed the format requested by her instructor, other students should check with their instructors about details such as the following:

Title: Some instructors prefer all capitals, and others prefer capitals and lowercase type. Do not use quotation marks or underlines.
Title page: Some instructors prefer that there be no title page. There are also many different preferences regarding its format.
Outline: Some instructors prefer it to be single spaced; others, double spaced.
Page numbers: Some instructors prefer them to be placed to the right. Others request that a full heading, including the title or your name, be used.
Bibliography: Some instructors prefer that it be called *bibliography* rather than *works cited*.

In all such matters, find out what your instructor prefers and do that. If your instructor states no preference, you may follow the format recommended in this chapter.

Overall Evaluation

Although we noted a number of weaknesses in the paper, most turned out to be minor and easily correctable. For example, the problem of the misleading title could be solved by either changing the title (to something like "Protests Continue over Killing of Harp Seal Pups") or expanding the subtopic about the pro and con arguments. The only serious problem is that the featured subtopic about the protests is unsubstantial and does not hang together very well. Fixing it would require further research and some rewriting.

Therefore, the paper seems successful in most respects, especially when we consider that the purpose of assigning term papers in a writing class is to teach library research, the writing of smoothly integrated papers from notes, and the use of scholarly format. On all these counts, the paper is successful.

Transitions: A Special Problem for the Pyramid of Surprise

As was mentioned earlier in the chapter, transitions from one subtopic to another can be a tricky problem when you organize by the pyramid of surprise. Most of us are accustomed to handling transitions with phrases such as "in the first place," "second," and "however." But the sections of the pyramid of surprise do not fit together in such a natural manner, and some other way must be found.

The two easiest methods are to begin each section with a heading or a rhetorical question. However, headings are not appropriate for short papers, and continual use of rhetorical questions can be repetitious. The feature story by Panzer illustrates a better way. If you look at the paragraphs that occur at the section breaks (paragraphs 3, 8, 12, 39–40), you will notice how skillfully one section has been blended into the next; the transition paragraph mentions an idea that is common to both sections. That is a skill you should aim to develop. In the meantime, try the plain style whenever you get stuck. For example, Panzer could have written paragraph 3 as follows: "Before we discuss this controversy about pesticides, let us cover some basic information on what gypsy moths are and where they come from." That may not be graceful, but it gets the job done.

Exercises on Writing the Second Draft

1. Write a second (and, if necessary, a third and fourth) draft of your paper. Each time, work on smoothing out the wording within sections and trying different methods of joining the sections.
2. When you have produced a draft that you like, work on the references,

both those in the text and on the "Works Cited" page. Remember, the references in the text give the exact page the material came from and use some device to let the reader know which item in the bibliography is the source. The bibliography, or works cited, then, is simply a list of the sources that you used in the paper. (Some students like to list every source they read, but there is little point to this in a student paper—unless you're just trying to impress your instructor.)

3. Reexamine your outline to see if it still conforms with the paper as it is finally written. Revise it where necessary.

4. Make a complete, semifinal draft of the paper with all the parts required: title page, outline, text, and works cited. Compare your draft to the sample paper in this chapter to ensure that you haven't omitted anything. (This draft can be typed or written longhand, but it should be legible.)

5. Show the draft to your instructor for comments. Make whatever revisions the instructor requests.

6. Type a final draft very neatly. If you have someone else do the typing, be sure to give complete directions. You, not the typist, are responsible for the paper.

7. Proofread, then make minor corrections neatly, in ink. Retype the page for a major correction. Turn in the paper.

SUPPLEMENTARY INFORMATION: EXAMPLES OF DOCUMENTATION

With the new style of documentation (no footnotes), you will be giving the full information on your sources only once, on the last page of your paper under "Works Cited." Therefore, in the body of your paper you need give only enough information to allow the reader to find the correct source and the exact page you are citing from that source. Below are some examples of both in-text documentation and entries for "Works Cited."

However, two additional comments should be made. First, there is insufficient space in this book to give examples of all possible types of works that could be cited. If you have sources that don't match any of the examples, you should either construct the entry in a logical manner or check the form in a larger manual. Second, you may still have "content footnotes" in which you add information that doesn't fit into the main text or comment on the main text in some way. Unless your instructor says otherwise, place content notes at the foot of the page.

Documenting within the Text

The preferred method of indicating sources within your text is to use the author's name in the attribution and then give the page number at the end of the citation:

According to Evelyn Cheesman, gypsy moth caterpillars travel by being blown along by the wind (73).

Note that the page number goes before the period. However, if the author were being quoted, the page number would go after the quotation marks:

According to Evelyn Cheesman, "Aeroplanes have caught these flying caterpillars at a height of 2,000 feet" (73).

Of course, this method assumes that you and your readers know who the author, Evelyn Cheesman, is—besides the fact that she wrote a particular book. If you don't, add a phrase of identification or omit the name from the sentence. These two options go as follows:

Their white coats are not for camouflage as some scientists have thought, according to David M. Lavigne, a Canadian zoologist (129).

Gypsy moths "travel" during the larval stage, when their light bodies and long hair allow them to be easily blown along by the wind (Cheesman 73).

Also use the latter form when the information is common knowledge. Finally, there will also be times when the author is anonymous. In such cases use a key word from the title of the article or book (whatever appears first on the "Works Cited" page). It does not have to be the first word of the title:

According to one newspaper, gypsy moths are now moving south into Delaware and Virginia ("Move" 5).

Forms to Use on "Works Cited" Page

One purpose of this page is to help the readers find your sources. Sometimes readers want to check on you, to see that you quoted or paraphrased someone correctly. More often, however, a reader will want to learn more about the topic. Your job, then, is to help the reader get hold of the sources. Use the following examples as guides to the proper format, but don't be afraid to add more information if you think it would help the reader.

BOOKS. Always give (1) author, (2) title, (3) place of publication, (4) publisher (abbreviate as much as possible), and (5) date of publication. If 3, 4, or 5 is missing, say so with n.p. or n.d. (for *no place, no publisher, no date*) in the appropriate place. Also give editor, edition, volume number, and name of series when available. Finally, if you cited someone other than the author or editor of the book, clearly indicate who was cited and what the person wrote.

Clausen, Lucy W. *Insect Fact and Folklore*. New York: Macmillan, 1954.

Powell, Jerry A. "Family RIODINIDAE: The Metalmarks." In *The Butterflies of North America*. Ed. William H. Howe. Garden City, NY: Doubleday, 1975: 259–72.

Deason, Hilary J. Foreword. *Familiar Insects of America*. By Will Barker. New York: Harper & Row, 1960.

Caborn, J. M. "The Measurement of Wind Speed and Direction in Ecological Studies." In *The Measurement of Environmental Factors in Terrestrial Ecology*. Ed. R. M. Wadsworth. British Ecological Society Symposium Number Eight. Oxford, G.B.: Blackwell Scientific Publications, 1968.

MAGAZINES.   Give (1) author, (2) title of article, (3) title of magazine, (4) date, and (5) page numbers the article covers. For scholarly magazines, give volume number and year, not month or day.

Cameron, E. Alan, and others. "Disruption of Gypsy Moth Mating with Microencapsulated Disparlure." *Science* 183 (1974): 972–3.

Begley, Sharon, and John Carey. "Plague of the Gypsy Moths." *Newsweek*. 8 June 1981: 86.

Masson, Walter. "Save Your Trees from the Gypsy Moth." *Organic Gardening* May 1982: 31–7.

NEWSPAPERS.   Give (1) author (if there is one), (2) title or headline, (3) name of newspaper, (4) full date, (5) section number, and (6) page number. For section and page numbers, follow the newspaper style (sec. 2: 5, B5, B–5, or whatever). When it would be helpful, also give the type of article: Editorial, Letter to the Editor, Associated Press news release, and so on.

Balgooyen, Warren. "Gypsy Moth Readying '80 Assault. *New York Times* 22 Mar. 1980, sec. 22: 16.

"Gypsy Moth: Not Much You Can Do." Story by Staff and Wire Service. *Sunday Democrat and Chronicle* (Rochester, N.Y.) 1 Feb. 1981: 1A, 2A.

OTHER SOURCES.   Pamphlets, encyclopedias, movies, recordings, and other sources come in a bewildering variety of formats and also vary widely in the amount of information they give about author or artist, title, date, sponsor, publication number, and so on. Use your common sense to provide the reader with as much information as will be needed to find the source, and give it in an order that most closely matches the following examples.

Beal, F.E.L. *Some Common Birds Useful to the Farmer*. Fish and Wildlife Service, U.S. Department of the Interior. Conservation Bulletin 18. Washington: GPO, 1948.

Davis, Don. "Gypsy Moth." *Encyclopedia Americana*. 1979 ed.

Acid Rain. EPA Research Summary. U.S. Environmental Protection Agency, Office of Research and Development. EPA 600/8-79-028. Washington: GPO, Oct. 1979.

Weir, Byrna, ed. *The Environmental Self-Guide*. Rochester, N.Y.: Rochester Committee for Scientific Information, Jan. 1972.

Teaching Tips on Current Environmental Problems. Curriculum Aid Prepared by Project S.P.R.U.C.E. Mimeographed pamphlet. New Paltz, N.Y.: Ulster County Board of Cooperative Educational Services, 1969.

Cohn, James M. Personal interview. Buffalo, N.Y. Mar. 23, 1974.

Ullman, Michael. Record Jacket. *Marian McPartland at the Festival*. Concord, Calif.: Concord Jazz, 1980. CJ-118.

Explaining and Proving

THE IMPORTANCE OF EXPLAINING AND PROVING

One of our ongoing efforts is to explain the world around us. We want to know how things are and why they are that way. For example, suppose at a fireworks display a family observes the explosion of an aerial bomb. A child, typically, wants to know why he or she sees the bright flash of the bomb before hearing the noise of the explosion. The parent explains: "Because light travels faster than sound."

Such an "explanation" is usually accepted by children and, if so, it can be regarded as an informative statement, a fact. But some inquisitive children go further. "How do you know that?" they ask. Now the explanation is being regarded as a thesis, that is, a statement that needs to be proved. Children learn at an early age that explanations need not be accepted unless they can be proved in some manner.

Explaining things and proving the explanations to be true is thus a basic and necessary human activity. There are, however, many ways of proving. Persuasion does it by means of appeals to emotions, biases, and carefully selected facts; literature does it by getting the reader to identify with a main character who goes through a certain experience. In this chapter, we will be doing it as the scientist does, through careful collection and interpretation of data.

This chapter, then, might be thought of as a chapter about science writing. We do not call it that because to many people science consists only of physics, chemistry, and biology; by contrast, we are interested here in principles that apply to any situation in which someone is trying to be rigorously objective, whether that person is studying a poem or a chemical compound. And we are assuming that the written report of the investigation will attempt to reflect that objectivity.

Of course, it is not possible for us to cover methods of investigation in any great depth. Each field of study has its own methods, and one of your primary, long-range tasks in college is to learn the methods of the field that you have chosen to major in. In other words, a history major learns to investigate historical events, an English major learns to investigate pieces of literature, a sociology major learns to investigate the behavior of groups of people, and so on. This chapter can only show you a few of the principles common to many fields so that you can carry out some simple investigations that will lead to papers for your writing course.

A second problem is that there are many different types of investigations and, therefore, different types of papers. Since not all of them can be covered here, just two of the most common types are explained, the statistical study and the case study. Statistical assignments are common in such courses as sociology, psychology, agriculture, quality control, and education. In such courses you are often asked to study a group of items (people, plants, machine parts, and so on), make a generalization about the nature of the group, and then write a report of your findings and your method of investigation. Case assignments are most often made in career-oriented courses such as law, social work, and business management. In such assignments you are given the facts about a particular problem and asked how you would solve the problem. Such cases are intended to give you some practical experience before you go out on the job. The papers that you write to defend your solutions are also good practice for the enormous amounts of paperwork such jobs normally entail.

Of course, even within these two types of papers, there are many variations in how actual organizations decide to write their reports (and many organizations are quite dogmatic about this), but the principles here should be adaptable for many courses and jobs.

SOME EXAMPLES OF EXPLAINING AND PROVING

As usual, there are two articles to read before we study the prewriting process. The first one ("Deceived Respondents: Once Bitten, Twice Shy") is an example of a statistical study, while the second ("Was It Ethical to Deny Baby Doe Medical Care?") is the result of a case study assignment. Both were written by students, the former by a group of three upper-division students, the latter by a freshman. However, since the statistical study was published in a professional magazine, we will consider it our professionally written article. A newspaper article served as the "case"

that the case study was written about, so that article has also been
included.

Study guides are provided for both articles because the two kinds of
writing are so different that we need to discuss the two methods simultaneously rather than waiting for the end of the chapter to discuss the student
essay.

Prereading Activities for "Deceived Respondents: Once Bitten, Twice Shy," by Thomas Sheets, Allen Radlinski, James Kohne, and G. Allen Brunner

ORGANIZATION.   This article reports on a statistical study that was
done to test an explanation. Like virtually all reports of such tests, it is
written according to a standard outline that is specified by nearly all
magazines that publish such papers. The outline begins with the explanation being tested, then moves into the method of carrying out the test. The
results of the test come next, and the results then allow the writers to
confirm or deny the original explanation. The outline of the article is as
follows (the numbers in parentheses are paragraph numbers):

    I.   Introduction (1–3)
        A. The problem: legitimate researchers worry about false surveys (1)
        B. Explanations for their concern (2)
        C. Comments and past research on the concern (3)

    II. Method of testing (4–8a)
        A. Hypothesis, or specific explanation to be tested (4–5)
        B. Selection of the people to be surveyed (6)
        C. Giving the false survey and the legitimate one (7)
        D. Counting the results (8a)

    III. The results (8b plus tables)

    IV. Conclusions (9–12)
        A. Confirmation of the hypothesis (9)
        B. Weaknesses of the test and recommendations for future tests (10–12)

VOCABULARY.   By and large, reports of statistical studies are
published in highly specialized magazines called *professional journals.*
Each field of study sponsors one or more such journals, primarily for the
specialists working in that field. The general public, in other words, is not
expected to read the articles.

As might be expected with such a specialized readership, the vocabulary of journals is often rather difficult for laypeople to read. The language not only can be highly technical, but authors also feel no need to simplify the language even for nontechnical matters. Study the vocabulary items below before you read the article.

marketing and other field-based research—tests conducted in real-life situations, outside of a laboratory

ploy, gambit—strategies used to gain advantage over one's opponent

decried—complained about; disparaged

homogeneous—uniform; similar in nature or kind

experimental group—a group of people or items upon whom an experiment is conducted

control group—a second group of people or items, matched to the experimental group, but not experimented upon

X^2—Chi Square, a statistical procedure designed to determine if two groups are alike or different

p—the abbreviation for "probability"

deleterious—injurious; harmful

pilot study—a small research project, used to experiment with a method of testing

STUDY QUESTIONS

1. We say that a statistical study is designed to test an explanation. What is being tested here, and how does it constitute an explanation?
2. As with most introductions, the precise explanation to be discussed in the article comes after some opening discussion. What does the opening discussion consist of?
3. See if you can explain in your own words how the study itself (i.e., the experiment) was done. Where does the description of the study occur in the article? How much detail is given about it?
4. After a study is done, some results are obtained. How are the results given in this paper?
5. What is the connection between the material in the introduction of the paper and that given in the section labeled "Conclusions"?
6. What else is in the section labeled "Conclusions"?

Prereading Activities for "Was It Ethical to Deny Baby Doe Medical Care?" by Ruth Goodhart

ORGANIZATION. At first glance, the second article bears much resemblance to a persuasive essay, and in truth, some persuasive essays use organizational patterns similar to the one employed here. As we shall see, however, there are some distinct differences.

One difference is that this pattern is fairly standardized and cut-and-dried, whereas persuasive essays are generally more free-form. This is not the only standard pattern that can be used for case essays, but it is a common one. It was originated in ancient Greece and still can be found in most law books and other places where legal arguments are published. The pattern is as follows (the numbers in parentheses are paragraph numbers):

I.   Introduction (1–8)
  A. The general problem to be explained (1–2)
  B. The facts of the case of Baby Doe (3–7)
  C. The specific ethical issue to be explained (8a)
  D. The explanation, or thesis (8b)

II. The argument (9–16)
  A. Direct support for the thesis (9)
  B. Arguments for the "other side" and rebuttals to each
    1. The argument for "quality of life" (10)
    2. Rebuttal (11)
    3. The burden on the parents (12)
    4. Rebuttal (13)
    5. The burden on society (14)
    6. Rebuttal (15–16)

III. Conclusion (17)

VOCABULARY.   Because this essay was written by a student, it does not contain much difficult language except for a few medical terms. However, several terms are being used in special ways. The term *ethics* as used here refers to the rules of right conduct toward other people. Under the definition the student is using, an action that causes no harm to anyone is not unethical.

To analyze a problem in ethics, such as the dispute about Baby Doe, one way is to identify the ideals, obligations, and consequences involved. *Ideals* are beliefs that a society has about the proper way to treat other people. *Obligations* are the duties or responsibilities that one person has toward another person. *Consequences* are the effects, or possible effects, that one person's actions may have on another person; generally, we believe that any action that causes harm to someone else is unethical. All three of these terms are used in the essay.

STUDY QUESTIONS

1. As can be seen from the outline, the problem or issue is explained twice, once in general terms (paragraphs 1 and 2) and then again in specific terms (paragraph 8a). Explain this difference in your own words.
2. Compare the student's summary of the facts with those given in the news story. What has the student included and omitted?
3. The only direct support for the thesis is in paragraph 9. How might the rest of the argument be considered indirect support?

4. Locate some of the ideals and obligations that are being used in various parts of the argument.
5. Locate an example of an argument based on consequences.

DECEIVED RESPONDENTS: ONCE BITTEN, TWICE SHY

Thomas Sheets, Allen Radlinski, James Kohne, and G. Allen Brunner*

1 For some time, people engaged in marketing and other field-based research have had to contend with the consequences of a fairly widely used ploy in the direct selling field: gaining a potential customer's attention and interest by requesting cooperation in some sort of false survey. Despite the efforts of the American Association for Public Opinion Research, the American Marketing Association, and other groups, and regardless of recent Federal Trade Commission orders, this gambit is still in use, although perhaps somewhat modified.

2 Two dimensions of false surveys concern legitimate researchers: ethical considerations and the effects of such sales techniques upon the efficiency of genuine research. Although we believe that this practice should be decried on ethical grounds, the following research deals only with its effect on legitimate research.

3 Many authors have speculated a probably negative effect of false surveys on the efficiency of field interviewing.[1] Others have provided insight into the matter by publishing data on the impact of sales efforts on market survey refusal rates.[2] Still others have suggested that the subject requires further study.[3]

The Study

4 Drawing upon these recommendations, speculations, and inferences the following hypothesis was developed and pilot tested using an experimental design:

5 A prior exposure to a false survey, i.e., a direct sales attempt, will significantly increase the refusal rate in a legitimate fixed-address survey.

[1] Rome G. Arnold, "The Interviewer in Jeopardy; a Problem in Public Relations," *Public Opinion Quarterly*, Vol. 28, 1964, pp. 119–123; and Richard Baxter, "An Inquiry into the Misuse of the Survey Technique of Sales Solicitors," *Public Opinion Quarterly*, Vol. 28, 1964, pp. 124–134.

[2] *Ibid*; and Alvin Schwarts, "Interviewing and the Public," *Public Opinion Quarterly*, Vol. 28, 1964, pp. 134–142.

[3] Alexander Biel, "Abuses of the Survey Research Technique: the Phony Interview," *Public Opinion Quarterly*, Vol. 31, 1967, p. 298; and Irving L. Allen and J. Colfax, "Respondents' Attitudes Toward Legitimate Surveys in Four Cities," *Journal of Marketing Research*, November 1968, pp. 431–433.

*Thomas Sheets, Allen Radlinski, and James Kohne were undergraduate students in a marketing research class directed by G. Allen Brunner, who is a professor of marketing at the University of Toledo. Mr. Sheets is currently in an industry-training program. Mr. Kohne is in real estate sales, and Lt. Radlinski is completing his tour in the U.S. Army.

6   In an effort to approximate field selling conditions, a homogeneous, middle-income, suburban housing development was chosen for the test. Within the selected area, all residences in a given block were randomly assigned to either the experimental or control groups. With the exception of those not at home, this procedure resulted in the identification of 104 experimental and 70 control units.

7   The members of the experimental group were asked to cooperate in a marketing research study. If they did so, the field interviewers proceeded to deliver a fairly low-key sales presentation for a totally fictitious encyclopedia (the Newtonian Encyclopedia). The individual in the selected residence was carefully identified at this time. The refusal rate—the proportion of persons who refused to cooperate in the false research—was approximately 50 percent for this phase of the study, as shown in Table 1.

8   At intervals of from two to four days after their exposure to the experimental treatment, the 54 persons who had cooperated in the initial phase were approached by a different interviewer and again asked to cooperate in the marketing research study. The 70 members of the control group were interviewed during this same period. The same opening statement was made in both the experimental and control interviews.[4] The results

TABLE 1   *Phase 1: Experimental Group Willingness
To Participate in False Market Research*

Response	Number	Percent
Consent	54	51.9%
Refusal	50	48.1
Total	104	100.0

TABLE 2   *Phase 2: Experimental and Control Group Willingness
To Participate in True Market Research*

	Experimental		Control	
Response	Number	Percent	Number	Percent
Consent	12	24.5%	36	51.4%
Refusal	37	75.5	34	48.6
Total[a]	49	100.0	70	100.0

[a]The total number in the experimental group who cooperated was reduced from the original 54 because 5 respondents were not available for the second phase of the study.

$X^2 = 8.554$; $p < .005$ (1 d.f.)

[4]The opening statement was: "Hi! My name is _____. We are conducting some marketing research in this area. I just have a couple of questions to ask you folks; it will only take a couple of minutes of your time."

of this effort are displayed in Table 2. While it is apparent that the refusal rates for the first stage of both the experimental and the control group are virtually identical (48.1 and 48.6 percent, respectively) the effect of the second exposure upon the consenting members of the experimental group is quite pronounced. Slightly more than 75 percent refused to cooperate in the research study. The difference in the refusal rate was significant with $p <$ .005.

Conclusion

9   The findings indicate support for the hypothesis: false market surveys have a deleterious effect upon respondent willingness to cooperate in subsequent market research studies. By inference, households that have been previously exposed to false research are half again as likely to refuse to cooperate in legitimate field research as those who have not. The implication for field researchers is either to stay away from areas that have had recent, heavy, direct sales efforts or to plan for higher refusal rates in such areas.

10   We regard this work as a pilot study partially because of the small size and homogeneous composition of the groups. However, of perhaps greater concern is the limit imposed upon interpretation because of the use of the same opening statement in all situations. While we regard this statement as fairly innocuous, it may have been a sufficient recall stimulus to contaminate the findings. Any further efforts to test the hypothesis should control for this possibility.

11   It is also possible that the results would have been the same if both contacts had been legitimate, that the effect stems essentially from annoyance about being bothered in the home rather than resentment of the sales strategies. Thus, two sales calls or two research contacts made under similar circumstances might have produced the same response noted by this study.

12   Finally, research should be conducted to determine the duration of such effects. Some of our interviews suggested that a number of respondents had no recollection of having been interviewed only two to four days previously. One may speculate that increased time between interview attempts would lead to a reduction in refusal rates.

CHARGES WEIGHED FOR PARENTS WHO LET BABY DIE UNTREATED

1   BLOOMINGTON, Ind., April 16 (UPI)—Prosecutors said today that they might file charges against the parents of a retarded infant who died at Bloomington Hospital after the parents were granted a court's approval to deny him food, water and medical aid.

2   "I have a responsibility as prosecutor, in a death of this nature, to examine the possibility of criminal culpability," said Barry Brown, the Monroe County Prosecutor. He said a decision on filing charges against the parents, whose names were not made public, would be made by next week. The infant was known only as "Baby Doe."

3   Dr. John Pless, the county coroner, is investigating the infant's death. "This is a direct killing," said Dr. J. C. Willke, president of the National Right to Life Committee. "Since when do we allow people to be killed just because they are handicapped?"

4   "I think it's really disgusting," said Janet Rebone, president of the Monroe County Right To Life. "We certainly don't think that child should have been allowed to die."

5   Dan Mills, a lawyer whose partner, Andrew Mallor, represents the baby's parents, said no charges should be filed against the couple. "I think it would be a gross miscarriage of justice for the prosecutor to waste his time like that." Mr. Mills said, "It has been a tremendous ordeal for the parents."

6   The 6-pound infant, who died Thursday night, was born with Down's syndrome and was unable to eat normally because his esophagus was not connected to his stomach. He was not fed intravenously.

7   "I guess those of us who were involved with the case feel sad about the death, which we were fighting so hard to prevent," said Lawrence Brodeur, Monroe County Deputy Prosecutor, who was the baby's court-appointed guardian.

8   The week-old infant died hours before Mr. Brodeur and an Indiana University law professor were to appear before Justice John Paul Stevens of the United States Supreme Court for a stay of a ruling by the Indiana Supreme Court. The state court refused to order treatment, upholding an earlier decision by two Monroe County judges.

9   Ten couples sought to adopt the infant. Shirley and Bobby Wright of Evansville filed a petition for legal guardianship. "We feel that we have lost this particular battle, but we are not going to stop fighting for the rights of handicapped children," said Mrs. Wright, who has a 3-year-old daughter with Down's syndrome.

WAS IT ETHICAL TO DENY BABY DOE MEDICAL CARE?

Ruth Goodhart

1   It is the hope of every expectant parent that their child will be born normal and healthy. Unfortunately, some infants are born with congenital abnormalities, which means that sometime during the early months of fetal development, some stage of development went awry. As a result, the part(s) of the fetus which is developing at that particular point will develop abnormally; that is, it will deviate from the normal pattern of growth. Sometimes this anomaly can be relatively simple to correct; sometimes the problem is correctable, though more life-threatening for the infant. But occasionally, the defect may be extremely severe, such as the case of infants born with spina bifida or Down's syndrome. For these children, the disease is not curable and complications are common. Immediate surgery to sustain life may be necessary, yet the prognosis for the infant's future is dim. There is little hope that these infants will survive, and if they do survive, they will always require constant care. The responsibilities and sacrifices parents face with infants

born with serious defects are far greater than those of parents with normal children.

2   In the United States, where great emphasis is placed on medical care and prolonging human life as much as possible, these children could be given surgical and medical care in an attempt to sustain their lives. Some parents, realizing their child's prognosis, would rather choose not to medically intervene with the child's life. In most cases, then, these children will not survive more than a few days. The issue, therefore, is whether it is ethical for a parent to deny medical intervention for a severely handicapped newborn, realizing the infant will not survive without that treatment.

3   This was the decision that two parents from Indiana had to make. According to a UPI release printed in the *New York Times*, the couple's newborn son was afflicted with a severe type of Down's syndrome. (Down's syndrome is caused by a malformation of the chromosomal structure. The children of Down's syndrome will be mentally retarded, with the retardation ranging from mild to very severe. The severely retarded child often dies before his/her third year of life, and those who survive will require much supervision and care.[1])

4   The child was also born with esophageal atresia, meaning that his esophagus was not connected to his stomach. The boy was unable to eat by normal methods. (Infants with esophageal atresia are fed intravenously for a short time until a gastrostomy is performed. This is a relatively simple procedure whereby a flexible tubing would be connected directly to the child's stomach through his abdomen. Feedings would go directly to the child's stomach via the tube. At a later date when the child is older, the atresia would be corrected. That procedure is much riskier than the gastrostomy, since it involves opening the chest cavity. Complications could arise from this procedure, including a mortality risk.[2])

5   These parents, whose names were withheld, decided not to medically intervene with the child's life. This meant that no gastrostomy would be ordered, nor would the infant be fed intravenously. They were granted a court order to uphold their decision, and hospital personnel were required to abide by that order.

6   Ten couples, hearing about the case, wanted to adopt the infant, who was known only as "Baby Doe." One couple, who already had a Down's syndrome child, filed to seek legal guardianship of Baby Doe.

7   In the meantime, a deputy prosecutor was court-appointed the legal guardian for the child. After the State of Indiana refused to order treatment, the prosecutor and an Indiana University law professor were preparing to take the case to the United States Supreme Court. Just hours before the case was to be heard, however, the week-old infant died.

8   Though the parents acted within their legal bounds, what exists is a highly questionable ethical situation. In view of the child's prognosis, did the

---

[1] Henry L. Barnett, M.D., *Pediatrics* (New York: Appleton-Century-Crofts, Educational Division Meredith Corporation, 1972), pp. 897–900.

[2] For this information, I am indebted to my husband, John, who patiently explained esophageal atresia. He is a Surgical Physician Assistant and has assisted with surgical cases similar to Baby Doe's.

parents act in an ethical manner by denying medical care for their infant, knowing that their decision would terminate the child's life? I would have to assume that the parents spent some agonizing moments weighing the situation, and in the end felt justified in their decision. However, I do not believe that they were justified, and the purpose of this paper is to prove why I think the couple's decision to refuse treatment for their child was unethical.

9   I believe this primarily because it is the obligation of all parents to meet the needs of their child. By needs, I mean that they should provide everything necessary for a child to survive—food, shelter, care, and medical attention. Society shuns parents who neglect the needs of a child, particularly when the child is too young or physically incapable of caring for himself. I realize that sometimes all the medical care available will not guarantee the life of a child, but if there is even a small chance of survival the child should be extended that care. Even though the probability of this child's survival was not ideal, the parents were obligated to try. Without medical care, the child could not receive nourishment and would die. They did not want their child to get the treatment necessary to survive, and therefore shunned their obligations as parents. In my opinion, this was an unethical act of neglect.

10   I realize that there are many people who believe that the parents' decision was justifiable. They might believe that there are times when a parent's obligations are not the most important issue. For example, I am sure that some people will say that it is wrong to insist upon sustaining a life whose quality of living would be extremely poor. They may argue that it was far more humane for the child to withhold medical treatment. Because the child was severely retarded, he would not have had even a modicum of quality life. To insist upon sustaining his life when there was such an obviously bleak future for him would have been wrong and unfair.

11   I have to agree that there are some valid points in this argument. It is true that this child would probably remain severely handicapped, and his participation in everyday activities would always be severely limited. However, we do not have the right to decide whether or not another person's life is worth living. If we began evaluating whether a newborn's life would be worth living, where would we draw the line? For example, would it be reasonable to deny medical attention for all Down's syndrome children? Or children born with heart problems? I don't think so. Quality of existence is an individual preference, and in our society we just cannot project our preferences onto another person when it concerns a choice of living or dying. Granted, this child would be mentally retarded; but it was wrong for the parents to deny him the opportunity to live when their decision was based on their personal opinion regarding quality of life.

12   Someone else may argue that it is unethical to commit an act if the consequences may cause harm to other people, and the act of sustaining the child's life could be harmful to the parents. The couple would be burdened with a tremendous responsibility—including the financial and emotional strain involved in caring for a child so seriously handicapped. The medical expenses could become very prohibitive. The child would need an unusual amount of care, most of which the parents would have to provide. Adding to these pressures would be the knowledge that the child could die at any time, since the chances of the child surviving were so slim. This would create an

intense, unwanted strain on the couple which could potentially endanger their marriage and/or their health. By medically intervening with the child's life, the consequences that the parents would face as a result would be potentially harmful; therefore, it would have been unethical.

13   I can understand that caring for such a severely handicapped child might be a hardship for some couples. We don't know the financial situation of this particular couple, but it could be a possibility that they would have financial problems. I will also concede to the possibility that the emotional strain of raising this child could be stressful. But to deny the child a chance to live based on those grounds is still wrongful, because they eliminated the ethical option of placing the child for adoption. In our society we allow parents the freedom of choosing either to raise their children, or to allow someone else to adopt their children, thereby relinquishing all obligations as a parent. These parents could have placed the child up for adoption, which would have relieved them of the strain involved in raising him. In fact, there were ten known couples who expressed desire to adopt this baby. It seems to me that it was unethical to deny the child the right to live simply because the parents did not choose to be obligated, particularly when they had another available option.

14   Finally, there will be people who will say that it would have been wrong to either place the child for adoption OR to obligate the parents to care for him. They will point out that if the child survives, there is a strong possibility that he may become a burden to society. For example, what if it becomes necessary to institutionalize the boy because he simply demands more care than a family can provide? Or suppose he outlives his parents—who will assume responsibility for him then? Society will then have to carry the financial and emotional burden of care, and society should not have to assume these responsibilities. After all, mental institutions are very often funded by the taxpayer's dollars and it is unfair to expect society to donate part of their income to care for someone who will never be capable of contributing to society. It is doubtful that this particular child will ever be able to assume any kind of responsibility—for himself OR to others—so it is unethical to expect society to care for him.

15   In all fairness, I can understand the objection some people may feel about having part of their wages used for the purpose of helping total strangers. In all probability, the resentment is part of a more generalized feeling that taxes are too high and that our society is trying to do more for people than it can afford. In spite of our dislike of taxes, however, no one has seriously proposed saving taxes by allowing handicapped people to die. That is, we continue willingly to pay for mental hospitals, schools for the blind and deaf, homes for the aged, and similar institutions for so-called burdensome people. We seem to believe that it is a basic ethical rule that no one should be required to die simply because he is a burden. Everyone has a right to live if possible, and it is the ethical duty not only of society in general but also of the individuals within society to protect this right. Therefore, Baby Doe's right to live should have been protected by his parents and, if they couldn't afford it, by the taxpayer's dollar. The fact that Baby Doe might have been a burden is not relevant.

16   Furthermore, the parents would have discovered, had they checked, that

Baby Doe was not absolutely doomed to be a burden. Esophageal atresia is correctable, so Baby Doe might have survived the operation to become a physically normal person. And as for the mental retardation resulting from Down's Syndrome, even this need not prevent a child from becoming a useful member of society or at least someone who can take care of himself. The rate at which people are institutionalized is decreasing as the awareness of the handicapped increases. It is a possibility that the community's responsibility to the child (if any existed at all) would have been reduced to a minimum.

17   Given the facts as presented in the newspaper article, as well as the reference materials used for this paper, I believe that the parents were unethical to deny their infant the necessary medical care. In my opinion, there did not seem to be any issue—obligation, ideal, or consequence—that could justify the parents' decision.

PREWRITING

Answering the study questions should have led you to observe the three main factors involved in testing a thesis, hypothesis, or other type of explanation. Remember, in this chapter we are examining methods of constructing rigorously objective tests that should result in proofs that do not involve persuasive appeals.

The three factors involved in a test can be traced to the three issues, or concerns, that stem from the communications triangle. The first issue, the *writer issue*, arises when the author discovers that the words we use in everyday life are not defined precisely enough to be used in rigorously logical arguments. For example, if a writer is going to prove that something is bad, he or she must define what he means by the word *bad*. To a great extent, writers may define words to suit themselves; thus the writer issue is one of *definitions of terms*.

The writer's second concern is the selection of the rules, or principles, by which evidence can be interpreted. These rules must be acceptable to all members of that audience of reasonable, objective people to whom these logical arguments are presumed to be directed. For example, if you can prove that someone has lied to you, you can "interpret" the lie with the rule that "lying is wrong," a rule most reasonable people would agree with. The *reader issue* thus involves the selection of the proper *rules of interpretation* to apply to the evidence.

Finally we have the *subject-matter issue*, which requires the writer to acquire an accurate view of the subject, or problem, under consideration. Ordinarily, we think of this step as the gathering of evidence (facts) about the subject. For example, in order to prove that someone has told a lie, we would need to establish exactly what the person said and then determine whether this statement was in accordance with the truth. If we can show that the truth was one way and the person said it was another way, then we have the possibility of proving that the person lied. (The final proof, of course, will depend upon how we decide to define a lie. The person could simply have been mistaken.) In all such cases, therefore, we need to find the truth—an accurate picture of reality—before we can write a good argument.

The solution of these three issues—definitions, rules of interpretation, and evidence—is thus essential to proving that explanations are true. The issues are illustrated on the communications triangle in Figure 5.1.

Although we will primarily be considering the three issues just discussed there is a fourth issue, logic, which is involved in the proving of explanations. We expect the proofs to be logical argumentation in a rigorous manner.

There is not enough room in this book to present an extensive treatment of logic, but we can mention a few essential principles. The first essential principle is that there are two main types of logic, induction and deduction. Most arguments use both types simultaneously, but it is probably safe to say that a particular argument will use more of one than of the other.

For example, the first article ("Deceived Respondents: Once Bitten, Twice Shy") mainly exhibits the use of *inductive logic*. Inductive logic involves making generalizations. In this case, the authors wanted to make a general statement about how *all people* would respond to false surveys; they believed that all people would be more reluctant to respond to legitimate surveys if they had first been tricked into taking a false survey. They decided to test this theory by subjecting people to a false survey and then following it up with a legitimate survey. However, it was not practical to use this test on all people, so they only chose a *sample* of people for the experiment. Then they intended to say that whatever was found to be true

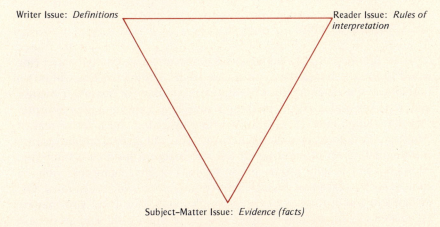

Writer Issue: *Definitions*   Reader Issue: *Rules of interpretation*

Subject-Matter Issue: *Evidence (facts)*

FIGURE 5.1. The three issues in explaining and proving.

about the sample of respondents would also be true of all respondents. This is the process of induction. It is not the only kind of induction, but it seems to have become the most common one.

The nature of *deductive logic* is illustrated in the essay about Baby Doe. Here the author takes facts and interprets them by applying a rule, or principle. For example, the fact is that Baby Doe's parents decided to deny him medical care. This fact is then interpreted with the rule that "it is the obligation of all parents to meet the needs of their child." (In the same paragraph, *medical care* is defined as a need.) From these two statements we can then *deduce* that the parents were wrong in their handling of the situation. A *deduction* usually consists of three statements:

> Evidence—Baby Doe's parents are denying him medical care, which is one of the baby's needs.
> Rule—It is the (ethical) obligation of all parents to meet the needs of their child.
> Conclusion—The parents were unethical.

A further characteristic of both induction and deduction is that there are rules for doing them properly. These are called the *rules of logic*. Some of these rules are discussed below, but you already know most of them intuitively. For the most part, you will be asked to use your intuition as you fulfill the assignments for this chapter.

You should now realize that the rules for induction are considerably different from the rules of deduction. This difference means that writing an inductive essay, such as the statistical study, is very different from writing a deductive one, such as the case study. For this reason, the directions for prewriting are divided into two sections, and two types of exercises are provided.

Choosing a Topic

The first step in choosing a topic is to recognize whether you are being asked to do a statistical study or a case study. Ordinarily, this will be no problem. If the assignment is for a statistical study, your instructor will ask you to go out and collect data about a sample of items and then interpret that data; some instructors will save time by giving you a set of real or "dummy" data to work with. Either way, you will recognize that you are working with a set of numbers. If the assignment is for a case study, the instructor will usually assign a case to you; in fact, many textbooks in courses such as business management contain dozens of case studies. Or, as happened with the student who wrote about Baby Doe, you may be asked to find your own case. News stories are often good sources of case material. Either way, you are asked to deal with a set of facts given in sentence form, and the facts indicate that a decision must be made to solve a problem.

For your course in composition, your instructor may decide to use any of the preceding methods. You may prefer an open-ended assignment, but if the instructor is very prescriptive, don't think that you are being "put upon" in some way. Not only will you save time, but you will be approximating what happens outside of college. Outside of college, papers of explanation and proof are usually written as part of your job, and the topics develop from the job situation. In other words, you do what you're assigned to do.

However, let us assume that the topic *has* been left open and that you will be asked to write both types of papers covered in this chapter, a statistical study (inductive) and a case study (deductive).

CHOOSING A STATISTICAL TOPIC.   If you have taken a course in statistics, you already know something about how to choose a topic for a statistical study, although what you mainly learned was what to do with data after collecting some. But if you have not taken such a course, it's best to stick to something simple. For example, do not set out to survey your entire student body unless yours is a very small college.

The best approach is to look for some sort of "curious phenomenon" that needs to be explained. For instance, one student noticed that he always drank from the water fountain closest to the men's rest room, even if he had to pass a fountain next to the women's rest room. He wonders if other people do the same curious thing. Another student, newly introduced to beer drinking at college, noticed that all brands of beer seemed to taste alike. If this is the case, he wonders, why do some of his friends insist on certain brands? Is there some difference that experienced drinkers can detect? A third student, mother of a two-year-old girl, dreaded having to leave the child in the college day-care center while attending classes. She was certain that the child would be unhappy, yet after some initial tears the little girl seemed to get along quite well. Is it possible that children may actually prefer being with other children?

These examples illustrate the kinds of curious phenomena that we all encounter now and then. Moreover, each phenomenon is open to several questions, and therefore at least one possible explanation to answer each question. For instance, the student who noticed the drinking fountain phenomenon could wonder how many people would do the same thing and why they would do so. He might think the explanation is that most people prefer the fountain next to the rest room appropriate to their sex in order to avoid the possibility of seeing something "embarrassing." (It was possible to see into the rest room from the drinking fountain when someone opened the door, although one could not see very much.)

Finally, the explanation must be one that you are capable of testing. Almost any explanation can be tested, but some tests require considerable expertise and money. Therefore, it will be best if you list several questions and explanations and then choose the one that seems within your capabilities to test. Your instructor should be able to help you decide.

Exercises on Choosing a Topic for a Statistical Study

1. **List two or three curious phenomena that you have noticed recently. Explain briefly, in writing, how you happened to notice each phenomenon and why it seems curious to you.**
2. **For each curious phenomenon, write two questions that might be asked about it.**
3. **For each question, write what seems to you to be the most logical explanation, or answer.**
4. **Show your list of phenomena, questions, and explanations to your instructor and some other students. Discuss which would be the most appropriate for a statistical study that you would be able to carry out.**
5. **Choose an explanation to test.**

CHOOSING A TOPIC FOR A CASE STUDY.   For a case study you need a topic for which a set of facts is already available. Your job will then consist of applying some rules of interpretation to this set of facts. In theory, you could choose a case appropriate to nearly any course you have taken. This is because most basic courses have as their primary goal to teach you the basic rules of a field; that is why the courses and/or textbooks are called by such names as *Principles of Accounting*, *Principles of Economics*, or *Principles of Social Work*. These "principles" are what we have been calling the rules of interpretation.

However, many students feel unsure of their grasp of courses they have taken and prefer to deal with something that does not require specialized knowledge. That is what Ruth Goodhart, the author of the essay on Baby Doe, did. She chose to write about an ethical problem since we assume that adults such as yourself already know the principles of ethics. To limit her task further, she wrote about a decision that had already been made. She was thus limited to an either/or situation—*either* the people involved had made the correct decision *or* they had not. Goodhart's explanation was that, in her opinion, Baby Doe's parents had not made the correct ethical decision, and her paper was then an attempt to prove this explanation.

In the exercises that follow, and in the prewriting exercises later in the chapter, it is assumed that you have followed Goodhart's example—you are writing about an ethical problem, and you are judging the ethical correctness of a decision that someone made.

*Exercises on Choosing a Topic for a Case Study About
an Ethical Problem*

1. **Find, in a newspaper or news magazine, the factual account of someone who faced an ethical dilemma and has decided how to handle it.**
2. **If the problem was reported in the mass media, there was probably something controversial about it. Briefly explain, in writing, why the problem was controversial.**
3. **Make a tentative judgment as to whether you agree with the decision of the person or persons involved. Write your judgment in the form of a sentence. Show both the sentence and the news story to your classmates and your instructor to obtain their opinions as to the appropriateness of the topic and the soundness of your judgment.**

The Three Principles Applied

Just as advice and exercises for choosing a topic were divided into two sections—one for a statistical study and the second for a case study—so is this section on prewriting. The prewriting steps have been arranged in a logical sequence, but you should keep in mind one caution made earlier: you will probably discover that there is some overlap between steps and that decisions made in later steps will require changes in the earlier steps. That is perfectly normal, because writing is not simply a linear process.

The Writer Issue: Defining Terms

Usually when we think of defining terms, we think of defining difficult words for someone who may not understand them. But that is not what is meant by defining terms in a paper of explanation and proof. In this case, what we do is "sharpen" the terms, that is, eliminate vague words and replace them with very precise terms. This is necessary throughout a logical argument, but for now we will concentrate on the most important terms, the words in the original explanation to be tested. (This original explanation is usually called the *hypothesis* of a statistical study and the *thesis statement* of a case study.)

DEFINING TERMS FOR THE HYPOTHESIS OF A STATISTICAL STUDY. Let us begin by seeing how this was done in "Deceived Respondents." The terms to be defined are first brought up when the authors are discussing the problem that needs to be explained. They describe the problem three times, each time getting a little more precise, as follows:

(The problem is) the consequences of a fairly widely used ploy in the direct selling field: gaining a potential customer's attention and interest by requesting cooperation in some sort of false survey.

(The problem is) the effects of such sales techniques upon the efficiency of genuine research.

(The problem is) a probably negative effect of false surveys on the efficiency of field interviewing.

Having explained the problem in general terms, the writers become more precise; the explanation must be given in a form that can actually be tested to see if it is true. Examining the general statements, we find that there are three key concepts, or terms, that need to be given this precision. First, the authors are worried about the *consequences* (or "effects" or the "probably negative effects") of false surveys. Now, what might these consequences be? They have to be something an experimenter can observe occurring, and the authors define the consequences this way: a significant increase in "the refusal rate in a legitimate fixed-address survey."

The second key term is *false survey*, which supposedly has such an ill effect. What do they mean by a false survey? They explain that it is in reality a "direct sales attempt," which is given as a "prior exposure."

Finally, the authors consider exactly what *thing* will be hurt by the false survey. They are worried about the effects on legitimate research, and they explain what type of legitimate research they have in mind: "a legitimate fixed-address survey."

There is a good reason why there are three key terms to define, no more and no less. They stem from the three key decisions that every researcher must make: (1) which population of items to study; (2) what method to use, that is, how to study this population; and (3) how to measure the outcome of the study. In this study the researchers decided the three key points this way: (1) that their population would include all people with fixed address; (2) that they would like to give the population a false survey, followed by a legitimate survey; and (3) that they would measure the effects of their method by counting the number of people who refused to participate in the legitimate survey as compared with the original amount of cooperation.

Putting all of this together, the researchers formulated a hypothesis that could be tested:

A prior exposure to a false survey, i.e., a direct sales attempt, will significantly increase the refusal rate in a legitimate fixed-address survey.

Before you begin to construct your own experiment, you should follow a similar procedure in writing your hypothesis. Isolate the three key terms, and then define each one so that you define the three key parts of a study: (1) the population you will study, (2) a reasonable and practical method of studying this population, and (3) your method of measuring the

STUDENT 1

Original explanation: When drinking fountains are located next to rest rooms, people usually prefer to drink from the fountain next to the rest room of their own sex.

Terms to be defined:	*Definitions:*
"people"	students, faculty, and staff of X college
"prefer to drink from the fountain next to the rest room of their own sex"	will be observed to drink from the fountain next to the rest room of their own sex, in cases where there are two adjacent rest rooms with a drinking fountain next to each one
"usually"	more often than they drink from the other fountain

Testable hypothesis: Students, faculty, and staff of X college will be observed to drink from the fountain next to the rest room of their own sex, in cases where there are two adjacent rest rooms with a drinking fountain next to each one; this will happen more often than not.

STUDENT 2

Original explanation: Most children in day-care centers seem to like the experience.

Terms to be defined:	*Definitions:*
"children in day-care centers"	children who have been in the day-care center of X college for at least three consecutive weeks and who come to the center at least three days a week for four hours per day
"seem to like the experience"	will not ask for their parents while in the day-care center
"most children"	at least three-fourths of them

Testable hypothesis: At least three-fourths of the children in the day-care center of X college will not ask for their parents while in the center; this will apply to children who have been in the center for at least three consecutive weeks and who come at least three days a week for four hours per day.

FIGURE 5.2. Examples of Student Problems

results of the study. Examine how two students did this (see Fig. 5.2) and then do the exercises that follow.

Exercises on Writing the Explanation to be Tested

1. **Examine the definitions written by the students above. Would you have defined the terms the same way? Why have the students defined the terms the way they did?**
2. **Examine the explanation you wrote during the "Choosing a Topic" exercise for the statistical study. Identify the three terms that need to be defined in order to make the explanation a testable one.**
3. **Write a definition for each term and then put everything together in one complete sentence, forming your hypothesis.**
4. **Check your hypothesis with your instructor and some of your classmates.**

DEFINING TERMS FOR THE THESIS OF A CASE STUDY. For the thesis of a case study, there are also three terms to define. You need to identify specifically *who* is being judged, the *act* to be judged, and the *field* in which the judging will take place.

We can see each of these in the essay about Baby Doe. First, there are several *who's* that could have been judged—the court, the parents of Baby Doe, the county prosecutor, and others. The student chose to judge the parents. Second, each of the *who's* performed one or more acts, and this includes the parents. The parents filed for the court's permission to let Baby Doe die, they apparently failed to seek someone to adopt Baby Doe, and they let the baby die. The student decided to judge the latter act. Finally, there were several fields in which the argument could take place. One could argue whether the court's decision was *legally* correct, whether letting the baby die was correct according to *religious* principles, whether the decision made *economic* sense, or whether the decision was *ethical*. The student, of course, chose ethics as the field.

Exercises on Defining Terms in the Thesis

1. **Look at the thesis you wrote earlier. Have you identified exactly who is being judged? Which other *who's* could you have judged? Why did you choose the person you did?**
2. **Did you identify which *act* is being judged? What other acts did the person perform that could have been judged? Why did you choose the act you did?**
3. **Did you specify that the field of judging is ethics?**
4. **Rewrite your thesis, where necessary, to identify explicitly the who, the act, and the field.**

The Reader Issue: Rules of Interpretation

RULES OF INTERPRETATION FOR A STATISTICAL STUDY. Every statistical study requires, first of all, the same basic rule of interpretation. To understand this rule, remember that you would like to study an entire population of items, but this is seldom possible. Instead, you have to choose a sample from the population and study only the sample. The key to success for a statistical induction is to choose a sample that is highly *similar to* the population. The sample must be similar because the basic rule of interpretation of all inductions is that *whatever is true of the sample is also true of the population.* For example, the researchers in "Deceived Respondents" wanted to be able to say that if their sample of respondents was adversely affected by the false survey, all other respondents, that is, the population, would be affected in the same way.

Of course, even under the best of circumstances a sample is not exactly like the population. In other words, the rule above should actually read, "Whatever is true of the sample is *approximately* true of the population." Thus statistical studies need a second rule of interpretation to allow for this approximation. There are many such rules, most of them mathematical formulas with strange-sounding names. The one used in "Deceived Respondents" is called *chi square*. These rules are what you would learn in statistics class, so we obviously cannot cover them here. For the purposes of the present assignment you will simply have to estimate how confident you can be when you say that whatever is true of your sample is true of the population.

The main purpose of the following exercises is to help you think about the population you will be studying. It is suggested that you keep the population small and local. That way, you have the best chance of being able to choose a good sample.

Exercises on Identifying Populations

1. Look back at the two student examples that precede the exercises on definition. What is the population being studied in each case? Could the students obtain samples that are representative of these populations?
2. Examine the hypothesis that you wrote earlier. What is the population that you intend to study? Is that a reasonable task for you to take on? In other words, do you have a reasonable chance of obtaining a representative sample to study? If not, redefine the population, and rewrite the hypothesis.
3. Identify someone in the class who has taken a course in statistics and who would be willing to explain to the class how *chi square* works in

"Deceived Respondents." Give the student a few days to prepare for this.

RULES OF INTERPRETATION FOR A CASE STUDY.   Rules of interpretation are even more important for the deductive arguments of a case study than for the inductions of a statistical study. To see why this is so, consider the following sentences from paragraph 9 of Ruth Goodhart's essay on Baby Doe:

> I believe this primarily because it is the obligation of all parents to meet the needs of their child. . . . They [the parents] did not want their child to get the treatment necessary to survive, and . . . in my opinion, this was an unethical act of neglect.

The rule of interpretation is "it is the obligation of all parents to meet the needs of their child." This rule is used to interpret the evidence. In this case, the evidence shows that the parents did not meet the needs of their child for medical care. By applying the rule to the evidence, Goodhart then concludes that the parents were unethical.

Many other rules can be seen throughout the essay. For example, Goodhart gives several rules by which the parents might defend themselves: (1) "It is wrong to insist upon sustaining a life whose quality of living would be extremely poor"; (2) "It is unethical to commit an act if the consequences may cause harm to other people" (harm to the parents, in this case); (3) It would be wrong to keep alive one who would "become a burden to society." These rules, then, are sometimes "answered" with other rules. For example, the writer answers the rule about "quality of living" with the rule that "we do not have the right to decide whether another person's life is worth living."

The arguing process in this essay shows what you should do to write such an argument. First, list all of the rules of interpretation that could possibly apply to your case. Second, choose the rule that seemed to support the hypothesis most strongly. Third, consider the rules that would lead to a denial of your thesis. Finally, construct the whole argument in order to determine whether the case for your thesis really holds water. If it does, work on revising the argument until it is as tight as possible. If not, abandon the thesis and try something else.

Above all, remember that judgments about these rules of interpretation must be made with an eye toward the audience of reasonable, objective readers who are presumed to be the ultimate judges of the case. It will do you no good to apply rules of interpretation that reasonable people do not accept or to say that one rule is more important than another if reasonable people do not agree. Writers may define terms as they please, but they must use rules that are widely accepted by reasonable people.

Exercises on Identifying Rules of Interpretation

1. Although we must apply rules of interpretation to evidence in order to draw conclusions, many of us have trouble stating explicitly the rules we use. The following minicases will give you some practice in doing this. For each case, decide whether the person was right or wrong according to the rules of ethics. Then try to write out the rules you used in drawing your conclusion. Compare your results with those of the rest of the class.
   a. Karen has a friend who is trying to quit smoking. The friend asks for a cigarette, and Karen gives her one.
   b. Kevin is the star of a college basketball team. Just before the final tournament, he quits the team to play professional ball.
   c. Tom has a grandmother who talks all the time. Since the grandmother lives with Tom's family, there is no way to get away from her. Finally, Tom says, "Shut up, you old bag! I can't stand it anymore!"
   d. A burglar broke into Sam's house and was sneaking through the bedroom. Sam grabbed a gun from the nightstand and shot the burglar without warning.
   e. Joe saw a car edging into traffic ahead of him. Since Joe had the right of way, he didn't slow down. The car kept coming, and Joe hit it.
   f. Andrew's wife is sick, and his car won't start. He borrows his neighbor's car without permission to take her to the hospital for emergency treatment. (The neighbor is at work.)
   g. Jane, a young policewoman, is assigned to be an undercover narcotics agent at a college campus. She befriends students and sets up arrests if she finds them using drugs.
   h. Susan knows that her sister once gave birth to an illegitimate child and gave it up for adoption. She tells this to her sister's new fiancé.
2. Identify the rules that could apply to the case you have chosen to write about. To do this, draw a line down the center of a sheet of paper, and use one column for rules to support your thesis and the other for rules that would disprove your thesis. (Your instructor may permit you to set up a debate in class on your topic. This will help you to think of the rules.)
3. Choose the single strongest rule that supports your thesis. Sharpen it by defining any vague terms. (Note how the student writer defined medical treatment as one of the needs of a child.)
4. Identify three or four rules that might be used in opposition to your strong rule. How would you counter each one?

Subject-Matter Issue: Gathering Evidence

When we want to prove something, we need some evidence (facts, data, statistics, and so on) with which to operate. This evidence must reflect the true nature of the case or the population that we are explaining, so one of our tasks is to gather such evidence.

GATHERING EVIDENCE FOR A STATISTICAL STUDY. The *subject* of a statistical study is the population you are studying. However, as we noted earlier, it is seldom possible to study an entire population, so what you must do is study a sample of the population instead. There are, as we also noted, three steps involved: (1) choosing the sample; (2) studying this sample; and (3) obtaining some numbers that are taken to be measurements of the sample. (A *statistic* is simply a number taken to be a measurement of some aspect of a sample or population.) Let us see how this was done in "Deceived Respondents."

The goal of sample selection, you will remember, is to select a sample that is *similar to*, or *representative of*, the population. There are three rules by which samples are usually selected; these are the rules of *numbers*, *variety*, and *randomness*. The rule of numbers requires that the sample be as large as is practical. The rule of variety means that the sample should include representatives from all the subgroups in the population. For example, in a human population, one might want to include representatives of the lower class, middle class, upper class, whites, blacks, old, young, and so on. The rule of randomness requires that every member of the population should have an equal chance of being chosen for the sample; in practice, the rule of randomness requires some sort of lottery system for choosing the sample.

Few researchers use all three rules to choose their samples, and "Deceived Respondents" is no exception. The sample here was fairly large, thus fulfilling the rule of numbers to some extent. However, only one subgroup is included (white, middle-class suburbanites), and randomness was used only in assigning people to control and experimental groups. The sample was therefore probably not very similar to the population; that is one reason why, in their conclusion, the authors express some reservations about their study.

The second step in evidence-gathering is to study the sample. There are two basic ways to do this: researchers can either simply observe the sample as it is in its natural state, or they can manipulate the sample to see how the various members of the sample react. The former method is called a survey; the latter, an experiment.

The authors of "Deceived Respondents" could have conducted their research either way. They could have conducted a survey in which they simply asked the respondents for their opinions about false surveys.

Instead, however, as the hypothesis indicates, they did an experiment in which they actually manipulated the sample by conducting a false survey and following it up with a legitimate survey. They were trying to see if the sample would react to the false survey by refusing to participate in the legitimate survey. (The control group was used for the purpose of discovering how a sample would normally respond to a legitimate survey.)

After studying the sample, the third step is to measure the outcome of the survey or experiment. This can be done in several ways. One common way is to rate the reaction according to a scale of some sort. For example, the researchers could have rated each respondent on a scale of 1 to 4, as follows: (1) strong refusal, (2) weak refusal, (3) weak acceptance, (4) enthusiastic acceptance. Another way, the one used in "Deceived Respondents," is simply to classify each member of the sample as either-or; either the respondent cooperated or refused. Then one simply counts the number of each type.

Whatever method of measurement you use, for a statistical induction you must end up with some numbers. The numbers are your facts, or evidence, about the sample. Then, by using one or more rules of interpretation, you generalize from the sample to the population.

To summarize, after you have written your hypothesis and chosen your rules of interpretation, you conduct your research. Using the hypothesis as a general guide, you choose a sample, manipulate or observe the sample, and measure the results. Each of these steps must be planned and executed carefully in order for you to be reasonably certain that the figures you come out with truly are factual statements about the sample.

Exercises on Planning the Research

1. **To see what would happen if you used only one of the rules of sample selection, try the exercises that follow. Consider the group of items in the box to be your population.**

```
X  0  0  X  #  0  #  X  X  X  0  0  #  X  0  $  X  #  X  #  0  0  0
X  X  X  #  X  X  0  $  $  X  0  0  X  0  #  $  0  0  X  X  X  X  X
#  0  $  #  X  0  $  #  X  0  0  0  X  X  $  X  #  0  X  #  0  0  0
X  0  0  X  X  X  0  0  0  0  X  #  #  $  X  $  0  0  $  X  X  X  0
0  0  0  X  #  0  0  $  X  X  X  $  0  0  0  X  X  $  #  X  X  X  0
X  0  X  $  X  #  #  0  $  X  $  $  $  0  0  X  #  #  0  X  X  0  $
```

    a. **How many subgroups are in the population? List them.**
    b. **Count the number of items in each subgroup. Compute the percentage of the population that each subgroup consists of.**

   c. Choose a number between 3 and 8. Choose it randomly, by flipping a coin or by drawing a number out of a hat. Beginning at the top row of the population, count over from the left the number that you chose and circle the item. Then count again and circle again. Keep doing this for the whole population. (Say that you chose the number 4. You would circle the fourth item, the eighth item, the twelfth item, and so forth.) You will than have chosen a sample by means of the rule of randomness.

   d. Now count up the number of circled items for each subgroup, determine the percentage of each subgroup in the sample, and compare this with the percentages obtained for Exercise 1b. Did you get a representative sample? Compare your sample with those of members of your class who drew a different beginning number. Did anyone get a representative sample?

   e. Draw a square box enclosing twenty items anywhere in the population. Count up the number of items from each subgroup inside the box, compute the percentage of each subgroup, and again compare to the figures obtained in Exercise 1b. Compare your results with those of your classmates.

   f. Now try the same thing (drawing a box) with larger samples, such as 30 or 40 items. Again compute percentages and compare with Exercise 1b.

2. Using your hypothesis as a guide, decide on a method of choosing a sample for your own research. Use at least one of the rules of sample selection well. Check your plan with your instructor and some other members of the class.

3. Decide whether you are going to conduct an experiment or survey. (If it's to be an experiment, decide whether you need a control group.) Then figure out a method of studying the sample. In other words, decide what you will do with the sample once you have it.

4. Still using your hypothesis as a guide, decide how to measure the outcome of your research.

5. Write up a one- or two-page outline of your proposed study and submit it to your instructor. (If you know of a faculty member who is an expert on this type of research, you might also check your plan with this person.) Your instructor may ask you to revise the plan and write a new version. Since instructors generally recommend that you simplify your plan, strongly consider taking this advice.

6. Conduct the research according to the plan. (You may want to "fiddle around" with your methods, trying them out on a small group before carrying out the whole plan. Such fiddling around is also highly recommended.)

   GATHERING EVIDENCE FOR A CASE STUDY. The evidence of a case study consists of the facts of the case. There are three problems in dealing with these facts: (1) establishing the truth of the facts as stated in the case assignment; (2) finding additional, existing evidence that is not given in the case; and (3) dealing with missing evidence. How you handle these problems will depend partly on the assignment given by your instructor and partly on whether you are using an assigned case or one that you found for yourself.

The first problem, establishing the truth of the facts stated in the case, is seldom necessary for an assigned case. You simply assume that they are true and go from there. (They are often "made-up" facts, anyway.) Your instructor may permit you to do the same with your own case, but if not, you will need to find other reports of the same case to check the facts. Some of the more respectable places to look are the *New York Times*, *Newsweek*, *Time*, and the *Christian Science Monitor*.

The second task, supplying additional evidence, may also not be necessary. However, even for assigned cases many instructors will expect you to make use of general information that you have learned in the course. For your own cases you may also want to bring in general knowledge. Ruth Goodhart, for instance, seemed to believe it necessary to know more about Down's Syndrome and esophageal atresia, so she looked up one of these terms in a medical book and asked her husband about the other. We can speculate that she was trying to find out just how serious these conditions are. It's possible that if she had found them to be truly hopeless conditions, she might have agreed with Baby Doe's parents.

Finally there is the problem of missing evidence—seldom a factor in assigned cases but frequently something you must deal with when you choose your own case. However, realizing that evidence is missing can be tricky business, and there is no adequate guide for doing so. Goodhart's instructor saw this as the only major fault of the paper. The student argued that the parents should have given Baby Doe up for adoption, but the instructor said there was no evidence that they were aware of this choice. In fact, he said that "common sense" would suggest that no one would want to adopt such a severely handicapped child.

Since there is no adequate guide to identifying missing evidence—or outside evidence either, for that matter—your best approach may again be to argue the case orally with some of your classmates.

Exercises on Examining the Evidence

1. **Locate at least one other account of your ethical problem. Compare it with the news article you chose earlier. If there are any differences in facts, decide which facts you will take to be the truth.**
2. **Identify at least one area of your case that might benefit from additional background information and seek the necessary facts. (For example, if the case involves child abuse, you could look up statistics on the incidence and causes of child abuse.) Decide whether this additional information helps you test the case in any way.**

3. By discussing your case with several other students, seek to determine whether some evidence is missing. If you decide that some is missing, make a reasonable guess as to what the facts are. How would it affect your argument if you turned out to be wrong?

Summary: Prewriting for the Three Issues

On pp. 150–151 are diagrams outlining the steps suggested here for thinking through the two types of papers for explaining and proving. Keep in mind, however, that while papers of explanation and proof can be planned to a greater extent than many other kinds of papers, they will still seldom work out exactly as you expected. You may find, for example, that you cannot study the population you wanted to study or that your method of conducting the study is too complicated for you to carry out. Or, in the case study, you may find that your initial decision as to who is right and who is wrong cannot be substantiated. Or during the actual writing of the paper, all sorts of additional arguments, counter arguments, and missing evidence may occur to you.

To reduce such problems, there is no substitute for constant consultation with your instructor and with other students. You cannot expect them to write the paper for you, but you can expect that they will test your ideas, bringing up other arguments and finding fault with your methods and ideas. Nor should you consider that this consultation is anything unusual. When you write such papers on the job, it is expected that you will check your work with fellow workers and supervisors. In fact, you may work as part of a team, or there may be a supervising committee to review your plans and the final paper.

ORGANIZING THE PAPER

At the beginning of this chapter we briefly examined the organizational patterns of the two sample essays. We noted then that the pattern of the statistical study (the inductive essay) is very different from the pattern of the case study (the deductive essay). Let us now examine each pattern in more detail, for the patterns of these essays are even more helpful in planning papers than are the patterns suggested for other types of essays. This is because they are fairly standardized, and each heading in the outlines can be regarded as a "slot" that must be filled. You haven't finished the job until every slot is filled.

Inductive Organization

The essay "Deceived Respondents" employs an organizational structure that is fairly typical of all essays about statistical studies. Turn back to p. 122 and review the outline so you can consider it in more detail.

Now that you have studied the prewriting process for a statistical study, you can see that "Deceived Respondents" is organized according to this process. In other words, it follows a *chronological* pattern, going from the initial problem or question, through the forming of the hypothesis and the testing procedure, to the collecting of data and drawing of conclusions. The ending even looks forward to the future, making suggestions for future research on the same problem. A generalized outline for such a paper follows. (The asterisks indicate sections your instructor may permit you to omit, either to save time or because you don't have the background to carry out the step.)

I. Introduction
    A. The problem or question to be explained
   *B. Summary of past research on this problem
    C. The hypothesis, or tentative explanation of the problem

II. Procedures for the research
    A. Selection of the sample (how you achieved randomness, numbers and/or variety)
    B. The experiment or survey, that is, what was done to the sample
    C. Method of measuring the results

III. Results
    A. Compiled data (given as percentages, averages, totals, and so on)
   *B. Interpreted data, that is, application of a rule of interpretation to account for the fact that a sample is not exactly representative of a population
    C. Discussion of the results
    D. Conclusions about the sample

IV. Conclusions
    A. Conclusions about the population, that is, application of the rule that "whatever is true of the sample is also true of the population"
    B. Limitations of the conclusions
    C. Recommendations for action and/or future research

Exercises on Organizing the Statistical Essay

1. Using the preceding general outline, plan your own statistical essay. Under each point of the outline, jot down some notes about the aspects of your own research that would be discussed in that section.
2. Write a draft of parts I and II of your paper. Discuss your draft with your instructor and some classmates.
3. You will probably want to wait awhile (until we have discussed the style of statistical papers) before drawing firm conclusions from your data, but give some initial thought to what your data seem to prove. Does it seem that your hypothesis will be confirmed?

Choosing a Topic	The Writer Issue: *Definitions*—the process of "sharpening up" terms until they specify exactly what you intend to prove	The Reader Issue: *Rules of Interpretation*—selecting means of interpreting facts, data, and so on (rules that would be acceptable to all objective readers)	The Subject-Matter Issue: *Evidence*—collecting evidence that accurately reflects the reality (population or case) that you are studying
		For a Statistical Study	
1. Notice a curious phenomenon that needs to be explained.	1. Give an initial explanation in commonsense terms.	1. Remember that you will apply the rule for generalizing: "Whatever is true of the population is also true of the sample."	1. Choose a sample according to the rules of numbers, variety, and randomness (trying to use one rule well, the others only as well as is practical).
2. Clearly state the problem or question to be explained.	2. Identify the three "key terms" that need to be defined more precisely.	2. Examine the population to ensure that you could actually obtain a sample of it.	2. Set up a method of studying the sample—a survey or an experiment.
	3. Define each key term so that you have identified the population, the method of studying the population, and results expected.	3. If necessary, redefine the population and rewrite the hypothesis.	3. Determine the best way to measure the results of the study.
	4. Write the hypothesis.	4. If you have taken a course in statistics, choose one of the rules (statistical formulas) that you learned for interpreting samples. (If you didn't take the course, you need to wait and estimate when the time comes.)	
	(Note: You will also discover other terms that need to be defined, but these are not likely to come up until later in the process.)		

For a Case Study

1. Examine the case, either one that was assigned or one that you found on your own.

2. "Jump to" a tentative decision (your thesis).

1. Identify the three *key terms* that need to be defined more precisely.

2. Define each key term so that you have identified the field in which the argument will take place, the act to be judged, and the person or persons to be judged.

3. Rewrite the thesis in precise terms.

(Note: Other terms to be defined will come up, especially as you work with rules of interpretation.)

1. List the rules of interpretation (from the defined field) that could apply to the case.

2. Choose the strongest rule supporting your thesis to use for the direct argument.

3. Identify several rules that could be used in opposition to your thesis.

1. If necessary, verify the facts given in the case.

2. If necessary, seek outside information to supply additional evidence.

3. Identify *missing evidence*—that which is not given in the case and is not available in other sources.

FIGURE 5.3. A Summary of the Prewriting Steps for Explaining and Proving

The Deductive Organization

The essay about Baby Doe is outlined on p. 124. Take a moment to review the outline.

As you can see, the introduction begins with a discussion of the problem in general terms, followed by a summary of the facts about Baby Doe's situation. All of the facts that will be used in the argument should be given here. Finally, the introduction ends with the specific issue to be discussed in the paper (whether the parents were ethical to allow the baby to die) and the thesis (no, they were not ethical).

Next comes the body of the essay, which contains the argument for the thesis. The author handles the argument, first, by offering a "line" of direct support for the thesis; this takes only one paragraph but could have taken more if necessary. This line contains what the author considers to be the most important pieces of evidence (the parents neglected to meet the needs of Baby Doe) and the strongest rule of interpretation that applies to the case (parents are obligated to meet the needs of their children). Also included is a definition of *needs* (*medical treatment* is defined as a need), plus further explanation and defense of the rule of interpretation. This paragraph may be called the *direct argument*.

The rest of the argument is handled by a method that may be called *counterargument and rebuttal*. That is, the author brings up several arguments that could be used in opposition to her thesis; these are the counterarguments. After stating each counterargument, the author then gives a rebuttal—an explanation of why she does not accept the counterargument. Each counterargument may consist of a piece of evidence, a rule of interpretation, and one or more definitions. Each rebuttal then attacks one component of the counterargument.

Finally, the essay ends with a brief conclusion that returns to the thesis and ties the argument back to the introductory material. The conclusion might also have contained an "escape clause" to deal with any missing evidence; the author might say that if the missing evidence is found and turns out to be different from what she had expected, the case would need to be reconsidered.

This is a standard outline for a case study and may be summarized as follows:

I.   Introduction
  A. The general problem (without mentioning the case at hand)
  B. The evidence, that is, the facts of the specific case to be discussed
  C. The specific issue
  D. The thesis

II. The argument
  A. Direct argument (including the strongest rule of interpretation, the evidence relevant to that rule, support for the rule, and definitions of terms in the rule)

      B. Counterarguments and rebuttals
        1. First counterargument
        2. Rebuttal to first counterargument
        3. Second counterargument
        4. Rebuttal to second counterargument and so on

  III.   Conclusion

Again, this is not the only way in which to organize a deductive argument. However, it is a very common one and is used in many persuasive essays as well. It will be worth your effort to learn to use it.

Exercises on Organizing the Deductive Paper

1. **Copy the preceding outline, leaving extra space for notes under each section. Then jot down some notes for each part to indicate what you will be discussing there.**
2. **Now try writing a first draft of the paper all the way through. Don't worry at this time about making it perfect, for you will probably have to write several drafts before you are satisfied.**
3. **Rewrite the paper a few times until you think it's worth showing to someone. Then submit a draft to your instructor and trade papers with classmates. Ask the classmates first to see if they can match each of your paragraphs with some part of the general outline. Then get one classmate to analyze several of your paragraphs, trying to identify your rule of interpretation, your evidence, and your definitions, if needed.**
4. **Working with the comments from your instructor and classmates, write another draft.**

STYLE IN EXPLAINING AND PROVING

Having planned the argument and the organization of the paper, your final concern is the proper style in which to write your essay. The basic rule is the same as for informative writing: to have an objective, impersonal style that does not intrude on the logic of the essay. This especially requires that no emotionally loaded language be used, but there are several additional characteristics to be considered.

    TECHNICAL LANGUAGE. We noted earlier in the chapter that both essays contain many undefined technical terms. For example, "Deceived Respondents" has terms such as *chi square*, *pilot study*, and *experimental group*. And the essay on Baby Doe does not define *ethics*, *obligations*, and *consequences*. This happens for two reasons. First, as we already noted, the process of defining terms in logical writing requires authors to make language more precise; there is no requirement to make language simpler.

The second, and main, reason for lack of definitions is that these terms are being used in a *technical* sense. This means that the articles are intended to be read by people who are specialists in the topics being discussed; these specialists know the meanings of the special terminology, or jargon, of their fields. For example, "Deceived Respondents" is intended for specialists in market research. These specialists must have a background in statistics and in the methodology of research. They already know what chi square is and do not need to have the term defined for them.

In addition to terms that are obviously technical, logical arguments may also contain common words that are being used in a technical sense. For example, the authors of "Deceived Respondents" find that there is a *significant difference* between the control and experimental groups. This is a common term that any of us might use in everyday conversation, as when we say that there is a significant difference between communism and capitalism. However, in "Deceived Respondents," *significant difference* is being used in a technical sense that may be roughly translated as meaning that the control and experimental samples belong to different populations. (The word *population* is itself being used in a technical sense.)

Therefore, technical language is one feature of logical discourse. The words need not be defined in most papers because the papers are intended for specialists. However, when the essays are aimed at nonspecialists, the words need to be either simplified or defined, if possible. In any case, it's not necessary to use technical language just to impress the reader.

TECHNICAL SENTENCE STRUCTURE. Just as logical arguments may employ technical terms, they also may employ a special type of sentence structure. This is illustrated in the following sentences from "Deceived Respondents":

> Drawing upon these recommendations, speculations and inferences, the following hypothesis *was developed* and *pilot tested* using an experimental design.

> In an effort to approximate field selling conditions, a homogeneous, middle-income, suburban housing development *was chosen* for the test.

The italicized verbs are in passive voice rather than the more common active voice. To get the passive voice the authors have reversed the "normal" sentence structure, which would have been something like "we developed and pilot tested the following hypothesis" and "we chose a . . . suburban housing development." In both cases, the normal subject of the sentence is "we," and this is followed by an active-voice verb and then a direct object. But it is a tradition of logical writing to curtail the use of personal pronouns such as *we*, and the most common method of eliminating them is to use passive verbs. Sentences with passive verbs are said to be hard to read, and many experts on writing decry them for this reason. However, many of the magazines that publish logical writing ban personal pronouns, so writers continue to use passive verbs.

TRANSITIONS.　All types of writing require transitions, but they are perhaps more critical in writing that uses careful reasoning. This is because reasoning is hard to follow, and transitions are necessary to help the reader follow the "trail" of the logic. Lack of transitions is probably the major weakness of early drafts of papers of explanation and proof.

EXPLICITNESS AND DETAIL.　If you have previously worked through the chapter on persuasive writing, you may remember that such writing often omits parts of the argument. The writer may omit certain inconvenient facts or fail to supply one premise of a deduction. Neither strategy is permitted in logical discourse. All of the relevant facts must be presented, even those that weaken the argument, and every rule of interpretation and definition must be stated explicitly, except when they are clearly implied. (When in doubt, play it safe by being explicit.) This means that every part of the paper, from the sentences to the paragraphs to the paper itself, tends to be longer and more detailed than if the same problem were treated in a persuasive paper. The paper will inevitably be somewhat tedious to read because of this, but being interesting is not a major concern in papers of explanation and proof.

The necessity for detail stems from two sources, practical and ethical. The practical reason for detail in a statistical study is that we do not consider a scientific conclusion to be confirmed unless another scientist can conduct the same study and reach the same conclusions. The reader therefore must be given sufficient detail to be able to repeat the study. The practical reason for detail in a case study is that, in many job situations, your argument will be opposed by someone defending the opposite thesis. Furthermore, your supervisor will be nearly as knowledgeable about the topic as you are. In such a case you dare not omit inconvenient facts or arguments. Your job is on the line.

Then there is the ethical component. Explaining and proving, as we noted earlier, is a type of scientific writing, and science is (or is supposed to be) a profession with a high sense of ethics. By revealing everything about your topic, the weaknesses as well as the strengths of your work, you demonstrate your ethics. Your colleagues will demand this and will disregard your work if you are found to be skipping important evidence.

NUMBERS, TABLES, AND GRAPHS.　A final aspect of the style of logical writing, especially statistical essays, can be seen in the section of "Deceived Respondents" that gives the results of the study. There are only five sentences that discuss the results; the bulk of the information about results is given in the two tables and in the footnote to Table 2.

This is typical practice for statistical papers. Numbers are difficult to comprehend, and to discuss all of the numbers in sentences would make the results section impossibly long. Therefore, the numbers are given in tabular form, and only the most important numbers are also mentioned in the text.

We can also notice that there are two types of numbers. The tables give totals and percentages; these may be called the *compiled data*. Then at the bottom of Table 2 are the following numbers: $X^2 = 8.554$; $p < .005$ (1 d.f.). These are the *interpreted data* that adjust for error in the selection of the sample and allow conclusions to be drawn. These data show that even after allowing for error, the control group is significantly different from the experimental group.

In addition to tables, many statistical papers also include *graphs* of one kind or another. (The main reason that "Deceived Respondents" has no graph is that the particular kind of data therein do not lend themselves to being placed on a graph.) Graphs are useful because they give the reader a *visual impression* of what happened in the research. In most cases, the graph is made from the compiled data and thus can reveal trends (e.g., downward or upward) more clearly than mere numbers can. Designing graphs and knowing when to use them are arts in themselves. However, graphs are part of the style of logical discourse, especially inductions, so your instructor may explain something about the arts if the occasion arises.

Exercises on Completing the Statistical Paper

1. As a result of your research, you have obtained some *raw data*. In consultation with your instructor, figure out a way to compile these data in order to reduce the amount of numbers that you have to work with. Then determine a way to arrange the numbers in a table and a method of displaying them on a graph.

2. Now, using your hypothesis as a guide, try to interpret the data. If you have taken a course in statistics, use a statistical formula. If not, just make an "eyeball judgment." Does the hypothesis seem to be true for your sample?

3. Now generalize from the sample to the population. Do you feel confident in saying that whatever is true of the sample is also true of the population? Express, in words or numbers, your confidence.

4. Write a draft of parts III and IV of the paper; then rewrite the whole paper.

5. Consider who might be interested in knowing the results of your research, and assume that you will be making copies of your paper and

distributing them to these people. Adjust your use of technical terminology and technical sentence structure to this potential audience.
6. Write a final draft of the paper.

Exercises on Revising the Case Study

1. Consider who might be interested in knowing the results of your reasoning and assume that you will be making copies of your paper and distributing them to these people. Reread your draft of the paper and adjust your use of technical terminology for this potential audience.
2. Using the comments obtained earlier from classmates and your instructor, determine whether you have sufficient transitions to enable readers to follow your reasoning. Revise sentences and paragraphs wherever you discover that readers did not understand you.
3. Write a final draft of the paper.

Exercises on Methodology for Statistical Studies

Each of the following problems involves several questions that could lead to statistical studies. For each question, suggest the answers to the following four problems of methodology: (1) What is the population you would have to study in order to answer the question? (2) How would you choose a sample from that population? (3) How would you study the sample? (4) How would you measure the results of the study? (Assume that you have adequate time, financial support, and expertise to conduct the study.)

1. City X needs to dispose of the sludge from its sewer plant. The city council has authorized the purchase of a farm so that the sludge can be spread over the farmland. However, many farmers in the vicinity of the proposed site object are saying that the sludge probably contains trace metals and other toxic chemicals that could get into streams and groundwater, thus contaminating everyone's land. How would you answer the following questions?
   a. Does the sludge contain toxic materials?
   b. If there are toxic materials in the sludge, would these substances get into the water supplies?
   c. Is it true that *many* farmers object to the plan?
2. College A provides a service to students who are having academic troubles. It is an advising service to which instructors send the names of students who aren't doing well in class. Advisors call in the students for individual consultation and then help them arrange for needed help such as psychological counseling, tutoring, financial aid, or learning study skills. The college administration wonders whether this service is worth

the cost. Shouldn't students be able to find this help on their own? How would you find the answers to the following questions?

a. How many of the students in need of help are actually referred by their instructors?

b. How many students who seek help from psychological counselors would not have done so without assistance from their advisors?

c. How many students show up for advice after being invited by the advising service?

d. Do students follow the advice they are given?

e. Does following the advice really help the students?

f. What happens to students who don't show up for counseling or who don't take the advice they were given?

Exercise on Analyzing Deductive Paragraphs

1. Following are paragraphs taken from longer essays by students. Most are the direct arguments of the essays, so they contain the thesis of the essay. For each paragraph, determine the thesis, the main evidence statement, and the main rule of interpretation. Some paragraphs also contain definitions and statements to back up the evidence or rule. See if you can also identify any of these.

a. It is highly probable that the fingerprint on the weapon belongs to the butler, Alexander. At least ten points of similarity have been noted between Alexander's fingerprint and the one on the murder weapon. General practice is to claim that ten points of correspondence are sufficient to identify a person's fingerprint; this is standard practice by the F.B.I. and has been accepted as valid by courts.

b. There is a general principle that the government may ban items that serve only harmful purposes, that is, items that cause or lead to much harm and have no corresponding good uses to balance the harm. The government may do this because of its responsibility to protect its citizens. This is why the government seems justified in banning those small, inexpensive handguns called *midnight specials*. Such handguns have been shown to serve only harmful purposes because they are useful only in robberies and other crimes and cannot be used for sporting purposes.

c. Many people have sought to have the book *Brave New World* banned from high school libraries, but I do not think it should be banned. Students who are reasonably mature—and I think high school students meet this criterion—should have access to any book that presents serious, legitimate opinions. After all, the main purpose of schools is to teach people to think for themselves, which they can't do if they aren't exposed to all types of ideas. In the case of *Brave New World*, court decisions have already established that the book presents serious and legitimate opinions.

d. Let us assume that any tool or symbol that does not function as it is supposed to may be safely discarded, and this is another reason why the grading system, as used in American schools, may be replaced. The system is supposed to reveal how students are doing, but it does this very imperfectly; an *A* in one class does not mean the same thing as an *A* in another class. It is also supposed to encourage students to do high-quality work, but it doesn't do that very well either; students go for grades in any manner possible and only resort to hard studying when all else fails.

FURTHER READINGS AND ANALYSIS

The following article will give you some additional practice in reading statistical studies. It was chosen partially because it's a famous article and partially because it employs no complicated mathematics or tables. However, it does contain one small deviation from the usual pattern because the author gives two possible explanations instead of one. Both are explanations to answer the question expressed in the first sentence. Read the article carefully and then answer the questions below. (Only about a third of the original article is reproduced here. The remainder discusses the results in more detail and describes other studies along the same line.)

STUDY QUESTIONS

1. It was noted that the author gives not one but two possible explanations to answer the initial question. What are they?
2. What population was studied? (It's *not* the pseudopatients.)
3. How was the sample chosen? Which of the three rules—randomness, variety, and numbers—was followed most closely?
4. What was the method of study? That is, what did the researcher do with the sample?
5. How were the results measured? That is, how did the researcher decide which hypothesis was true?
6. What did the author conclude about the detection of sanity and insanity?
7. Reconsider the sample and the population. Can we safely say, in this case, that "whatever is true of the sample is also true of the population"?

ON BEING SANE IN INSANE PLACES

D. L. Rosenhan

1   If sanity and insanity exist, how shall we know them?

2   The question is neither capricious nor itself insane. However much we may be personally convinced that we can tell the normal from the abnormal, the evidence is simply not compelling. It is commonplace, for example, to read about murder trials wherein eminent psychiatrists for the defense are contradicted by equally eminent psychiatrists for the prosecution on the matter of the defendant's sanity. More generally, there are a great deal of conflicting data on the reliability, utility, and meaning of such terms as "sanity," "insanity," "mental illness," and "schizophrenia" (1). Finally, as early as 1934, Benedict suggested that normality and abnormality are not universal (2). What is viewed as normal in one culture may be seen as quite aberrant in another. Thus, notions of normality and abnormality may not be quite as accurate as people believe they are.

3   To raise questions regarding normality and abnormality is in no way to question the fact that some behaviors are deviant or odd. Murder is deviant. So, too, are hallucinations. Nor does raising such questions deny the existence of the personal anguish that is often associated with "mental illness." Anxiety and depression exist. Psychological suffering exists. But normality and abnormality, sanity and insanity, and the diagnoses that flow from them may be less substantive than many believe them to be.

4   At its heart, the question of whether the sane can be distinguished from the insane (and whether degrees of insanity can be distinguished from each other) is a simple matter: do the salient characteristics that lead to diagnoses reside in the patients themselves or in the environments and contexts in which observers find them? From Bleuler, through Kretchmer, through the formulators of the recently revised *Diagnostic and Statistical Manual* of the American Psychiatric Association, the belief has been strong that patients present symptoms, that those symptoms can be categorized, and, implicitly, that the sane are distinguishable from the insane. More recently, however, this belief has been questioned. Based in part on theoretical and anthropological considerations, but also on philosophical, legal, and therapeutic ones, the view has grown that psychological categorization of mental illness is useless at best and downright harmful, misleading, and pejorative at worst. Psychiatric diagnoses, in this view, are in the minds of the observers and are not valid summaries of characteristics displayed by the observed (3–5).

5   Gains can be made in deciding which of these is more nearly accurate by getting normal people (that is, people who do not have, and have never suffered, symptoms of serious psychiatric disorders) admitted to psychiatric hospitals and then determining whether they were discovered to be sane and, if so, how. If the sanity of such pseudopatients were always detected, there would be prima facie evidence that a sane individual can be distinguished from the insane context in which he is found. Normality (and presumably abnormality) is distinct enough that it can be recognized wherever it occurs, for it is carried within the person. If, on the other hand,

the sanity of the pseudopatients were never discovered, serious difficulties would arise for those who support traditional modes of psychiatric diagnosis. Given that the hospital staff was not incompetent, that the pseudopatient had been behaving as sanely as he had been outside of the hospital, and that it had never been previously suggested that he belonged in a psychiatric hospital, such an unlikely outcome would support the view that psychiatric diagnosis betrays little about the environment in which an observer finds him.

6   This article describes such an experiment. Eight sane people gained secret admission to 12 different hospitals (6). Their diagnostic experiences constitute the data of the first part of this article; the remainder is devoted to a description of their experiences in psychiatric institutions. Too few psychiatrists and psychologists, even those who have worked in such hospitals, know what the experience is like. They rarely talk about it with former patients, perhaps because they distrust information coming from the previously insane. Those who have worked in psychiatric hospitals are likely to have adapted so thoroughly to the settings that they are insensitive to the impact of that experience. And while there have been occasional reports of researchers who submitted themselves to psychiatric hospitalization (7), these researchers have commonly remained in the hospitals for short periods of time, often with the knowledge of the hospital staff. It is difficult to know the extent to which they were treated like patients or like research colleagues. Nevertheless, their reports about the inside of the psychiatric hospital have been valuable. This article extends those efforts.

Pseudopatients and Their Settings

7   The eight pseudopatients were a varied group. One was a psychology graduate student in his 20's. The remaining seven were older and "established." Among them were three psychologists, a pediatrician, a psychiatrist, a painter, and a housewife. Three pseudopatients were women, five were men. All of them employed pseudonyms, lest their alleged diagnoses embarrass them later. Those who were in mental health professions alleged another occupation in order to avoid the special attentions that might be accorded by staff, as a matter of courtesy or caution, to ailing colleagues (8). With the exception of myself (I was the first pseudopatient and my presence was known to the hospital administrator and chief psychologist and, so far as I can tell, to them alone), the presence of peudopatients and the nature of the research program was not known to the hospital staffs (9).

8   The settings were similarly varied. In order to generalize the findings, admission into a variety of hospitals was sought. The 12 hospitals in the sample were located in five different states on the East and West coasts. Some were old and shabby, some were quite new. Some were research-oriented, others not. Some had good staff-patient ratios, others were quite understaffed. Only one was a strictly private hospital. All of the others were supported by state or federal funds or, in one instance, by university funds.

9   After calling the hospital for an appointment, the pseudopatient arrived at the admissions office complaining that he had been hearing voices. Asked what the voices said, he replied that they were often unclear, but as far as he could tell they said "empty," "hollow," and "thud." The voices were

unfamiliar and were of the same sex as the pseudopatient. The choice of these symptoms was occasioned by their apparent similarity to existential symptoms. Such symptoms are alleged to arise from painful concerns about the perceived meaninglessness of one's life. It is as if the hallucinating person were saying, "My life is empty and hollow." The choice of these symptoms was also determined by the *absence* of a single report of existential psychoses in the literature.

10   Beyond alleging the symptoms and falsifying name, vocation, and *employment*, no further alterations of person, history, or circumstances were made. The significant events of the pseudopatient's life history were presented as they had actually occurred. Relationships with parents and siblings, with spouse and children, with people at work and in school, consistent with the aforementioned exceptions, were described as they were or had been. Frustrations and upsets were described along with joys and satisfactions. These facts are important to remember. If anything, they strongly biased the subsequent results in favor of detecting sanity, since none of their histories or current behaviors were seriously pathological in any way.

11   Immediately upon admission to the psychiatric ward, the pseudopatient ceased *any* symptoms of abnormality. In some cases, there was a brief period of mild nervousness and anxiety, since none of the pseudopatients really believed that they would be admitted so easily. Indeed, their shared fear was that they would be immediately exposed as frauds and greatly embarrassed. Moreover, many of them had never visited a psychiatric ward; even those who had, nevertheless had some genuine fears about what might happen to them. Their nervousness, then, was quite appropriate to the novelty of the hospital setting and it disappeared rapidly.

12   Apart from that short-lived nervousness, the pseudopatient behaved on the ward as he "normally" behaved. The pseudopatient spoke to patients and staff as he might ordinarily. Because there is uncommonly little to do on a psychiatric ward, he attempted to engage others in conversation. When asked by staff how he was feeling, he indicated that he was fine, that he no longer experienced symptoms. He responded to instructions from attendants, to calls for medication (which was not swallowed), and to dining-hall instructions. Beyond such activities as were available to him on the admissions ward, he spent his time writing down his observations about the ward, its patients, and the staff. Initially these notes were written "secretly," but as it soon became clear that no one much cared, they were subsequently written on standard tablets of paper in such public places as the dayroom. No secret was made of these activities.

13   The pseudopatient, very much as a true psychiatric patient, entered a hospital with no foreknowledge of when he would be discharged. Each was told that he would have to get out by his own devices, essentially by convincing the staff that he was sane. The psychological stresses associated with hospitalization were considerable, and all but one of the pseudopatients desired to be discharged almost immediately after being admitted. They were, therefore, motivated not only to behave sanely, but to be paragons of cooperation. That their behavior was in no way disruptive is confirmed by nursing reports, which have been obtained on most of the patients. These reports uniformly indicate that the patients were "friendly," "cooperative," and "exhibited no abnormal indications."

The Normal Are Not Detectably Sane

14   Despite their public "show" of sanity, the pseudopatients were never detected. Admitted, except in one case, with a diagnosis of schizophrenia (10), each was discharged with a diagnosis of schizophrenia "in remission." The label "in remission" should in no way be dismissed as a formality, for at no time during any hospitalization had any question been raised about any pseudopatient's simulation. Nor are there any indications in the hospital records that the pseudopatient's status was suspect. Rather, the evidence is strong that, once labeled schizophrenic the pseudopatient was stuck with that label. If the pseudopatient was to be discharged, he must naturally be "in remission"; but he was not sane, nor, in the institution's view, had he ever been sane.

15   The uniform failure to recognize sanity cannot be attributed to the quality of the hospitals, for, although there were considerable variations among them, several are considered excellent. Nor can it be alleged that there was simply not enough time to observe the pseudopatients. Length of hospitalization ranged from 7 to 52 days, with an average of 19 days. The pseudopatients were not, in fact, carefully observed, but this failure clearly speaks more to traditions within psychiatric hospitals than to lack of opportunity.

16   Finally, it cannot be said that the failure to recognize the pseudopatients' sanity was due to the fact that they were not behaving sanely. While there was clearly some tension present in all of them, their daily visitors could detect no serious behavioral consequences—nor, indeed, could other patients. It was quite common for the patients to "detect" the pseudopatients' sanity. During the first three hospitalizations, when accurate counts were kept, 35 of a total of 118 patients on the admission ward voiced their suspicions, some vigorously. "You're not crazy. You're a journalist, or a professor [referring to the continual note-taking]. You're checking up on the hospital." While most of the patients were reassured by the pseudopatient's insistence that he had been sick before he came in but was fine now, some continued to believe that the pseudopatient was sane throughout his hospitalization. The fact that the patients often recognized normality when staff did not raises important questions.

References and Notes

1. P. Ash, *J. Abnorm. Soc. Psychol.* **44**, 272 (1949); A. T. Beck, *Amer. J. Psychiat.* **119**, 210 (1962); A. T. Boisen, *Psychiatry* **2**, 233 (1938); N. Kreitman, *J. Ment. Sci.* **107**, 876 (1961); N. Kreitman, P. Sainsbury, J. Morrisey, J. Towers, J. Scrivener, *ibid.*, p. 887; H. O. Schmitt and C. P. Fonda, *J. Abnorm. Soc. Psychol.* **52**, 262 (1956); W. Seeman, *J. Nerv. Ment. Dis.* **118**, 541 (1953). For an analysis of these artifacts and summaries of the disputes, see J. Zubin, *Annu. Rev. Psychol.* **18**, 373 (1967); L. Phillips and J. G. Draguns, *ibid.* **22**, 447 (1971).
2. R. Benedict, *J. Gen. Psychol.* **10**, 59 (1934).
3. See in this regard H. Becker, *Outsiders: Studies in the Sociology of Deviance* (Free Press, New York, 1963): B. M. Braginsky, D. D. Braginsky, K. King, *Methods of Madness: The Mental Hospital as a Last Resort* (Holt, Rinehart & Winston, New York, 1969); G. M. Crocetti and P. V. Lemkau, *Am. Sociol. Rev.* **30**, 577 (1965); E. Goffman, *Behavior in Public Places* (Free Press, New York, 1964); R. D. Laing, *The*

Divided Self: A Study of Sanity and Madness (Quadrangle, Chicago, 1960); D. L. Phillips, *Amer. Sociol. Rev.* **28**, 963 (1963); T. R. Sarbin, *Psychol. Today* **6**, 18 (1972); E. Schur, *Amer. J. Sociol.* **75**, 306 (1969); T. Szasz, *Law, Liberty, and Psychiatry* (Macmillan, New York, 1963); *The Myth of Mental Illness: Foundations of a Theory of Mental Illness* (Hoeber Harper, New York, 1963). For a critique of some of these views, see W. R. Gove, *Amer. Sociol. Rev.* **35**, 873 (1970).

4. E. Goffman, *Asylums* (Doubleday, Garden City, N. Y., 1961).
5. T. J. Scheff, *Being Mentally Ill: A Sociological Theory* (Aldine, Chicago, 1966).
6. Data from a ninth pseudopatient are not incorporated in this report because, although his sanity went undetected he falsified aspects of his personal history, including his marital status and parental relationships. His experimental behaviors therefore were not identical to those of the other pseudopatients.
7. A. Barry, *Bellevue Is a State of the Mind* (Harcourt Brace Jovanovich, New York, 1971); I. Belknap, *Human Problems of a State Mental Hospital* (McGraw Hill, New York, 1956); W. Candill, F. C. Redlich, H. R. Gilmore, E. B. Brody, *Amer. J. Orthopsychiat.* **22**, 314 (1952); A. R. Goldman, R. H. Bohr, T. A. Steinberg, *Prof. Psychol.*, **1**, 427 (1970); unauthored, *Roche Report,* **11** (No. 13), 8 (1971).
8. Beyond the personal difficulties that the pseudopatient is likely to experience in the hospital, there are legal and social ones that, combined, require considerable attention before entry. For example, once admitted to a psychiatric institution, it is difficult, if not impossible, to be discharged on short notice, state law to the contrary notwithstanding. I was not sensitive to these difficulties at the outset of the project, nor to the personal and situational emergencies that can arise, but later a writ of habeas corpus was prepared for each of the entering pseudopatients and an attorney was kept "on call" during every hospitalization. I am grateful to John Kaplan and Robert Bartels for legal advice and assistance in these matters.
9. However distasteful such concealment is, it was a necessary first step to examining these questions. Without concealment, there would have been no way to know how valid these experiences were; nor was there any way of knowing whether whatever detections occurred were a tribute to the diagnostic acumen of the staff or to the hospital's rumor network. Obviously, since my concerns are general ones that cut across individual hospitals and staffs, I have respected their anonymity and have eliminated clues that might lead to their identification.
10. Interestingly, of the 12 admissions, 11 were diagnosed as schizophrenic and one, with the identical symptomatology, as manic-depressive psychosis. This diagnosis has a more favorable prognosis, and it was given by the only private hospital in our sample. On the relations between social class and psychiatric diagnosis, see A. deB. Hollingshead and F. C. Redlich, *Social Class and Mental Illness: A Community Study* (Wiley, New York, 1958).

Case-study essays, as we noted earlier in the chapter, are more often than not written in school or on the job and therefore are not published. (The main exceptions are legal decisions by judges.) This is especially true of essays about ethical problems because those written for the general public tend to be persuasive discourse rather than the more objective arguments we have been studying here.

The essay reprinted below does have some persuasive elements, particularly the emotional language in the closing paragraphs, but the logic of the argument is carefully worked out. It also follows approximately the organization we have been studying. However, there are two exceptions. First, the introduction is compressed since the author seems to believe that readers are familiar with the facts of the case. Second, the direct argument is longer than usual and is split into two sections. The first section, immediately following the thesis, explains and defends the rule of interpretation. The second part of the direct argument follows the counterarguments and rebuttals; it explains and defends the evidence statement.

Read the essay and then try to answer the study questions. Analyzing the essay is difficult, so you may want to do the analysis as a group project.

STUDY QUESTIONS

1. What is the issue under discussion, according to the introduction?
2. What is the thesis of the essay?
3. In order to identify the parts that discuss the rule of interpretation and the evidence, first locate the section that gives the counterarguments and rebuttals. Try to explain each counterargument and rebuttal in your own words.
4. In the first part of the direct argument (immediately following the thesis) Russell says that there are two possible theories of law-abiding behavior by which people can justify their actions. What are these two theories, and which one does Russell say is the correct one? This is his rule of interpretation.
5. The evidence follows the section giving counterarguments and rebuttals. What is the main evidence statement and how does it fit in with the rule of interpretation?

THE COMMITTEE OF 100

Bertrand Russell

1 The Committee of 100, as your readers are aware, calls for nonviolent civil disobedience on a large scale as a means of inducing the British Government (and others, we hope, in due course) to abandon nuclear weapons and the protection that they are supposed to afford. Many critics have objected that civil disobedience is immoral, at any rate where the government is democratic. It is my purpose to combat this view, not in general, but in the case of nonviolent civil disobedience on behalf of certain aims advocated by the Committee of 100.

2 It is necessary to begin with some abstract principles of ethics. There are, broadly speaking, two types of ethical theory. One of these, which is exemplified in the Decalogue, lays down rules of conduct which are supposed to hold in all cases, regardless of the effects of obeying them. The other theory, while admitting that some rules of conduct are valid in a very great majority of cases, is prepared to consider the consequences of actions and to permit breaches of the rules where the consequences of obeying the rules are obviously undesirable. In practice, most people adopt the second point of view, and only appeal to the first in controversies with opponents.

3 Let us take a few examples. Suppose a physically powerful man, suffering from hydrophobia, was about to bite your children, and the only

way of preventing him was to kill him. I think very few people would think you unjustified in adopting this method of saving your children's lives. Those who thought you justified would not deny that the prohibition of murder is *almost* always right. Probably they would go on to say that this particular sort of killing should not be called "murder." They would define "murder" as "unjustifiable homicide." In that case, the precept that murder is wrong becomes a tautology, but the ethical question remains: "What sort of killing is to be labeled as murder?" Or take, again, the commandment not to steal. Almost everybody would agree that in an immense majority of cases it is right to obey this commandment. But suppose you were a refugee, fleeing with your family from persecution, and you could not obtain food except by stealing. Most people would agree that you would be justified in stealing. The only exceptions would be those who approved of the tyranny from which you were trying to escape.

4   There have been many cases in history where the issue was not so clear. In the time of Pope Gregory VI, simony was rife in the Church. Pope Gregory VI, by means of simony, became Pope and did so in order to abolish simony. In this he was largely successful, and final success was achieved by his disciple and admirer, Pope Gregory VII, who was one of the most illustrious of Popes. I will not express an opinion on the conduct of Gregory VI, which has remained a controversial issue down to the present day.

5   The only rule, in all such doubtful cases, is to consider the consequences of the action in question. We must include among these consequences the bad effect of weakening respect for a rule which is usually right. But, even when this is taken into account, there will be cases where even the most generally acceptable rule of conduct should be broken.

6   So much for general theory. I will come now one step nearer to the moral problem with which we are concerned.

7   What is to be said about a rule enjoining respect for law? Let us first consider the arguments in favour of such a rule. Without law, a civilized community is impossible. Where there is general disrespect for the law, all kinds of evil consequences are sure to follow. A notable example was the failure of prohibition in America. In this case it became obvious that the only cure was a change in the law, since it was impossible to obtain general respect for the law as it stood. This view prevailed, in spite of the fact that those who broke the law were not actuated by what are called conscientious motives. This case made it obvious that respect for the law has two sides. If there is to be respect for the law, the law must be generally considered to be worthy of respect.

8   The main argument in favour of respect for law is that, in disputes between two parties, it substitutes a neutral authority for private bias which would be likely in the absence of law. The force which the law can exert is, in most such cases, irresistible, and therefore only has to be invoked in the case of a minority of reckless criminals. The net result is a community in which most people are peaceful. These reasons for the reign of law are admitted in the great majority of cases, except by anarchists. I have no wish to dispute their validity save in exceptional circumstances.

9   There is one very large class of cases in which the law does not have the merit of being impartial as between the disputants. This is when one of the disputants is the state. The state makes the laws, and unless there is a very

vigilant public opinion in defence of justifiable liberties, the state will make the law such as suits its own convenience, which may not be what is for the public good. In the Nuremberg trials war criminals were condemned for obeying the orders of the state, though their condemnation was only possible after the state in question had suffered military defeat. But it is noteworthy that the powers which defeated Germany all agreed that failure to practise civil disobedience may deserve punishment.

10   Those who find fault with the particular form of civil disobedience which I am concerned to justify maintain that breaches of the law, though they may be justified under a despotic régime, can never be justified in a democracy. I cannot see any validity whatever in this contention. There are many ways in which nominally democratic governments can fail to carry out principles which friends of democracy should respect. Take, for example, the case of Ireland before it achieved independence. Formally, the Irish had the same democratic rights as the British. They could send representatives to Westminster and plead their case by all the received democratic processes. But, in spite of this, they were in the minority which, if they had confined themselves to legal methods, would have been permanent. They won their independence by breaking the law. If they had not broken it, they could not have won.

11   There are many other ways in which governments, which are nominally democratic, fail to be so. A great many questions are so complex that only a few experts can understand them. When the bank rate is raised or lowered, what proportion of the electorate can judge whether it was right to do so? And, if anyone who has no official position criticizes the action of the Bank of England, the only witnesses who can give authoritative evidence will be men responsible for what has been done, or closely connected with those who are responsible. Not only in questions of finance, but still more in military and diplomatic questions, there is in every civilized state a well-developed technique of concealment. If the government wishes some fact to remain unknown, almost all major organs of publicity will assist in concealment. In such cases it often happens that the truth can only be made known, if at all, by persistent and self-sacrificing efforts involving obloquy and perhaps disgrace. Sometimes, if the matter rouses sufficient passion, the truth comes to be known in the end. This happened, for example, in the Dreyfus Case. But where the matter is less sensational the ordinary voter is likely to be left permanently in ignorance.

12   For such reasons democracy, though much less liable to abuses than dictatorship, is by no means immune to abuses of power by those in authority or by corrupt interests. If valuable liberties are to be preserved there have to be people willing to criticize authority and even, on occasion, to disobey it.

13   Those who most loudly proclaim their respect for law are in many cases quite unwilling that the domain of law should extend to international relations. In relations between states the only law is still the law of the jungle. What decides a dispute is the question of which side can cause the greatest number of deaths to the other side. Those who do not accept this criterion are apt to be accused of lack of patriotism. This makes it impossible not to suspect that law is only valued where it already exists, and not as an alternative to war.

14   This brings me at last to the particular form of nonviolent civil disobedi-

ence which is advocated and practised by the Committee of 100. Those who study nuclear weapons and the probable course of nuclear war are divided into two classes. There are, on the one hand, people employed by governments, and, on the other hand, unofficial people who are actuated by a realization of the dangers and catastrophes which are probable if governmental policies remain unchanged. There are a number of questions in dispute. I will mention a few of them. What is the likelihood of a nuclear war by accident? What is to be feared from fall-out? What proportion of the population is likely to survive an all-out nuclear war? On every one of these questions independent students find that official apologists and policy-makers give answers which, to an unbiased inquirer, appear grossly and murderously misleading. To make known to the general population what independent inquirers believe to be the true answers to these questions is a very difficult matter. Where the truth is difficult to ascertain there is a natural inclination to believe what official authorities assert. This is especially the case when what they assert enables people to dismiss uneasiness as needlessly alarmist. The major organs of publicity feel themselves part of the Establishment and are very reluctant to take a course which the Establishment will frown on. Long and frustrating experience has proved, to those among us who have endeavoured to make unpleasant facts known, that orthodox methods, alone, are insufficient. By means of civil disobedience a certain kind of publicity becomes possible. What we do is reported, though as far as possible our reasons for what we do are not mentioned. The policy of suppressing our reasons, however, has only very partial success. Many people are roused to inquire into questions which they had been willing to ignore. Many people, especially among the young, come to share the opinion that governments, by means of lies and evasions, are luring whole populations to destruction. It seems not unlikely that, in the end, an irresistible popular movement of protest will compel governments to allow their subjects to continue to exist. On the basis of long experience, we are convinced that this object cannot be achieved by law-abiding methods alone. Speaking for myself, I regard this as the most important reason for adopting civil disobedience.

15   Another reason for endeavouring to spread knowledge about nuclear warfare is the extreme imminence of the peril. Legally legitimate methods of spreading this knowledge have been proved to be very slow, and we believe, on the basis of experience, that only such methods as we have adopted can spread the necessary knowledge before it is too late. As things stand, a nuclear war, probably by accident, may occur at any moment. Each day that passes without such a war is a matter of luck, and it cannot be expected that luck will hold indefinitely. Any day, at any hour, the whole population of Britain may perish. Strategists and negotiators play a leisurely game in which procrastination is one of the received methods. It is urgent that the populations of East and West compel both sides to realize that the time at their disposal is limited and that, while present methods continue, disaster is possible at any moment, and almost certain sooner or later.

16   There is, however, still another reason for employing nonviolent civil disobedience which is very powerful and deserves respect. The programmes of mass extermination, upon which vast sums of public money are being

spent, must fill every humane person with feelings of utter horror. The West is told that communism is wicked; the East is told that capitalism is wicked. Both sides deduce that the nations which favour either are to be "obliterated," to use Krushchev's word. I do not doubt that each side is right in thinking that a nuclear war would destroy the other side's "ism," but each side is hopelessly mistaken if it thinks that a nuclear war could establish its own "ism." Nothing that either East or West desires can result from a nuclear war. If both sides could be made to understand this, it would become possible for both sides to realize that there can be no victory for either, but only total defeat for both. If this entirely obvious fact were publicly admitted in a joint statement by Khrushchev and Kennedy, a compromise method of coexistence could be negotiated giving each side quite obviously a thousand times more of what it wants than could be achieved by war. The utter uselessness of war, in the present age, is completely obvious except to those who have been so schooled in past traditions that they are incapable of thinking in terms of the world that we now have to live in. Those of us who protest against nuclear weapons and nuclear war cannot acquiesce in a world in which each man owes such freedom as remains to him to the capacity of his government to cause many hundreds of millions of deaths by pressing a button. This is to us an abomination, and rather than seem to acquiesce in it we are willing, if necessary, to become outcasts and to suffer whatever obloquy and whatever hardship may be involved in standing aloof from the governmental framework. This thing is a horror. It is something in the shadow of which nothing good can flourish. I am convinced that, on purely political grounds, our reasoned case is unanswerable. But, beyond all political considerations, there is the determination not to be an accomplice in the worst crime that human beings have ever contemplated. We are shocked, and rightly shocked, by Hitler's extermination of six million Jews, but the governments of East and West calmly contemplate the possibility of a massacre at least a hundred times greater than that perpetrated by Hitler. Those who realize the magnitude of this horror cannot even seem to acquiesce in the policies from which it springs. It is this feeling, much more than any political calculation, that gives fervour and strength to our movement, a kind of fervour and a kind of strength which, if a nuclear war does not soon end us all, will make our movement grow until it reaches the point where governments can no longer refuse to let mankind survive.

Exploring

THE IMPORTANCE OF EXPLORING

In this book you study several ways of proving a thesis—everything from persuasive proofs to the rigidly logical proofs of scientific writing. In almost all such cases you learn to prove a thesis that you already believe is true; your task is to figure out a way to get readers to agree with you.

Proving beliefs that you hold is one of the basic activities of life, and in order to be influential on a job and in other situations, it is a skill you must have. But another important skill that you also need is the ability to discover new answers when you suspect that old answers are not adequate. This skill has many names, such as *problem-solving* or *invention*, but here we shall call it *exploring*.

All writing is exploratory to some extent. As has been pointed out elsewhere, we often don't know what we are going to write until we write it, and we frequently don't understand our own ideas clearly until we have written them down. Furthermore, we sometimes need to explore to find topics for papers or arguments to support a thesis. However, this chapter does not use the term *exploring* to refer to any of these common steps in writing. Here it is being used to refer to the "discovery of new ideas"— ideas that neither you nor anyone else may have thought of before.

Exploring is thus, on one level, the highest of intellectual endeavors. While nearly anyone can be trained to test or prove an existing idea, discovering new ideas requires creativity and an open mind. On another level, however, problem-solving is something that we all must do at one time or another because we find ourselves "stuck" in situations where our old, tried-and-true answers do not work. Then we must create a new answer. For example, suppose you are canoeing miles from civilization and lose a paddle; you are, as the saying goes, "up a creek without a paddle" and must find a new way to move and steer the canoe. Like it or not, you have a problem to solve. Of course, some people are better than others at solving such problems, but we all face similar situations, large or small, daily.

Although explorations are common, written exploratory essays are uncommon. This is because explorations take place mainly in the mind; and when a new idea is discovered, the tendency is to write only a proof for the new idea, not an explanation of how it came into being. Or, if the idea is discovered during writing, the tendency is to rewrite the paper several times to clarify and streamline the proof for the idea and eliminate the evidence of the fumbling steps that preceded the discovery. Although both tendencies are understandable, and even necessary in some situations, it is unfortunate that more explorations are not preserved in writing. Accounts of explorations are often fascinating, and sometimes the retelling of an exploration can be more convincing than a formal proof for a new idea.

Besides its scarcity, another characteristic of written exploration is that the essay is seldom in itself an exploration. It is the *remembrance* of an exploration that was done mostly in the mind. In this way, exploratory writing is different from other types of writing. For example, when you have written a persuasive essay, that essay *is* persuasion; or when you write a poem, the poem *is* literature. But when you write an exploratory essay, the exploration has probably already taken place and the essay merely recounts the exploratory process as best you can remember. It is true that you will engage in a kind of exploratory thinking as you write—making ideas more clear, developing proofs, and so on—but this happens in every kind of writing. This also means that your written account of the exploration is likely to be neater and more systematic than the original mental process, both because you forget some of the mistakes you made in thinking and because you must create an organized paper for the reader.

In summary, exploration is a very important process because it is our means of solving problems and discovering new ideas. Exploratory essays are not common, although we frequently see condensations of explorations in the introductions of some other types of essays. Exploratory writing is worth studying because written exploration sometimes serves as the only practical kind of proof of a new idea. In fact, while there are several types of exploratory essays, it is the exploratory essay that serves as proof for an otherwise unprovable idea that we are concerned with here.

SOME EXAMPLES OF EXPLORATORY ESSAYS

The professional example of an exploratory essay in this chapter is the first chapter from *Kon-Tiki* by Thor Heyerdahl. Heyerdahl, a Norwegian, has become famous for his attempts to trace the origins of primitive peoples. He has written several books about this theories, and his attempts to prove his theories have been the subjects of at least two motion pictures (*Kon-Tiki* and *The Voyages of Ra*). In the chapter reprinted here,

Heyerdahl tells us how he became interested in primitive people and how he discovered his first theory.

The second essay, "What Is Progress?", is more typical of the type of essay a student might write, since the exploration was carried out only with the aid of the instructor, the library, and classmates. It does not pretend to contain a fully developed theory, nor does it cover all of the possible steps involved in a complete exploration. It is also the result of a highly structured assignment, one that practically guaranteed each student a successful exploration. (The assignments in this chapter are not so tightly organized; depending on the nature of the class, your instructor may wish to be more directive.)

Prereading Activities for "A Theory," by Thor Heyerdahl

ORGANIZATION.   It is quite clear that this essay has a narrative (chronological) organization, telling a story in sequence. It is also obvious that the author uses the *flashback* technique, in which he begins in the middle of the story and then goes back to the beginning. This is not the only way to organize an exploratory essay, but narrative order is extremely common, and the flashback technique is used in many kinds of narratives addressed to popular audiences, to hook the readers' interest. This organization does not follow exactly the sequence of exploratory steps that we will study, but it comes close. The organization is as follows:

  I.   Introductory episode—on a raft in the Pacific Ocean (1–14)

 II.   How it all started (15–28)
        A. Living on Fatu Hiva Island (15–17)
        B. Noticing important details
            1. The east wind (18–21)
            2. The story by Tei Tetua (22–24)
            3. The similarity of the monoliths (25–26)

III.   Changing careers (29–30)

 IV.   Information about the Polynesians, discovered by reading (31–39)
        A. Polynesians' first contacts with Europeans (31)
        B. Theories about the origins of the Polynesians (32–34)
        C. How the Polynesians reached the islands (35)
        D. Writing, religion (36)
        E. Genealogies (37)
        F. The Polynesians' Stone Age culture (38–39)

  V.   Forming the new theory (40–50)
        A. Looking toward the New World (40)
        B. The "white gods" of the Incas (41)

C. The white ancestors of the Polynesians (42)
D. Tracing the origins of Tiki (43–44)
E. Discovery of Kon-Tiki (45–46)
F. Completing the theory (47–50)

VOCABULARY. Heyerdahl's essay is easy to read, but a few place names and other terms may be unfamiliar to some readers. The numbers in parentheses refer to the paragraphs in which the words first appear.

sextant (9)—a device used in navigation of the oceans. It helps the navigator determine his position by reference to the positions of stars and planets.
fathom (13)—a unit of length equal to six feet; used mainly to measure depth of water
Polynesian (24)—pertaining to the people of Polynesia, a group of islands scattered over the Pacific Ocean, from Hawaii to Australia
monolith (26)—a large block of stone, or a figure carved from a single, large stone
the Caucasus (32)—a region in the Soviet Union between the Black and Caspian seas
Atlantis (32)—a legendary island in the Atlantic Ocean, west of the island of Gibraltar, that supposedly sank beneath the sea
hieroglyphs (36)—pertains to a system of writing in which figures or objects are used to represent syllables
Melanesia (39)—a group of islands in the southwestern Pacific Ocean, south of Fiji
Pitcairn (40)—a small island in the South Pacific between Easter Island and Tahiti; settled by the mutineers from the *Bounty*
Semitic (42)—having to do with the Semites, especially Jews or Arabs
Lake Titicaca (45)—a lake in the Andes mountains of South America, between Peru and Bolivia

STUDY QUESTIONS. Read the following list of questions, keep them in mind as you read the essay, and then go back and try to answer them in some detail. The questions will help you understand the exploratory nature of the essay.

1. Where is Heyerdahl as the story begins? What is he doing there?
2. What two facts or events aroused Heyerdahl's interest in the origin of the Polynesian people?
3. What was Heyerdahl's state of mind when he noticed these facts or events?
4. What question does Heyerdahl want to answer?
5. What were the first theories advanced by "specialists" to answer this question?
6. How does Heyerdahl know that these theories must be incorrect?
7. What theory has been advanced out of the imagination of nonscientific people? How does Heyerdahl know that this theory is also wrong?
8. In his "armchair studies" of the Polynesians, what did Heyerdahl learn about the language and origins of these people?
9. What other things did Heyerdahl learn by visiting actual archeological sites?

10. At what point does Heyerdahl begin to focus on Peru as the original home of the Polynesians? What discovery confirms his suspicion?
11. Why does Heyerdahl continue to work on his theory after he becomes certain that the original Polynesians came from Peru?
12. Given that this is only the first chapter of the book, what do you suppose the remainder of the book contains?

A THEORY

Thor Heyerdahl

1   Once in a while you find yourself in an odd situation. You get into it by degrees and in the most natural way but, when you are right in the midst of it, you are suddenly astonished and ask yourself how in the world it all came about.

2   If, for example, you put to sea on a wooden raft with a parrot and five companions, it is inevitable that sooner or later you will wake up one morning out at sea, perhaps a little better rested than ordinarily, and begin to think about it.

3   On one such morning I sat writing in a dew-drenched logbook:

—May 17. Norwegian Independence Day. Heavy sea. Fair wind. I am cook today and found seven flying fish on deck, one squid on the cabin roof, and one unknown fish in Torstein's sleeping bag. . . .

4   Here the pencil stopped, and the same thought interjected itself: This is really a queer seventeenth of May—indeed, taken all round, a most peculiar existence. How did it all begin?

5   If I turned left, I had an unimpeded view of a vast blue sea with hissing waves, rolling by close at hand in an endless pursuit of an ever retreating horizon. If I turned right, I saw the inside of a shadowy cabin in which a bearded individual was lying on his back reading Goethe with his bare toes carefully dug into the latticework in the low bamboo roof of the crazy little cabin that was our common home.

6   "Bengt," I said, pushing away the green parrot that wanted to perch on the logbook, "can you tell me how the hell we came to be doing this?"

7   Goethe sank down under the red-gold beard.

8   "The devil I do; you know best yourself. It was your damned idea, but I think it's grand."

9   He moved his toes three bars up and went on reading Goethe unperturbed. Outside the cabin three other fellows were working in the roasting sun on the bamboo deck. They were half-naked, brown-skinned, and bearded, with stripes of salt down their backs and looking as if they had never done anything else than float wooden rafts westward across the Pacific. Erik came crawling in through the opening with his sextant and a pile of papers.

10   "98° 46' west by 8° 2' south—a good day's run since yesterday, chaps!"

11   He took my pencil and drew a tiny circle on a chart which hung on the

bamboo wall—a tiny circle at the end of a chain of nineteen circles that curved across from the port of Callao on the coast of Peru. Herman, Knut, and Torstein too came eagerly crowding in to see the new little circle that placed us a good 40 sea miles nearer the South Sea islands than the last in the chain.

12   "Do you see, boys?" said Herman proudly. "That means we're 850 sea miles from the coast of Peru."

13   "And we've got another 3,500 to go to get to the nearest islands," Knut added cautiously. "And to be quite precise," said Torstein, "we're 15,000 feet above the bottom of the sea and a few fathoms below the moon."

14   So now we all knew exactly where we were, and I could go on speculating as to why. The parrot did not care; he only wanted to tug at the log. And the sea was just as round, just as sky-encircled, blue upon blue.

15   Perhaps the whole thing had begun the winter before, in the office of a New York museum. Or perhaps it had already begun ten years earlier, on a little island in the Marquesas group in the middle of the Pacific. Maybe we would land on the same island now, unless the northeast wind sent us farther south in the direction of Tahiti and the Tuamotu group. I could see the little island clearly in my mind's eye, with its jagged rust-red mountains, the green jungle which flowed down their slopes toward the sea, and the slender palms that waited and waved along the shore. The island was called Fatu Hiva; there was no land between it and us where we lay drifting, but nevertheless it was thousands of sea miles away. I saw the narrow Ouia Valley, where it opened out toward the sea, and remembered so well how we sat there on the lonely beach and looked out over this same endless sea, evening after evening. I was accompanied by my wife then, not by bearded pirates as now. We were collecting all kinds of live creatures, and images and other relics of a dead culture.

16   I remembered very well one particular evening. The civilized world seemed incomprehensibly remote and unreal. We had lived on the island for nearly a year, the only white people there; we had of our own will forsaken the good things of civilization along with its evils. We lived in a hut we had built for ourselves, on piles under the palms down by the shore, and ate what the tropical woods and the Pacific had to offer us.

17   On that particular evening we sat, as so often before, down on the beach in the moonlight, with the sea in front of us. Wide awake and filled with the romance that surrounded us, we let no impression escape us. We filled our nostrils with an aroma of rank jungle and salt sea and heard the wind's rustle in leaves and palm tops. At regular intervals all other noises were drowned by the great breakers that rolled straight in from the sea and rushed in foaming over the land till they were broken up into circles of froth among the shore boulders. There was a roaring and rustling and rumbling among millions of glistening stones, till all grew quiet again when the sea water had withdrawn to gather strength for a new attack on the invincible coast.

18   "It's queer," said my wife, "but there are never breakers like this on the other side of the island."

19   "No," said I, "but this is the windward side; there's always a sea running on this side."

20   We kept on sitting there and admiring the sea which, it seemed, was loath to give up demonstrating that here it came rolling in from eastward,

eastward, eastward. It was the eternal east wind, the trade wind, which had disturbed the sea's surface, dug it up, and rolled it forward, up over the eastern horizon and over here to the islands. Here the unbroken advance of the sea was finally shattered against cliffs and reefs, while the east wind simply rose above coast and woods and mountains and continued westward unhindered, from island to island, toward the sunset.

21   So had the ocean swells and the lofty clouds above them rolled up over the same eastern horizon since the morning of time. The first natives who reached these islands knew well enough that this was so, and so did the present islanders. The long-range ocean birds kept to the eastward on their daily fishing trips to be able to return with the eastern wind at night when the belly was full and the wings tired. Even trees and flowers were wholly dependent on the rain produced by the eastern winds, and all the vegetation grew accordingly. And we knew by ourselves, as we sat there, that far, far below that eastern horizon, where the clouds came up, lay the open coast of South America. There was nothing but 4,000 miles of open sea between.

22   We gazed at the driving clouds and the heaving moonlit sea, and we listened to an old man who squatted half-naked before us and stared down into the dying glow from a little smoldering fire.

23   "Tiki," the old man said quietly, "he was both god and chief. It was Tiki who brought my ancestors to these islands where we live now. Before that we lived in a big country beyond the sea."

24   He poked the coals with a stick to keep them from going out. The old man sat thinking. He lived for ancient times and was firmly fettered to them. He worshiped his forefathers and their deeds in an unbroken line back to the time of the gods. And he looked forward to being reunited with them. Old Tei Tetua was the sole survivor of all the extinct tribes on the east coast of Fatu Hiva. How old he was he did not know, but his wrinkled, bark-brown, leathery skin looked as if it had been dried in sun and wind for a hundred years. He was one of the few on these islands that still remembered and believed in his father's and his grandfather's legendary stories of the great Polynesian chief-god Tiki, son of the sun.

25   When we crept to bed that night in our little pile hut, old Tei Tetua's stories of Tiki and the islanders' old home beyond the sea continued to haunt my brain, accompanied by the muffled roar of the surf in the distance. It sounded like a voice from far-off times, which, it seemed, had something it wanted to tell, out there in the night. I could not sleep. It was as though time no longer existed, and Tiki and his sea-farers were just landing in the surf on the beach below. A thought suddenly struck me and I said to my wife:

26   "Have you noticed that the huge stone figures of Tiki in the jungle are remarkably like the monoliths left by extinct civilizations in South America?"

27   I felt sure that a roar of agreement came from the breakers. And then they slowly subsided while I slept.

28   So, perhaps, the whole thing began. So began, in any case, a whole series of events which finally landed the six of us and a green parrot on board a raft off the coast of South America.

29   I remember how I shocked my father and amazed my mother and my friends when I came back to Norway and handed over my glass jars of beetles and fish from Fatu Hiva to the University Zoological Museum. I wanted to give up animal studies and tackle primitive peoples. The unsolved

mysteries of the South Seas had fascinated me. There must be a rational solution of them, and I had made my objective the identification of the legendary hero, Tiki.

30   In the years that followed, breakers and jungle ruins were a kind of remote, unreal dream which formed the background and accompaniment to my studies of the Pacific peoples. Although the thoughts and inclinations of primitive man can never be rightly judged by an arm-chair student, yet he can, in his library bookshelves, travel wider beyond time and horizons than can any modern outdoor explorer. Scientific works, journals from the time of the earliest explorations, and endless collections in museums in Europe and America offered a wealth of material for use in the puzzle I wanted to try to put together. Since our own race first reached the Pacific islands after the discovery of South America, investigators in all branches of science have collected an almost bottomless store of information about the inhabitants of the South Seas and all the people living round about them. But there has never been any agreement as to the origin of this isolated island people, or the reason why this type is only found scattered over all the solitary islands in the eastern part of the Pacific.

31   When the first Europeans at last ventured to cross this greatest of all oceans, they discovered to their amazement that right out in the midst of it lay a number of small mountainous islands and flat coral reefs, isolated from each other and from the world in general by vast areas of sea. And every single one of these islands was already inhabited by people who had come there before them—tall, handsome people who met them on the beach with dogs and pigs and fowl. Where had they come from? They talked a language which no other tribe knew. And the men of our race, who boldly called themselves the discoverers of the islands, found cultivated fields and villages with temples and huts on every single habitable island. On some islands, indeed, they found old pyramids, paved roads, and carven stone statues as high as a four-story house. But the explanation of the whole mystery was lacking. Who were these people, and where had they come from?

32   One can safely say that the answers to these riddles have been nearly as many in number as the works which have treated of them. Specialists in different fields have put forward quite different solutions, but their affirmations have always been disproved later by logical arguments from experts who have worked along other lines. Malaya, India, China, Japan, Arabia, Egypt, the Caucasus, Atlantis, even Germany and Norway, have been seriously championed as the Polynesians' homeland. But every time some obstacle of a decisive character has appeared and put the whole problem into the melting pot again.

33   And where science stopped, imagination began. The mysterious monoliths on Easter Island, and all the other relics of unknown origin on this tiny island, lying in complete solitude halfway between the easternmost Pacific islands and the coast of South America, gave rise to all sorts of speculations. Many observed that the finds on Easter Island recalled in many ways the relics of the prehistoric civilizations of South America. Perhaps there had once been a bridge of land over the sea, and this had sunk? Perhaps Easter Island, and all the other South Sea islands which had monuments of the same kind, were remains of a sunken continent left exposed above the sea?

34   This has been a popular theory and an acceptable explanation among

laymen, but geologists and other scientists do not favor it. Zoologists, moreover, prove quite simply, from the study of insects and snails on the South Sea islands, that throughout the history of mankind these islands have been completely isolated from one another and from the continents round them, exactly as they are today.

35   We know, therefore, with absolute certainty that the original Polynesian race must at some time, willingly or unwillingly, have come drifting or sailing to these remote islands. And a closer look at the inhabitants of the South Seas shows that it cannot have been very many centuries since they came. For, even if the Polynesians live scattered over an area of sea four times as large as the whole of Europe, nevertheless they have not managed to develop different languages in the different islands. It is thousands of sea miles from Hawaii in the north to New Zealand in the south, from Samoa in the west to Easter Island in the east, yet all these isolated tribes speak dialects of a common language which we have called Polynesian.

36   Writing was unknown in all the islands, except for a few wooden tablets bearing incomprehensible hieroglyphs which the natives preserved on Easter Island, though neither they themselves nor anyone else could read them. But they had schools, and the poetical teaching of history was their most important function, for in Polynesia history was the same as religion. The people were ancestor-worshipers; they worshiped their dead chiefs all the way back to Tiki's time, and of Tiki himself it was said that he was son of the sun.

37   On almost every island learned men could enumerate the names of all the island's chiefs back to the time when it was first peopled. To assist their memories they often used a complicated system of knots on twisted strings, as the Inca did in Peru. Modern scientists have collected all these local genealogies from the different islands and found that they agree with one another with astonishing exactness, both in names and number of generations. It has been discovered in this way, by taking an average Polynesian generation to represent twenty-five years, that the South Sea islands were not peopled before about 500 A.D. A new cultural wave with a new string of chiefs shows that another and still later migration reached the same islands as late as about 1100 A.D.

38   Where could such late migrations have come from? Very few investigators seem to have taken into consideration the decisive factor that the people who came to the islands at so late a date was a pure Stone Age people. Despite their intelligence and, in all other respects, astonishingly high culture, these seafarers brought with them a certain type of stone ax and a quantity of other characteristic Stone Age tools and spread these over all the islands to which they came. We must not forget that, apart from single isolated peoples, inhabiting primeval forests, and certain backward races, there were no cultures in the world of any reporductive capacity which were still at the Stone Age level in 500 or 1100 A.D., except in the New World. There even the highest Indian civilizations were totally ignorant at least of the uses of iron, and used stone axes and tools of the same types as those used in the South Sea islands right up to the time of the explorations.

39   These numerous Indian civilizations were the Polynesians' nearest neighbors to the east. To westward there lived only the black-skinned primitive peoples of Australia and Melanesia, distant relations of the Ne-

groes, and beyond them again were Indonesia and the coast of Asia where the Stone Age lay farther back in time, perhaps, than anywhere else in the world.

40 Thus both my suspicions and my attention were turned more and more away from the Old World, where so many had searched and none had found, and over to the known and unknown Indian civilizations of America, which no one hitherto had taken into consideration. And on the nearest coast due east, where today the South American republic of Peru stretches from the Pacific up into the mountains, there was no lack of traces if one only looked for them. Here an unknown people had once lived and established one of the world's strangest civilizations, till suddenly, long ago, they had vanished as though swept away from the earth's surface. They left behind them enormous stone statues carved in the image of human beings, which recalled those on Pitcairn, the Marquesas, and Easter Island, and huge pyramids built in steps like those on Tahiti and Samoa. They hewed out of the mountains, with stone axes, stone blocks as large as railway cars and heavier than elephants, transported them for miles about the countryside, and set them up on end or placed them on top of one another to form gateways, huge walls, and terraces, exactly as we find them on some of the islands in the Pacific.

41 The Inca Indians had their great empire in this mountain country when the first Spaniards came to Peru. They told the Spaniards that the colossal monuments that stood deserted about the landscape were erected by a race of white gods which had lived there before the Incas themselves became rulers. These vanished architects were described as wise, peaceful instructors, who had originally come from the north, long ago in the morning of time, and had taught the Incas' primitive forefathers architecture and agriculture as well as manners and customs. They were unlike other Indians in having white skins and long beards; they were also taller than the Incas. Finally they left Peru as suddenly as they had come; the Incas themselves took over power in the country, and the white teachers vanished forever from the coast of South America and fled westward across the Pacific.

42 Now it happened, when the Europeans came to the Pacific islands, they were quite astonished to find that many of the natives had almost white skins and were bearded. On many of the islands there were whole families conspicuous for their remarkably pale skins, hair varying from reddish to blonde, blue-gray eyes, and almost Semitic, hook-nosed faces. In contrast to these the genuine Polynesians had golden-brown skins, raven hair, and rather flat, pulpy noses. The red-haired individuals called themselves *urukehu* and said that they were directly descended from the first chiefs on the islands, who were still white gods, such as Tangaroa, Kane, and Tiki. Legends of mysterious white men, from whom the islanders were originally descended, were current all over Polynesia. When Roggeveen discovered Easter Island in 1722, he noticed to his surprise what he termed "white men" among those on shore. And the people of Easter Island could themselves count up those of their ancestors who were white-skinned right back to the time of Tiki and Hotu Matua, when they first came sailing across the sea "from a mountainous land in the east which was scorched by the sun."

43 As I pursued my search, I found in Peru surprising traces in culture, mythology, and language which impelled me to go on digging ever deeper

and with greater concentration in my attempt to identify the place of origin of the Polynesian tribal god Tiki.

44   And I found what I hoped for. I was sitting reading the Inca legends of the sun-king Virakocha, who was the supreme head of the mythical white people in Peru. I read:

45   . . . Virakocha is an Inca (Ketchua) name and consequently of fairly recent date. The original name of the sun-god Virakocha, which seems to have been more used in Peru in old times, was Kon-Tiki or Illa-Tiki, which means Sun-Tiki or Fire-Tiki. Kon-Tiki was high priest and sun-king of the Incas' legendary 'white men' who had left the enormous ruins on the shores of Lake Titicaca. The legend runs that the mysterious white men with beards were attacked by a chief named Cari who came from the Coquimbo Valley. In a battle on an island in Lake Titicaca the fair race was massacred, but Kon-Tiki himself and his closest companions escaped and later came down to the Pacific coast, whence they finally disappeared oversea to the westward . . . .

46   I was no longer in doubt that the white chief-god Sun-Tiki, whom the Incas declared that their forefathers had driven out of Peru on to the Pacific, was identical with the white chief-god Tiki, son of the sun, whom the inhabitants of all the eastern Pacific islands hailed as the original founder of their race. And the details of Sun-Tiki's life in Peru, with the ancient names of places round Lake Titicaca, cropped up again in historic legends current among the natives of the Pacific islands.

47   But all over Polynesia I found indications that Kon-Tiki's peaceable race had not been able to hold the islands alone for long. Indications that seagoing war canoes, as large as Viking ships and lashed together two and two, had brought Northwest Indians from the New World across the sea to Hawaii and farther south to all the other islands. They had mingled their blood with that of Kon-Tiki's race and brought a new civilization to the island kingdom. This was the second Stone Age people that came to Polynesia, without metals, without the potter's art, without wheel or loom or cereal cultivation, about 1100 A.D.

48   So it came about that I was excavating rock carvings in the ancient Polynesian style among the Northwest Coast Indians in British Columbia when the Germans burst into Norway in 1940.

49   Right face, left face, about face. Washing barracks stairs, polishing boots, radio school, parachute—and at last a Murmansk convoy to Finnmark, where the war-god of technique reigned in the sun-god's absence all the dark winter through.

50   Peace came. And one day my theory was complete. I must go to America and put it forward.

The Student Essay

The following essay, by a student, explores a problem of definition rather than one of fact. However, it follows much the same sequence as the passage by Heyerdahl, ending with a proposal, or hypothesis, that will need to be tested or proved in some way. Since the essay will be discussed in detail only toward the end of the chapter, no study questions are given.

WHAT IS PROGRESS?

Andrew Eibl

1   From the beginning of life on earth till now there has been change, such as from the first microorganism to the first land animal to humans. The question is whether such change can be considered progress toward a specific goal in the future. The definition of progress could be the hardest of all definitions, for it must take into consideration the whole of the cosmos. Let us take a closer look at this idea called progress.

2   When I first thought about progress, I believed it could be defined as the social and technological advancement of society brought on by new ideas to create new art, new music, and new technological know-how for the betterment of society. However, when others read my definition it became evident that my definition of progress failed to take several problems into consideration. Progress, critics said, was not always for the betterment of the people. New technology can create new ways to kill people or new ways for large corporations to exploit people or the environment to make a profit. Therefore progress as we have conceived of it may not be good for the people. People also may not be ready for progress, and that could result in future shock where technology has progressed further and faster than our social and moral ideas. Do we have true progress if we do not have progress of human intelligence to a higher plane of thought?

3   Because of these objections, it seems I will have to find a better, more complete definition of progress, one that does not lead people to believe, as I did, that progress is automatically good. We also need to distinguish progress from mere change.

4   Some alternatives to my original definition can be inferred from the criticisms of it and found in dictionaries. Progress could be defined as any general advancement, whether it's good or bad for the people or the environment. However, this doesn't sound very good because of its extremely general nature. What is an "advancement" and how do we separate it from change? There could also be an advancement that doesn't affect people or their environment. Another alternative is the idea that progress is like repeating history but not making the mistakes our ancestors did. This seems to me to be an insufficient definition because it does not include new ideas, thoughts, or actions. It's good to avoid repeating mistakes, but some new things, like better health care, ought to be included as progress.

5   The *Random House Dictionary* defines progress as the movement or advancement to a goal or to a higher stage with continuous improvement. This definition sounds good, but there is one problem. How do we know when something is really an improvement? We may think that there is an improvement in one area, such as when we generate electricity, but the

improvement may cause things to get worse in another area, the way that generating electricity pollutes the environment. The *Harper Dictionary of Modern Thought* states that progress could represent the moral or social improvement of the human condition. I like this definition better than the one from the other dictionary, but it leaves out scientific progress.

6   Since none of the definitions I have found or inferred seem adequate, let me take a look at some things we have called progress. For example, we, the human race, have progressed from stone users to metal users. We have gone from man-power transportation to animal-powered transportation to vehicular transportation. These things were accomplished by using and accepting new ideas. It was also called progress when we moved from farms to the city, and eventually adopted the forty-hour week. This freed us from working all the time and gave us more time for leisure. It was called social progress but was permitted by the Industrial Revolution, which came from scientific progress. Other things referred to as social progress were advances in sanitation and health care to allow us to live longer, changes in our attitudes toward handicapped and other kinds of disadvantaged people to allow them a more normal life, and changes in government to allow more people to participate in making the laws. Some of these, it is true, came about partially because of scientific advances, but others seem to be real improvements in man's morals.

7   What it seems to me that we have here is a problem of connotations. We have come to think that everything labeled as progress is good, but scientific progress is neither bad nor good, not automatically. It does not deserve its good connotations. But social progress, if it is real, *is* good. The situation is a lot like the words "dam" and "damn." A dam used to be considered always good and so the word had good connotations, but this is no longer true. Now the word "dam" just refers to an object and we take a close look at each proposal for a dam to see whether it's good or bad. The word "damn," however, will always have connotations (negative in this case) and deserves them.

8   We could split up the definition of progress in the same way, even changing the spelling for one of the definitions. The word with its present spelling would refer only to scientific or technological change, and we could teach people that this word has no positive or negative connotations. Each example of such progress has to be looked at to see if it's good or bad. Then we would have a new word, "progresse," to refer to social progress, which I define as an improvement in the condition of people resulting from better moral attitudes. I don't think the improvement would be permanent unless attitudes did change.

9   I don't mean to imply that people wouldn't still misuse the new word. They would do such things as putting more people in jail for smoking pot and calling that "progresse." But people always do that with words with strong connotations. You have to educate people to watch out for it. But the other side of the coin is that when you do find a real example of progresse, you can use the good connotations of the word to sell the idea to even more people.

PREWRITING

Several Preliminary Considerations

A complete exploration about a topic weighty enough for a college paper can take months or even years. For this reason you will seldom be asked to write a paper about a whole exploration but will instead be assigned to discuss only part of the process. Or the assignment may be left open so that you can choose the part you wish to do. Therefore, this chapter will explain how to write several types of papers. So that you will understand each type and where it fits into the exploratory process, let us first make a survey of the whole process.

We can organize this survey by reference to three issues discussed in previous chapters. First comes the reader issue, that, in the case of exploration, is the requirement that you demonstrate that an exploration is needed. You must do this because your readers will likely believe that there is no problem and that the important questions about your topic have already been answered. You, obviously, believe that the old answers are wrong, but you must prove this to your readers. You may not be able to prove it conclusively, but you must at least raise enough doubt in the readers' minds so that they will grant the possibility of a need for an exploration. This first stage is called *raising the question*.

Once you have disproved the old answer and raised the question, the next step, quite logically, is to *search for a new answer*. We call this the writer issue because you, as the explorer, must be granted the right to explore in your own way. Some people are plodding and methodical in their searches, while others skip around, trying this and that. Some people can go right to the heart of the problem, while others must fumble around. Whatever your method may be, your mental workings will inevitably find their way into the paper that you eventually write; readers must put up with this, even though their own minds may work differently, and follow you as best they can.

Finally, if you do manage to find a new answer that seems reasonable, you come to the last stage of exploration, *testing the new answer*. Since this is the subject-matter issue, you are required to test and prove the new answer in as fair and logical a manner as you can devise. Persuasive, expressive, or literary proofs will not do for exploration; you must employ some sort of scientific test such as those discussed in the preceding chapter, "Explaining and Proving."

When you have tested your new answer and proved that it is true—or, at least, that it is better than the old answer—you have come to the end of the exploration. The three stages are illustrated on the diagram in Figure 6.1.

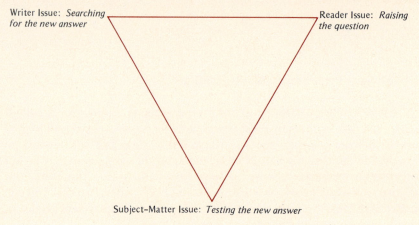

FIGURE 6.1. The stages of exploration.

THE RELATIONSHIP BETWEEN "EXPLORING" AND "EX-PLAINING AND PROVING." We noted above that the last stage of exploration, testing the new answer, must use the same scientific techniques as those discussed in the preceding chapter. But you may have also noticed that there are other similarities between an exploration and a scientific proof. For example, we saw in Chapter 5 that many scientific papers begin by stating a problem and then giving a hypothesis, or tentative answer to the problem, two steps that also occur in exploration. This similarity exists because many scientific papers really are the third stages of explorations, and their introductions, therefore, constitute a condensed version of the first and second stages. The condensation may be done to save space, or because the writer doesn't think anyone would be interested in the entire exploration, or because the original exploration has been published elsewhere.

However, the main reason for the shortness of a scientific introduction is that most hypotheses for such papers do not result from genuine explorations. Most of the time the hypothesis is simply a commonsense explanation that the writer wishes to test, a logical extension of previous research, or an answer that immediately occurred to the writer upon first encountering the problem. Thus, most scientific papers are not related to exploration and cannot be said to be the third stages of exploratory activities.

Because, however, the hypothesis resulting from a real exploration is usually tested in the same manner as hypotheses from other sources, we will not take the time here to discuss again how to conduct the test. If you wish to test an exploratory hypothesis, or if you wish to conduct scientific research as any part of an exploration, refer to Chapter 5 for some helpful advice.

Exercises on Recognizing Exploration

1. A number of people have written about the "myth of American invincibility." What was this myth and what questions were raised about it?

2. List five statements that you believe to be true. Try to provide an assortment of types of statements—at least one of a factual nature ("the earth goes around the sun"), one a matter of policy ("abortion should be made illegal"), and one of values ("death is better than slavery"). Then list two or three reasonable questions that someone might use to challenge each of your beliefs. For example, someone might ask, "How can it be practical to pass a law against abortion when more than half of the population disagrees with such a law?"

3. We all have many beliefs that we do not recognize, in other words, that we take for granted. For each of the following common objects, write one statement that you believe to be true about the object. Try for an assortment of types of beliefs; don't make them all factual.
   a. lawns
   b. hair
   c. the shirt or blouse you are wearing
   d. parking meters
   e. maple trees
   f. the sky

4. Think of some personal questions that you are trying to answer right now. List two or three of them, and then try to remember how they came up. Did any of them arise because something you once believed is now recognized as untrue?

5. Tell the class about a great idea that you have. Also try to remember how you got this idea.

CHOOSING A TOPIC FOR AN EXPLORATORY PAPER. Now that you know a little about all three major stages of exploration, you can see why it is seldom practical or possible to write a paper that covers a complete exploration. Your paper may cover all of the first or second stage or just a part of one of these stages. This means that several kinds of topics are available.

For a paper covering all or part of the first stage, the best topic is a belief that you already suspect is not true. You can then write a paper examining and raising questions about this belief. It should preferably be a belief that, unlike the laws against marijuana, for example, has not already come into widespread controversy. It's far more interesting to raise questions about something everyone else regards as true than to rake over, once again, a tired old topic.

If you cannot think of such a new topic, you can take almost any popular belief and subject it to scrutiny. You can do this because nearly all of what we believe to be true is not true, or, at the very least, is not perfectly true. Everything is open to question if one simply has the courage and open-mindedness to take a fresh look at it. Of course, we all have some areas we wish to keep "off limits" to questions—religious or political views, for example. That is as it should be. Even then, any given writer still has many other topics worth exploring.

If, instead of doing something on the first stage, you would prefer to engage in the second stage—the search for a new answer—you will need a different kind of topic. This should be a topic for which the old answer, if one exists, has already been disproved to your satisfaction, so the remaining task is to find a new answer. The question that you want to answer can be a personal one such as "What shall I major in?" or a wider one such as "What causes allergic reactions?" Furthermore, it could be a question of fact ("Who killed Mr. X?"), a question of policy ("What shall we do about inflation?"), a question of values ("Is animal experimentation morally right?"), or many other types of questions. In any case, however, the question should be one about which you can become sufficiently knowledgeable in the time available to have a reasonable chance of finding an answer. You may not find an answer, of course, but if the topic is limited enough you can still do some productive writing.

Exercises on Choosing a Topic

1. Think of a personal problem that came about because you were trying to do what our society says is right for a person like yourself (in terms of age, sex, family relationships, ethnic background, and so on). Write a belief explanation of what you were trying to do and why it didn't work out for you.

2. When you came to college, you probably encountered people with beliefs that were different from those your parents taught you. Identify one of these situations and then briefly explain, in writing, (a) how you happened to find out that the belief was different, (b) what your belief is, and (c) what your new acquaintance's belief is.

3. If your local community is like most others, the people there are resisting some sort of change that has been suggested by local leaders, the state government, or the federal government. Or there may be a problem that obviously needs to be solved, but the people refuse to do anything about it. Briefly explain, in writing, the problem and why the community isn't doing anything about it.

4. College students sometimes seek to change college regulations or procedures. Identify a proposed change at your own college and briefly explain, in writing, the regulation or procedure under challenge, the proposed change, and the reasons for the proposal.

5. When you came to college, you probably encountered some aspects of college that seemed foolish to you—a regulation, a requirement, or some

such thing. Identify one such "foolishness" and explain it in writing. Also explain why you don't like it.
6. Identify any belief (other than those previously covered) that you once held but now have come to doubt. Briefly explain, in writing, the belief and why you now doubt it.
7. Now make a tentative choice about your topic, choosing the one from the preceding exercises that looks most promising. You also need to decide, again tentatively, whether you are going to write a paper that raises questions about an existing belief or one that attempts to find a new answer. Write a brief explanation of what you have decided to do and discuss it with your instructor.

Raising Questions About Accepted Beliefs

Assume that you have decided to write a paper that covers all or part of the first exploratory stage, raising questions. Further assume that you have chosen a topic—a belief—that you wish to write about, one that you are willing to question or that you have already begun to question.

Heyerdahl, in *Kon-Tiki*, chose such a topic, or rather, as happens in a great many explorations, the topic chose him. He happened to be in the right place at the right time, and he noticed some curious phenomena that prompted him to begin thinking. Heyerdahl does not clearly indicate what he knew or believed in the beginning about the origin of the Polynesians, but one thing is clear: according to all previous theories and beliefs, the Polynesians had come from the west, either by sea or by means of a now-sunken "land bridge."

This preexisting belief is called the *dogma* of an exploration. A dogma is usually defined as an idea or belief authoritatively regarded as true. Your first task, then, is to understand this dogma as well as you can. You need to understand not only the basic, dogmatic belief itself but also the reasoning behind it. It would not be fair to the belief or to the people who hold it to begin asking questions about something you do not completely understand. And the paper you eventually write will hardly be convincing to a reader if it is clear that you did not give the dogma a fair shake.

Of course, the amount that you say about the dogma in your paper will depend on the topic and the intended readers. Heyerdahl was able to skip rather lightly over the dogma or dogmas about the Polynesians because it was not likely that the intended readers knew or cared very much one way or the other about previous theories. But if you are discussing a belief that your readers do know about and care about, you will need to do a more complete job. In either case, you must at least have a good understanding in mind, whether or not you eventually put on paper everything you know about the dogma.

When you understand the dogma and the reasons for it as well as you can, it is time to raise questions about it. You do this by noting *anomalies*, facts that cannot be explained by the dogma or that appear to contravene it. For example, Heyerdahl notices that the wind always blows from the east. How, then, could the Polynesians have come from the west, since they had no engines and, probably, no sailing ships either? He also notices the stone monoliths. How could anyone say that people from the west carved those monoliths when all similar examples exist on the continent to the east? Finally, he notes that the Polynesians claim that they came across the sea. Why, then, do some people insist that the Polynesians arrived by means of a land bridge?

You will find similar anomalies in the dogma you are exploring, assuming that you have picked a topic within your capability and that you have learned as much as you can about it. You will no doubt come across some anomalies in your reading, while others will occur to you as you think about the dogma. Thus it may seem that you will need some luck to find anomalies, and to a certain extent this is true. However, you are probably investigating a dogma for which you had already noticed important anomalies. In other words, as happened to Heyerdahl, the topic picked you rather than vice versa. Few people go around hunting for dogmas to investigate. People find themselves in dilemmas, and when the standard solutions (the dogmas) don't solve the dilemmas, questions begin to arise.

Noticing anomalies precipitates the third step of the raising questions part of the exploration. This is the *crisis*, so called because the questioning of accepted beliefs is risky and upsetting—and exciting, too, as Heyerdahl remembers. Heyerdahl couldn't sleep; what he had noticed continued to "haunt my brain."

Exploration causes a crisis because to admit the existence of an anomaly is to admit the possibility that the dogma might be wrong. Since settled beliefs are safe and comforting, attempts to question them are inevitably met with resistance. In fact, some crises never seem to go away for some people. The theory of evolution, which replaced the older theory of creation, is still the subject of occasional controversy among those who wish to believe that the Bible is literally true.

Of course, a student trying to write a required paper may not experience the crisis of a true explorer. However, the central requirement of the crisis can still be accounted for. This is the decision about whether to reject the dogma. In other words, you must decide whether the anomalies are so convincing that the dogma must be regarded as untrue. Although you have found anomalies, deciding to reject the dogma is not automatic. Every dogma has some anomalies, and most of the time we ignore them or decide that they are not serious enough to worry about. Or we may believe that some minor adjustment is necessary in the dogma but no such radical move as outright rejection is warranted.

In the end, the decision about whether to reject the dogma is yours alone. If you decide to reject it, you may have to do so based as much on your feelings as on the facts. You may simply have a hunch that the dogma is wrong, hoping that some later explorer will discover the new answer that will vindicate your hunch.

Thus, when you write an exploratory paper, you cannot hope to convince every reader to agree with your final decision, especially if you decide to reject the dogma. However, if you treat the dogma fairly, showing that you understand it well, the fairminded reader will stay with the paper. Then when you point out the flaws in the dogma, the reader will be inclined at least to continue reading and to accept the anomalies as genuine. Finally, a reader who agrees with your rejection of the dogma may be inspired to do what you have not yet done—to look for the new answer.

This first type of paper may be regarded as "planting the seed." You first plant the seed of doubt in your mind as you research the dogma and its anomalies. Then when you write the paper, you hope to raise similar doubts in the minds of your readers, believing that the seed eventually will flower into a new and better theory to replace the old one.

Exercises on Raising the Question

1. Identify the dogma in your topic, and write it out. Show it to your classmates to see if they agree that your statement accurately reflects the belief as generally held. Rewrite it until all or most of the class agree that you have it right.
2. List the facts and reasons that support the dogma. Show your list to the class to see if other students can add to it. Your instructor may also suggest that you go to the library and read some material about the topic to discover more reasons why people believe the dogma.
3. List and briefly explain the anomalies that you have noticed in the dogma. Ask some classmates if they have noticed the same problems. Also ask if anyone sees additional anomalies.
4. As you think about your topic and discuss it with others, look for emotional reactions (i.e., a crisis atmosphere) in yourself and others. Jot down some notes about the signs that you observe. If you see no signs of crisis, try to find other people who ought to be upset about what you're doing, and casually mention your project to them. (If you see no signs of crisis anywhere, perhaps it's not appropriate to write a "raising the question" paper about your topic. Consider writing a "search for a new answer" instead.)
5. Consider whether the dogma needs to be rejected outright or simply adjusted a little. Give some thought as to what the adjusted dogma or the new answer might look like.
6. Write a first draft of the paper. Do this even if (as is probable) you could

not do some of the preceding exercises. (Remember, writing itself is exploratory in many ways, so you can expect appropriate material to come to you as you write.) Write the story of your exploration simply and directly, putting yourself into the story. Don't worry about organization or editing at this time.

The Search for a New Answer

The kind of search discussed here is a continuation of the preceding process; in other words, we are interested in how to find a new answer to replace the now-repudiated old answer. However, there are several other kinds of searches that also can be called exploratory. One is the *choices* search, where you explore for the best choice among several known alternatives. Choosing a college to attend is an example; the choices are already available, and you must choose the right one for your needs. Another kind of exploration is the *new problem* type, in which you are suddenly faced with a problem that you have never encountered before and for which you have no well-known answer. Solving such a problem requires "starting from scratch" by learning as much as you can; you will probably find that the answer existed all the time, but you were just too inexperienced to know it. Thus both of these other types of exploration can be fairly straightforward: once you have learned enough about the problem, the answer probably becomes obvious.

But when you search for a new answer to replace the old one, simply learning more about the problem, while a necessary step, is seldom enough. You will also need some luck, some genius, and some time. Where do you start? There's an old saying that "chance favors the prepared mind," so you must first prepare your mind.

We will assume that you have chosen to explore a problem you are somewhat familiar with, so you probably know something about the original dogma and the reasons it has been rejected. However, unless you are an expert on the topic, you need to know more, and so you will start by reading some essays that explain the dogma and its anomalies. Such essays should be available in your library. If you need help in finding them, check with your instructor or a librarian.

As you work to understand the history of the problem and then to begin the search, remember that exploration seldom moves in a straight line. While we study a step-by-step process here, you will probably not cover all the possible steps, nor will you finish each step before beginning another. The anomalies, for example, may help you develop the new answer, so it would be valid to say that the search may actually begin anywhere.

Let's examine the search stage of exploration *as* if it moved in a straight line. These are the possible steps you may take.

One early step worth taking is to *clarify the question* that you are trying to answer. This may not be as easy as it seems, for the question may change as you search. For example, Heyerdahl originally set out to discover the origins of the Polynesians, but soon found that there were several migrations, not all from the same place. So he clarified his question by settling on the problem of the origin of the "legendary white men" who were the first Polynesians. Then he narrowed this even further, deciding that if he could find the origins of Tiki, the legendary sun-god, the rest of the answer would fall into place—which is what happened. In other words, Heyerdahl progressively simplified his task by narrowing his question, choosing a question that would prove to be the key to the whole problem.

Changing the question is fairly common in exploration. You will see instances in which someone worked for months to answer a question, only to find that he or she had been asking the wrong question and had to begin again. An exploratory paper that preserves all of these false starts will actually look like a series of explorations.

Having asked what you hope is the right question, the next step is to look around for attempts by previous thinkers to answer that question. There is, after all, very little that's new in this world, and if you have a question, it's likely that others have also asked it. This step requires that you *examine tentative answers that others have already proposed* as solutions to your problem.

In his chapter, Heyerdahl does not clearly separate this step from the original dogma, so when he gives the list of older theories, we cannot tell which ones he knew at the beginning of his exploration and which he came across during the search stage. He may have forgotten, or, as we speculated earlier, he may have realized that most readers knew very little about the Polynesians and there was therefore no reason to clearly specify the dogma.

It may happen, as you read about attempts by others to answer the question, that you will discover a tentative answer that seems plausible. If so, you can skip the rest of the search stage and simply look for additional evidence to support this theory. Then you can write about the other person's theory, adding information, evidence, and ideas you have come across.

More likely, however, you will decide that none of these tentative answers is correct. Therefore, you will move into the next step of the search. *reexamining the reality in question.* This step requires that you take a fresh look at whatever real items are involved in the problem, hoping to discover some new facts about these items overlooked by other explorers. For Heyerdahl, the reality in question was the Polynesian people themselves, so he set out to learn as much as he could about them. He studied their language, their genealogies, their culture, and the historical accounts of their first encounters with Europeans. At first he did this just through library sources, but when his reading confirmed his original hunch that the

Polynesians came from the east, from the Americas, he went to America for some first-hand study. He bagan in British Columbia and worked his way south to Ecuador and Peru until he found what he was looking for, that clue to the origin of Tiki.

Heyerdahl was fortunate in having a clear idea of what he was looking for and in being able to find the documents he needed. He was then able to complete his theory in a systematic and straightforward manner. Some luck and some genius were involved, of course, for he had to be lucky enough to find the right document and smart enough to recognize the missing facts when he saw them. However, it was mainly a case of "chance favoring the prepared mind," for he had done his homework and there was no luck involved in his readiness to see something important in a document that many others must have read and passed over.

Preparing the mind, while a necessary step in all explorations, does not necessarily lead straight to a theory. A number of intervening steps can be taken, methods of helping the facts sort of rearrange themselves into a theory that answers the question. There is not enough space here to discuss all of the various theories of creative problem-solving, so we will focus on just one of the most common methods, which we will call the technique of *the borrowed model.* A model is a method of seeing or organizing reality, but since that is a rather abstract definition, some examples may explain the term more clearly.

Two well-known examples function in the controversy over abortion. The controversy may be seen as a conflict between models, for we seem to have only two ways of seeing and organizing living human tissue. Either the tissue is not a person—as an appendix, for example, is not a person—and there is no moral issue involved in cutting it out and throwing it away. Or the tissue is a person, such as a baby, in which case it has certain rights and cannot be killed without a moral issue being raised. Both of these ways of treating human tissue are models; we can say that there is an appendix model and a person model. In most cases, we already know which model to apply to a given situation, but in the case of a fetus we are not so certain. Is a fetus to be treated like an appendix or like a person? The answer is not clear because a fetus is a fetus; it's not a bodily organ and, especially at the early stages, it looks nothing like a person either. One way out of the dilemma, used by the Supreme Court, has been to compromise: the appendix model is applied until the fetus reaches a certain stage of growth, and thereafter the person model is applied. This compromise, however, has satisfied no one, and one suspects that the controversy will not be settled until someone invents an entirely new model, or, more likely, borrows a third model that applies more successfully to fetuses.

This is what is meant by borrowed models. We take a known way of structuring and treating one kind of reality and use it to interpret an unsettled type of reality or to change the view of a reality that has been structured badly. Thus you can become more creative if you develop an awareness of models and then use a model you know well to structure or restructure the problem you are exploring.

In writing "What Is Progress?" Andrew Eibl can be observed using a borrowed model. He was looking for a way to restructure a definition; in other words, he had given up the "old model" (i.e., the dogma) for defining progress and was casting around for a new structure. Instead of creating a new answer "out of nowhere," he borrowed the model of the two other words, *dam* and *damn*, and redefined progress in the image of these two examples.

Coming up with this idea involved two creative steps. First, Eibl had to invent the idea that there are two kinds of progress, so different from each other that the same word should not be used for both. Yet he didn't want to invent new words; a simple change in spelling would do the job. This idea then became a *projection* for the type of model to borrow. Thus he used one more step than Heyerdahl needed, for Heyerdahl projected the type of answer he needed (the origin of Tiki) but then went directly to finding the answer without, apparently, borrowing a model.

In working on your own exploration, you can try to take these steps consciously. After you have reexamined the reality in question and collected some facts about it, try projecting the kind of answer you will need. Then look for a model you can borrow to meet your needs. This conscious attempt at creativity may not be successful, but your subconscious will go to work on the problem and could come up with the answer. Even if you don't get the answer, a paper about your search is still worth writing because it may help someone else's search.

When you have finally decided upon a plausible model to borrow, you may well feel satisfied, for you have passed the most important step of the search; you have been lucky and have demonstrated a touch of genius. But there are two more steps that can be taken. First, you could develop your idea into a complete theory. This is usually not difficult, for you can simply apply various parts of the borrowed model to the new problem, assuming that whatever parts exist in the borrowed model can also be incorporated into your new model. When you have done this, you have a *theory*. Finally, you can, if you wish, develop some testable *hypotheses* from the theory. These should be single statements that can be scientifically verified.

We can see these steps in "What Is Progress?" The borrowed model, of the word *dam* (and *damn*), suggests to the writer how to develop his theory for the definition of progress. He divides *progress* into two words, keeping the same pronunciation but changing the spelling of one. Then he proposes that one of the words has no connotations, while the other would retain the positive connotations that the word *progress* always had. He also includes at least one idea that is subject to verification; we could, for instance, conduct a scientific study to determine whether good social changes are accompanied by improved moral attitudes.

Once you have worked out the new model—the theory and some

testable hypotheses—for your problem, your work on this second major stage of the exploration is finished. You can now write your paper. Remember, though, that several types of papers can result from this stage, depending on how far you progressed into the stage or how much was done by others before you began. Other influences that determine the type of paper to write are your assignment, the amount of time you have, and plain old luck.

Exercises on Searching for a New Answer

1. First consider how well you understand the original dogma of concern in your paper and the reasons it was rejected. If you have not already done so, write a brief discussion of this matter. Should your understanding prove to be inadequate, read some essays about the problem.
2. Have any new answers already been proposed? If so, list them and briefly explain, in writing, the strengths and weaknesses of each. Show your list to your classmates to see if they can add other possibilities.
3. State the problem in question form. You're looking for a question that, if answered, would give you the new model that you need. Show your question to your instructor and classmates and, if necessary, rewrite it to clarify it or to narrow your task.
4. Identify the key reality in question. That is, identify the objects (for example, Polynesians, fetuses) you must study in order to gain a fresh look at them. Identifying the correct reality is trickier than it sounds, so you may want to check your decision with your instructor. When you think you have identified the key reality, figure out a method for reexamining it. First-hand examination is best (for instance, someone interested in unemployment could interview some unemployed people), but reading about the reality in reference books may suffice.
5. Try to project the kind of answer you need. Begin with the following sentence: "An appropriate answer to my question will have the following characteristics." Then list the characteristics.
6. Look around for a model that has the characteristics you need. Try this consciously but expect that your subconscious will make the final choice for you. Give yourself plenty of time so that the subconscious can work.
7. Eureka! You have the new model. If it is based on a borrowed model, list the characteristics of the borrowed model and next to each one explain how it would be transferred into the new model. (Remember, you need not apply every part of the borrowed model.) If you did not use a borrowed model, still list the characteristics of the new model. If there is any way that you can diagram the new model, do so, for diagrams are excellent ways to develop theories; they also help you write the paper.
8. Write a first draft of the paper. Do this even if (as is probable) you could not do some of the preceding exercises. Remember, writing itself is

exploratory in many ways, so you can expect appropriate material to come to you as you write. Write the story of your exploration simply and directly, putting yourself into the story. Don't worry about organization or editing at this time.

AN OUTLINE OF THE EXPLORATORY PROCESS

STAGE I: Raising Questions (the reader issue)
- A. Dogma
  - 1. Recognize and understand the dogma.
  - 2. Understand the supporting arguments for the dogma.
- B. Anomaly
  - 1. Note evidence (facts, objects, beliefs) that does not fit the dogma or cannot be explained by it.
  - 2. Note weaknesses in the arguments for the dogma.
  - 3. Find other analyses of the dogma's weaknesses.
- C. Crisis
  - 1. Seriously question the truth of the dogma.
  - 2. Express feelings of discord and excitement.
  - 3. Reject the dogma.

STAGE II: Searching for a New Answer (the writer issue)
- 1. Specify the question to be answered.
- 2. Examine other attempts to answer the question. Reject these suggested answers.
- 3. Reexamine the reality in question, collecting more evidence about it.
- 4. Project the nature of the answer you need. This may require narrowing the question.
- 5. Borrow and try out several models.
- 6. EUREKA! You identify the model that works.
- 7. Develop the theory.

STAGE III: Testing the New Answer (the subject-matter issue)
- 1. Identify a testable hypothesis from your theory.
- 2. Conduct research to test the hypothesis, or try to construct a satisfactory argument to support it.
- 3. Confirm, deny, or modify the theory in accordance with your findings.

ORGANIZING THE PAPER

In contrast to other types of writing for which the organizational pattern is specified by tradition or by editors, written exploration has no recommended pattern. (Patterns *have* been established for oral explorations, such as panel discussions, but that's another matter.) This is partly because the idea of writing exploratorily is fairly new and partly because many explorations are incomplete, being picked up in the middle of things, so to speak, or dropped before an answer is found or tested.

Let us first take a look at the organizations of the two essays included with this chapter, and then make a few general recommendations about how you can organize your paper. Now that we have some terminology for what occurs in an exploration, we can label the parts of each outline. (The numbers in parentheses are paragraph numbers.)

THE ORGANIZATION OF "A THEORY" (THE FIRST CHAPTER OF KON-TIKI)

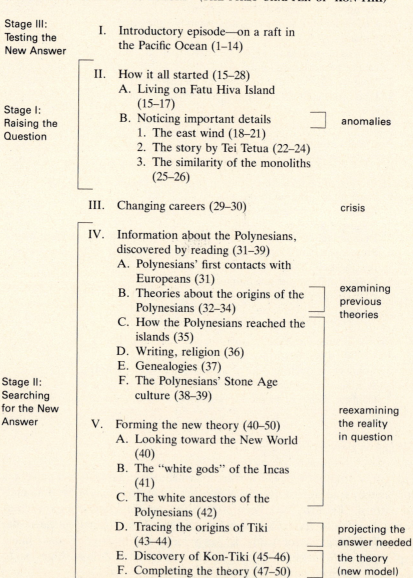

Stage III:
Testing the
New Answer

I. Introductory episode—on a raft in the Pacific Ocean (1–14)

Stage I:
Raising the
Question

II. How it all started (15–28)
   A. Living on Fatu Hiva Island (15–17)
   B. Noticing important details   anomalies
     1. The east wind (18–21)
     2. The story by Tei Tetua (22–24)
     3. The similarity of the monoliths (25–26)

III. Changing careers (29–30)   crisis

IV. Information about the Polynesians, discovered by reading (31–39)
   A. Polynesians' first contacts with Europeans (31)
   B. Theories about the origins of the Polynesians (32–34)   examining previous theories
   C. How the Polynesians reached the islands (35)
   D. Writing, religion (36)
   E. Genealogies (37)
   F. The Polynesians' Stone Age culture (38–39)

Stage II:
Searching
for the New
Answer

      reexamining the reality in question

V. Forming the new theory (40–50)
   A. Looking toward the New World (40)
   B. The "white gods" of the Incas (41)
   C. The white ancestors of the Polynesians (42)
   D. Tracing the origins of Tiki (43–44)   projecting the answer needed
   E. Discovery of Kon-Tiki (45–46)   the theory
   F. Completing the theory (47–50)   (new model)

ORGANIZATION OF "WHAT IS PROGRESS?"

I. Introduction—the problem of
    defining progress (1)

**Stage I:
Raising
the
Question**

II. The initial definition
    A. The writer's original definition
       (2a) — dogma
    B. Criticism of the writer's definition
       (2b) — anomalies
    C. Rejection of the definition (3a) — crisis
    D. The kind of new definition
       needed (3b) — projection of
       answer needed

III. Alternative definitions
    A. Alternatives inferred from the
       criticisms (4)
    B. Definitions from dictionaries (5) — examination of
    proposed and
    existing
    theories

**Stage II:
Searching
for the
New
Answer**

IV. Examples of progress
    A. Scientific and technological
       examples (6a)
    B. Social examples (6b) — reexamination
    of the reality
    in question

V. The problem of connotations
    A. Types of progress that do and do
       not deserve good connotations
    B. Analogy to *dam* and *damn* — borrowed model

VI. The new definitions
    A. Scientific and technological
       progress (8a)
    B. Social *progresse* (8b) — new model
    C. Strengths and weaknesses of the
       definition of *progresse* (9)

As you can see from these outlines, both essays are organized sequentially, moving in a fairly straight line through the exploratory stages. This is a narrative pattern in which the authors tell the story, step by step, of their thinking. Perhaps the original thoughts of the authors were not quite this neat, but the sequence has been arranged to make everything sound fairly logical.

There are only a few minor exceptions to the sequential pattern. Heyerdahl's chapter begins in the middle of Stage III (testing the new answer), then "flashes back" to the beginning of the exploration. Heyerdahl also actually begins the exploration with the anomalies rather than the dogma, a reasonable variation since recognition of anomalies logically precedes the realization that there is a dogma to be explored. (Eibl, who was simply assigned to investigate the definition of progress, started with the dogma, as the outline indicates.) Finally, we cannot separate the dogma of Stage I in Heyerdahl's essay from the "other suggested answers" at the beginning of Stage II. Perhaps this occurs because the writer himself forgot what he knew in the beginning.

Also worth noting is the amount of space the two authors spend on the various parts of the exploration. Heyerdahl gives the most space to anomalies and the reexamination of the reality in question (i.e., the Polynesians). Eibl also gives considerable space to anomalies but devotes the largest portion of his paper to examination of existing alternative definitions. In Heyerdahl's case the reason for his space allotment is easy to infer. Since he was writing for a general audience, he spends his time on those aspects of the search most interesting to a general audience. If he were writing for a more scientifically minded audience, he would have had to expand the discussion of the existing theories to disprove them more definitively. Eibl's case is more difficult to explain. Perhaps the best guess is that he uses so much space on the existing alternatives because that is where he spent most of his own time during the exploration.

When you begin to revise the rough draft that you have written, you can use the two samples discussed here to help you. Very likely, your paper is too long and rambles too much. Furthermore, some parts are inadequately developed and others use too much space retelling what everyone already knows. Your job of organizing will involve expanding some parts and condensing others and rearranging material to improve the sequence.

Perhaps your best starting point for accomplishing these two steps is to choose an audience for the paper. For most topics there are two likely audiences: those who could implement your idea and those who could pressure the authorities to implement it. For example, if your idea is for a change in college regulations to benefit students, you could write for those in charge (e.g., the student government or the board of trustees) or to the students themselves. Then your next task, choosing what to expand or condense, would be guided by what the chosen audience already knows and believes. For instance, some people who follow a given dogma don't know that they are doing so. You would then expand the part of the paper that explains the dogma, demonstrating that a dogma, supported by certain facts and reasons, does exist. Other people might know that they are following dogma but might not be aware that serious anomalies exist; so you would concentrate on anomalies. Each part of the paper, each stage of exploration, is thus open to being expanded or condensed depending on the audience you have chosen.

When revising the sequence of your paper, consider doing more than just putting it in a more logical order; also consider what is necessary to keep the audience reading the paper through to the end. For instance, if you suspect that they will be greatly offended by your questioning of the dogma, you might put the anomalies first, and then when you have demonstrated the truth of them, you could point out that these anomalies just might be construed as disproving the dogma. Or, if you have readers who are aware of both the dogma and the anomalies but don't seem worried enough to make any changes, you could start with the crisis; showing the readers that a great many people are upset about the situation might arouse sufficient interest to keep them reading in order to see what solution you can offer.

Exercises on Revising the Paper

1. Reread your draft carefully and identify the various parts of the exploration. Label the parts in the margin.
2. Choose an audience for the paper and then consider the following questions about the audience: (a) Do they know that a dogma exists? (b) How strongly do they hold the dogma? (c) How much do they know about the anomalies? (d) Do they recognize the existence of a crisis? What is their attitude toward the crisis? (e) Which of the existing proposals for changes in the dogma does the audience know about? (f) How much do they know of the realities in question? (g) To what extent must your theory be worked out in order to seem plausible?
3. Outline the paper that you have written and then revise it in accordance with the needs and beliefs of the audience. In the new outline, indicate not only a revised sequence of material but also the parts that will be expanded and condensed. (This need not be a formal outline, just something to use for a guide as you rewrite the paper.)
4. Write the revised version. Use the outline as a guide, but feel free to depart from it if better ideas occur to you.

THE STYLE OF EXPLORATORY WRITING

Since most explorations are oral or mental, most comments about style in exploration have concentrated on these models. It has been pointed out that such explorations are characterized by arguments, questions, fumblings, and other signs of search.

Written explorations are seldom so informal. Yet they still contain a few marks of style that give the writing a distinctively exploratory flavor. For example, much of the language is the same objective, denotative language that is found in informative or explaining-and-proving papers. This is only to be expected, since exploration, like information and explaining and proving, is one of the referential aims. But within this general aura of objectivity certain other stylistic features occur that are less common in the other referential aims.

Perhaps the most obvious deviation from pure objectivity is that exploratory writers put themselves into the story. We learn, for example, of Heyerdahl's sojourn in the South Seas, of his wife and parents, and his military service in World War II. The author of "What Is Progress?" intrudes less, but we still learn that Eibl sought criticism of his initial definition of progress and that he likes some definitions and doesn't like others.

A second obvious mark of style is an aura of *tentativeness* in which the authors demonstrate their exploratory attitudes. When they are not certain, or were not at a particular time, they say so, using words such as *it seems* and *perhaps*. They ask questions and propose tentative answers that they label *suspicions* and *theories*. In these ways, the authors seek to remind their readers that they are making a proposal and not proving a thesis.

Exercises on Revising for Style

1. Reread your paper to see that the style marks it as exploratory. Put yourself into the story, but don't overdo it. Wherever you are, or were, unsure of your ideas, retain the phrases that demonstrate your uncertainty. If you eliminated them from previous drafts, put them back in. Finally, keep the overall tone reasonably objective.
2. Rewrite the paper one more time, all the way through, to incorporate changes you made in the style. Feel free to make additional changes in content and organization if they seem appropriate.

Supplementary Exercises

1. Mixing models: The groups listed below can be seen as organizations; most are run as hierarchies, with some levels of the organization higher or lower than others. And at each level of the hierarchy, there is a model representing the duties, rights, and responsibilities of people at that level. Choose two of these organizations, one that you believe works well and another that seems to need improving. Then write an essay in which you "borrow" from the successful model to improve the other one. Either suggest changes in the overall hierarchy or just seek to improve one level of the organization.

   For example, suppose that you think your college is a hopeless mess, organizationally, but you were in the army and liked the way the army worked. Consider how you could borrow some features of the army to improve the college.

ORGANIZATIONS

a. The army	f. A factory
b. The U.S. federal government	g. A store
c. The United Nations	h. A high school
d. A college	i. A family
e. A religious sect	j. A corporation

2. **Redefining a word or phrase: At the end of these instructions is a list of words or phrases that have controversial or slippery definitions. Choose one of them (preferably one that you're personally involved with) and explore it to pin down a satisfactory definition. The following steps are suggested as a way of approaching the task:**

   a. **Write out the definition that you have in mind at the top of a blank sheet of paper. Do this without using a dictionary.**

   b. **Pass the sheet around the class, and ask each student to write comments on your definition. You are looking for criticisms.**

   c. **Study the comments, and try to summarize them. In particular, look for the following kinds of anomalies:**

      (1) **The boundaries of the definition are fuzzy. People are not certain what is included or excluded from the definition.**

      (2) **Connotations are wrong or confusing, which causes some people to have improper attitudes toward the things the word stands for.**

      (3) **People differ in what things they apply the word to.**

      (4) **The definition popularly given in dictionaries or elsewhere is not the one people actually use.**

   d. **Look up the word in several dictionaries. If your topic is a phrase, you may have to try some other reference works.**

   e. **Find and read at least one essay on your topic.**

   f. **Make a list of things that the word stands for. Also list some things that are closely related but that your word does *not* stand for.**

   g. **Think of a word or phrase that has problems similar to yours but where the definition is satisfactory.**

   Now write an exploratory essay on your topic. In general, follow the model provided by the student essay in this chapter.

POSSIBLE TOPICS

death	crime	deviancy
pornography	dangerous drug	educated person
freedom	victimless crime	privacy
adult	profession	equality
work	musician	peace
the good life	objectivity	national security

3. On the following pages is an exploratory essay about the decline in SAT
    scores. Read the essay, and then try to answer the questions below.
    a. What is the dogma raised in the essay?
    b. What is the principal anomaly in the dogma?
    c. Identify words and phrases that indicate a crisis. Is this the author's
        crisis or a larger one?
    d. The author says that he is going to "raise some possible explana-
        tions." Before one explains the answer to a question, it's helpful to
        know what the question is. What *is* the question? (Try to be more
        precise than the title of the essay.)
    e. The possible explanations are given as phrases at the beginnings of
        several paragraphs. Are these mainly revisions of the dogma or are
        they suggestions for new answers to the question?
    f. What is the relationship of Dr. Upton's experiment to the problem at
        hand?
    g. Is there a new hypothesis? If so, what is it? If not, what *is* the purpose
        of the last paragraph?

SAT SCORES: WHAT HAPPENED TO THE BEST AND THE BRIGHTEST?

Fred M. Hechinger

1   According to popular as well as psychological folklore, each new American
generation is not only taller but also smarter than any of its predecessors.
Thus, it was not surprising that the monitors of the 1960's youth culture
proclaimed adolescents of the era as the best and the brightest.

2   Against such a background, what is the country to make of the recent
disclosure by the College Entrance Examination Board (CEEB) that high
school students have been scoring steadily worse on the Scholastic Aptitude
Tests (SATs) administered to most college applicants? The initial reaction to
the news that the scores have been in a ten-year downhill slide is one of
shock and disbelief.

3   The tests, which the Educational Testing Service at Princeton, New
Jersey, administers for the CEEB, are the pride of objective testing. The
separate scores for verbal and mathematical aptitude run from a low of 200
to a maximum of 800. In 1962–63 the mean scores had been 478 (verbal) and
502 (mathematical); in 1972–73 they were 445 and 481 respectively. Over one
million students took the tests last year.

4   "At first, the news hit me square between the eyes," said Ernest L.
Boyer, chancellor of the State University of New York. "The experts had told
us not only that the kids were brighter and more sophisticated, but also that
the difference constituted something like a quantum jump upward."

5   After the initial shock, however, Boyer and other observers began to
raise questions—about the tests and the schools as much as about the

youngsters. Even though none of the questions have as yet been satisfactorily answered, they are beginning an appraisal without which these startling statistics could be grossly misinterpreted and abused. For the anti-youth forces, who have been waiting for an opportunity to cut the kids down to size, the new statistics are an invitation to vindictiveness.

6   Because any hasty, unproven conclusion that "they don't make either the kids or the schools like they used to anymore" could set off another round of acrimonious controversy, a sensible reaction would be to raise some possible explanations for dispassionate discussion.

8   "More is worse." The dramatic increase in college applicants during the 1960's should have been expected to lower the scores, particularly since a greater proportion of the new candidates came from the lower socioeconomic sector. If James S. Coleman is right in saying that home background is the most important factor in school achievement, then it is more than likely that the environment would also affect a student's aptitude. Indeed, CEEB statistics also confirm that students from high-income families score higher on the SATs.

9   Tempting as it is to accept the demographic logic of that explanation and to drop the matter, the answer turns out to be less than airtight. One informed CEEB source points out that the number of test-takers actually had stabilized at about one million several years ago. Yet the decline in the scores continued. Clearly, other possible contributing factors must be considered.

10   The McLuhan generation. The new generation's minds have been shaped far more by the electronic than by the print media. Children today see and hear more (and understand at least some of it at an often frighteningly early age), but they read less and have less time for reflection. After his first year of teaching English in a middle-class section of Brooklyn, a young man complained: "If I give them fifty pages of overnight reading, I have a revolution on my hands."

11   The other side of the coin was revealed in the sudden, startling comment by our own son when he was only five years old. "You're nicer than the average mummy." On investigation, it turned out that he had been a steady viewer of television's Yogi Bear, who is "smarter than the average bear."

12   High school students have grown up amid a steady onrush of national and international crises that call for sophisticated responses, and amid an equally steady decline in measurable norms of intellectual and social standards established by society and school. Such uncertainty makes it harder to answer objective questions.

13   Nonverbal classrooms. The schools have adjusted to the new style by sacrificing much of the analytical part of learning to mere spontaneity. Under the onslaught of critics who consider all drill autocratic, teachers have moved away from parsing sentences, analyzing ideas, and preparing outlines. Modern languages enrollment has declined sharply. Yet those are the activities that sharpen the talents that lead to high SAT scores.

14   In 1960, Dr. Albert Upton, professor of English at Whittier College, subjected 280 freshmen to a regimen of examining the relationship between "words and things." After eight months of such training, the students' I.Q.s had been raised by an average of ten and one-half points. SATs are related

closely enough to I.Q. tests to make it quite likely that a decline in the schools' emphasis on the analytical skills may lower the scores of even bright and sophisticated students.

15   The easy way out would be simply to charge that the tests have not kept pace with a changing generation of youngsters. While that is probably true, it evades the real issue—how damaging a retreat from analytical, print-oriented schooling will be in the long run. The greater sophistication of the New Generation, with instant experience and instant reaction, could be an enormous asset. But unless its experience is cross-fertilized with the deliberative and analytical skills of the pre-electronic age, that generation may go intellectually soft—all heart and little mind.

16   Nothing quite so alarming need yet be indicated by the decline in the SAT scores. The trend does not necessarily prove that the new generation is not as bright as its admirers had thought. But it does suggest that the alignment between students, schools, society, and tests may no longer be in balance. A simplistic response would be to fiddle with the tests; a more fruitful approach would be to try to learn more about the relationship between young people and the intellectual environment that dominates their education and indirectly affects their aptitudes.

Writing Poems and Stories

THE IMPORTANCE OF LITERARY DISCOURSE

This is a chapter concerned with literary discourse—with "creative" writing—and specifically with the writing of poems and stories. We have had literary discourse ever since the first person became intrigued with the possibility of manipulating and arranging language for the purpose of creating something new out of it. Something different. Art.

The Greeks referred to literary discourse as *poetry*, a word derived from their verb *to make*. For us as for them, a writer of literary discourse is a maker, a person who uses language with imagination and care. It is precisely the chance to create a new language object—the story or poem, however long or short—that motivates the writer or poet to take pen in hand at all. Without the artist's motivation to go beyond conventional discourse, there could be no literature. A writer, Joan Didion tells us, is "a person whose most absorbed and passionate hours are spent arranging words on pieces of paper."

The product of this process, the original work of art crafted from the language, bears witness to the artist's toil:

Good friend for Jesus' sake forbear,
To dig the dust enclosed here.
Blest be the man that spares these stones,
And curst be he that moves my bones.

These are the words on Shakespeare's grave, and they say much more than "Hands off, please (or else)!" That message was old even in Shakespeare's time—but not the unique shape and flow of the words through which it's sent, a shape and flow that say, "here lies a man whose passion was to arrange words on pieces of paper."

The working assumption behind this chapter, then, is that while poems and stories can be expressions of the writer's personality (self-expression), representations of reality (sources of reference and information), or attempts to instruct or convince (persuasion), poems and stories are above all unique language structures in and of themselves (creations). It is only because the object of art itself exists that we can say that the writer's expression was creative, that a message of some kind was conveyed, and that the reader's intelligence and emotions were affected.

Literary discourse is important, then, as an aim, a process, and the product of the writer's play with language.

SOME EXAMPLES OF POETRY AND FICTION

No attempt is made here to present the full range of possibilities inherent in the idea of literary discourse. The selections provided are simply meant to exemplify poetry and fiction as types of discourse and to suggest the kinds of creative options open to a potential writer of poems and stories. Four poems and three stories are included; one example of each type was written by a student.

In reading each poem and story, you should attempt to answer as many of the following questions as possible and to develop connections among your answers:

1. What is the governing principle of organization of this selection? How is this principle reflected in patterns of language and structure?
2. Into what parts or units might this selection be broken? What are its basic units of construction—clauses or images, phrases or sentences, stanzas or paragraphs?
3. What are some of the stylistic features of this selection? Comparison? Contrast? Repetition? Surprise?
4. How does the title contribute to the poem or story as a whole?
5. What is the relationship between meaning and style in this selection?
6. What choices in diction, punctuation, and grammar has the writer made?
7. What basic knowledge of culture (or more specific context) must the reader share with the writer in order to understand the selection?
8. How does the writing of this selection differ from writing done for one of the other aims of discourse (to self-express, to persuade, to inform, to explain, to explore)?
9. Finally, how are the poems similar to or different from one another *as poems*, and how are the stories like or unlike one another *as stories*?

DESIGN

Robert Frost

     I found a dimpled spider, fat and white,
     On a white heal-all, holding up a moth
     Like a white piece of rigid satin cloth—
     Assorted characters of death and blight
5   Mixed ready to begin the morning right,
     Like the ingredients of a witches' broth—
     A snow-drop spider, a flower like a froth,
     And dead wings carried like a paper kite.

     What had that flower to do with being white,
10 The wayside blue and innocent heal-all?
     What brought the kindred spider to that height,
     Then steered the white moth thither in the night?
     What but design of darkness to appall?—
     If design govern in a thing so small.

                         (1936)

NOT WAVING BUT DROWNING

Stevie Smith

     Nobody heard him, the dead man,
     But still he lay moaning:
     I was much further out than you thought
     And not waving but drowning.

5   Poor chap, he always loved larking
     And now he's dead
     It must have been too cold for him his heart gave way,
     They said.

     On no no no, it was too cold always
10 (Still the dead one lay moaning)
     I was much too far out all my life
     And not waving but drowning.

                         (1962)

A HEIFER CLAMBERS UP

Gary Snyder

a heifer clambers up
    nighthawk goes out
        horses
trail back to the barn.
5   spider gleams in his
        new web
dew on the shingles, on the car,
    on the mailbox—
the mole, the onion, and the beetle
10   cease their wars.
        worlds tip
into the sunshine, men and women
    get up, babies crying
children grab their lunches
15   and leave for school.
the radio announces
    in the milking barn
        in the car bound for work
"tonight all the countries
20   will get drunk and have a party"
russia, america, china,
        singing with their poets,
pregnant and gracious,
    sending flowers and dancing bears
25   to all the capitals
fat
    with the baby happy land
          (1968)

THE DINER

Susan Morrison

Sitting at the counter
surviving another night of filmy coffee.
it's here or a flat on South Clark—
    it doesn't matter which apartment
5   they all have mice and dirty-beige walls.

so it's here
    and the girl
        of blue eyelids and weary strawberry curls
        and the empty-faced man in an ancient suit
10   pulling a cigarette from his yellowed sock.

it's here, or nothing.
          (1980)

Next, the stories. Remember that what the stories share with one another is not theme or subject matter but creative impulse, the aim that made them possible.

THE UNICORN IN THE GARDEN

James Thurber

1   Once upon a sunny morning a man who sat in a breakfast nook looked up from his scrambled eggs to see a white unicorn with a golden horn quietly cropping the roses in the garden. The man went up to the bedroom where his wife was still asleep and woke her. "There's a unicorn in the garden," he said. "Eating roses." She opened one unfriendly eye and looked at him. "The unicorn is a mythical beast," she said, and turned her back on him. The man walked slowly downstairs and out into the garden. The unicorn was still there; he was now browsing among the tulips. "Here, unicorn," said the man, and he pulled up a lily and gave it to him. The unicorn ate it gravely. With a high heart, because there was a unicorn in his garden, the man went upstairs and roused his wife again. "The unicorn," he said, "ate a lily." His wife sat up in bed and looked at him, coldly. "You are a booby," she said, "and I am going to have you put in the booby-hatch." The man, who had never liked the words "booby" and "booby-hatch," and who liked them even less on a shining morning when there was a unicorn in the garden, thought for a moment. "We'll see about that," he said. He walked over to the door. "He has a golden horn in the middle of his forehead," he told her. Then he went back to the garden to watch the unicorn; but the unicorn had gone away. The man sat down among the roses and went to sleep.

2   As soon as the husband had gone out of the house, the wife got up and dressed as fast as she could. She was very excited and there was a gloat in her eye. She telephoned the police and she telephoned a psychiatrist; she told them to hurry to her house and bring a straitjacket. When the police and the psychiatrist arrived they sat down in chairs and looked at her, with great interest. "My husband," she said, "saw a unicorn this morning." The police looked at the psychiatrist and the psychiatrist looked at the police. "He told me it ate a lily," she said. The psychiatrist looked at the police and the police looked at the psychiatrist. "He told me it had a golden horn in the middle of

its forehead," she said. At a solemn signal from the psychiatrist, the police leaped from their chairs and seized the wife. They had a hard time subduing her, for she put up a terrific struggle, but they finally subdued her. Just as they got her into the straitjacket, the husband came back into the house.

3   "Did you tell your wife you saw a unicorn?" asked the police. "Of course not," said the husband. "The unicorn is a mythical beast." "That's all I wanted to know," said the psychiatrist. "Take her away. I'm sorry, sir, but your wife is as crazy as a jay bird." So they took her away, cursing and screaming, and shut her up in an institution. The husband lived happily ever after.

4   *Moral: Don't count your boobies until they are hatched.*

THE DACHAU SHOE

W. S. Merwin

1   My cousin Gene (he's really only a second cousin) has a shoe he picked up at Dachau. It's a pretty worn-out shoe. It wasn't top quality in the first place, he explained. The sole is cracked clear across and has pulled loose from the upper on both sides, and the upper is split at the ball of the foot. There's no lace and there's no heel.

2   He explained he didn't steal it because it must have belonged to a Jew who was dead. He explained that he wanted some little thing. He explained that the Russians looted everything. They just took anything. He explained that it wasn't top quality to begin with. He explained that the guards or the kapos would have taken it if it had been any good. He explained that he was lucky to have got anything. He explained that it wasn't wrong because the Germans were defeated. He explained that everybody was picking up something. A lot of guys wanted flags or daggers or medals or things like that, but that kind of thing didn't appeal to him so much. He kept it on the mantelpiece for a while but he explained that it wasn't a trophy.

3   He explained that it's no use being vindictive. He explained that he wasn't. Nobody's perfect. Actually we share a German grandfather. But he explained that this was the reason why we had to fight that war. What happened at Dachau was a crime that could not be allowed to pass. But he explained that we could not really do anything to stop it while the war was going on because we had to win the war first. He explained that we couldn't always do just what we would have liked to do. He explained that the Russians killed a lot of Jews too. After a couple of years he put the shoe away in a drawer. He explained that the dust collected in it.

4   Now he has it down in the cellar in a box. He explains that the central heating makes it crack worse. He'll show it to you, though, any time you ask. He explains how it looks. He explains how it's hard to take it in, even for him. He explains how it was raining, and there weren't many things left when he got there. He explains how there wasn't anything of value and you didn't want to get caught taking anything of that kind, even if there had been. He explains how everything inside smelled. He explains how it was just lying out in the mud, probably right where it had come off. He explains that he ought to keep it. A thing like that.

5   You really ought to go and see it. He'll show it to you. All you have to do is ask. It's not that it's really a very interesting shoe when you come right down to it but you learn a lot from his explanations.

TOGETHER AGAIN

Bruce Ouderkirk

1   "Where do *you* suppose he is, then?" asked Mr. Waubly.

2   Mrs. Kendall, wearing a stiff pair of blue jeans, stood leaning over the kitchen sink, staring out the back window. She brought her menthol cigarette to her lips and blew one faulty smoke-ring at the screen. "I suppose he just ran away," she said, without turning.

3   "Ran *away*?" he said, in a voice that carried a frown. "What for? Because of *me*?"

4   Shrugging, she turned toward the kitchen table to face him, a short man in his mid-forties with bushy red sideburns. A Budweiser T-shirt, strained over his big belly, fell about an inch short of his hairy navel. She saw that he had his right foot—his club—propped on another chair, and that he was frowning at the new black cowboy boot it wore.

5   "It's nothing to worry about," she said.

6   He ran a hand over his thin hair, which was still flattened from the brown felt cowboy hat now resting on the table. "Maybe I shouldn't have moved in at all. Maybe it was a mistake." He twisted his boot, groaning. "This puppy's gonna take some breaking in."

7   She put both hands behind her on the countertop and lifted herself up onto the counter. Dangling her long legs, she smiled at him. "It wasn't a mistake. He just needs to get used to it."

8   "What's so bad about me that needs getting used to?" he asked, scratching his navel. "Don't I measure up to what's-his-name?"

9   "He didn't even *know* him. He was only three years—"

10   "Didn't I buy him a new bike, just like the other two? You don't hear them complaining."

11   "He's different," she said. "It'll just take him a little time. Don't worry."

12   "I don't know," he said, yawning. "Get me a Bud?"

13   Mrs. Kendall hopped down from the counter. She clicked open the refrigerator and tossed a can underhand to him. Flipping it over, he snapped off the tab and sipped the rising foam. "Should we call the police?" he asked.

14   "What for?"

15   "To find the kid. What else?"

16   She shook her head. "I think I know where he is." Leaning over the sink, she peered out the window again. "He takes off every other month, steady as clockwork."

17   "How come?"

18   "Got me," said Mrs. Kendall. She knocked the ash of her cigarette onto a little pile in the sink. "Last time a kid down the street told him his ears stuck

out. Time before that, Mary Weaver said her doll didn't like him. God only knows what sent him off this time.''

19   ''Jesus,'' said Mr. Waubly. ''I'll cure him of that in a hurry. A good whipping's all he needs.'' He clanked the can down on the table, and asked in a tired voice, ''Where is he?''

20   ''I'll get him.'' She pointed out the window. ''Down there, past the neighbors' trees, there's a little creek. Wall Creek. Whenever he skips off, he heads straight down there. He sits on this bench-like thing dug out of the bank. Just sits there and stares at the water till I go get him.''

21   ''And you always do it?'' he asked, pulling at his boot.

22   ''Sure.'' She tapped her ash again onto the little mound in the sink. ''It's just his way of telling me something's wrong.''

23   He took a long swallow of beer, pounded his fist on his chest, and belched loudly. Seeming rather pleased, he belched again, but with little result. ''Where's the other two?'' he asked. ''If we don't leave pretty quick, the whole beach'll be mobbed.''

24   ''They're down at the park.'' She squeaked the faucet on and washed the ashes down the drain. ''Why don't you go pick them up while I get Noel. I'll meet you back here quick as I can.''

25   He nodded. Pushing himself up from his chair, he downed the last swallow of beer and flipped the can at the wastebasket; it bounced off the edge and clanged on the floor.

26   She chased down the rolling can and, dropping it in the wastebasket, stepped to Mr. Waubly. She tugged down his T-shirt so that it covered his navel. Then she put a hand on his shoulder. ''Glen, will you talk to Willie when you get him? When I came in the kitchen this morning, I saw him dart out the door with one of his friends, and I'm sure he had a can of beer in his hand.''

27   ''That little bastard,'' he said with a smile. ''You bet I will. Sneaking off with my beer. You bet.''

28   She patted his pot belly. ''I wish you wouldn't keep any in the house. But if you have to, at least scare him away from it.'' She smiled. ''And don't worry about this,'' she said. ''It'll just take them a little while to get used to it. But I'm glad to have you here, and I know they really are, too.''

29   ''I'm not worrying,'' he said, tapping his fingers on his thigh. ''I'll be back in a few minutes. You see if you can talk some sense into that one,'' he added, nodding toward the window. The T-shirt rose again as he stretched his shoulders. Then he turned and tap-clumped away, the new boots making him moan softly with every other step.

30   Mrs. Kendall stopped a moment when she reached the shade of the towering oaks. She took a deep breath of the cool air, listened closely to a blue jay singing overhead, brushed back her dishwater-blond hair which the breeze was slightly ruffling, and then moved on toward the creek. The legs of her stiff blue jeans whispered to each other, and she whistled bird-calls, as she walked. At last she reached the familiar cluster of bushes behind which, she knew, on the bank of the creek, a dirt bench had been dug out. She fought her way through the passage between the bushes, snagging and freeing her shirt sleeve, and stepped down onto the bench.

31   Her son's name, in big shaky capitals, was scratched in the dirt at the foot of the bench, but he was nowhere in sight. She whistled five shrill whippoorwill calls, and then stood frozen, listening. She heard nothing. She frowned at her watch, then scanned the trees and bushes, squinting her near-sighted eyes. Finally, she glimpsed a patch of white, about fifty yards down the bank. In her flimsy sandals, she stumbled toward it, cursing the sharp white rocks that stubbed her toes, until the patch took shape at last as the T-shirt of her son.

32   Letting out a whistling sigh, she passed between two thick oaks, entering a clearing where a short log lay half-buried in the ground, its top sheared off as flat as a bleacher seat. Her son Noel was squatting at the far end, holding his knees in his hands and staring at the water. She plopped down at the other end and looked at him with mock surprise.

33   "Fancy meeting you here," she said. "I thought I had this log reserved."

34   The boy kept staring at the creek, which trickled cool and clear in the shade. Besides the T-shirt, he was wearing a baggy pair of cut-off jeans, blue tennis shoes, no socks. Without looking at it, he scratched a large mosquito bite on one of his pale ankles.

35   "Beggars can't be choosers," she said. "I guess we'll have to share."

36   As he just scratched and stared, she began to whistle bird-calls. "Purple martin." She whistled again. "That's a new one. Blue jay."

37   "There's dirty bird feathers there," the boy said.

38   "What?"

39   "Bird feathers," he repeated, looking at her for the first time. "Dirty ones. Where you're sitting."

40   She stood up, brushed off the seat of her jeans, and looked beneath her. "By George. The blue jays been at it again. They raid nests, you know. And fight like the devil." With two fingers she picked up a couple straggly feathers and tossed them to the side, then sat back down and looked at her son. He was staring at the creek again. Propped against the log next to him was a stuffed, yellowed pillowcase with a rubber band wrapped around the top.

41   "I have a look?" she asked, nodding at it.

42   He shrugged, his eyes on the water.

43   She lifted the small pillowcase, peeled off the rubber band, and peered inside. There were three pieces of chalk; two shiny nickels; a small stack of children's books tied together with string, the story of Humpty Dumpty on top; a plastic bag filled with marbles; a shaggy tennis ball; a molar in a clear plastic case.

44   "All your good stuff," she said. "I guess you plan to stay away for keeps."

45   The boy was scratching his name in the dirt with a stick.

46   "Know how to skip a rock?" she asked.

47   He looked up at her and shook his head.

48   "About time you learned, then." She hunted for a flat rock, but at last settled for a rounded one. "Here's how it's done," she said, standing beside him and indicating a side-arm motion. "Nothing to it." Then she let the rock sail; it plunked into the creek.

49   "Didn't skip a bit," he said, clearly let down.

50   "What do you mean it didn't skip?"

51   "It just didn't."

52   "I guess you're right," she said. "But it's not my fault. *First* of all, if you're going to do it right, you need a flat rock. *Secondly*, if you're any kind of rock-skipper at all—not one of these amateurs that aren't worthy of the name—you need more water, a lake for instance. But beggars can't be choosers."

53   She weighed another rock between her fingers, and then side-armed it. Out of the corner of her eye, she saw the boy watch its flight. It churned into the water without a skip.

54   She dropped back down on the log, a little closer to him than before, and shook her head. "A professional rock-skipper would just *cry* at these conditions." Seeing him reach for his stick, she asked, "So why'd you run away?"

55   He started drawing squiggles under his name.

56   "Know why Humpty Dumpty fell off that wall?" She waited, while he paused in his drawing and then started again. "If you don't care, I better not let the secret out. There's no telling what'd happen if it got around that I snitched."

57   The boy stopped drawing. He tapped his stick. "Robert's mom says you're bad."

58   Mrs. Kendall cracked the knuckles of her left hand, then of her right. "Why would she say something like that?"

59   "His dad does, too. Robert told me."

60   "I wonder why they say that," she said, slipping a cigarette pack out of her jeans pocket.

61   "Mr. Waubly."

62   She straightened a bent cigarette between two fingers, then lit it. "What's wrong with Mr. Waubly? I thought you liked him."

63   "You're not Mrs. Waubly. That's why they say it."

64   She looked at the creek. "So you want me to get married?"

65   He drew more squiggles with his stick, and finally shrugged.

66   "Don't you remember how we felt when your father left?" she said, trying vainly to catch his eye. "How we waited for him to come back? We don't want to go through that again, do we? When you're married to someone, you expect him to stick around. We don't have to expect anything from Mr. Waubly. He can come or go as he pleases."

67   "They say it's bad. Robert heard them."

68   She took a reflective puff on her cigarette. "They don't know what it was like before Glen moved in. Now we can pay the rent. And you got a new bike. And Willie has to behave. I'd say it's better than it was. Wouldn't you?"

69   The boy scratched at his mosquito bite. When it began to bleed, he looked up at his mother. "But Robert heard them. He told me. She says you're bad. His dad, too."

70   Wincing, she took one last puff on her cigarette, and flipped the butt creekward. Then she slid down the log next to him. "I bet you think you're an expert on Humpty Dumpty," she said. "I bet you think you know everything anybody could *ever* know about him. Well, I'll let you in on a little secret." She peered along the bank as if fearing spies, then spoke in slightly more

than a whisper: "They don't tell *half* the story in that book. Not the half of it."

71   "What don't they?"

72   "Lots of things. Like how he happened to fall off that wall. But since you don't care—" She picked up her son's stick and drew a large egg, with a mouth drooping at the corners and slippered feet, in the dirt beside his name. She could feel him watching her.

73   "How did he?" he said at last.

74   "How'd who what?"

75   "How'd he fall off the wall?"

76   Smiling, she dropped the stick and held one of his hands. "You won't find this in the book," she said, "but *actu*ally he didn't fall."

77   "Didn't?"

78   "*Actu*ally, he was pushed. It was no accident. But it was still his fault. Know why?"

79   He shook his head.

80   "Because he *let* them push him off. He didn't say a word. Know what he should've done? He should've said, 'You cut that out right now! I won't stand for any of that!' But he didn't. He just let them push him around. And pretty soon they pushed him right off the wall and smashed him in a million pieces."

81   Her son watched a frog hop along the bank. "Couldn't they *ever* put him back together again?"

82   "Not that I heard of. All those king's horses and men tried their darndest. He just shouldn't have let people push him around." She picked up the stick and drew a wide jagged crack across the frowning egg. "He was too fragile. He was a fragile egg, like somebody I think I know."

83   The boy dropped his head.

She reached out and lifted up his chin. "I was like that, too," she said.

84   "Long ago. When I was a girl, I was as fragile as they come. And I used to let people push me around. I had lots of close calls."

85   "Did you ever get cracked?" he asked, looking at the egg.

86   "Almost."

87   "How?"

88   "Well, there was a girl that lived next door. Rhonda *Roode*." She made a sour face and shook her head until her son smiled. "This Rhonda *Roode* was just the meanest, snottiest little brat that ever snitched on the face of the earth. Know what she used to do? She used to tell all the kids at school that I couldn't go to heaven because my mother wasn't married when she had me. And I always let her get away with it. Heck, I believed her. When I said my prayers I used to ask God, if I couldn't go to heaven, wouldn't he at least, please, not let me die."

89   She crossed her legs and, with a thumbnail, deftly picked a pebble from the sole of her sandal. "One day I went home and told my mother all about it. I thought at least she'd take my side. But she just got mad. She said, 'Susanna, if you let people say things like that without screaming blue murder, it's your own fault and you deserve what you get.' So the next day when Rhonda Roode started up her old song, I told the kids that her mom tried to give her to the Salvation Army when she was a baby, but they only

took her diapers and rattle and sent her back blubbering. All the kids loved it. And you know what, after that Rhonda Roode never said another bad word about me. She acted like I was her long-lost friend.''

90   Mrs. Kendall took out a crinkled cigarette and lit its curled tip. ''That's the way it is,'' she said.

91   The boy looked at his elbow a moment, then turned back to her, folding his hands. ''What other ones? What other close calls?''

92   She shrugged. ''There were lots.''

93   ''What other?''

94   ''Well, like my cousin Maureen. When I was in sixth grade, we lived with my aunt and uncle and my stuck-up cousin Maureen. She didn't like me because I moved into her precious paneled room with her. Pink paneling. Know what she used to do?''

95   He shook his head.

96   ''When we were getting ready for school, she used to watch me pick out the clothes I was going to wear—I didn't have much. She'd wait till I was all dressed and we had to leave for school that very minute, and then she'd whisper in my ear, 'Susan, you look just *horrid.*' I wouldn't know whether to go to school or drown myself on the way. Whenever I saw anybody coming down the hall at school, I'd hug the wall so tight I nearly skinned my nose, hoping they wouldn't see me.''

97   She took a puff on her cigarette, and with her sandaled foot rubbed out the crack on her drawing. ''One day when I was just about to drown myself, I remembered old Rhonda Roode. So the next morning when Maureen leaned over and said, 'Susan, you look just *horrid,*' I batted my eyes and told her, 'Why, Maureen, that's just what Randy Hefner was saying about you yesterday.' He was her dream boy, you see, but he didn't really care a gnat for her and she knew it. It shut her up for good. After that, when I met somebody in the hall, I just smiled my brightest. I knew I didn't really look the least bit horrid, she'd only been saying it because she had to share that pink-paneled room with me.''

98   The boy glanced again at his elbow. ''What other ones?''

99   ''Other ones?'' Looking down at the egg, she rubbed her forehead and sighed. ''I don't know. There were lots. But you get the idea, you're no dummy. You just can't let people push you around.'' She patted his hand gently.

100   ''Like Robert?''

101   ''Like Robert, like his mom and dad, like that snotty Rhonda Roode. Those kind just try to push us off the wall. They break more eggs than blue jays.'' She brushed the hair out of his eyes. ''Shells get thicker with time, but yours is still tender. They could smash you in a million pieces like old Humpty Dumpty.''

102   After a moment, the boy shook his head. ''Not Robert. His mom and dad are nice. They built him a clubhouse with real curtains on the window. You pull a string and they open. Then you pull the other side and they close, and nobody can see inside.''

103   ''You never can tell,'' she said. ''I bet they helped push poor Humpty Dumpty off that wall. I wouldn't doubt it a minute.''

104   ''They never *could* put him back together again,'' he said, and looked out

at the creek. His mother followed his gaze. A frog leaped from the edge of the bank, plopped into the middle of the creek, and swimming slowly at first, then more swiftly, disappeared with the cold current. Finally he turned back to her. "I got a scratch."

105   "Let's see."

106   He stretched out his elbow to her. She bent her head down and squinted to see the scratch.

107   "I think I need a Band-Aid."

108   "I guess we better go back and get you one. Then, know what? Mr. Waubly's going to take us all to the lake, and I'll show you how to *really* skip a rock."

109   "Really?"

110   "Sure." She got up and lifted him to his feet. "I'll race you back," she said. "Last one there's a rotten egg."

PREWRITING

Choosing Topics for Poems and Stories

Literary discourse is *creative* because of the writer's individual need to create out of language something different, something new. But the truth is that most writers of poems and stories rarely begin with fully developed topics in mind—let alone fully structured forms. Rather, most writers begin with an inkling of a theme, a reaction to an event, a striking detail, a single poetic line, or a fragment of dialogue. The inkling, reaction, or single piece of what will eventually be the finished product is a kernel, or seed, from which the poem or story grows.

Furthermore, while creative writers may choose their topics, it is just as common for topics to choose writers. For even if we could all get together on what the "right" topics for poetry and fiction are, we'd still have a difficult time limiting our concerns to only these. After all, human experience can be chancy and unpredictable and is inevitably a matter of more than love and life, wine and roses. So no theme or topic is inherently good or bad, with or without potential for a poem or story. It is the writer's job to be acutely attentive to all aspects of experience (positive or negative, expected or unexpected) and to identify and select its most promising kernels and nurture them in the mind.

Topics, then, are not invented or even planned so much as perceived and identified—that is, located in and taken from the memory, imagination, and actual experience of the writer.

How do you know when you've identified a topic? It's easiest, perhaps, when a complete line of poetry or an unmistakably compelling concept comes to mind. You may be lucky enough, at the beginning, to come up with a line such as Stevie Smith's "Not waving but drowning" or a controlling idea like Bruce Ouderkirk's of Humpty Dumpty not falling but being pushed. But barring such a fortunate turn (good luck plays a minimal role in successful writing, no matter what kind), look for that kernel of experience in a striking image or detail. Even if you've begun writing with a general mood or emotion in mind (depression, for example, or sheer love of life, or guilt), ask yourself what concrete detail or image or analogy has caused that mood or emotion to enter and remain in your head—and might enable you to transfer it into the reader's. It might be a spider or a moth (or both), a heifer, a unicorn, a shoe. It might be the diner down the street or a nursery rhyme you'd almost forgotten about.

A good poem or story is always a fusion of detail and topic, so in finding at least one detail that works you'll be starting out well. Of course, the more details the better, and a sure sign that you've got a good topic is that you are able to come up with a list of details that might find their way into the poem or story. Images and details ultimately have a relationship in terms of sequence and shape, but the writer must have more than one to work with. "A dimpled spider, fat and white" is intriguing, but even more so when linked with "dead wings carried like a paper kite."

In fact, a poem or story, like any other piece of writing, is a whole made up of many parts: details and images, words and sounds, feelings and ideas. It is the writer's job to combine all of these in a way that makes clear their relationship to each other. For Frost the key images are of the white spider, flower, and moth; for Susan Morrison the key details are the tainted coffee, walls, cigarette, and sock. For W. S. Merwin the worn-out Dachau shoe is the controlling detail for a series of related facts, including the Russians and the kapos, the German grandfather and the Jews, the sense and the smell of persecution and death.

The Logic of Creativity

Creativity, whether in art, architecture, music, or writing, always moves toward a structure. This structure can be functional, of course—a bridge or a concert hall—but it is considered an object of art only if the parts have a sensible and attractive relationship to the whole, a logical and aesthetic relationship to each other. Thus logic and creative impulse, usually considered to be in opposition to each other, are intimately connected by the concept of coherent form.

In both poetry and fiction, *consistency* and *choice* are the keys to coherence and esthetic form. Choice is important because creativity does not automatically entail selection. In fact, it is often when your mind is being the most inventive in remembering and imagining that it is least capable of choosing and organizing details. Ideally, a writer begins with a small treasure of important, but not necessarily functional, material (like that pillowcase full of "good stuff" in Ouderkirk's story)—a treasure that needs to be sifted through in order to determine the best and to eliminate material that, no matter how relevant to the writer's experience, may not finally be useful in the poem or story.

Choice is also important in that a commitment to one word or phrase, one image or idea, one sound or meaning naturally serves to open up relationships with others and to eliminate the likelihood of associations with many more. Choice should always be governed by the rule of consistency. For example, when Frost commits himself to a spider, a flower, and a moth at the edge of a garden, he drastically reduces the logical possibility that he will be able to introduce (let us say) a whale or a baseball game into his poem, though both have been the subjects of poems of their own by other poets. When Ouderkirk chooses to present Mr. Waubly in terms of a cowboy hat, a T-shirt, and a can of beer, he decreases the chance that Mr. Waubly will later be seen drinking from a demitasse or quoting Dostoyevsky. By the same token, when Frost chooses to write about "dark design" in the form of a sonnet and ends his first line with the word *white*, he is obliged by the rules of sonnets to find several rhymes for *white* later on in the poem.

In summary, every choice made by the writer opens up new ones and eliminates a host of others, and the logic of literary discourse asks that all choices of material to be included in a poem or story be consistent with the subject, format, and tone established by what has already been written.

Since, as your reading of the sample pieces has just shown, the forms of poetry and fiction differ significantly from each other, the following discussions of logic, organization, and style will be separated according to literary type.

Exercises on Choosing Topics and Material for Poems and Stories

1. Identify a mood, situation, conflict, or problem that might be presented in a poem or story. Make a list of ten relevant concrete details or specific images that might prove useful to you in writing a poem or story concerning the mood, situation, conflict, or problem.

2. Examine the list of details and images developed for the preceding exercise. Which three of these seem central to the topic and perhaps focal points for its organization and development? Why? Do any of your images or details now seem peripheral, out of place, or otherwise expendable? Why? Replace the expendable details or images with an equal number of new ones.

3. Identify and describe an appropriate larger context in which the details and images from the previous exercise might appear. That is, describe a setting for your material, whether or not that description would actually appear in your finished poem or story.

4. **Briefly explain why the context or setting described in the previous exercise would be appropriate in subject, scope, and tone for your details and images.**

WRITING STORIES: LOGIC, ORGANIZATION, AND STYLE

The Logic and Organization of Stories

As a mode of discourse, a story is narration. That is, a story is a sequence of actions or events that take on significance because of their relationships in time. "Noel ran away and his mother found him and brought him home" is a story—in this case, two events reported in sequence as they occurred in time (chronologically). Typically, however, neither writers nor readers are satisfied with stories as simple as this one; we prefer stories that tell us not only what happened, but *why*, and that take us beyond simple sequences of events to the causes and *consequences* of that action.

"Together Again" is one example of the kind of story that makes us want to read fiction. Its basic units can be identified as follows (the numbers in parentheses refer to paragraphs):

1. *A conflict or problem is presented,* along with some sense of its source: Noel has run off, quite possibly in response to the beer-guzzling, fist-pounding Mr. Waubly. (1–29)
2. The *conflict becomes clearer but* is also revealed to be *more complex* than originally assumed: Mrs. Kendall searches for Noel, finds him, and discovers that his running away is in reaction to her relationship with Mr. Waubly and other people's response to it—"Robert's mom says you're bad." (30–57)
3. The *problem* is more clearly and completely defined and *brought to a climax*: Noel, like Humpty Dumpty—in his mother's rendition, at least—has "Let them push him around." (58–80) But now his mother gives him both courage and a strategy for fighting back. (81–103)
4. The *conflict* between the principal characters is *resolved*: Noel finds a scratch for his mother to tend to, she squints hard enough to locate it, and "together again" they go for the Band-Aid and home. (104–110)

The logic and organization of "The Dachau Shoe" are less obvious. At first glance there seems to be little organization because nothing much seems to happen in it; no one runs away and no one is taken to the booby hatch. The narrator simply describes his cousin's Dachau shoe and then passes on to us the cousin's explanation of how he came to get it and some of the people and events it's connected to.

Yet organization is important here, beginning with the description of the shoe itself (paragraph 1), which makes the reader ask "why?" In fact, the logic of time (chronology) is implicit in the story as soon as Dachau is mentioned, since the author assumes the reader will recognize it as the name of one of the German concentration camps set up during World War II for the persecution and extermination of the Jews. The fact of Dachau (and, by extension, the other death camps) is the controlling detail of Merwin's story. In understanding what Dachau was, we see that the shoe is a legacy of "a Jew who was dead," a remembrance (but not a trophy) of the war. Gene didn't feel bad about picking it up, "because the Germans were defeated" and because saving the Dachau shoe wasn't like the looting the Russians did or even like the souvenir-hunting for "flags or daggers or medals" typical of American troops (paragraph 2). It is in the light of Dachau (in all, over 6 million Jews died in the camps) that we understand that Gene is torn between a sense of justice and outrage on one hand (it was "a crime that could not be allowed to pass") and pathos and guilt on the other ("it's no use being vindictive . . . we share a German grandfather . . . we couldn't always do just what we would have liked to do"). We understand both why Gene once picked up the shoe and why he now keeps it in a drawer—pain is his primary concern, not dust. Finally (paragraph 4), we come to understand that Merwin's story is about the total experience the Dachau shoe represents—the death camps themselves, the rain and mud, the smell; the Jew who wore it once and the American soldier who found it and feels obliged to keep it; and finally, how hard it is to take all this in, to comprehend its magnitude and the fact that it actually happened ("A thing like that").

In short, the shoe itself is not very interesting because the story is in Gene's explanations and in the relationships—within individual paragraphs and the story as a whole—that these explanations involve. The details have a logic and order because they are all related to each other in terms of Gene's guilt, anger, sympathy, and regret. In this story the basic conflict is between the part of Gene (and the reader) that feels obliged to remember Dachau and the part that wishes it could forget.

In summary, note that a story typically involves the presentation, elaboration or complication, climax, and resolution of a conflict through the use of interrelated details and incident.

Exercises on the Logic and Organization of Stories

1. In a paragraph, describe a conflict situation that focuses on one of the following: money, work, pain, authority, pleasure, alcohol, tradition or habit, insecurity, failure.
2. Outline a story that will involve the conflict you described in the previous exercise. Use the conflict-complication-climax-resolution breakdown for the major sections of your outline.

3. Write any one of the major sections (paragraph or paragraphs) of the story for which you have developed an outline in the previous exercise.

The Style of Narration

You may have noted that Thurber's fable is composed of fairly short sentences. Of course, the fable format makes us expect this, but we can see that the ordinary and matter-of-fact nature of the sentences helps to emphasize by contrast the rather fantastic nature of the action itself. Note also that Thurber (unlike Merwin) has chosen to incorporate dialogue directly into his story, in particular the words of the wife that come back to haunt her in the end. Finally, note that the most striking (and memorable) stylistic twist of Thurber's story may be the way he makes a small but crucial switch in the particular short sentence that constitutes his moral, a switch that uses a word right out of the angry woman's mouth. And, if we can define surprise as a combination of insight and pleasure (except, in this case, for the wife herself), we experience additional surprise in recognizing that Thurber's story is not about unicorns so much as the creative use of the imagination. (One mark of literature is that it often teaches us something we didn't really expect.) When we fully understand what "The Unicorn in the Garden" is about, we come to appreciate its method: a simple chronological presentation and a surprise ending, coupled with the updated moral borrowed from Aesop's fable.

"Together Again" offers even further evidence that good stories need not depend on lengthy or elaborate sentences. In addition, Ouderkirk's story is noteworthy in that it effectively (and more than the other two) blends narration, description, and dialogue in the creation of character and action (development from conflict to resolution). Merwin's story is essentially the paraphrased dialogue of cousin Gene; there is little narration or story line and little description. Thurber's fable contains brief and simple dialogue and little description. By contrast, Ouderkirk makes use of story, setting, individual characters, and dialogue in creating action that develops, as in drama, before our eyes.

Finally, the most important—because controlling—stylistic device in each of the sample stories is what we call point of view. *Point of view* is the specific relationship the author develops with the material of his or her story as reflected in the perspective and manner of the narration. "The Unicorn in the Garden" is told from the point of view of an *omniscient*, or all-seeing and all-knowing, narrator. An omniscient narrator, who speaks in the third person, has the potential to tell us everything about the characters and action of the story—what is done, thought, and said. Thurber's narrator is able to inform us not only of what the man sees in his garden but that the man "had never liked the words 'booby' and 'bobby-hatch,'" a fact that perhaps even his wife doesn't know. Similarly, at the end, Thurber's omniscient narrator tells us that "The husband lived happily ever after," a piece of information not likely to be available from any of the characters in the story except the man himself (who isn't telling it).

The omniscient narrator clearly controls, by consciously choosing, what we as readers are actually told about the characters and their story. And these choices are crucial. In fact, the two most obvious pitfalls of omniscient point of view are (1) telling the reader so much that the story becomes cluttered by a narrator "showing off" a privileged position and (2) telling the reader so little that the story is obscure in its sparseness and the narrator is resented for being coy. Omniscience, then, is a particularly powerful but potentially hazardous two-edged sword in the writer's hands: it allows the author to tell the reader, in a number of different ways, what the story means (an explicit moral is one of these); but it also makes possible the errors of under- or overtelling.

Effective use of the omniscient point of view requires that the writer understand the degree to which the all-knowing and all-seeing privilege can be taken advantage of in any given story.

"Together Again" exemplifies another kind of point of view, the *objective*. The objective point of view, like the omniscient, is presented in the third person, but is limited in what it knows and can tell the reader. The objective point of view is that of the narrator as spectator (seer) but not commentator. That is, the objective narrator can report or show, as a movie camera or particularly perceptive eavesdropper might, but cannot tell the reader "what the story is about." Thus we are *shown* the story of Mrs. Kendall, Mr. Waubly, and Noel, but without any commentary on the part of Ouderkirk's narrator; we have to figure out the meaning of the story on our own. The objective point of view must obviously make the most of description, dialogue, and action, since these are the writer's only methods for explaining things to the reader.

"The Dachau Shoe" exemplifies yet a third kind of point of view, the *first-person* point of view. In first-person narration the writer tells the story through one of the characters in it. That is, a specific character (but not necessarily one of the major ones) is the reader's particular witness to what happens—what is seen, heard, and done. Thus Merwin's narrator (who is never even given a name) passes on to us what he knows of cousin Gene and his Dachau shoe—in this case making more use of description and dialogue than any striking action in its own right. This point of view, like the objective, is limited in what it can offer to the reader. One result of this is that the writer is given a specific way to limit and focus the information passed on to the reader. Another result is that the choice of narrator, no matter how limited in knowledge, can make the telling of the story as simple or complex and as objective or subjective in its telling as human character permits. That is, any story told by an eyewitness is only as complete and unbiased as that particular eyewitness is, and the author who uses the first-person point of view should always remember that *who* the narrator is has everything to do with *what version* of any given story can be told and *how* it can be passed on to the reader.

A fourth type of point of view is that of *limited omniscience*, presented by an anonymous narrator but limited to the perspective of a specific character in the story. Virginia Woolf's "The Legacy," one of the additional readings at the end of this chapter, is written using the limited omniscient point of view. In using limited omniscience, the writer takes advantage of being able to see into the mind of a particular character (the novelist Henry James called this a "center of consciousness"), but *voluntarily limits the narration* only to a third-person rendering of what this particular character thinks, witnesses, says, and does. Thus "The Legacy" is a combination of objective narration concerning what happens as Gilbert Clandon reads his late wife's diary and omniscient observations on his unspoken thoughts as well as his conversation. Woolf lets us see into Clandon's mind, but because of the limitations of that particular consciousness, the pace and meaning of the story are determined by Clandon's understanding (or misunderstanding) of his wife's diary. Limited omniscience is extremely difficult to use, since it blends the limitations as well as the advantage of both first-person and objective narration.

Your choice of point of view in writing a particular story should depend on what that story is and how you believe it can most effectively be told. (Theoretically, any story can be told from any one of the four points of view described.) As a writer it is both your prerogative to pick the right point of view for your story and your obligation to the reader to stick consistently to that point of view throughout the telling.

Exercises on Narrative Style

1. **Rewrite the story of the Dachau shoe in the style of James Thurber's unicorn fable, using an omniscient narrator. You might consider beginning with the ending—that is, by writing out the moral of the story of the Dachau shoe.**
2. **Rewrite a familiar fairy tale from a point of view different from that in the original.**
3. **Write a one-paragraph *objective* description of a one-room setting for a story. Write a one-paragraph *subjective* description (either strongly positive or strongly negative) of the same setting.**

Further Suggestions for Writing Stories (Refer to Exercise 1 on page 221 for possible story focuses.)

1. **Write a story in which a character is in conflict with some aspect of the natural world—an animal or insect, some form of plant life, snow, sand, water, and so on.**

2. Write a story in which the action takes no more than three minutes to occur.
3. Write a story that develops like "Together Again," almost entirely in terms of dialogue.
4. Write a story in which the central character is in conflict with his or her physical environment. Consider as a possible environment the one-room setting you described in the third exercise on narrative style.

WRITING POEMS: LOGIC, ORGANIZATION, AND STYLE

The Logic and Organization of Poems

The organization of poetry—so obvious in visual terms as we read it on the page—may actually be its most striking feature:

I was much too far out all my life
And not waving but drowning.   [SMITH]

a heifer clambers up
   nighthawk goes out
      horses
trail back to the barn.   [SNYDER]

Whereas in stories the basic units of organization and understanding are sentences and paragraphs, in poems these units are individual lines. Sometimes these lines are complete sentences, as in "a heifer clambers up." Often, however, these lines are only phrases or individual words, made to stand out on their own for emphasis and focus, but in the end linked to each other to complete their meaning: ". . . horses / trail back to the barn."

When we read a poem, it is the arrangement of the lines on the page that creates a *rhythm* in our minds, an emphasis and movement that combines with the meanings of the separate words to give us the total experience of the poem. Writing poems is a matter of creating a synthesis of rhythm and meaning (sound and sense) that is both interesting as a statement but also unique as a language structure.

Any given poem "reads" in terms of a *pattern*, either a pattern handed down from earlier poets (as in the case of Frost's sonnet, "Design") or a pattern established in and for the particular poem (as with "a heifer clambers up"). But the poem is a unique creation only when the pattern is used creatively, when variations are developed out of traditional forms, and when poetic rules accommodate change. Poetic pattern should not lead to the predictable or trite in either structure or meaning. In fact poems, like stories, can delight both writer and reader *because* of their capacity to surprise—as in "Design," where something happens to our expectation that the last two lines of the sonnet (the couplet) will give us a sense of completeness and the "security" a conclusion brings:

> What brought the kindred spider to that height,
> Then steered the white moth thither in the night?
> What but design of darkness to appall?—
> If design govern in a thing so small.

Instead of an answer, we get a question—and a troubling one at that. Poets, like writers of stories, enjoy playing with words.

Another striking observation we can make concerning the logic and organization of poetry is that in a poem, the patterns of meaning are those of *associations* more than those of literal and rational statement. A writer of poetry thinks not only in terms of the denotative meanings of words but also of their connotations, implications, and interactions. In writing "Design," for example, Frost was aware of the connotations (for most readers, anyway) of the words *dimpled* and *witches' broth*. A dimple may literally be "a slight depression in a surface," but the poet knows that most readers associate dimples with cute babies—certainly not with a spider, "fat and white"—and that we will find it disconcerting to see dimple and spider combined. Similarly, a witches' broth is a macabre brew, and by likening the spider, the flower, and the moth to such a mixture Frost forces us to ask who or what has made the macabre tableau possible.

The *sounds* of a poem's words also help to create associations of detail and meaning. When Snyder tells us that "a *h*eifer clambers up / night*h*awk goes out / *h*orses / trail back to the barn," he links these creatures by repeating the sound of *h*. Frost reinforces the semantic connections of *moth*, *cloth*, *broth*, and *froth* through the use of rhyme. Poets combine the salient sounds of language with its extended meanings to make us perceive them as bound together; associations that we may have denied, been only half conscious of, or never thought possible now seem somehow sensible and correct.

Governing the way individual sounds and meanings interact in the various lines is the prevailing rhythm that controls the poem's movement. Since the creation of poetic rhythm is finally as complex and sophisticated as the writer wishes it to be (entire books have been written on the subject), only a basic introduction is presented here.

One kind of poetic rhythm is based on the systematic, but not necessarily ironbound and monotonous, repetition of stresses (or accents) and syllables in the lines of a poem as it develops. This repetition creates the poem's meter. What is usually called *accentual-syllabic meter* is based on a repeated pattern of strongly and weakly stressed syllables in lines whose lengths also form a pattern. In much poetry in English—and in Frost's "Design" and Shakespeare's "Sonnet 71" (at the end of this chapter)—the meter is a pattern developed out of variations and combinations of what is called the *iambic foot*—one light (˘) and one heavy (ˊ) stress combined.

Shăll Í   cŏm páre   thĕe tó   ă súm-   mĕr's dáy?

Thŏu árt   mŏre lóve-   lў ańd   mŏre tém   pĕr áte;

Note here that the basic pattern is of five feet to a line, with each foot composed of one soft/light and one hard/heavy accent. (Each line also contains ten syllables.) In Frost's sonnet, the basic pattern is the same, but there is more variation from the norm (◡ ´) in the individual feet.

Ĭ foúnd   ă dim-   plĕd spí   dĕr, fát   ańd white,

Ŏn ă white   hĕal-áll,   hóld ińg   úp   ă móth

However, just as accentual-syllabic meter allows for variations from the iambic foot, it also allows for more or less than five feet per line, a variety of line lengths in an individual poem, and (even within strict forms, such as the sonnet) quite a bit of latitude in the use of rhyme. Any collection of modern poetry will reveal a wide range of variations and combinations of all of these elements.

The other basic type of poetry is called *free verse*. Free verse is essentially free of the obligation to use rigid patterns of stresses and syllables in developing a poem. Within the basic flow of the English language itself, which seems to be dominated by a kind of iambic rhythm anyway, free verse develops in terms of words, lines, and their relationships to each other. Writers and readers of free verse find it convenient to refer to its movement in terms of overall rhythm or cadences. The poems by Stevie Smith, Gary Snyder, and Susan Morrison are all examples of free verse, as is the poetry of Walt Whitman, e.e. cummings, and many others.

Since writing poetry in one of the traditional accentual-syllabic forms (the sonnet, for example) requires the poet to read and study both the basic patterns and the work of many others, most beginning poets are attracted toward free verse as a form. In light of our understanding of the poet as "maker," this impulse is both natural and limiting. There's no reason for the writer who wishes to create to think of poetry only in terms of established writers and forms; but we should keep in mind that Frost once likened writing free verse to playing tennis with the net down. In poetry, as in other human endeavors, newness and innovation have their fullest meaning only when consciously measured against traditions and norms. Surprises are possibly only on a background of regularity, and freedom has meaning only in a context of expectations and rules.

Exercises on the Logic and Organization of Poems

1. **Write out two lists of descriptive details, one denotative and one connotative, of a setting with which you are familiar. Then, write a poem of 8 to 14 lines that makes use of both lists but stresses the connotative. (You might find a rereading of "The Diner" helpful.)**

2. Write out two lists of seven words each, one concrete and one abstract, that you associate with one of the following feelings or conditions: gluttony, egotism, fear, jealousy, smugness, cynicism. Then, write a poem of 8 to 14 lines that makes use of two or more concrete terms for every abstract one. (In developing the poem, feel free to introduce words not included on your original lists.)
3. Write a couplet—a two-line, end-rhymed poem in iambic pentameter—that makes a statement in one line and asks a question in the other.
4. Find out what a limerick is, and write one on a public figure or current affairs topic.

The Style of Poetry

Good poetry is a highly compressed type of discourse. A poet generally strives to evoke strong perceptions and emotional associations by using as few words as necessary. Writers of short stories are constantly aware of their need to tighten their writing; for poets this need seems even more intense. How, in practice, is this need fulfilled?

In good poetry, as in good prose, *every word counts*. This is because every additional word in a poem has the potential to (1) introduce a whole cluster of new (and perhaps unwanted) associations, and (2) cause the central point of the poem to be lost in a garble of irrelevant material.

In theoretical terms, "every word counts" should remind you that wordiness and repetition are particularly incompatible with the writing of poems. After all, the line is the basic unit of the poem, and even a long poetic line can (and should) only contain so much material. In practical terms, "every word counts" means that the words and combinations of words you use must mean exactly what you want them to mean, neither more nor less; your diction must be precise. Further, "every word counts" means that virtually every line of a poem must offer the reader something concrete. Nothing is more inefficient than losing the reader, and nothing loses the reader more quickly than abstractions or generalizations divorced from concrete detail. Thus a good poet makes constant use of the specifics of life and the facts brought into the mind through our senses. For Susan Morrison filmy coffee, mice, and dirty walls are details that evoke grubbiness, boredom, and fatigue. For Gary Snyder life itself is evoked by simple but concrete details of the everyday—heifer and hawk, spider and mole, mailbox and radio.

In addition, "every word counts" means that every word of the poem must not only be significant and necessary in its own right, but appropriate to the poem as a whole. Every word must be not only consistent with the logic of the subject (as just explained), but also appropriate to the particular theme and tone the writer wishes to convey and compatible with every other word. Having made the choice to present a tableau of "death and blight," Frost cannot violate the tone of this particular poem with the lightheartedness we see in other examples of his work. Having committed himself to a rather free-swinging and joyous poem, Snyder must take care not to let a discouraging word sneak in. In writing poems of your own, always be sure that every word checks out as compatible and consistent within its context—that is, in relation to the other words that surround it, the poem as a whole.

Note that the specific details of our lives and the experiences of our senses are most often conveyed to us through nouns and verbs. It should come as no surprise, then, that nouns and verbs are given even more weight in poems than in stories and that other types of words are given less. "I found a dimpled spider," Frost tells us, and Snyder observes that "a heifer clambers up." And note that even when Morrison doesn't use the noun-verb combination in "Sitting at the counter" and "pulling a cigarette from his yellowed sock," she is actually using a verb in the form of a noun, and the effect is much the same. Finally, recall that the logic of poetry is the logic of associations—connections of comparison, contrast, and implication—and that this logic is partly reflected in the arrangement of a poem's lines. For this reason, poetry has much less need for conjunctions and prepositions than prose does. Conjunctions and prepositions are most often used in prose to connect words and phrases and to otherwise show their relationship to each other.

A few words about poetic license. You no doubt noticed that both Snyder and Morrison not only write free verse but have also taken certain liberties with capitalization and punctuation. Your question may inevitably be: In writing a poem, how much of this sort of freedom can I take? The answer is: As much freedom as is fitting with your need to keep your audience. When poetic license becomes offensive and distracting because it makes you seem self-indulgent or your poem confusing and obscure, you've taken too much.

If you really want to develop as a writer of poems and stories, keep reading the poems and stories of other writers, especially those that have been published. Analyze their work to see how they solve the kinds of problems you come up against in your own efforts to make something new for the language. In addition, see what other writers and other teachers of writing have to say in books and articles on creative writing. Be ready for a wide variety of suggestions and tactics; some of them will be contrary to each other and some of them will be potentially useful to you.

Exercises on Poetic Style

1. **Write a poem of 8 to 14 lines on hostility, guilt, or fatigue in which every line contains at least one concrete term.**
2. **Reduce the poem written in the preceding exercise to 6 to 10 lines; that is, cut your poem by 2 to 4 lines. In addition to deleting words and lines, consider adding or substituting material.**

Further Suggestions for Writing Poems

1. Write a poem of 8 to 14 lines that, like Shakespeare's "Sonnet 71," expresses a specific attitude toward a specific person. For example, see the untitled poem by Jane Freese at the end of this chapter.
2. Write a poem of 8 to 14 lines that conveys the experience of reading "The Dachau Shoe."
3. Write a poem that conveys the mood of the audience at a rock concert.
4. Read "The Legacy," at the end of this chapter, and write a poem of 8 to 14 lines in which Angela speaks to Gilbert Clandon concerning their relationship.

FURTHER READING AND ANALYSIS

Below are more examples of literature for you to read and use as sources of ideas for your own work. After reading the pieces, answer the discussion questions that follow them.

THE LEGACY

Virginia Woolf

1   "For Sissy Miller." Gilbert Clandon, taking up the pearl brooch that lay among a litter of rings and brooches on a little table in his wife's drawing-room, read the inscription: "For Sissy Miller, with my love."

2   It was like Angela to have remembered even Sissy Miller, her secretary. Yet how strange it was, Gilbert Clandon thought once more, that she had left everything in such order—a little gift of some sort for every one of her friends. It was as if she had foreseen her death. Yet she had been in perfect health when she left the house that morning, six weeks ago: when she stepped off the kerb in Piccadilly and the car had killed her.

3   He was waiting for Sissy Miller. He had asked her to come; he owed her, he felt, after all the years she had been with them, this token of consideration. Yes, he went on, as he sat there waiting, it was strange that Angela had left everything in such order. Every friend had been left some little token of her affection. Every ring, every necklace, every little Chinese box—she had a passion for little boxes—had a name on it. And each had some memory for him. This he had given her; this—the enamel dolphin with the ruby eyes—she had pounced upon one day in a back street in Venice. He could remember her little cry of delight. To him, of course, she had left nothing in particular, unless it were her diary. Fifteen little volumes, bound in green leather, stood behind him on her writing table. Ever since they were married, she had kept a diary. Some of their very few—he could not call them quarrels, say tiffs—had been about that diary. When he came in and found her writing, she always shut it or put her hand over it. "No, no, no," he could

hear her say. "After I'm dead—perhaps." So she had left it him, as her legacy. It was the only thing they had not shared when she was alive. But he had always taken it for granted that she would outlive him. If only she had stopped one moment, and had thought what she was doing, she would be alive now. But she had stepped straight off the kerb, the driver of the car had said at the inquest. She had given him no chance to pull up. . . . Here the sound of voices in the hall interrupted him.

4   "Miss Miller, Sir," said the maid.

5   She came in. He had never seen her alone in his life, nor, of course, in tears. She was terribly distressed, and no wonder. Angela had been much more to her than an employer. She had been a friend. To himself, he thought, as he pushed a chair for her and asked her to sit down, she was scarcely distinguishable from any other woman of her kind. There were thousands of Sissy Millers—drab little women in black carrying attaché cases. But Angela, with her genius for sympathy, had discovered all sorts of qualities in Sissy Miller. She was the soul of discretion; so silent; so trustworthy, one could tell her anything, and so on.

6   Miss Miller could not speak at first. She sat there dabbing her eyes with her pocket handkerchief. Then she made an effort.

7   "Pardon me, Mr. Clandon," she said.

8   He murmured. Of course he understood. It was only natural. He could guess what his wife had meant to her.

9   "I've been so happy here," she said, looking round. Her eyes rested on the writing table behind him. It was here they had worked—she and Angela. For Angela had her share of the duties that fall to the lot of a prominent politician's wife. She had been the greatest help to him in his career. He had often seen her and Sissy sitting at that table—Sissy at the typewriter, taking down letters from her dictation. No doubt Miss Miller was thinking of that, too. Now all he had to do was to give her the brooch his wife had left her. A rather incongruous gift it seemed. It might have been better to have left her a sum of money, or even the typewriter. But there it was—"For Sissy Miller, with my love." And, taking the brooch, he gave it her with the little speech that he had prepared. He knew, he said, that she would value it. His wife had often worn it. . . . And she replied, as she took it almost as if she too had prepared a speech, that it would always be a treasured possession. . . . She had, he supposed, other clothes upon which a pearl brooch would not look quite so incongruous. She was wearing the little black coat and skirt that seemed the uniform of her profession. Then he remembered—she was in mourning, of course. She, too, had had her tragedy—a brother, to whom she was devoted, had died only a week or two before Angela. In some accident was it? He could not remember—only Angela telling him. Angela, with her genius for sympathy, had been terribly upset. Meanwhile Sissy Miller had risen. She was putting on her gloves. Evidently she felt that she ought not to intrude. But he could not let her go without saying something about her future. What were her plans? Was there any way in which he could help her?

10   She was gazing at the table, where she had sat at her typewriter, where the diary lay. And, lost in her memories of Angela, she did not at once answer his suggestion that he should help her. She seemed for a moment not to understand. So he repeated:

11   "What are your plans, Miss Miller?"

12   "My plans? Oh, that's all right, Mr. Clandon," she exclaimed. "Please don't bother yourself about me."

13   He took her to mean that she was in no need of financial assistance. It would be better, he realized, to make any suggestion of that kind in a letter. All he could do now was to say as he pressed her hand, "Remember, Miss Miller, if there's any way in which I can help you, it will be a pleasure . . . ." Then he opened the door. For a moment, on the threshold, as if a sudden thought had struck her, she stopped.

14   "Mr. Clandon," she said, looking straight at him for the first time, and for the first time he was struck by the expression, sympathetic yet searching, in her eyes. "If at anytime," she continued, "there's anything I can do to help you, remember, I shall feel it, for your wife's sake, a pleasure . . . ."

15   With that she was gone. Her words and the look that went with them were unexpected. It was almost as if she believed, or hoped, that he would need her. A curious, perhaps a fantastic idea occurred to him as he returned to his chair. Could it be, that during all those years when he had scarcely noticed her, she, as the novelists say, had entertained a passion for him? He caught his own reflection in the glass as he passed. He was over fifty; but he could not help admitting that he was still, as the looking-glass showed him, a very distinguished-looking man.

16   "Poor Sissy Miller!" he said, half laughing. How he would have liked to share that joke with his wife! He turned instinctively to her diary. "Gilbert," he read, opening it at random, "looked so wonderful. . . ." It was as if she had answered his question. Of course, she seemed to say, you're very attractive to women. Of course Sissy Miller felt that too. He read on. "How proud I am to be his wife!" And he had always been very proud to be her husband. How often, when they dined out somewhere, he had looked at her across the table and said to himself, "She is the loveliest woman here!" He read on. That first year he had been standing for Parliament. They had toured his constituency. "When Gilbert sat down the applause was terrific. The whole audience rose and sang: 'For he's a jolly good fellow.' I was quite overcome." He remembered that, too. She had been sitting on the platform beside him. He could still see the glance she cast at him, and how she had tears in her eyes. And then? He turned the pages. They had gone to Venice. He recalled that happy holiday after the election. "We had ices at Florians." He smiled—she was still such a child; she loved ices. "Gilbert gave me a most interesting account of the history of Venice. He told me that the Doges . . ." she had written it all out in her schoolgirl hand. One of the delights of travelling with Angela had been that she was so eager to learn. She was so terribly ignorant, she used to say, as if that were not one of her charms. And then—he opened the next volume—they had come back to London. "I was so anxious to make a good impression. I wore my wedding dress." He could see her now sitting next old Sir Edward; and making a conquest of that formidable old man, his chief. He read on rapidly, filling in scene after scene from her scrappy fragments. "Dined at the House of Commons. . . . To an evening part at the Lovegroves'. Did I realize my responsibility, Lady L. asked me, as Gilbert's wife?" Then, as the years passed—he took another volume from the writing table—he had become more and more absorbed in his work. And she, of course, was more often

home. . . . It had been a great grief to her, apparently, that they had had no children. "How I wish," one entry read, "that Gilbert had a son!" Oddly enough he had never much regretted that himself. Life had been so full, so rich as it was. That year he had been given a minor post in the government. A minor post only, but her comment was: "I am quite certain now that he will be Prime Minister!" Well, if things had gone differently, it might have been so. He paused here to speculate upon what might have been. Politics was a gamble, he reflected; but the game wasn't over yet. Not at fifty. He cast his eyes rapidly over more pages, full of the little trifles, the insignificant, happy, daily trifles that had made up her life.

17   He took up another volume and opened it at random. "What a coward I am! I let the chance slip again. But it seemed selfish to bother him with my own affairs, when he had so much to think about. And we so seldom have an evening alone." What was the meaning of that? Oh, here was the explanation —it referred to her work in the East End. "I plucked up courage and talked to Gilbert at last. He was so kind, so good. He made no objection." He remembered that conversation. She had told him that she felt so idle, so useless. She wished to have some work of her own. She wanted to do something—she had blushed so prettily, he remembered, as she said it, sitting in that very chair—to help others. He had bantered her a little. Hadn't she enough to do looking after him, after her home? Still, if it amused her, of course he had no objection. What was it? Some district? Some committee? Only she must promise not to make herself ill. So it seemed that every Wednesday she went to Whitechapel. He remembered how he hated the clothes she wore on those occasions. But she had taken it very seriously, it seemed. The diary was full of references like this: "Saw Mrs. Jones . . . She has ten children. . . . Husband lost his arm in an accident. . . . Did my best to find a job for Lily." He skipped on. His own name occurred less frequently. His interest slackened. Some of the entries conveyed nothing to him. For example: "Had a heated argument about socialism with B. M." Who was B. M.? He could not fill in the initials: some woman, he supposed, that she had met on one of her committees. "B. M. made a violent attack upon the upper classes. . . . I walked back after the meeting with B. M. and tried to convince him. But he is so narrow-minded." So B. M. was a man—no doubt one of those "intellectuals," as they call themselves, who are so violent, as Angela said, and so narrow-minded. She had invited him to come and see her apparently. "B. M. came to dinner. He shook hands with Minnie!" That note of exclamation gave another twist to his mental picture. B. M., it seemed, wasn't used to parlourmaids; he had shaken hands with Minnie. Presumably he was one of those tame working men who air their views in ladies' drawing-rooms. Gilbert knew the type, and had no liking for this particular specimen, whoever B. M. might be. Here he was again. "Went with B. M. to the Tower of London. . . . He said revolution is bound to come. . . . He said we live in a Fool's Paradise." That was just the kind of thing B. M. would say—Gilbert could hear him. He could also see him quite distinctly—a stubby little man, with a rough beard, red tie, dressed as they always did in tweeds, who had never done an honest day's work in his life. Surely Angela had the sense to see through him? He read on. "B. M. said some very disagreeable things about—." The name was carefully scratched out. "I told him I would

not listen to anymore abuse of—'' Again the name was obliterated. Could it have been his own name? Was that why Angela covered the page so quickly when he came in? The thought added to his growing dislike of B. M. He had had the impertinence to discuss him in this very room. Why had Angela never told him? It was very unlike her to conceal anything; she had been the soul of candour. He turned the pages, picking out every reference to B.M. ''B. M. told me the story of his childhood. His mother went out charring. . . . When I think of it, I can hardly bear to go on living in such luxury. . . . Three guineas for one hat!'' If only she had discussed the matter with him, instead of puzzling her poor little head about questions that were much too difficult for her to understand! He had lent her books. *Karl Marx, The Coming Revolution.* The initials B. M., B. M., B. M., recurred repeatedly. But why never the full name? There was an informality, an intimacy in the use of initials that was very unlike Angela. Had she called him B. M. to his face? He read on. ''B. M. came unexpectedly after dinner. Luckily, I was alone.'' That was only a year ago. ''Luckily''—why luckily?—''I was alone.'' Where had he been that night? He checked the date in his engagement book. It had been the night of the Mansion House dinner. And B. M. and Angela had spent the evening alone! He tried to recall that evening. Was she waiting up for him when he came back? Had the room looked just as usual? Were there glasses on the table? Were the chairs drawn close together? He could remember nothing—nothing whatever, nothing except his own speech at the Mansion House dinner. It became more and more inexplicable to him—the whole situation: his wife receiving an unknown man alone. Perhaps the next volume would explain. Hastily he reached for the last of the diaries—the one she had left unfinished when she died. There, on the very first page, was that cursed fellow again, ''Dined alone with B. M. . . . He became very agitated. He said it was time we understood each other. . . . I tried to make him listen. But he would not. He threatened that if I did not . . .'' the rest of the page was scored over. She had written ''Egypt. Egypt. Egypt,'' over the whole page. He could not make out a single word; but there could be only one interpretation: the scoundrel had asked her to become his mistress. Alone in his room! The blood rushed to Gilbert Clandon's face. He turned the pages rapidly. What had been her answer? Initials had ceased. It was simply ''he'' now. ''He came again. I told him I could not come to any decision. . . . I implored him to leave me.'' He had forced himself upon her in this very house. But why hadn't she told him? How could she have hesitated for an instant? Then: ''I wrote him a letter.'' Then pages were left blank. Then there was this: ''No answer to my letter.'' Then more blank pages, and then this: ''He has done what he threatened.'' After that—what came after that? He turned page after page. All were blank. But there, on the very day before her death, was this entry: ''Have I the courage to do it too?'' That was the end.

18   Gilbert Clandon let the book slide to the floor. He could see her in front of him. She was standing on the kerb in Piccadilly. Her eyes stared; her fists were clenched. Here came the car. . . .

17   He could not bear it. He must know the truth. He strode to the telephone.

20   ''Miss Miller!'' There was silence. Then he heard someone moving in the room.

21   ''Sissy Miller speaking''—her voice at last answered him.

22   ''Who,'' he thundered, ''is B. M.?''

23   He could hear the cheap clock ticking on her mantelpiece; then a long drawn sigh. Then at last she said:

24   "He was my brother."

25   He *was* her brother; her brother who had killed himself. "Is there," he heard Sissy Miller asking, "anything that I can explain?"

26   "Nothing!" he cried, "Nothing!"

27   He had received his legacy. She had told him the truth. She had stepped off the kerb to rejoin her lover. She had stepped off the kerb to escape from him.

Questions on "The Legacy"

1. What do you feel is the topic of Woolf's story? What is the "legacy" of the title?
2. What are the most striking details of the story? Why?
3. What are the principal aspects of Gilbert Clandon's life, as reflected in the story? Which of these did he share with his late wife? Which did he not share? Why?
4. How would you describe Gilbert Clandon's relationship to Sissy Miller? How would you describe Angela's relationship to Sissy? What explains the differences?
5. In light of question 3, explain the logic of Gilbert Clandon's life. Discuss Angela Clandon's legacy to her husband in terms of motivation, method, consequence, and surprise.
6. Discuss the extent to which the logic of the story can help the reader see its key revelation before Gilbert Clandon does.
7. How should we interpret the meaning of the words "Egypt. Egypt. Egypt"? Is it useful to assume Angela's writing here alludes to Shakespeare's *Antony and Cleopatra* (Act IV, Scene xv), in which Antony, who has just stabbed himself, speaks these lines to the Egyptian queen: "I am dying Egypt, dying, only / I here importune death awhile, until / Of many thousand kisses the poor last / I lay upon thy lips"? (In Act V Cleopatra herself commits suicide.)
8. Discuss Woolf's use of limited omniscience as a point of view in "The Legacy." How appropriate is her choice of limited omniscience here, and how might a different point of view have affected the story?

SONNET 71

William Shakespeare

No longer mourn for me when I am dead
Than you shall hear the surly sullen bell
Give warning to the world that I am fled

From this vile world, with vilest worms to dwell:
5   Nay, if you read this line, remember not
The hand that writ it; for I love you so,
That I in your sweet thoughts would be forgot,
If thinking on me then should make you woe.
Oh, if, I say, you look upon this verse
10   When I perhaps compounded am with clay,
Do not so much as my poor name rehearse,
But let your love even with my life decay;
Lest the wise world should look into your moan,
And mock you with me after I am gone.

UNTITLED

Jane Freese

so i stroked your hair,
        and you knew . . .

thought you were asleep.
thought beer and oblivion held you,
5   securely protected from knowing

so i stroked your hair,
        and you knew all the time.

                              (1978)

Questions on the Poems

1. Jane Freese's untitled poem:
   a. Describe the logic and organization (including word associations and pat-
      terns of words and sounds) of this poem.
   b. Describe the style (including diction and repetition) of this poem.
2. Shakespeare's "Sonnet 71":
   a. Describe the logic and organization (including word associations and pat-
      terns of words and sounds) of this poem.
   b. Describe the style (including meter and rhyme) of this poem.
3. The poems by Shakespeare and Freese are addressed to specific people. In each
   case, how does this strategy affect the author's logic, organization, and style?
   For example, what might have been different in the poem due to Freese's
   addressing not the person she does but the reader, concerning the person
   addressed?

Exercises on Combining the Writing of Poems and Stories with the Modes of Writing

1. Poems and stories and description: Write either a poem of 8 to 14 lines or 150 words of prose in which you describe one of the following so as to evoke a specific mood, feeling, or attitude:
   a. a train or subway station at a specific time of day or night
   b. the atmosphere in the room before a final exam
   c. a wedding rehearsal or reception
   d. a locker room an hour after a game
   e. the bedroom of a younger brother or sister

2. Poems and stories and classification/definition: Write either a poem of 8 to 14 lines or a 250-word story in which you classify one of the following in order to explain what it is or why it is important:
   a. test anxiety
   b. a cockroach
   c. the crowd at a baseball game
   d. personal rejection
   e. a social climber or smoker

3. Poems and stories and narration: Write either a narrative poem or a story synopsis of 1 to 2 pages in which one of the following pairs is involved in conflict and change in a period of two days or less:
   a. two sisters or two brothers
   b. an animal and a human being
   c. a person under sixteen and a person over 60
   d. an employee and a supervisor or boss
   e. a young man and an older woman (or vice versa)

4. Poems and stories and evaluation: Write either a poem of 8 to 14 lines or a short story of 3 to 4 pages in which a value judgment is made on some human action; or, write a 2-page evaluation of a poem or story written by someone else in your class. (Review the criteria for poems and stories discussed in this chapter.)

THE MODES OF WRITING

PART II

The Modes of Writing

The first seven chapters of this book deal with the aims of writing. We have distinguished different purposes that determine differences in logic, organization, and style. But another primary influence on each of these areas is the way a writer looks at the subject matter under discussion. We are all aware that a *narration* or story about a basketball player is not the same thing as a *description* of the same player. And a *classification* of kinds of restaurants is not the same thing as an *evaluation* of them. When we distinguish among narration, description, classification, and evaluation we are talking about different ways of looking at objects and experience. These different ways of looking are called *modes*.

How important are the modes of writing? The modes control the organization and development of any piece of writing. For example, a narrative must follow the rules of narrative structures whether it is a short story, a historical account, a parable in the gospel, or a very personal chronicle of what happened on the ski slopes in Colorado. The modes of writing also influence some aspects of prose style, and the choice of a mode even determines to some extent the choice of a writer's subject matter.

FOUR WAYS TO LOOK AT A SUBJECT

In the field of law and rhetoric, the following example, somewhat fictionalized, has long been used to illustrate the necessity of focusing on a particular aspect of a subject. Assume it is March 16, in the year 44 B.C. Cicero, the prominent Roman lawyer, is disturbed early in the morning by a knock on his door. He opens it and admits his friend, Brutus.

"I desperately need a lawyer," confides Brutus. "I'm certain you've heard about Caesar's death, yesterday in the senate. Now the people are accusing Cassius and me of murder and of conspiracy against the state."

"Yes, I heard," replies Cicero. "Did you actually kill Caesar? Or were you somewhere else at the time, and could we obtain witnesses to prove this?"

"Unfortunately, the whole senate saw me there and would certainly witness against me on that question. And, yes, I and several others did kill Caesar. And many senators will witness to that also," answered Brutus.

"So the fact of the killing must be admitted," Cicero concedes. "I can't defend you on the issue of the facts. What about the reason for the killing? Did Caesar attack you first, and did you and Cassius react by counterattacking?"

"I know what you are trying to do—change the category of the act from murder to self-defense—and I wish it could be done," again replies Brutus. "But the fact of the matter is that, although Caesar turned down the requests of Tillius Cimber and several others, and that, although Tillius pulled Caesar's robe from his neck, Caesar certainly did not initiate the violence. And many will testify to that. I'm afraid we can't plead self-defense."

But Cicero hasn't finished. He asks, "Was there a general uproar when Tillius pulled the robe? And did those who defended Caesar fight against those who attacked him? Could we argue that in the heat of the moment many got excited, and that, although Caesar was murdered, it was the result of a general confusion and turmoil?"

Brutus has to discourage this approach also. "Maybe it was unfortunate, but no one came to his assistance. All the witnesses would have to testify that the only people who came armed with daggers were those who killed Caesar. And I am afraid that the act was planned and premeditated. I am afraid it will be judged murder, murder by conspiracy."

"So we must concede the facts and the legal category," worries Cicero. "You did kill Caesar, and it was murder. And for the masses Caesar represents the state, although you and I and others do not see him in that light."

"No, of course not," agrees Brutus. "You know my past and my hatred of tyranny. We conspired not against the state, but to save the state."

"That will be my defense," breaks in Cicero. "I concede the facts of the killing. I concede the category of murder—it was planned and premeditated. But it was a good murder, a conspiracy to save the state. The quality of the act, the value of the murder to the state will constitute a solid defense. That's where we'll take our stand."

So much for Cicero and Brutus. As you may know, history did not follow the course planned by Cicero here. The next year, Antony and Octavius assassinated Cicero, and a short time later, Antony and Octavius defeated Brutus and his army on the plains of Philippi.

But here we are interested in how Cicero chose the aspect of the situation that he would use for the defense of Brutus. At first he hoped that the issue would be a *matter of fact*. If Brutus had been elsewhere and if this could be established by witnesses, Cicero could repudiate the entire charge. The facts, however, were against Brutus. So Cicero then tried to reclassify the charge to one of self-defense: a *matter of definition*. But the *classification* of the act had to be conceded; it was a planned murder. Finally, Cicero decided to attempt the defense by considering the acknowledged facts of the killing and the acknowledged definition of murder at the level of *matters of value*. That is, the killing and the recognition of the killing as murder could be conceded if the murder was a valuable act to the state.

Matters of fact, matters of definition and classification, and matters of value are the concerns of the next four chapters. Eventually, we will divide matters of fact into matters of descriptive fact and matters of narrative fact, so that there will be four matters to consider. But the same issues that Cicero considered in his rhetorical treatise—matters of fact, definition, and value—are crucial questions for us to consider when learning how to narrow a topic down to the relevant issue at hand.

SOME EXAMPLES OF THE MODES OF WRITING

Let us take a more careful look at these *matters*, as they are traditionally called. Some fairly simple examples might help to give us some working distinctions. Read the following selections with two questions uppermost in your mind: (1) What object or objects are being talked about? and (2) What aspects of the objects are given prominence in the writing?

THE GOOSE THAT LAID THE GOLDEN EGG

Aesop

1   There was a man who owned a goose that laid a golden egg every morning. By selling these precious eggs, the man was able to accumulate a store of wealth.

2   But the richer he grew, the greedier he became. He began to be dissatisfied with only one egg a day.

3   "Why not two eggs?" he thought, "or five or six? As a matter of fact, if I cut that bird open, I shall probably find a hundred eggs, and then I can retire and live in luxury for life!"

4   So thinking, he killed his goose, cut her open, and, of course, found nothing.

5   *He who wants more often loses all.*

HIPPARCHUS' CLASSIFICATION OF STARS ACCORDING TO BRIGHTNESS

Meir H. Degani

1   The ancient Greek astronomers classified the visible stars according to their apparent brightness, into six classes. This basic classification, in the main, is still valid. To Hipparchus, who lived on the island of Rhodes in the second century B.C., goes the credit for this classification. The twenty brightest stars known to him were arbitrarily designated as stars of the *first magnitude*; and the next fifty in order of apparent brightness were designated as stars of the *second magnitude*; and so on. The designation of sixth magnitude was given to several hundred stars barely visible to the normal eye. . . . Thus a completely arbitrary classification of stars, according to their brightness, was obtained. These magnitudes are, however, only *apparent* magnitudes. Some stars are actually bright, but appear faint because of their great distance. *Decimal Division of Apparent Magnitudes.* In the 19th century, the decimal division was introduced. In this classification, a star of magnitude 5.5 has an apparent brightness half-way between that of a star of magnitude 5.0 and that of a star of magnitude 6.0. Similarly, to state that the North Star (Polaris) has a magnitude of 2.1, signifies that its apparent brightness is only slightly less than the brightness of a star of magnitude 2.0. Increasingly, the decimal method of denoting magnitudes has been applied more extensively and made more precise.

WHO IS JAMES K. POLK?

Bernard DeVoto

1   . . . So presently the telegraph announced that George Bancroft, with the assistance of Gideon Pillow and Cave Johnson and the endorsement of Old Hickory in the Hermitage, had brought the delegates to agree on the first dark horse ever nominated for the Presidency, Mr. Pillow's former law partner, James K. Polk.

2   "Who is James K. Polk?" The Whigs promptly began campaigning on that derision, and there were Democrats who repeated it with a sick concern. The question eventually got an unequivocal answer. Polk had come up the ladder, he was an orthodox party Democrat. He had been Jackson's mouthpiece and floor leader in the House of Representatives, had managed the anti-Bank legislation, had risen to the Speakership, had been governor of Tennessee. But sometimes the belt line shapes an instrument of use and precision. Polk's mind was rigid, narrow, obstinate, far from first-rate. He sincerely believed that only Democrats were truly American, Whigs being either the dupes or the pensioners of England—more, that not only wisdom and patriotism were Democratic monopolies but honor and breeding as well.

"Although a Whig he seems a gentleman" is a not uncommon characterization in his diary. He was pompous, suspicious, and secretive; he had no
humor; he could be vindictive; and he saw spooks and villains. He was a
representative Southern politician of the second or intermediate period
(which expired with his Presidency), when the decline but not the disintegra-
tion had begun.

3   But if his mind was narrow it was also powerful and he had guts. If he
was orthodox, his integrity was absolute and he could not be scared,
manipulated, or brought to heel. No one bluffed him, no one moved him with
direct or oblique pressure. Furthermore, he knew how to get things done,
which is the first necessity of government, and he knew what he wanted
done, which is the second. He came into office with clear ideas and a fixed
determination and he was to stand by them through as strenuous an
administration as any before Lincoln's. Congress had governed the United
States for eight years before him and, after a fashion, was to govern it for the
next twelve years after him. But Polk was to govern the United States from
1845 to 1849. He was to be the only "strong" President between Jackson and
Lincoln. He was to fix the mold of the future in America down to 1860, and
therefore for a long time afterward. That is who James K. Polk was.

HAWAII MUSICAL A 'DRAB DISASTER'

William Glover

1   (New York, AP) Hawaii is the unlucky locale of "Heathen!" a drab musical
disaster that premiered Sunday night at Broadway's Billy Rose Theater.

2   The peculiarly pallid theatrical piece was written by Sir Robert Help-
mann, the noted English ballet master, and Easton Magoon Jr. of Honolulu.
The alleged score and lyrics were provided by Magoon, who did similar
disservice to the craft a decade ago here with "13 Daughters," which lasted
one performance.

3   "Heathen!" tries to take a composite look at the Pacific islands in 1819,
when a missionary from Boston arrives to redeem and remains to romance,
and 1972, when descendants of the prior characters come into renewed
collision.

4   Trying to fuse those narrative segments into some sort of meaningful
entertainment has daunted everyone involved, including the program printer
who hasn't been able to keep up with changes in scenes and songs for the
guidance of anyone wondering what happens where and when.

5   Every white man-pagan stage confrontation entails certain obligatory
items. So there's the pidgin English scene with happy, laughing natives
learning a new language; there's the grass-skirted Mother Courage spouting
lusty wisdom, and an episode in which the parson's converts do their quaint
version of some Biblical lore. An eruption of Muana Loa occurs offstage.

6   Tastelessly running underneath all the surface clutter, in performance as
well as text, is a homosexual enthusiasm.

7   Physically "Heathen!" is the ugliest production of a good many seasons,

scenically misdesigned by Jack Brown, ludicrously costumed by Bruce Harrow.

8   The best thing about the show is that it finally ends.

Modes Record Different Aspects of a Subject

Let us take one of the examples previously given and examine alternatives that the author chose not to write about. Meir Degani, the author of the selection on Hipparchus, chose to discuss stars from the perspective of their classification on the basis of brightness. In another context, Degani could have viewed stars from quite another standpoint, such as their origin, development, and eventual destruction. Indeed, modern astronomy has made this facet of stars one of its main claims to glory; although as late as the Renaissance, stars were looked upon as eternal, unchanging entities, at the present time stars are talked about in terms of a birth, a life, and a death. In yet another situational context, Degani might have written about stars from a descriptive perspective. Given our present capabilities, it is possible to describe individual stars in terms of their unique characteristics. Degani might have isolated the polar star, described its position in the visible universe, and discussed its individual peculiarities of size, brightness, chemical makeup, and so on. Finally, instead of merely describing Polaris, Degani might have evaluated it from several different viewpoints: its unique position and stability in the northern celestial sphere (which make it particularly valuable for navigation in the northern half of the globe), its proximity for future cosmic exploration, its potential for rare chemical substances, and so on.

Why did Degani choose to ignore the history of the stars, or the structure of any one given star, or the value of any given star? Because, given his purpose and interests at the time, these other concerns were not relevant. Later on in his book some of these concerns are taken up; his ignoring them at first simply means that he was not, at that moment, interested in them. In short, focusing on any one aspect of a subject necessarily holds off from consideration, at that time, other aspects of that subject. Consequently, it is quite appropriate to say that *any one mode* is an abstraction; that is, any one mode, or consideration of any one aspect of a subject, *draws away from* the other aspects (this is the literal meaning of the term *abstraction*).

A Theoretical Basis for the Modes

So far we have seen that each of the examples given to illustrate the four modes looks at the subject matter in a different light and records a different aspect of this subject. But, you might ask, aren't the different perspectives from which a given subject may be viewed almost infinite in number? After all, a physicist, for example, looks at a moving projectile differently from the way an artillery officer who sends one on its way does; a person living in the area in which the projectile will hit takes a quite different view from either the physicist or the officer; and so on. Can a study of composition reduce these perspectives to only four?

Yes. And there is a rational basis for doing this. The basic ways of looking at subjects are inherent in the basic kinds of writing a person can do about them. *Narratives* report changes in objects; *classification* groups objects having some characteristics in common; *description* details the individual characteristics of a particular object; and *evaluation* rates the performance of an object in light of some goal. One of the key bases for these distinctions in modes of discourse is the difference between viewing objects as static or as dynamic. Both description and classification view the object under discussion as static, stable, and unchanging. We saw this in the analysis of the sample readings concerning James K. Polk and the stars. By contrast, narration and evaluation are concerned with changing objects, happenings, and events—as in both the story told in the musical *Hawaii* and the evaluation of that musical as a performance or event.

In other words, description and classification have to do with the static; narration and evaluation have to do with the dynamic.

Next, consider what constitutes the difference between the two types of discourse about objects viewed statically, that is, between description and classification. In the case of objects being classified, for example in the piece about the stars, the objects are only considered insofar as they are members of a group. Polaris, as a special star, is cited in the given selection only because it is an example of the class of stars having a brightness index of 2.1. That is, the focus of the classification is on membership in the group, not on the individuality of one member of the group. In the case of description, however, James K. Polk is important in the piece by Bernard DeVoto precisely because he is a unique individual, not because he was a Democrat or among those in the class of "strong" presidents. In Figure 8.1 these distinctions are graphically indicated on the lower and right side of the square.

Finally, what is the difference between narration and evaluation? In narration the interest is in action or change *as change*: a weather report is simply a report of the changes in the weather. But evaluation is concerned with action or change as measured by some kind of norm or goal; the announced rain may be viewed as good by a farmer whose crops need water or bad by a golfer looking forward to a pleasant day on the links. These differences between the dynamic modes are graphically presented in the upper and left quadrants of the square.

The differences among the modes are explained in more detail in the following chapters: In the meantime, however, the lists on page 249 should prove helpful to you in seeing the differences among the modes in terms of the kinds of writing that can occur in each.

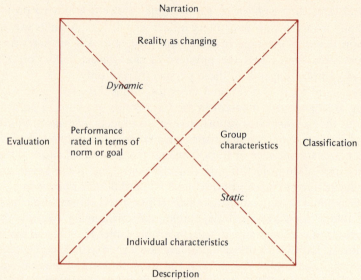

FIGURE 8.1   The modes as four ways of looking at objects.

Overlap of the Modes

Figure 8.1 indicates, through the use of broken lines, the important fact that the modes overlap. Each mode overlaps with the other three. A more careful look at our sample reading confirms this. For example, take just the second paragraph of the story about the goose that laid the golden egg: "But the richer he grew, the greedier he became. He began to be dissatisfied with only one egg a day." It is obvious that the story line advances in these sentences: something changes, something happens. There is a narrative.

But it is also obvious that this story classifies. The owner of the goose belongs to the group or class of the "rich" and also the class of the "greedy"; eventually he belongs to the class of those who lose all. Classification is important to this story, particularly in terms of its lesson or moral. In addition, the narrative describes individually, in terms of particulars, the man who owns the goose: he keeps a goose, he is rich, he is greedy, he is foolish, he wants to live in luxury for life, he kills and cuts open his pet, he loses all. Finally, it should be clear that "richer" and "greedier" have value associations for most people: being rich is often viewed as good and desirable, whereas greed is often viewed as bad and to be avoided. In the story of the goose, greed is eventually punished by a loss of wealth. A value system is brought to bear on the owner of the goose in order to make a point. In considering each of the other readings, you will find that one of the modes is dominant, but that the others are evident as well.

The overlap of modes is another justification for seeing each mode as

EXAMPLES OF EACH MODE

Narration

Biography
History
News stories
Novels
Short stories
Dramas
Case histories in psychology or
    medicine
Sports reporting
Accounts of process

Description

The makeup of a cell
A town or country
Geological formations in a canyon
Organization of books, plays
Plot structure of a novel
People
Structure of a population
Structure of a government, an
    industry

Classification

Definitions of democracy, novel,
    obscenity, freedom, change
Classifications of diseases, skiers, fish,
    governments, languages
Comparisons and/or contrasts of
    religions, governments, dramas,
    dialects, writers

Evaluation

Political systems
Religious systems
Techniques of producing something
Farming methods
Football teams
Actors
Politicians
Clothing
Toothpastes
Actions of individuals or groups
Books
Heroes
Cements
Buildings

an abstraction. There are two further justifications. First, the skills required for writing in one mode are not the same skills as required for writing in another. This means that in learning to write, it is useful to abstract and isolate each mode and learn the skills involved in it just as you could focus on the skill of serving in tennis as distinct from the skill of using a backhand. Second, by understanding the differences among the modes, a writer can see what skills and approaches are called for by a particular writing assignment.

THE RELATIONSHIP BETWEEN THE AIMS AND MODES OF WRITING

You have probably noticed that little has been said in this chapter about the aims of writing. You should not assume, however, that the aims and modes bear no relationship to each other. On the contrary, you should understand that every writing situation involves—and every writer faces—a concern for both overall purpose and a particular way of viewing and conveying the subject—in short, a simultaneous concern for aim and mode.

In this chapter, we have been discussing specimens of the four modes. But the piece from the astronomy text, which we analyzed here as an example of classification, also has a purpose. It's informative in purpose, as is much of the writing in textbooks generally. The fable, on the other hand, is literary in aim, with a strong element of persuasion tied in, particularly at the end. The review of the musical reflects the usual combination of literary and persuasive aims, with some information thrown in.

By the same token, it should be clear that each mode can be applied to any one of the aims. For example, there are persuasive narrations, such as the parables of the Gospel, and there are persuasive classifications: "Now, you aren't going to vote for a Socialist, are you?" There are persuasive descriptions, such as a chamber of commerce description of a city, and there are persuasive evaluations: "You deserve only the best, so why not buy _____?" Put simply: Every piece of writing has a purpose or aim and exemplifies at least one mode or way of looking at reality. Consequently, it is possible to construct a grid to indicate the major combinations of aims and modes in writing.

The table illustrates 24 basic combinations of the aims and modes. In addition, it also makes clear that even a simple writing assignment presents

Primary Combinations of Aims and Modes of Writing

Aims

Modes	Self-Expression	Convey Information	Prove a Point	Explore a Subject	Persuasion	Literature
		Exposition				
Description						
Classification and Definition						
Narration						
Evaluation						

the writer with two distinct initial tasks: one, determining the dominant aim; and the other, selecting the dominant mode.

Exercises on the Modes of Writing

1. Keep a record of the dominant modes of the various items you read on a typical day. For example, a novel or short story would be dominantly narrative, and a movie review would be dominantly evaluative. An article concerning the reduction of athletic injuries might be both descriptive and classificatory in mode or perhaps descriptive and evaluative. Be prepared to discuss your reasons for determining the dominant mode or modes in each case, including cases in which you see strong modal overlaps.
2. Choose a relative or close friend and write a short (100–150 word) description of him or her. Then, write a short piece evaluating some aspect of the same person.
3. Write a short narrative about someone you know well; then write a short piece about the different groups or classes of people to which he or she belongs (political, religious, ethnic, and other groups). When you classify, be sure to define terms or groups with which your reader may not be familiar.
4. Reread the section of this chapter in which the story of the gold-producing goose is analyzed for overlaps among the modes. Then, briefly record how each of the other readings—the pieces on Polk, the stars, and the musical that flopped—also reflects the use of more than one mode.
5. Reexamine the four texts about the Williams family used to discuss the aims of writing in Chapter 1. Which mode of writing seems to dominate in Mrs. Williams' letter? Which seems to dominate in the poem? Which mode dominates in the lawyer's speech? In any of these cases, is more than one mode dominant? What conclusion, regarding the relationship between the modes and any given subject matter, can you make based on your analysis of the various Williams texts?

Describing

THE IMPORTANCE OF DESCRIBING

The first seven chapters of this text are devoted to the aims or purposes of writing. But, as the preceding chapter explains, a second dimension of the task always faces the writer—the subject matter about which he or she writes and the particular view taken of this subject matter. We have called the various views taken of subject matters the modes of writing. The determination of specific mode and aim often occur at the same time, but for practical purposes we have considered aims and audiences before talking about narrowing down the topic to a given aspect or mode relevant to a particular situation. Actually, we have been using modes all along, but now we need to isolate them for particular consideration.

We begin with the descriptive mode for several purposes. First, a good portion of the writing the average person is called upon to do is descriptive. In a business course you may be asked to describe the structure of a particular corporation; in a government course you may be asked to outline the structure of the British parliament; in a geology class you may have to present the details of various strata of the Grand Canyon. In fact, every discipline requires descriptive assignments, and in most disciplines they are basic and important.

Second, from a learner's point of view, description is possibly the easiest of the modes to master. Description even precedes narration psychologically, because before we see that something is changing, we must see that the object is first in a certain condition it is changing *from*. And before we can group an object into a class, we must first have seen the object as it is in itself; thus description precedes division and classification. Finally, as a condition to evaluate an object, we must first observe it, so description precedes evaluation. Many teachers of composition recommend addressing description before the other modes because it is not as abstract and complex as the other types of writing.

SOME EXAMPLES OF DESCRIPTION

Let's examine carefully two examples of descriptive writing. The first is by the great Russian novelist Alexandr Solzhenitsyn, and it comes from his investigative study of the political prisons of the Soviet Union, *The Gulag Archipelago*. The second is a description of a typewriter by a college student. Both examples are good illustrations of good descriptive writing techniques. As you read them, ask yourself what makes them effective descriptions.

Prereading Activities

VOCABULARY. The first reading assignment may, at first sight, seem to contain more than the usual number of unfamiliar words. However, by identifying a few Russian place names and writers, we can remove most of the strange and unfamiliar tones of the passage.

Fourteen different prison camps are mentioned in the selection: Kolyma, Samarka, Katlos-Volkuta, Kaluga, Karlag, Kraslag, Sakhalin, Ust-Vym, Ukhta, Burepolon, Akatui, Omsk, Nerchinski, and Vorkuta. Some of these are twentieth-century Soviet camps and others were nineteenth-century Czarist camps; the context usually distinguishes them.

Solzhenitsyn refers to some other writers who have described Czarist or Soviet prison camps. Chekhov, Doestoyevksy, and Gorky are classic writers of Russian literature who have treated the topic. Shalanov and Dobryak are contemporary writers who have dealt with the issue, and Yakubovich is a writer from the latter part of the nineteenth century who also wrote on Czarist prison camps.

The following are other words that might give trouble to some readers (the number in parentheses is the number of the paragraph in which the word first appears).

Gulag—acronym for Chief Administration of Corrective Labor Camps
Archipelago—a group of islands or a sea with a group of islands in it
socialism (3)—the system of state ownership of property and production and distribution of goods; in this case, one could substitute Russian communism
OSO (4)—special boards empowered to sentence "socially dangerous" persons without trial
impregnate (4)—to fill or saturate

hummocks (4)—ridges of land in a swamp
vetch (8)—climbing plants of the pea family, chiefly used for fodder
camomile (11)—plant of the aster family
Stakhanovite—a status title given to a worker with high production norms
zeks (15)—prisoners in the camps
kasha (13)—soup ration
bast (23)—fiber used in making ropes, mats, and other goods
skewbald (25)—having irregular markings, usually said of horses

There should be no vocabulary problems with the student selection.

Organization of the Two Selections.   The first four volumes of *The Gulag Archipelago* include 42 chapters about different aspects of life in the Soviet prison camps, and the section anthologized is part of one of these chapters. The first two volumes treat the procedures of arrest, trial, and intimidation; the history of the camps and of the changes in laws to justify them; the transporting of prisoners; and the different kinds of prisons. Volumes 3 and 4 expand the history of the camps and discuss the women and children in the camps, the spies, and so on. The section anthologized comes from Volume 3.

The chapter has a strong internal organization. You ought to be able to identify the following sections easily (the numbers at the end of each line are the paragraph numbers).

I.   General introduction to way of life (1,2)

II.   Work (3–10)
    A. Introduction (3)
    B. Kinds of work (4)
    C. Logging (5–7)
    D. Contrast to Czarist work norms (8,9)
    E. Raising work norms (10)

III.   Food (11–18)
    A. General (11)
    B. Ration cut when norms were not met (12)
    C. Danger of extra rations (13,14)
    D. Contrast to Czarist food rations (15,16)

IV.   Dress and shoes (19–26)
    A. Introduction (19–20)
    B. General description (21)
    C. Patches (22)
    D. Shoes (23)
    E. Conclusion to dress and shoes (24–26)

V.   Barracks (27–30)

    VI. Miscellaneous (31–32)
       A. Impermanence (31)
       B. Lack of privacy (32)

   VII. Conclusion (32–35)

The organization of the student's essay is also easy to discern. The following parts should be fairly clear.

     I. Introduction (1)

    II. General description (2)

   III. Keyboard (3)

   IV. Keys (4)

    V. Ribbon (5)

   VI. Carriage (6)

   VII. Conclusion (7)

STUDY QUESTIONS. While reading the selections, keep in mind the following questions. You should be able to answer them after a careful reading. They lead directly to the principles of describing discussed in the section following the anthologized selections.

1. Does the author manage to present the object he describes as a whole or merely as a collection of parts?
2. Is the object being described presented as unified in some way or other?
3. Is the object being described as something separate and unique?
4. From what point of view does the author present the description? Does he speak as an insider, an outsider, an angry person, or a neutral observer? Does he speak in his own voice or does he present the views of others? Do the two descriptions differ in some of these respects?
5. Does the author seem to have a purpose that determines what facets of the objects are going to be presented to the reader in the description? Does the description seem one-sided or neutral?

THE WAY OF LIFE AND CUSTOMS OF THE NATIVES

Alexandr I. Solzhenitsyn

1   To describe the native life in all its outward monotony would seem to be both very easy and very readily attainable. Yet it is very difficult at the same time. As with every different way of life, one has to describe the round of living

from one morning until the next, from one winter to the next, from birth (arrival in one's first camp) until death (death). And simultaneously describe everything about all the many islands and islets that exist.

2   No one is capable of encompassing all this, of course, and it would merely be a bore to read whole volumes.

3   And the life of the natives consists of work, work, work; of starvation, cold, and cunning. This work, for those who are unable to push others out of the way and set themselves up in a soft spot, is that selfsame *general work* which raises socialism up out of the earth, and drives us down into the earth.

4   One cannot enumerate nor cover all the different aspects of this work, nor wrap your tongue about them. To push a wheelbarrow. ("Oh, the machine of the OSO, two handles and one wheel, so!") To carry hand barrows. To unload bricks barehanded (the skin quickly wears off the fingers). To haul bricks on one's own body by "goat" (in a shoulder barrow). To break up stone and coal in quarry and mine, to dig clay and sand. To hack out eight cubic yards of gold-bearing ore with a pick and haul them to the screening apparatus. Yes, and just to dig in the earth, just to "chew" up earth (flinty soil and in winter). To cut coal underground. And there are ores there too—lead and copper. Yes, and one can also . . . pulverize copper ore (a sweet taste in the mouth, and one waters at the nose.) One can impregnate ties with creosote (and one's whole body at the same time too). One can carve out tunnels for railroads. And build roadbeds. One can dig peat in the bog, up to one's waist in the mud. One can smelt ores. One can cast metal. One can cut hay on hummocks in swampy meadows (sinking up to one's ankles in water). One can be a stableman or a drayman (yes, and steal oats from the horse's bag for one's own pot, but the horse is government-issue, the old grass-bag, and she'll last it out, most likely, but you can drop dead). Yes, and generally at the *"selkhozy"*—the Agricultural Camps—you can do every kind of peasant work (and there is no work better than that: you'll grab something from the ground for yourself).

5   But the father of all is our Russian forest with its genuinely golden tree trunks (gold is mined from them). And the oldest of all the kinds of work in the Archipelago is logging. It summons everyone to itself and has room for everyone, and it is not even out of bounds for cripples (they will send out a three-man gang of armless men to stamp down the foot-and-a-half snow). Snow comes up to your chest. You are a lumberjack. First you yourself stamp it down next to the tree trunk. You cut down the tree. Then, hardly able to make your way through the snow, you cut off all the branches (and you have to feel them out in the snow and get to them with your ax). Still dragging your way through the same loose snow, you have to carry off all the branches and make piles of them and burn them. (They smoke. They don't burn.) And now you have to saw up the wood to size and stack it. And the work norm for you and your brother for the day is six and a half cubic yards each, or thirteen cubic yards for two men working together. (In Burepolom the norm was nine cubic yards, but the thick pieces also had to be split into blocks.) By then your arms would not be capable of lifting an ax nor your feet of moving.

6   During the war years (on war rations), the camp inmates called three weeks at logging *"dry execution."*

7   You come to hate this forest, this beauty of the earth, whose praises have been sung in verse and prose. You come to walk beneath the arches of pine and birch with a shudder of revulsion! For decades in the future, you only have to shut your eyes to see those same fir and aspen trunks which you have hauled on your back to the freight car, sinking into the snow and falling down and hanging on to them tight, afraid to let go lest you prove unable to lift them out of the snowy mash.

8   Work at hard labor in Tsarist Russia was limited for decades by the Normative Statutes of 1869, which were actually issued for free persons. In assigning work, the physical strength of the worker and the degree to which he was accustomed to it were taken into consideration. (Can one nowadays really believe this?) The workday was set at seven hours (!) in winter and at twelve and a half hours in summer. At the ferocious Akatui hard-labor center (Yakubovich, in the 1890's) the work norms were *easily fulfilled* by everyone except him. The summer workday there amounted to eight hours, including *walking to and from work*. And from October on it was seven hours, and in winter only six. (And this was even before any struggle for the universal eight-hour workday!) As for Dostoyevsky's hard labor in Omsk, it is clear that in general they simply loafed about, as any reader can establish. The work there was agreeable and went with a swing, and the prison administration there even dressed them up in *white* linen jackets and trousers! Now, how much further could they have gone? In our camps they used to say: "You could even put on a white collar"—which meant things were very, very easy and there was absolutely nothing to do. And they had . . . even white jackets! After work the hard-labor convicts of the "House of the Dead" used to spend a long time *strolling* around the prison courtyard. That means that they were *not* totally fagged out! Indeed, the Tsarist censor did not want to pass the manuscript of *The House of the Dead* for fear that the *easiness* of the life depicted by Dostoyevsky would fail to deter people from crime. And so Dostoyevsky added new pages for the censor which demonstrated that life in hard labor was *nonetheless* hard![1] In our camps only the trusties went strolling around on Sundays, yes, and even they hesitated to. And Shalamov remarks with respect to the *Notes of Mariya Volkonskaya* that the Decembrist prisoners in Nerchinsk had a norm of 118 pounds of ore to mine and load each day. (One hundred and eighteen pounds! One could lift that all at once!) Whereas Shalamov on the Kolyma had a work norm per day of 28,800 pounds. And Shalamov writes that in addition their summer workday was sometimes sixteen hours long! I don't know how it was with sixteen, but for many it was thirteen hours long—on earth-moving work in Karlag and at the northern logging operations—and these were hours on the job itself, over and above the three miles' walk to the forest and three back. And anyway, why should we argue about the length of the day? After all, the *work norm* was senior in rank to the length of the workday, and when the brigade didn't fulfill the norm, the only thing that was changed at the end of the shift was the convoy, and the work sloggers were left in the woods by the light of searchlights until midnight—so that they got back to the camp just before

_____

[1] Letter of I. A. Gruzdev to Gorky. Gorky Archives. Vol. XI, Moscow, 1966, p. 157.

morning in time to eat their dinner along with their breakfast and go out into the woods again.[2]

9   There is no one to tell about it either. They all died.

10   And then here's another way they raised the norms and proved it was possible to fulfill them: In cold lower than 60 degrees below zero, workdays were written off; in other words, on such days the records showed that the workers had not gone out to work; but they chased them out anyway, and whatever they squeezed out of them on those days was added to the other days, thereby raising the percentages. (And the servile Medical Section wrote off those who froze to death on such cold days on some other basis. And the ones who were left who could no longer walk and were straining every sinew to crawl along on all fours on the way back to camp, the convoy simply shot, so that they wouldn't escape before they could come back to get them.)

11   And how did they feed them in return? They poured water into a pot, and the best one might expect was that they would drop unscrubbed small potatoes into it, but otherwise black cabbage, beet tops, all kinds of trash. Or else vetch or bran, they didn't begrudge these. (And wherever there was a water shortage, as there was at the Samarka Camp near Karaganda, only one bowl of gruel was cooked a day, and they also gave out a ration of two cups of turbid salty water.) Everything any good was always and without fail stolen for the chiefs (see Chapter 9), for the trusties, and for the thieves—the cooks were all terrorized, and it was only by submissiveness that they kept their jobs. Certain amounts of fat and meat "subproducts" (in other words, not real food) were signed out from the warehouses, as were fish, peas, and cereals. But not much of that ever found its way into the mouth of the pot. And in remote places the chiefs even took all the *salt* for themselves for their own pickling. (In 1940, on the Kotlas-Vorkuta Railroad, both the bread and the gruel were unsalted.) The worse the food, the more of it they gave the zeks. They used to give them horse meat from exhausted horses driven to death at work, and, even though it was quite impossible to chew it, it was a feast. Ivan Dobryak recalls today: "In my own time I have pushed no small amount of dolphin meat into my mouth, also walrus, seal, sea bear, and all kinds of other sea animal trash. [I interrupt: we ate whale meat in Moscow, at the Kaluga Gates.] I was not even afraid of animal feces. And as for willow herbs, lichens, wild camomile—they were the very best of dishes." (This means he himself *went out and added* to his rations.)

12   It was impossible to try to keep nourished on Gulag norms anyone who worked out in the bitter cold for thirteen or even ten hours. And it was completely impossible once the basic ration had been plundered. And this was where Frankel's satanic mixing paddle was put into the boiling pot: some sloggers would be fed at the expense of others. The *pots* were divvied up; if less than 30 percent of the norm (and in each different camp this was

---

[2]Those who increase work norms in industry can still deceive themselves into thinking that such are the successes of the technology of production. But those who increase the norms of *physical labor* are executionary *par excellence!* They cannot seriously believe that under socialism the human being is twice as big and twice as muscular. They are the ones . . . who should be tried! They are the ones who should be sent out to fulfill those work norms!

calculated in a different way) was fulfilled, the ration issued you was a punishment block ration: 10½ ounces of bread and a bowl of gruel a day; for from 30 to 80 pecent of norm they issued a penalty ration of 14 ounces of bread a day and two bowls of gruel; for from 81 to 100 percent you got a work ration of from 17½ to 21 ounces of bread and three bowls of gruel; and after that came the shock workers' pots, and they differed among themselves, running from 24½ to 31½ ounces of bread a day and supplementary kasha portions—two portions—and the *bonus dish*, which was some kind of dark, bitterish, rye-dough fingers stuffed with peas.

13 And for all this watery food which could not possibly cover what the body expended, the muscles burned up at body-rending toil, the shock workers and Stakhanovites went into the ground sooner than did the malingerers. This was something the old camp veterans understood very well, and it was covered by their own saying: *Better not to give me an extra kasha—and not to wake me up for work!* If such a happy stroke of fortune befalls you . . . as to be allowed to stay on your bunk for lack of clothing, you'll get the "guaranteed" twenty-one ounces. If they have dressed you up *for the season* (and this is a famous Gulag expression!) and taken you out to work on the canal—even if you wear your sledge hammer down to a chisel, you'll never get more than ten and a half ounces out of the frozen soil.

14 But the zek was not at liberty to stay on his bunk.

15 Of course, they did not feed the zeks so badly everywhere and always, but these are typical figures for Kraslag in wartime. At Vorkuta in that same period the miner's ration was in all likelihood the highest in all of Gulag (because heroic Moscow was being heated with that coal): it was 45½ ounces for 80 percent of norm underground or 100 percent on the surface. And in that most horribly murderous Tsarist hard-labor Akatui on a *nonworking* day (spent "on the bunk") they used to give out 2½ Russian pounds of bread (35 ounces) as well as 32 zolotniks (in other words, 4.65 ounces) of meat. And on a working day there they gave out 3 Russian pounds (43 ounces) of bread and 48 zolotniks (7 ounces) of meat. Was that not maybe higher than the front-line ration in the Red Army? And the Akatui prisoners carted off their gruel and their kasha by the tubful to the jailers' pigs. And P. Yakubovich found their thin porridge made from buckwheat kasha (! Gulag never ever saw that!) "inexpressibly repulsive to the taste." Danger of death from malnutrition is something else that never hung over the hard-labor convicts of Dostoyevsky's book. And what can you say if geese went wandering around (!!) in their prison yard ("in the camp compound") and the prisoners didn't wring their necks?[3] The bread at Tsarist Akatui was set out on their tables *unrestricted,* and at Christmas they were given a *pound* of beef and unlimited butter for their cereal. On Sakhalin the Tsarist prisoners working on roads and in mines during the months of the most work

---

[3]On the basis of the standards of many harsh camps Shalamov justly reproached me: "And what kind of a hospital *cat* was it that was walking around where you were? Why hadn't they killed it and eaten it long before? And why does Ivan Denisovich in your story carry a *spoon* with him, even though it is well known that everything cooked in camp can easily be drunk down as a liquid by *tipping up the bowl?*"

received each day 56 ounces of bread, 14 ounces of meat, 8¾ ounces of cereal! And the conscientious Chekhov investigated whether these norms were really enough, or whether, in view of the inferior quality of the baking and cooking, they fell short. And if he had looked into the bowl of our Soviet slogger, he would have given up the ghost right then and there.

16   What imagination at the beginning of our century could have pictured that "after thirty or forty years," not just on Sakhalin alone, but throughout the entire Archipelago, prisoners would be glad to get even more soggy, dirty, slack-baked bread, with admixtures of the devil only knew what—and that 24½ ounces of it would be an enviable *shock-worker* ration?

17   No, even more! That throughout all Russia the collective farmers would even envy that prisoners' ration! "We don't get even that, after all!"

18   Even at the Tsar's Nerchinsk mines they gave a supplementary "gold prospectors'" payment for everything over the government norm (which was always moderate). In our camps, for most of the years of the Archipelago, they either paid nothing for labor or just as much as was required for soap and tooth powder. Only in those rare camps and in those short periods when for some reason they introduced *cost accounting* (and only from one-eighth to one-fourth of the genuine wage was credited to the prisoner) could the zeks buy bread, meat, and sugar. And all of a sudden—oh, astonishment!—a crust would be left on the mess hall table, and it might be there for all of five minutes without anyone reaching out a hand to grab it.

19   And how were our natives dressed and shod?

20   All archipelagoes are like all archipelagoes: the blue ocean rolls about them, coconut palms grow on them, and the administration of the islands does not assume the expense of clothing natives—they go about barefoot and almost naked. But as for our cursed Archipelago, it would have been quite impossible to picture it beneath the hot sun; it was eternally covered with snow and the blizzards eternally raged over it. And in addition to everything else it was necessary to clothe and to shoe all that horde of ten to fifteen million prisoners.[4]

21   Fortunately, born outside the bounds of the Archipelago, the zeks arrived here not altogether naked. They wore what they came in—more accurately, what the *socially friendly* elements might leave of it—except that as a brand of the Archipelago, a piece had to be torn off, just as they clip one ear of the ram; greatcoats have their flags cut off diagonally, Budenny helmets have the high peak cut off so as to leave a draft through the top. But alas, the clothing of free men is not eternal, and footgear can be in shreds in a week from the stumps and hummocks of the Archipelago. And therefore it is necessary to clothe the natives, even though they have nothing with which to pay for the clothing.

22   Someday the Russian stage will· yet see this sight! And the Russian cinema screen! The pea jackets one color and their sleeves another. Or so

---

[4]According to the estimates of the encyclopedia *Rossiya-SSSR*, there were up to fifteen million prisoners at a time. This figure agrees with the estimate made by prisoners inside the U.S.S.R., as we ourselves have added it up. Whenever they publish more proven figures, we will accept them.

many patches on the pea jacket that its original cloth is totally invisible. Or a *flaming* pea jacket—with tatters on it like tongues of flame. Or patches on britches made from the wrappings of someone's food parcel from home, and for a long while to come one can still read the address written in the corner with an indelible pencil.[5]

23   And on their feet the tried and true Russian "lapti"—bast sandals—except that they had no decent "onuchi"—footcloths—to go with them. Or else they might have a piece of old automobile tire, tied right on the bare foot with a wire, an electric cord. (Grief has its own inventiveness. . . .) Or else there were "felt boots"—"burki"—put together from pieces of old, torn-up padded jackets, with soles made of a layer of thick felt and a layer of rubber.[6] In the morning at the gatehouse, hearing complaints about the cold, the chief of the camp would reply with his Gulag sense of humor:

24   "My goose out there goes around barefoot all winter long and doesn't complain, although it's true her feet are red. And all of you have got rubber overshoes."

25   And then, in addition, bronze-gray camp faces will appear on the screen. Eyes oozing with tears, red eyelids. White cracked lips, covered with sores. Skewbald, unshaven bristles on the faces. In winter . . . a summer cap with earflaps sewn on.

26   I recognize you! It is you, the inhabitants of my Archipelago!

27   But no matter how many hours there are in the working day—sooner or later sloggers will return to the barracks.

28   Their barracks? Sometimes it is a dugout, dug into the ground. And in the North more often . . . *a tent*—true, with earth banked and reinforced hit or miss with boards. Often there are kerosene lamps in place of electricity, but sometimes there are the ancient Russian "splinter lamps" or else cotton-wool wicks. (In Ust-Vym for two years they saw no kerosene, and even in headquarters barracks they got light from oil from the food store.) It is by this pitiful light that we will survey this ruined world.

29   Sleeping shelves in two stories, sleeping shelves in three stories, or, as a sign of luxury, "vagonki"—multiple bunks—the boards most often bare and nothing at all on them; on some of the work parties they steal so thoroughly (and then sell the spoils through the free employees) that nothing government-issue is given out and no one keeps anything of his own in the barracks; they take both their mess tins and their mugs to work with them (and even tote the bags containing their belongs—and thus laden they dig in the earth); those who have them put their blankets around their necks (a film scene!), or else lug their things to trusty friends in a guarded barracks. During the day the barracks are as empty as if uninhabited. At night they might turn over their wet work clothes to be dried in the drier (if there is a drier!)—but undressed like that you are going to freeze on the bare boards! And so they dry their clothes on themselves. At night their caps may freeze to the wall of

---

[5]In Tsarist Akatui the prisoners were given fur overcoats.

[6]Neither Dostoyevsky, nor Chekhov, nor Yakubovich tells us what the prisoners of their own Tsarist times wore on their feet. But of course they were doubtless shod, otherwise they would have written about it.

the tent—or, in a woman's case, her hair. They even hide their bast sandals under their heads so they won't be stolen off their feet. (Burepolom during the war.) In the middle of the barracks there is an oil drum with holes in it which has been converted into a stove, and it is good when it gets red-hot—then the steamy odor of drying footcloths permeates the entire barracks—but it sometimes happens that the wet firewood in it doesn't burn. Some of the barracks are so infested with insects that even four days' fumigation with burning sulphur doesn't help and when in the summer the zeks go out to sleep on the ground in the camp compound the bedbugs crawl after them and find them even there. And the zeks boil the lice off their underwear in their mess tins after dining from them.

30   All this became possible only in the twentieth century, and comparison here with the prison chroniclers of the past century is to no avail; they didn't write of anything like this.

31   It is necessary to add to all this the picture of the way the brigade's bread is brought on a tray from the bread-cutting room into the mess hall under guard of the huskiest brigade members carrying staves—otherwise other prisoners will grab it, tear it apart, and run off with it. And the picture should also be added of the way food parcels from home are knocked out of the zeks' hands at the very moment they leave the parcel office. And also the constant alarm whether the camp administration is going to take away the rest day (and why talk about the war if for a whole year before the war they had not had one day off on the "Ukhta State Farm," and no one in Karlag could remember any rest days from 1937 right through 1945?). Then on top of everything one has to add the eternal impermanence of camp life, the fear of change: rumors about a prisoner transport; the prisoner transport itself (the hard labor of Dostoyevsky's time knew no prisoner transports, and for ten or even twenty years people served out their term in one prison, and that was a totally different kind of life); then some sort of dark and sudden shuffling of "contingents"—either a transfer "in the interests of production," or a *"commissioning"* by a medical review board, or inventory of property, or sudden night searches that involve undressing and the tearing apart of all the prisoners' meager rags—and then beyond that the thorough individual searches before the big holidays of May 1 and November 7 (the Christmas and Easter of hard labor in the past century knew nothing like this). And three times a month there were the fatal, ruinous baths. (To avoid repetition, I will not write about them here; there is a detailed story-investigation in Shalamov, and a story by Dombrovsky.)

32   And later there was that constant, clinging (and, for an intellectual, torturing) *lack of privacy*, the condition of not being an individual but a member of a brigade instead, and the necessity of acting for whole days and whole years not as you yourself have decided but as the brigade requires.

33   And one must remember as well that everything that has been said refers to the established camp in operation for some time. But that camp had to be *started* at some time and by someone (and by whom if not by our unhappy brother zeks, of course?): they came to a cold, snowy woods, they stretched wire on the trees, and whoever managed to survive until the first barracks knew those barracks would be for the guard anyway. In November, 1941, near the station of Reshoty, Camp No. 1 of Kraslag was opened (over a

ten-year period they increased to seventeen). They drove 250 soldiers there, removed from the army to strengthen it morally. They cut timber, they built log frames, but there was nothing to cover the roofs with, and so they lived with iron stoves beneath the sky. The bread brought them was frozen, and they chopped it up with an ax, and gave it out in handfuls—broken up, crushed up, crumby.Their other food was heavily salted humpback salmon. It burned their mouths, and they eased the burning with snow.

34   (When you remember the heroes of the War of the Fatherland, do not forget these!)

35   Now that is the way of life of my Archipelago.

DESCRIPTION OF A MECHANISM: THE TYPEWRITER

Maurice Algazi

1   There is no doubt that the typewriter is the most used machine in the business world. Since it is a true physical mechanism, it can be described better than some of the abstract theoretical constructions used in business— such as an organizational chart, for example—among other reasons, because, unlike these, it has an actual physical appearance. A typewriter is a machine for printing characters on paper; smaller and easier to operate than a regular printing press, it is widely used in businesses and private households, mostly to type letters and works not intended for widespread distribution among the public.

2   While there are many different kinds of typewriters, the easiest way to give a general idea of their structure and appearance is by describing a specific one: a portable, mechanically operated, "flat" and compact typewriter of the kind that has been widely used since the 1920's—my Remington, for example. One of its main parts, the metal frame, holds together the other parts, and gives the machine its general shape and size. It is a boxlike structure, with an almost square bottom measuring about ten inches on each side; it is not cubical, its height being only around four inches. While the frame encloses the bottom and sides of the typewriter, it only covers a portion of the top, leaving apparent the other main parts of the machine: the keyboard, which forms a slant on the near side of the box's top; the type bars, which form a "basket" in its center; the carriage, an elongated structure that slides along a horizontal axis on the far side of the structure; and an inked ribbon, which runs between two spools located on the right and left of the body, in front and parallel to the carriage.

3   The keyboard of the typewriter consists of four rows of keys and a space bar, all parallel to the carriage. Each key is marked with the letter, character or special device it controls. There is a key for each of the 26 letters of the alphabet, for most punctuation marks such as the period, comma, and colon, and for each of the numerals from one to nine. The two last kinds of keys are each marked with a second character, such as the percent sign, the asterisk, or the dollar sign, which can be printed by pressing on the respective key while holding one of the two "shift" keys down; the same procedure is also

used to print the capitals of the letters. The shift keys can be prevented from bouncing back up by simultaneously pressing the "shift lock" key. The rest of the keys activate other special devices of the typewriter; for example, the back spacer key moves the carriage to the right one space. The space bar, which is located below the bottom row of keys, does the opposite of the back spacer; the space bar moves the carriage one space to the left. The margin release key, when pressed, allows the writer to type beyond the preset margin (see below). The tabulator key releases the carriage, which travels until it is stopped by a preset tabulator stop. These are small metal nails which can be placed at any point of the carriage to make it stop there by simply pressing the tabulator key. "Tab" stops are set by pressing a small lever located to the left of the numeral keys (it is pressed down to remove the tab stops).

4   The metal type bars are each about 3 inches long and are attached to a pivot under the roller (see below). They rest on a narrow pad located just behind the keyboard. Each of them is connected to a key; its free end, on which the type is located, strikes the paper whenever its respective key on the board is pressed.

5   The inking ribbon is a half-inch wide ink-soaked cloth ribbon that runs between two spools, as described above; one of these unwinds while the other receives the used ribbon. When a key is pressed, the ribbon rises in front of the carriage so that the end of the type bar, when struck, presses it against the paper, thus leaving the imprint of the particular type character.

6   The carriage is a metal frame, as wide as the typewriter's body, that slides along a rail attached to a horizontal axis. The carriage is composed of several parts: a black rubber cylinder called the roller, which turns on a metal axis whose two ends fit into two holes on each side of the carriage. The sheet of paper to be typed on is fastened on it and the roller provides support for the paper when it is struck by the type bars. Other basic parts are also located on the carriage; the first of these is the paper release lever, which allows the paper to move freely around the roller instead of being tightly pressed against it, as in normal typing. The second is the paper bail, a metal rod that normally rests on the roller and keeps the paper pressed against it; the bail can be raised to remove or adjust the paper. Next is the line spacer, a long metal handle attached to the left end of the carriage and pointing towards the keyboard. It allows the typist to turn the roller one or two lines, depending on the position of the "double-space" lever located at the same end of the carriage. There are also the carriage release levers on each side of the carriage; when pressed, these cause it to slide freely on its rail. Finally, there are the margin stops, two small metal "dogs" which can be moved along a notched bar on top of the carriage. If the margin release key is not pressed, the carriage will be unable to move beyond each of the preset stops, thus allowing the typist to create neat margins on each side of his text.

7   A typewriter contains many more parts, some hidden, others of secondary importance; only a more extensive description could cover them all. Those parts which were described hopefully present a brief view of the looks and functioning of a typewriter.

PREWRITING: THREE EARLY PROCESSES

Choosing a Topic

Often the student faced with a descriptive assignment says, "But what am I going to describe?" It might be instructive to ask how Solzhenitsyn came to his topic. As a young writer before World War II, Solzhenitsyn had written in a somewhat aimless way, searching for story themes. In 1945 he was arrested and for the next 11 years was subjected to prison camps, "rehabilitation," and interrogations—in fact, the kind of treatment he describes in one of the selections you have just read. During this time he discovered his subject and his aim. Nearly everything he has written since that time has been to let the world, especially the Russian people, know about the prison camps scattered throughout their land. He has made a career of this topic.

Solzhenitsyn's topic was, in a very real sense, thrust upon him by events—events not even of his own choosing. He reacted to these events and found his topic. He also found his audience and he found his purpose. He realized that he knew something important that others should know about and didn't.

Your own topics for description (and for everything else that you write voluntarily) will be written better if you follow Solzhenitsyn's example. Is there something about which you are in a position to know a good deal and about which you have some strong feelings? Is there an audience of readers who do not know about this object and that you feel should know about it? When *you, the writer*, feel thus qualified to describe a given *object* about which you are knowledgeable to an *audience* that is not acquainted with the object, you are in a position to write. You may not feel knowledgeable enough at the outset, but you can remedy this drawback through investigation and research. As usual, there are writer, reader, and subject-matter issues—and description poses particular concerns for each.

The writer must choose, as much as possible, the best *point of view*; the reaction of the reader to the description will be determined by the details of the object selected from reality and incorporated into the description by some sort of a *selection principle*; and the subject matter of the writing will be determined initially by the *object* itself that is being described. Figure 9.1 illustrates the relationship among the three topics, which we will relate to the three components of the communication process.

Let us consider the three issues separately, although in the actual prewriting process, the three are closely interwoven.

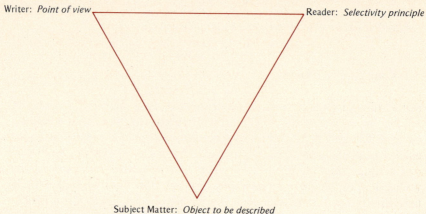

FIGURE 9.1   The issues in describing.

The Subject-Matter Issue: The Object to Be Described

Outside of the classroom, as we have said before, the thing to be described is determined by the occasion: by the context of the situation. If I want my brother to meet Dr. Eysenck at the airport, I have to describe Dr. Eysenck. If I want my friend to pick up my car at the parking lot, I must describe my car. Notice, in each case, that if the description is successful, the described object emerges as separate, distinct, and unique among other objects in its environment.

In the classroom, there is not the immediate urgency to separate Dr. Eysenck from the many other people getting off the same plane, nor to distinguish my car from the hundred others in the parking lot. Nevertheless, in learning to describe, it is important that you choose an object that is important to you in real life, if at all possible. Also, it helps if someone can check the accuracy of the description against the real thing.

How does the student writer manage to separate, isolate, and distinguish the object he or she is attempting to describe? The example of Solzhenitsyn can be very instructive. He uses three particular techniques: he identifies separate parts of the object; he shows how these parts are unified into a whole; and he shows that this whole is in some ways unique. The student also identifies the separate parts of the whole of a unique object.

The parts of "The Way of Life and Customs of the Natives" are fairly obvious from a quick reading of the selection. They are, in order, the suffering arising from work, the suffering arising from poor food or lack of food, the suffering because of inadequate dress and shoes, the suffering due to the poor housing of the barracks, and the psychological suffering from isolation. Each of these topics gets a fairly lengthy treatment: eight paragraphs for work, eight for food, eight for dress and shoes, four for barracks, and two for isolation. Later on we will see how Solzhenitsyn links these topics together in the order in which they occur.

At the moment we are interested in how Solzhenitsyn unifies these parts into a whole. This is always a problem for readers of description; the writer has seen the object as a unity, but the reader only gets the object parceled out in parts, word by word. The reader has to have some way of putting them together. Solzhenitsyn uses two techniques in this case. One is a common idea or theme; the other is an overall "umbrella" image.

The theme is that of "suffering," and it is for that reason that we can call each of the parts "the suffering from. . . ." This unifying notion ties all of these parts together into a common whole. Except for paragraph 19, which is a transition paragraph, every paragraph calls attention to the unrelenting, painful treatment of the prisoners. Sometimes this suffering is detailed in a succession of grim mental images, such as those of work in general (paragraph 4), of work in the forests (paragraph 5), or of food (paragraphs 11 to 17). Sometimes the picture is just suggested to the reader, who is expected to fill in the details: "There is no one to tell about it either. They all died" (paragraph 9).

These parts are all bound together in *The Gulag Archipelago* by two related images: that of an archipelago and that of a continent. The various prisons of the Russian concentration system are fused together by these two metaphors. Here is an excellent example:

> And the Kolyma was the greatest and most famous island, the pole of ferocity of that amazing country of Gulag which, though scattered in an Archipelago geographically, was, in the psychological sense, fused into a continent—an almost invisible, almost imperceptible country inhabited by the zek people.
>
> And this Archipelago crisscrossed and patterned that other country within which it was located, like a gigantic patchwork, cutting into its cities, hovering over its streets. Yet there were many who did not even guess at its presence and many, many others who had heard something vague. And only those who had been there knew the whole truth. ("Preface," pp. ix–x)

This metaphor recurs in 23 of the 35 paragraphs of the selection as well as in the title of the chapter and, of course, in the title of the book.

Finally, Solzhenitsyn makes the object look unique. What is unique in the picture of the concentration camps of the Soviet system is the singular extremity of the suffering in these concentration camps, especially when they are compared with those of the Czars. The special type of socialism in Russia (paragraph 2), the extreme work norms of the lumberjacks in Burepolon (paragraph 5), logging as "dry execution" (paragraph 6), hating the beautiful Russian forest (paragraph 7), cheating at workloads by making the prisoners work at temperatures lower than 60 degrees below zero (paragraph 10), the unbelievable food rations (paragraphs 10–17), and so on—all of these are conditions of singular extremity. Solzhenitsyn summarizes this uniqueness in paragraph 30:

> All of this became possible only in the twentieth century, and comparison here with the prison chroniclers of the past century is to no avail; *they didn't write of anything like this* [italics added].

The student had a much easier job than did Solzhenitsyn. His object was an actual physical object, the parts and the functions of which were much simpler to identify. Nonetheless, he did isolate the major parts at the outset. After a brief sketch of the whole, he enumerates the parts that he will describe in detail (paragraph 2). This enumeration then provides the structure of the remainder of his essay. In each of the subsequent parts, he again begins with the subordinate whole and describes the constituent parts. There is therefore a whole-part structure to the entire essay and to each of the subordinate sections. The student did not have such a singularly unique object to describe as did Solzhenitsyn, but even his typewriter may strike the reader as somewhat antiquated and strange, judged by modern standards of the electric or electronic typewriter, or by those of the computer-printer.

Exercises on the Subject-Matter Issue

These exercises are presented here in order to help you select an area of interest, narrow it down to a topic, and begin to work on the subject matter of a paper in which you will describe something. The paper could be a major assignment of some 10 to 20 pages (even a library paper), or it might be a small paper of only a few pages. But the process of prewriting and writing should follow the same development. It would be desirable to read and consider all of these exercises, even though you might limit yourself to only a few of them, because they give you a general procedure for developing your description.

1. **Choose an area of interest.** Your description ought to be about something in which you have some special involvement. It might be your academic discipline; it might be a personal problem area; it might be a political, economic, or religious issue of current significance; or it might be a concern that doesn't fit into any of these categories but that you feel is of some importance.

   Within your area of interest, pick out some object that is central to the issue and that a reader ought to be acquainted with and often isn't. The object may be a physical thing, but it might not be; for instance, it might be a governmental structure such as communism—a real entity, but not a physical object. Some examples of general types of objects that could be described are given in the following groups. When the general category is given, immediately narrow it down to a particular object of that general type with which you are familiar. Thus for engine, you should think 1982 Ford Maverick, 6-cylinder; for church, you should think St. Mark's Episcopal, on Sixth Avenue; and so on.

Here are some illustrative suggestions: (1) Natural sciences and engineering: an engine, a geographical location, a geological formation, a chemical substance, a famous bridge or other structure, an industrial plant; (2) Social sciences: a village, a city, a foreign country, a tribe, an industrial organization, a government agency, a church (either physical or conceptual), a teaching method (this overlaps with process and narration), a psychiatric case, a subculture; (3) Humanities and fine arts: a particular painting, a symphony (or other musical piece), a musical instrument, a short story, a poem, a play, a person, a historical personality (not a history but a character sketch); (4) Personal and topical areas: a town, a valley, a resort, a tourist site, a factory, a zoo, a personality, a relative, a local politician, an actor, an athlete.

2. Limit yourself generally to the descriptive features. Remember that this is an exercise in description, that is, you are to record the basic characteristics that will identify the object under consideration. In an important sense, your topic has already been significantly narrowed down already because this is an exercise in description. Except incidentally or by way of illustrating a stable descriptive feature, you are not writing a history of the object, or defining it, or even evaluating it—although all of these processes will be incidentally involved.

Make a list of the object's unique or distinctive features, especially those features that differentiate it from other members of the same general class. Emphasize these in the description.

3. Isolate the important parts, and try to figure out their relationships to each other and to the whole. It may be worth your while to go to a general dictionary, an encyclopedia, or a general reference work to get an overview of the object you are describing or of one like it. This can help put your view of the object in a more comprehensive perspective and at least suggest to you some aspects of the object that you can stress and some you can ignore.

When you have analyzed the parts, try to state the unifying facets or principles that cause the parts to adhere as a whole. Then try to verbalize the relationships of the parts to each other.

Any of these exercises can be carried out through discussion in class or among members of a cluster group working on the same kind of description. And, in the case of personal topics and some academic topics, an oral interview or a visit to the site being described may be worth three trips to the library.

The Reader Issue: The Selectivity Principle

Given an object that is to be presented to a set of readers, the next issue is: How much of what you see do you pass on to your readers? It is immediately clear that not all of what you see (or hear, or touch, or emotionally feel) can be passed on. To describe anything exhaustively would be difficult and impractical. Some selection must be made from the multitude of facets of the object you perceive. A good deal of the object will be screened out from your desciption.

What generates this screen of the selectivity principle? Suppose you are trying to induce a friend to join you at your present college. Your description of the college will tend to emphasize its favorable features. By contrast, if the members of a local environmental group are opposed to realtors putting up a housing development in a wilderness area immediately west of town, they will tend to stress the disadvantages of the area for the projected development. A scientist, on the other hand, wishing to obtain an accurate idea of the geological makeup of a piece of land, will attempt to make as representative a report of the land as he or she can manage. In each case, *the selectivity principle is determined by the aim of the writing*.

And the aim of the writing is the response the writer hopes to elicit with regard to the readers. At this juncture, we can see the close connection that the aims of writing, established in Chapter 1, have with writing a description.

Following the categories established in Chapter 1, we can say that descriptions will be expository, persuasive, literary, or expressive—and the meanings given to these words will be the meanings sketched in the previous chapters. And, of course, there can be overlaps of these aims. For example, a persuasive description in an advertisement can also incorporate information in order to persuade.

The selectivity principle operates very differently according to each aim. In general, an expository description tries to give as accurate a picture of the perceived object as possible. Scientists, for example, go to a great deal of trouble to make sure that their samples of a population are representative. Newswriters try to be objective in describing scenes they report. In persuasion, on the contrary, the writer often consciously biases the picture to emphasize aspects favorable to his or her attitude to the scene and to deemphasize unfavorable aspects. In literature, writers often have to transform the characters, settings, and events they see in real life to fit the patterns of their fictional creation. In expressive description, the writer emphasizes the aspects of the scene that caused vivid personal reactions. Each of these is a very different kind of selectivity principle.

There are three ways to discover a writer's selectivity principle. We can ask the author, we can ask the reader, and we can ask the text. Assuming that the author tells the truth and is aware of what he or she is

doing, his or her own statements about the purpose in selecting some items
and excluding others are usually reliable. Solzhenitsyn's dedication to the
book (p. vii) indicates his intention and his selection principle:

> I dedicate this
> to all those who did not live
> to tell it.
> And may they please forgive me
> for not having seen it all,
> for not having divined all of it.

He wants to *inform* his readers about *all* of the scene. In a sense, the
description is to be as accurate as possible. This implication is reinforced
by the subtitle of the book: *The Gulag Archipelago, 1918–1956: An
Experiment in Literary Investigation*. Even though it is literary, the book is
similar in nature to a journalist's investigation or that of a scientist. It is
clear from the text that it contains a massive collection of information
about the prison camps. But it is also clear that the information is not just
neutrally presented. There is a heavy dose of persuasion in the book, and
any reader can verify this. All of the marks of a persuasive text, as distinct
from the merely informative, are present. (We have seen these systematically in the chapter especially devoted to persuasion.)

The tone of the book is often highly emotional (and the reader feels
that this is completely justified). The effective repetitions in paragraphs 4,
5, and 7, for example, are not just objective reporting. The author
continually intrudes and so does the reader. In paragraph 5, there are 16
references to "you" or "your." But this *you* is also the speaker, the
inhabitant of the Archipelago. He is addressed in paragraph 16: "I
recognize you. It is you, the inhabitants of my Archipelago."

Some of the omissions of the text are characteristic omissions of
persuasive writing. For example, if anything pleasant happened in any of
the camps, it is almost universally ignored. And there are no sustained
comparisons to the camps of China, Nazi Germany, or any other country.
As mentioned above, the controlling purpose of this text is the unifying
theme behind the description: everything in the camps is inhuman and
ruthless and produces suffering.

Finally, we can ask the reader what he or she thinks the purpose of a
text is. You are only one reader, but you can check for yourself about the
purpose or purposes you see in this text. You will probably agree with
many other students who have read this selection: they see that persuasion
is one of the major effects elicited by the text.

The purposes of the student essay are not as complex. The emotional
tone of Solzhenitsyn, the one-sided choice of materials, and the unifying
imagery are all absent. The student is clearly much more neutral and
merely informational—he does not have the strong emotional commitment

to his Remington typewriter that Solzhenitsyn has to Russia. Consequently, there is no selective principle ruling out major components of the typewriter—with one exception: the student is giving an outside view of the typewriter. The internal hidden parts, which a technician might emphasize, are not talked about in this report (see the last paragraph). Thus the selectivity principle is the same as the point of view, that of an external observer, viewing the typewriter from the front. And the purpose is much more obviously informative—there is no hidden agenda.

Exercises on the Reader Issue

1. **Visualize your reader. Don't write for an indefinite or abstract audience. Outline a set of characteristics of the people whom you would consider the audience you are trying to reach. What are their ages, interests, and prior information about the subject matter involved? If possible, try to visualize an average reader; better still, if you consider one of the members of the class or one of your acquaintances such a person, approach him or her and try out your description at various stages of the draft.**

2. **What reaction do you expect from your typical reader if your description is fully successful? At this stage of the process, you should determine which of the basic aims of writing you will be working on in your description. Is the description going to be a fully documented scientific report that proves a point with complete evidence; is it only an informative piece; is it intended to be emotionally persuasive; is it intended to be humorous or tragic; or is your description an expressive reaction to something you feel quite strongly about? Or is it a combination of some of these purposes?**

    These aims are the issues of the first half of this text. The decisions you make in these areas will seriously affect the tone and structure of your description, as the preceding chapters have shown. But the decisions will also allow you to use some of the basic writing techniques you learned in these chapters. Thus, if you decide to do a persuasive piece, at this stage of the process you ought to give some strong thought to your ethical, emotional, and logical arguments, as they were called in Chapter 3. If you have been asked to write a scientific report, you might have to set up a rigid inductive system to test the various aspects of the object you will describe.

3. **What effects will your aim have upon the selection of details from the object you are describing? For example, if you are writing an attack upon the zoo in your area, what derogatory aspects of the zoo will you emphasize in your report? The principle of selectivity will affect your choice of details in a drastic way; your subject matter will be heavily influenced by the audience. This is as it should be.**

The Writer Issue: Point of View

Given a subject matter and a purpose in presenting it to the reader, a writer has to make a third critical decision in preparing material for a description. What he or she says about the object will be determined by the position from which it is viewed. This position is usually called the *point of view of the describer*. If I describe the football stadium at 4:00 P.M. on a Saturday in October from the point of view of an enthusiastic sports reporter occasionally using binoculars from a privileged place in a press box on the 50-yard line 60 rows from the playing surface, I convey a very different perspective from what I would if I were a faculty member adamantly opposed to intercollegiate athletics who looks out of the window of the university library several blocks away, sees only the tall, unsightly, double-decked concrete structure surrounded by blocks of parked cars, and hears only semisavage yells of despair or exultation. The two descriptions would be of the same object, but the different points of view would almost make the two scenes unrecognizable in terms of each other.

Notice the different dimensions of point of view. It includes attitude to the object being described—sympathetic, antipathetic, or even neutral; it includes possibly the intervention of a medium (binoculars), one of many media that can be used, including the reports of others and secondary sources; it includes the time of day and the season of the year; it even includes the possibility, in some kinds of writing, of adopting a fictional or an opponent's point of view.

Solzhenitsyn's use of point of view is very useful as a model in many ways. For example, he tells the reader explicitly in the Preface, in a passage already quoted, that he is describing from the point of view of an *insider*: "And only those who have been there know the whole truth" (paragraph 6). He frequently speaks in the first person: "I interrupt: we ate whale meat in Moscow, at the Kaluga gates" (paragraph 11); "In our camps only the trusties went strolling around on sundays, yes, and even they hesitated to" (paragraph 8—you can also check paragraphs 3, 8, 18, 19, 28, 31, 33, and 35).

He is thus speaking from the point of view of a prisoner; the first-person approach lends strong credibility to his description, in this instance. In other cases, as we will see in later chapters, it is sometimes advisable to take an outsider, and sometimes an impersonal, third-person approach.

But Solzhenitsyn is not speaking just in his own voice. Many of the first-person references given above are to "we" and "our." And often in such cases, he is speaking as a Russian: "But the father of all is our Russian forest" (paragraph 5, and see for further references to this Russian point of view paragraphs 3, 7, 16, 17, 22, 23, 28, 33, and 35). More specifically he speaks as a contemporary Russian; he systematically contrasts the present prison camps with those of the Czarist period in Russia. We have already seen several of these contrasts (see also paragraphs 8, 15, 16, 18, 22, 23, and 30). The general argument behind all of these contrasts is simple: The Russian people have always been told how terrible life was under the Czars, but today life is really much worse.

Solzhenitsyn does not limit himself to his own experiences. He tells us in the Preface that he used material from 227 witnesses in the prison camps, as well as the work of 36 other Soviet writers (see paragraphs 13, 19, and 21). By using this technique he manages to have more than just a stationary, limited point of view; he can describe many of the islands of the Archipelago. For instance, in this chapter he describes customs in 14 different camps.

Sometimes Solzhenitsyn speaks as a prisoner to other prisoners and addresses them as "you" and even includes himself in the *you*. Sometimes the *you* whom Solzhenitsyn is addressing is the entire Russian people and maybe even humanity at large. (For examples of the use of *you* as a technique in his point of view, see paragraphs 4, 5, 7, 8, 12, 13, 15, 29, 32, and 34.) Ordinarily, in expository papers this technique is not used. But in persuasion and in literature, it is frequent and often very effective—as it is here.

Perhaps the most important feature of Solzhenitsyn's point of view is its all-pervading negative tone. Of the 35 paragraphs, only 2 are not dominated completely by a pessimistic attitude. The two exceptions are paragraphs 2 and 19, and both of these are brief transitional paragraphs. A persistent pessimism characterizes not only this chapter but is dominant in all of the published volumes. It is surprising how sustained this tone is. There are many humorous passages, it is true, but the humor is grim and frightening. Even the treatment of the children in the Archipelago, "The Kids," is depressing.

Your point of view will not generally be as personal, all-pervasive, or negative as is Solzhenitsyn's. In fact, it is much more likely to be like that of Maurice Algazi, the author of the student essay, especially if you write an expository description. However, if you choose a persuasive description, your tone will move much closer to that of Solzhenitsyn. Normally, however, even in a persuasive piece, students will not have to describe such depressing objects to an unbelieving audience. As the two examples illustrate, your choice of point of view will be determined by the two most important considerations in any description: the purpose of the writing and the makeup of the audience.

Exercises on Point of View

1. **Before determining your point (or points) of view, consider the various alternatives in light of your purpose and subject matter. Physically you can have a stationary or a roving point of view or a single or a plural**

point of view (several different people's views presented along with your own); you can involve the intervention of one or several media (such as the naked eye or the microscope); and you can use the effects of points of view at different times of day or at different seasons. Which of these or which combination will most effectively enable you to select the facets that will contribute to your purpose? Draw a diagram showing your points of view relative to the topic.

2. Psychologically speaking, you can use either the omniscient point of view (it's assumed that the writer, or the speaker of the piece, knows everything) or the first-person point of view. For literary purposes the omniscient is allowed, but for all others, the first-person is almost required. It is possible to adopt another person's point of view and channel all of the writer's biases and interpretations through this adopted point of view. Such a technique is useful in literature and in persuasion, but it is not usually recommended for expository writing. Write a brief section of your paper in several points of view and then choose the best one.

3. Rhetorically, your point of view should emphasize your purpose. If you are writing a persuasive piece, it should reflect the thesis you are attempting to establish. Solzhenitsyn's selection is an admirable example of such reflection. In an expository piece, the neutral objectivity of the researcher or reporter should come through in the point of view. Using the point of view chosen in the previous exercise, try both the persuasive and neutral points of view. Choose the best one for your purpose.

ORGANIZING THE DESCRIPTION

Given a topic, purpose, and definite point of view, how does the writer go about organizing the object he or she perceives and wants to pass on to the reader? Both the student and the professional essay are typical and useful in this regard. Since the student essay is simpler, let us start with it.

In the prereading activities, the general structure of the description of the typewriter was sketched. After an introductory paragraph, there is a quick overview of the typewriter as a whole in paragraph 2. This is followed by a paragraph on each of the main parts: keyboard (paragraph 3), keys (paragraph 4), ribbon (paragraph 5), and carriage (paragraph 6). This body of the essay is succeeded by a conclusion (paragraph 7).

The essay is therefore made up of an introduction, a body, and a conclusion. The body is made up of the whole, then the parts in order. The order of the parts can be explained in two different ways. The keyboard is closest to the typist and movement is away from the typist: first comes the keyboard, then the keys, then the ribbon, and finally the carriage. This order is also the order of the action of the typewriter: the typist first strikes the keyboard; this activates the keys; the keys strike the ribbon; and the ribbon leaves the impression on the paper, which is rolled around the carriage. Now the point of view of the description is that of the typist; such a point of view enables the writer both to inform the reader about the looks of the typewriter and to arrive at an understanding of its function. In this case, therefore, the purpose of the writer, his point of view, and his organization are all closely tied together.

Solzhenitsyn's example is more complicated, but the same basic principles are in operation. Figure 9.2 is one way of explaining the general structure of the selection on "The Ways of Life and Customs of the Natives." The outside broken line with *The Gulag Archipelago* printed above it stands for the whole work of Solzhenitsyn on the prison camps. Chapter 7 of Volume 3, "The Ways of Life and Customs of the Natives," is shown as being one part of this larger whole (the chapter is represented by the large solid rectangle). Included within this chapter are the various

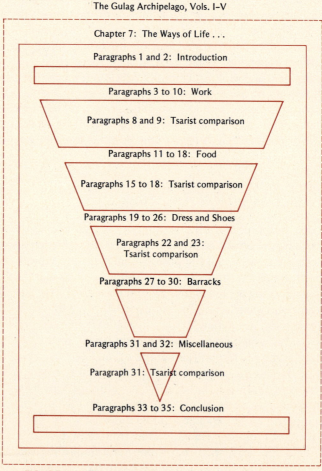

FIGURE 9.2 The organization of Solzhenitsyn's chapter.

paragraph groupings, labeled Introduction, Work, Food, Dress and Shoes, Barracks, Miscellaneous, and Conclusion.

What we are interested in is how the whole structure is put together: What determines what comes first, second, third, and so on?

The title and the first two paragraphs do at least two important things. First, both the title and the first paragraph continue the metaphor of the entire book: the camps constitute an archipelago and the prisoners are to be compared (and contrasted) to the natives of a South Sea archipelago. Thus the title and the first paragraph *link* the chapter to the five volumes as a whole.

Second, the introductory paragraph sets the tone and limits the topic—it would be impossible to describe everything in this somber sequence from birth to death. And both paragraphs hint at an outward monotony, and suggest, by implication, that beneath it may be some inward matters not at all boring. Thus the introduction suggests a large and partially inaccessible whole and captures the attention of the reader by suggesting that the sections to be covered will be an interesting and critical part of the whole picture. The last three paragraphs repeat the same ideas.

Consequently, the introduction and conclusion present the whole of the chapter; they relate this to the larger whole of the entire book and to the smaller parts of the chapter and remind the reader of the somber picture of Russia that he or she is to get (or has just gotten). In effect, they *frame* the rest of the parts, as the diagram indicates.

How are the internal parts organized? Why does *work* come first, *food* second, and so on? And why are impermanence and privacy (under *Miscellaneous*) last? Work seems to come first because it appears to be the dominant theme of the entire experience. The introductory sentence of paragraph 3 sounds this theme: "And the life of the natives consists of work, work, work." Notice that eight paragraphs are devoted to work and to food, four to dress, four to shoes, four to barracks, and one each to impermanence and lack of privacy.

In addition to the mere quantity of space devoted to the various sections, something else is noticeable, particularly in the earlier sections. The idea of death is first suggested in the introduction. But it is hinted at in the last line of paragraph 3, and in paragraph 6 logging is called "dry execution." The long contrast of paragraph 8 is summarized in one line: "*There is no one to tell about it either. They all died*" [italics added].

Death is also mentioned in the next paragraph. There are five ominous references to death in the first ten paragraphs. This theme returns in paragraph 15, where death in the gulags is twice contrasted to its relative absence in the Czarist camps. Death reminders are absent from the sections on dress and shoes and barracks, but in the conclusion, in the remembrance of the heroes of the War of the Fatherland, there is a final hint at the death motif.

In other words, the theme of death is present in the larger and earlier section on work and food and in the introduction and conclusion. We can see that there is a tone-setting and controlling grimness in the earlier sections that is not present in the later ones. For this reason the earlier sections are more important.

Writers in journalism have a name for this putting of the most important items in a story first and then working on down to increasingly less important elements. They call this structure the *inverted pyramid*; it is the structure of the majority of news stories in the typical American newspaper. And it is clear that Solzhenitsyn has used this principle for the internal ordering of the parts of his chapter. That is why the internal sections compose an inverted pyramid in the diagram.

The diagram brings out another noteworthy organizational technique in the reading. At the end of each section, several paragraphs or parts of a paragraph are devoted to contrasting the Gulag experiences with experiences in the Czarist camps. In each instance, of course, the Soviet camps are made to look immeasurably more inhuman. This internal contrast within each section gives another dimension to the organization.

Finally, in working down to the latter elements of his description, Solzhenitsyn continually uses key ideas or phrases to link his smaller parts to the preceding parts and to the various levels of whole sections as represented in the diagram.

There are therefore four major principles operating in the organization of the Solzhenitsyn piece: (1) careful relations of parts to wholes; (2) an inverted pyramid of importance, relating the parts of the prison life to the whole; (3) within each of these parts a contrast of the Soviet and Czarist experiences; (4) a careful interlinking of the various parts.

The relationships of parts to wholes is the typical organization pattern for description, but connections among the parts, and between parts and whole may differ widely with objects being described. For example, if you want to describe a plantation, the spatial layout of the plantation will probably determine the order of the material presented. If a steel mill is being described, the process of milling will probably determine the sequence of presentation; in this case description will move close to process or narrative writing. In further contrast, if the government of the United States, an institution, is to be described, the three basic parts (legislative, executive, and judicial) would first be sketched and then their various subdivisions would be presented in detail. This is a quite different example of parts and whole relationships than that of either the plantation or the steel mill.

The smaller units of Solzhenitsyn's organization can be seen in the makeup of the longer paragraphs. For example, paragraph 4 is made up of two long series of examples of different kinds of work. The first series consists of a list of infinitives: "To push . . . To carry . . . To unload . . . To haul . . . ," and so on—nine in all. The second is a series of "You can . . ." sentences—nine in all. Paragraph 5 is composed of three sentences leading up to the job of the lumberjack in the forest. The remaining sentences sketch the process of cutting down a tree, from the stamping down of the snow around the tree to the final splitting of the parts of the tree into blocks. The organization is that of the process. Paragraph 8 has a long comparison-and-contrast ministructure, contrasting the workloads of the Czarist camps with the Soviet prison camps. Three examples are given for the Czarist camps (Akatui, Omsk, and Merchinsk), and two examples are given for the Soviet camps (Kolyma and Karlag). Each example is backed up by an authority who had been in the camp and could testify to the facts.

Structures like these are studied in detail in other chapters of this book: examples in "Explaining and Proving"; process in "Narrating"; and comparison and contrast in "Defining and Dividing." There are only a limited number of such small structures, and these three are among the more important ones. (Of course, the whole-part structure of description, illustrated by the overall organization of Solzhenitsyn's chapter, is another of these basic patterns.) Your own materials can probably be handled in terms of one of these organizing principles. If not, follow the structure itself of the object you are describing, for frequently it will suggest a type of organization. For example, Washington, D.C., can be described by first talking about northwest Washington, then northeast Washington, then southeast Washington, then southwest Washington, and finally the center of the city.

Exercises on Organization

1. **Use the whole-part organizing principle. In considering how to organize the various materials you have collected for your description, you should first consider the most *natural* principle dictated by the nature of description itself—the presentation of the whole and the parts and their relationships to each other. This is the method Solzhenitsyn used.**

   If this method seems a workable one, then your problem is to determine how to present the whole initially in a quick way and then how to present the parts in some sort of order that will present the object to the reader in a manner that achieves the purpose of the presentation. The student used a spatial structure, which was also an action sequence; the professional writer used the journalistic hierarchy of importance structure. Frequently, the structure of the object being described will immediately suggest the order in which the parts should be presented. The description of a plantation or of a city will frequently follow a spatial order; the description of an industrial plant will naturally follow an action or process sequence.

2. **Look for the unifying principle in the object. If the object is more complex, as was the system of prison camps for Solzhenitsyn, look for a**

glue that cements all of the separate parts into a whole. In Solzhenitsyn's case, it is the universal suffering throughout the camps, as we have seen. Usually, in persuasive, literary, and expressive descriptions, and even in expository descriptions that are attempting to prove a point, the unifying glue will be closely related to the thesis of the paper.

3. Organize following aims techniques. The linking of the unifying principle in the object to the thesis presents the possibility that the order of presentation of the whole and the parts may follow one of the techniques of organization studied in the chapters on the aims of discourse. Thus a description that arrives at a generalization about the object can follow the inductive procedures of the chapter on explaining and proving. Another likely alternative might be the exploratory structure suggested in Chapter 6. Finally, if you are doing a story for a newspaper, you could well consider the informative structure of the inverted pyramid used by Solzhenitsyn and outlined in Chapter 4, though inverted.

Of course, if you are writing a poem or if your description is part of a short story or is a character sketch, then quite different organizing principles, those examined in Chapter 7, will be relevant.

STYLE IN DESCRIBING

To get a sense of different styles used in describing, contrast the style of the barracks description in Solzhenitsyn's paragraphs 27–30 with the following classified ad:

> $4,200 DOWN 449 PITI 4-2, Forest North; about 1500 sq ft. SLA. Fireplace. Or lease with option, #395. 836–1423

Then, contrast both of these styles with some lines from "The Grave of King Arthur," written by a British poet, Thomas Warton, in 1777:

> Illuming the vaulted roof,
> A thousand torches flam'd aloof:
> From massy cups, with golden gleam
> Sparkled the red metheglin's stream:
> 5   To grace the gorgeous festival,
> Along the lofty-window'd hall,
> The storied tapestry was hung;—
> With minstrelsy the rafters rung
> Of harps, that with reflected light
> 10   From the proud gallery glitter'd bright.

Despite the fact that all three of these passages are descriptions of dwellings, the tone of each is quite distinct. The tones are so dissimilar because the three dwellings are all from diverse cultures, separated in space and time. Also, the tones are so varied because the three pieces are attempting to do different things with language. Solzhenitsyn is writing an investigation of the Russian prison camps and attempting to convince other Russians that the Soviet government (and especially its prison camps) is at least as bad as that of the Czars. The anonymous piece in the newspaper attempts to provide information to contemporary readers and buyers about a house in as succinct and economical a way as possible because the author is paying by the word. Warton's poem of the late eighteenth century hopefully will delight the reader by its mood, its images, and its sound structures. The three different aims (investigative persuasion, information, and poetic delight) permit—in fact, dictate—very different styles; and these differences are enhanced by the culture and media differences.

Usually the descriptions you will be asked to write will be something of a cross between the style of Solzhenitsyn and that of the newspaper. (Of course, your English instructor would probably be enchanted if you could turn out something like Warton's description, but a geology instructor who asked for a description of Gunnison Canyon wouldn't.) In fact, Solzhenitsyn's description incorporates many of the stylistic characteristics the typical descriptive assignment should exhibit.

Let us, therefore, look at some of these. In a striking way, Solzhenitsyn's description illustrates the major concern of all description, and from this major concern nearly all of the stylistic attributes of description follow almost necessarily. A writer has to describe something to a reader because the reader, in his or her life situation, has not encountered that object. The reader is a stranger to one aspect of the writer's life situation; in a limited sense, therefore, the writer can be said to belong to another subculture. And the problem of descriptive style is always the problem of translating an object from a familiar subculture to an alien subculture.

Solzhenitsyn's description of the customs of the natives in the Soviet prison camps exhibits this concern in two distinct layers. He first faces the problem of telling his Russian readers about the very existence of the other subculture—a subculture of some fifteen million people. To dramatize the existence of this subculture, he gives it a name, gives the inhabitants a name, and paints a vivid picture of the entire little world he is describing. Precisely because "there were many who did not even guess at its presence and many, many others . . . had heard something vague" (Preface, p. 6), Solzhenitsyn continually had to recall these terms and that strange world.

Stylistically, he does this by painting picture after picture with words. Such word pictures are called *images*; and therefore imagery is one of the main stylistic assets of the describer. Such imagery will usually be concrete and specific, not abstract and general. Notice the vivid images created in paragraph 11 when Solzhenitsyn is speaking of food: water, pot, unscrubbed small potatoes, black cabbage, beet tops, trash, vetch, bran, one bowl of gruel, two cups of turbid salty water, fat and meat "subproducts," salt, horse meat, exhausted horses, dolphin meat, walrus, seal, sea bear, sea animal trash, whale, animal feces, willow herbs, lichens, wild camomile. For another effective use of images, notice the almost rapid-fire slide-show imagery of paragraph 4, when Solzhenitsyn presents the different kinds of work.

Another obvious feature of Solzhenitsyn's style is his use of the subculture jargon. And he always tells the reader what the strange terms mean: *burki* (felt boots, paragraph 23), *lapti* (bast sandals, paragraph 23), *vagonki* (multiple bunks, paragraph 28), *kasha* (gruel, paragraphs 13, 15), and so on. Such words help to convey to us the other world of the subculture.

A third technique that Solzhenitsyn uses to give a concrete picture of the camps is his use of numbers. Paragraph 12 is a good example of this; the last 13 lines of the paragraph contain 14 numerical references. Paragraphs 8, 13, 16, 17, and 18—about food—also use numbers effectively. So does footnote 4, about the number of prisoners in the camps (paragraph 20).

Color images, of course, can be used to highlight a picture. Notice, for instance, the colors in these lines from paragraphs 24 and 25:

"My goose out there goes around barefoot all winter long and doesn't complain, although it's true her feet are red. And all of you have got rubber overshoes."

And then, in addition, bronze-gray camp faces will appear on the screen. Eyes oozing with tears, red eyelids. White cracked lips, covered with sores. Skewbald, unshaven bristles on the faces. In winter . . . a summer cap with earflaps sewn on.

One of the most interesting stylistic features of these paragraphs in general is their almost total absence of sound. The vivid pictures are displayed almost as if they were a silent movie. The silence emphasizes the loneliness and isolation of the Gulag.

Figures of speech are also used in this piece to heighten the images. Thus, in the paragraphs cited, there is the personification of a speaker in the first and the metaphor of the cinema in the second. Sometimes the contrast between the strangeness of the object being described and the ordinary world of the reader suggests to the writer humorous, paradoxical, or satirical ways of identifying the object. Thus, even though food was so scarce that starvation was often a real danger, Solzhenitsyn points out the paradox of shock workers turning down the extra ration—only to avoid the grueling extra work and grab a few extra hours of sleep (paragraph 13).

Exercises on Style

1. **Contrast the two language worlds to be embodied in the description. You are in a somewhat handicapped position to realize this contrast if you take both worlds for granted. Try to separate out the jargon of the**

described object so that you will not use it without explanation in the description. Possibly even a list similar to that preceding the Solzhenitsyn reading can be drawn up (see p. 253). If you decide to use this language of the subculture, translate it to the reader. Some of it, of course, will give a flavor and tone to the description. But too much of it, especially if it is technical, can discourage the reader.

2. **Make a sort of imagery inventory.** In order to exploit all of the concrete possibilities of the object, you might do either or both of the following exercises: (a) Systematically go through all of the five senses and list the sights (colors and shapes), sounds, smells, tastes, and touch sensations of the world of the object; (b) Isolate the important *parts* of the whole and alongside each part, list the images that accompany it.

3. **Don't neglect graphic aids.** Don't neglect the assistance, in rendering the object concrete, that photos, charts, graphs, figures, and so forth, can give you. The pictures in the *National Geographic* almost tell us as much as the words of the text.

ADDITIONAL EXERCISES ON DESCRIBING

Analyzing Descriptions

In the preceding pages of this chapter, we have carefully analyzed Alexandr Solzhenitsyn's description of some aspects of the Soviet prison camps and Maurice Algazi's description of a common typewriter. Now it is your turn to do the analysis yourself. For your analysis, a typical entry from the *Illustrated World Encyclopedia*, edited by Edward Bobley and others, has been chosen. It is not difficult reading, since it is intended for an average adult audience. Read the piece keeping in mind what has been said about the nature of description in this chapter. In particular, try to determine the following: the point of view of the author, the selection principle of the author, the structure of the described object, the organization of the entire piece, and the style of the writer in this piece.

PARIS, FRANCE

1   Paris is the capital and largest city of France. It is on the Seine River. It is one of the best-known and most beautiful capitals in the world, and people go there to see its sights, to study, and to enjoy its gay life. It is called the "City of Light." Many writers and painters have gone there to study or live. Paris is also a great fashion center, and some of the world's most famous designers of women's clothing are in Paris.

2   About three million people live in Paris. There are factories that make women's clothing, perfume, hats, and jewelry, for which Paris is famous.

There are big plants that make automobiles, machinery, chemicals, and dyes. Paris prints more books, magazines and newspapers than any other city in France.

What Paris Is Like

3   A person visiting Paris can spend months enjoying all its sights. The city is known for its wide, tree-lined boulevards, its gardens and fountains, and its sidewalk cafés, where people may sit at tables outdoors in the warm weather.

4   Perhaps the most famous sight in Paris is the Eiffel Tower, the tallest structure in Europe. With its TV antenna, it is 1,056 feet high. One of the best-known streets is the Champs Elysées. At one end of this boulevard stands the Arch of Triumph (about which you can read in the article on ARCH). Another noted street is the Rue de la Paix, where people shop in luxurious stores as they do on Fifth Avenue in New York City.

5   Paris has many historic churches, museums, and buildings. Every year thousands visit Notre Dame Cathedral, a splendid example of Gothic architecture. It is on a little island in the Seine called the *Ile de la Cité* (Island of the City). Many also visit a building with a high dome called *Les Invalides* where the body of Napoleon rests. Few leave Paris without seeing the world-renowned museum, the Louvre, or the magnificent Opéra. Another popular place is Montmartre, the colorful entertainment section of Paris, with its steep, narrow streets. Montmartre is a hill, the highest point in Paris, and at the top stands the Sacré Coeur, a beautiful white church from which a person can get a wonderful view of the entire city. All through Paris are monuments to French patriots and heroes.

6   Paris has a number of important colleges and universities. The University of Paris is one of the oldest in the world. One of its schools, the Sorbonne, is more than 750 years old. Students from many countries study there. The University of Paris is on the side of the Seine River called the Left Bank. Many painters live in the section called the Left Bank, and visitors may see some of them painting out-of-doors and selling their works on the sidewalks.

7   Paris is one of the communications and travel centers of Europe. Railroads and highways branch out into all directions to other capitals and large cities. Airplanes from Britain, North America, the Middle East, North Africa and from other European cities land at its big airports. Paris is an inland port, and ships can travel on the Seine River to the English Channel. Paris has a large subway system called the Métro. The Paris stock exchange, called the Bourse, is one of the most important in the world.

Paris in the Past

8   Paris is a very old city. It was a little fishing village in ancient Roman times, two thousand years ago. Eight hundred years ago it had already become a great center of learning and was the capital of the kings of France.

9   During World War I, the Germans came close to capturing Paris but never took it. In World War II, the Germans did take the city and occupied it until 1944. All during the war, many of the people of Paris worked in

underground groups and fought the Germans as best they could. Paris was not damaged much during the war except in the suburbs where the large factories stood.

The Treaties of Paris

10   Many important treaties in history have been signed in Paris. In 1763, the treaty ending the French and Indian Wars between the French and the British was signed in Paris. The signing of the treaty that ended the Revolutionary War between Great Britain and the American colonies, making the United States an independent nation, was signed in Paris in 1783. The defeat of Napoleon in the Napoleonic wars ended in a treaty signed in Paris in 1814. In the following year, a second treaty was signed after Napoleon's final defeat at Waterloo. The Crimean War, between Russia on one side and France, England, Turkey and Sardinia on the other side, ended in a treaty signed in Paris in 1856. In 1898 Paris was chosen as the place to sign the treaty between the United States and Spain after the Spanish-American War. After World War I, the Peace Conference met in Paris and in nearby places where treaties with the various countries were signed. The famous treaty with Germany in 1919 was signed at Versailles, outside Paris. After World War II, several treaties were signed in Paris.

PARIS, FRANCE. Population (1969 estimate) 2,607,625. Capital and largest city of France. On Seine River.

The following exercises can be done either in written or in oral form. They might first be discussed by the class or a small group and then turned into written exercises.

Exercises on "Paris, France"

1. **Point of View**
   a. **What is the general point of view of the author of this piece? Do the editors think it is an important entry? In the same encyclopedia in which this entry occupies two columns, Tokyo occupies one column, Moscow one column, and London and Washington, D.C., three columns. What do these facts suggest about the point of view of the editors?**
   b. **Is the point of view neutral or biased? Is there an American partisanship? Of the treaties of Paris (this section occupies one-fourth of the article), how many relate to America? Can you detect a cultural, industrial, or political bias, negative or positive?**
2. **Selectivity Principle**
   a. **What are the three major subdivisions of the article? Why these three? What others might you want to have seen covered? Does the**

article tell you anything about the social classes of France or anything directly about the religion of the people? Why not?

b. What is the basic aim of this piece? Is it to entertain, to persuade, to prove something, or to inform?

c. What assumptions about the reader have been made in this piece? What level student could read this selection? Why is *Ile de la Cité* translated and *Les Invalides* not translated? Is the selection of material for the article based on what your concept of the general reader of that level would desire to know in a short article?

3. The Structure of the Object Described

a. In what part of the article is the whole of Paris described? The parts of Paris considered in the article are "What Paris is Like," "Paris in the Past," "The Treaties of Paris." Do these parts give you a comprehensive view of Paris? Would the same whole and parts apply to your own city or town?

b. What notion unifies the entire article, other than the general notion of Paris itself? If half of the article can be said to be about the present Paris and the other half about Paris in the past, do you consider this a justified view of the city?

4. Organization of the Article

a. What is the place of the article on Paris in the overall organization of the encyclopedia? What functions are achieved by putting the articles in alphabetical order? Does the phrase "everything from a to z" imply anything about purpose in an organizational scheme? (This issue was considered in Chapter 4.)

b. In the introductory section, the main elements emphasized (at least by space) are fashions, industries, and communication. Why do you think this is so?

c. In the section "What Paris is Like," half of the space is devoted to the sights (three paragraphs), one paragraph to the colleges and universities, and one paragraph to communications. Do these three parts seem to represent the present Paris?

5. Style

a. Would you say that this style is intended to persuade, to entertain, to explain, to prove, to inform, or to express the intense personal feelings of the writer about Paris?

b. Does the style seem to achieve the intended aim?

c. Would you characterize the article as personal or objective? As concrete or abstract? As partly affected by the culture of Paris? As intense or neutral? Do you think that Solzhenitsyn would describe Moscow in *The Gulag Archipelago* in this sort of style? Check some of the many references to Moscow in the *Gulag* and compare his treatment of the capital of Russia to this treatment of the capital of France.

Writing Descriptions

In each case, before you settle down to write, you should determine in advance your audience, your purpose, your medium (letter, article in a magazine, and so on), and the situation in which you would write such a piece. Then, you should go to some trouble to acquaint yourself with the object you are describing. Try to determine in advance your point of view (physical and mental), your selection principle, the whole and parts of your object, and the organizational pattern you will follow. Given all of these, what will be the tone of your style?

Exercises on Writing Descriptions

1. Describe something with which you are familiar to someone who is quite unfamiliar with it. Consider your hometown, your automobile, your college, your church, and so on.
   a. Try a persuasive purpose, that is, try to persuade a friend to visit your hometown, buy a similar automobile, switch to your college, or consider attending your church. This will enable you to select the favorable facets of your object and downplay the unfavorable. It will also enable you to use some emotional appeals and language. In other words, you have several options and resources in your appeals and in your style.
   b. If someone else in your class is from the same town, drives the same type of automobile, or is in the same academic department as yourself, have him or her take the same facts you used for the persuasive piece and incorporate them into an informative piece for the same audience. Or you may write both versions.
   c. If you have some poetic instincts, try to write a poem about your hometown, church, or college. Incorporate a good deal of description in the poem.
2. Take some object that might be studied in your major field and describe its structure. This time consider your audience to be an instructor in that field. Some suggested topics are the following: the structure of a bank, a firm, or an industry; the structure of a church; the structure of a city, state, or national government area; the structure of an organism; the structure of a poem or of a short story.
3. The preceding exercise would normally be written with an informative aim; that is, your audience would not expect you to prove that your description is accurate. In this exercise, try to establish that your description is reliable by giving evidence for its accuracy. The evidence may be based upon your own observations or those of witnesses whom

you have personally contacted and whose reports you have reason to trust; or it might be based upon secondary evidence, such as library materials and documents.

This theme might be a discourse analysis, with the reader being supplied with the discourse you are using. Thus, if you are analyzing a short poem, the accuracy of your structural descriptions can be readily checked by the reader.

4. One of the most frequent types of descriptions is the character sketch. These have been favorites of writers for centuries. Try your hand at this genre. Select a particular person that you can visualize to yourself, although you may want him or her to represent a general type of person. Don't be afraid to use incidents to illustrate the characteristics you are describing; in this genre description and narration come together quite comfortably. Historically, the character sketch has been used either for persuasive or for literary purposes, or for a combination of the two purposes. But if you prefer, it is also possible for you to write an informative description.

Narrating

THE IMPORTANCE OF NARRATION

A narrative is a story or description of actual or fictional events. This is the most familiar context of *narration*—the writing process that results in narrative prose. However, for the purposes of writing themes of your own and analyzing the writing of others, you should keep in mind the somewhat broader conception of this mode as defined in Chapter 8. Narration is a mode of organization in which experience is treated in dynamic terms, that is, as something that changes in the course of time. In a narration, something happens: people interact and change (physically, emotionally, and psychologically), processes are carried out, and the causes and effects of action are of central importance. In short, narration is the mode of stories, descriptions of processes, and accounts or analyses of causes and effects. Narration is the mode of myths and legends, stories and novels, news items, lab reports, many logical proofs, and exploratory investigations.

Since narration is based on a sense of experience as a sequence of events in time, its importance for most people should not be difficult to understand. We are constantly affected by and participate in events that occur within time, so we come to accept time as a significant factor in our lives. We have an interest in what happens, how it happens, and why. Narration, as an account of what is, was, or could be, enables us to understand, analyze, and perhaps even alter what happens. Narrative prose accounts for both sequence and consequence.

In this context you can see that the impulse on the part of many people to keep diaries or write journals is rooted in their need to keep a record of what has happened to them and to have a basis for figuring out why. Similarly, our need to write (as well as read) news stories and directions on how to do things is based on our assumption that passing on what we know is a significant human function. Our interest in telling stories about "once upon a time" is not only a way of reporting consequences but also of examining motives; it is not only a way of telling about the past but also of speaking to the present. Finally, our need to record evidence of events in the laboratory or in the social or political body or even in outer space is often the basis for hypotheses concerning events whose endings are not yet known—and can initially be known or proven only through inference. We record experiments, keep track of trends, write history, and project results, using what we know to draw conclusions about what we would like to know. Narration is a mode through which we deal with experience as a dynamic process, from beginning to middle to end.

SOME EXAMPLES OF NARRATION

For most readers, the most familiar forms of narration are the short story and the novel. But since the emphasis in this chapter (and in this book as a whole) is on nonfictional prose, the central examples of narration here will be essays rather than stories. (Narration, as considered in the writing of poetry and fiction, is further discussed in Chapter 7, "Writing Poems and Stories.") However, both examples reflect the central concepts of the narrative mode; both reflect an understanding of chronology, causation, and change.

The first reading in narration is an essay by Bruno Bettelheim, a psychologist and teacher at the University of Chicago. In reading the essay you will find that it is not strictly chronological (events are not presented strictly in the order of their occurrence) and that the essay is not strictly narrative in mode; that is, we are told about some of the effects of action before their causes are explained and a significant amount of descriptive (including analytical) material accompanies the narration. In reading, consider how the essay is affected because it was written in this manner.

Prereading Activities

VOCABULARY.   Your successful reading of the essay will require an understanding of the following terms (numbers in parentheses refer to paragraphs):

autism (2)—a form of childhood schizophrenia characterized by acting out and withdrawal

schizophrenia (4)—a psychotic reaction characterized by withdrawal from reality, accompanied by affective, behavioral, and intellectual disturbances

orthogenic (3)—pertaining to the correction or treatment of mental and emotional abnormalities in children

imperious (5)—domineering or overbearing

ingestive (5)—pertaining to the taking in or swallowing of food

megalomania (7)—a psychopathological condition characterized by fantasies of wealth, power, or omnipotence

colic (9)—severe abdominal pain in infants, due to gas in the alimentary canal

fey (10)—fated, or full of the sense of approaching death

STUDY QUESTIONS

As you read the essay, keep in mind the following questions.

1. How does concern with chronology govern the development of the narrative sections of this essay?
2. What is the effect of the descriptive sections? What do you believe was the author's reason for putting them in?
3. Where and how is this essay a story? Where and how is it an explanation of a process? Where and how is it a statement concerning cause and effect?
4. What is the point of view of this essay? How would you describe the narrator?
5. What is the point of the essay? Is there more than one? Is the point explicit or implicit in the essay?

JOEY: A "MECHANICAL BOY"

Bruno Bettelheim

1 Joey, when we began our work with him, was a mechanical boy. He functioned as if by remote control, run by machines of his own powerfully creative fantasy. Not only did he himself believe that he was a machine but, more remarkably, he created this impression in others. Even while he performed actions that are intrinsically human, they never appeared to be other than machine-started and executed. On the other hand, when the machine was not working we had to concentrate on recollecting his presence, for he seemed not to exist. A human body that functions as if it were a machine and a machine that duplicates human functions are equally fascinating and frightening. Perhaps they are so uncanny because they remind us that the human body can operate without a human spirit, that body can exist without soul. And Joey was a child who had been robbed of his humanity.

2 Not every child who possesses a fantasy world is possessed by it. Normal children may retreat into realms of imaginary glory or magic powers, but they are easily recalled from these excursions. Disturbed children are not always able to make the return trip; they remain withdrawn, prisoners of the inner world of delusion and fantasy. In many ways Joey presented a classic example of this state of infantile autism.

3 At the Sonia Shankman Orthogenic School of the University of Chicago it is our function to provide a therapeutic environment in which such children may start life over again. I have previously described the rehabilitation of

another of our patients ["Schizophrenic Art: A Case Study"; *Scientific American*, April, 1952]. This time I shall concentrate upon the illness, rather than the treatment. In any age, when the individual has escaped into a delusional world, he has usually fashioned it from bits and pieces of the world at hand. Joey, in his time and world, chose the machine and froze himself in its image. His story has a general relevance to the understanding of emotional development in a machine age.

4   Joey's delusion is not uncommon among schizophrenic children today. He wanted to be rid of his unbearable humanity, to become completely automatic. He so nearly succeeded in attaining this goal that he could almost convince others, as well as himself, of his mechanical character. The descriptions of autistic children in the literature take for their point of departure and comparison the normal or abnormal human being. To do justice to Joey I would have to compare him simultaneously to a most inept infant and a highly complex piece of machinery. Often we had to force ourselves by a conscious act of will to realize that Joey was a child. Again and again his acting-out of his delusions froze our own ability to respond as human beings.

5   During Joey's first weeks with us we would watch absorbedly as that at once fragile-looking and imperious nine-year-old went about his mechanical existence. Entering the dining room, for example, he would string an imaginary wire from his "energy source"—an imaginary electric outlet—to the table. There he "insulated" himself with paper napkins and finally plugged himself in. Only then could Joey eat, for he firmly believed that the "current" ran his ingestive apparatus. So skillful was the pantomime that one had to look twice to be sure there was neither wire nor outlet nor plug. Children and members of our staff spontaneously avoided stepping on the "wires" for fear of interrupting what seemed the source of his very life.

6   For long periods of time, when his "machinery" was idle, he would sit so quietly that he would disappear from the focus of the most conscientious observation. Yet in the next moment he might be "working" and the center of our captivated attention. Many times a day he would turn himself on and shift noisily through a sequence of higher and higher gears until he "exploded," screaming "Crash, crash!" and hurling items from his ever present apparatus—radio tubes, light bulbs, even motors or, lacking these, any handy breakable object. (Joey had an astonishing knack for snatching bulbs and tubes unobserved.) As soon as the object thrown had shattered, he would cease his screaming and wild jumping and retire to mute, motionless nonexistence.

7   Our maids, inured to difficult children, were exceptionally attentive to Joey; they were apparently moved by his extreme infantile fragility, so strangely coupled with megalomaniacal superiority. Occasionally some of the apparatus he fixed to his bed to "live him" during his sleep would fall down in disarray. This machinery he contrived from masking tape, cardboard, wire and other paraphernalia. Usually the maids would pick up such things and leave them on a table for the children to find, or disregard them entirely. But Joey's machine they carefully restored: "Joey must have the carburetor so he can breathe." Similarly they were on the alert to pick up and preserve the motors that ran him during the day and the exhaust pipes through which he exhaled.

8   How had Joey become a human machine? From intensive interviews with his parents we learned that the process had begun even before birth. Schizophrenia often results from parental rejection, sometimes combined ambivalently with love. Joey, on the other hand, had been completely ignored.

9   "I never knew I was pregnant," his mother said, meaning that she had already excluded Joey from her consciousness. His birth, she said, "did not make any difference." Joey's father, a rootless draftee in the wartime civilian army, was equally unready for parenthood. So, of course, are many young couples. Fortunately most such parents lose their indifference upon the baby's birth. But not Joey's parents. "I did not want to see or nurse him," his mother declared. "I had no feeling of actual dislike—I simply didn't want to take care of him." For the first three months of his life Joey "cried most of the time." A colicky baby, he was kept on a rigid four-hour feeding schedule, was not touched unless necessary and was never cuddled or played with. The mother, preoccupied with herself, usually left Joey alone in the crib or playpen during the day. The father discharged his frustrations by punishing Joey when the child cried at night.

10   Soon the father left for overseas duty, and the mother took Joey, now a year and a half old, to live with her at her parents' home. On his arrival the grandparents noticed that ominous changes had occurred in the child. Strong and healthy at birth, he had become frail and irritable; a responsive baby, he had become remote and inaccessible. When he began to master speech, he talked only to himself. At an early date he became preoccupied with machinery, including an old electric fan which he could take apart and put together again with surprising deftness.

11   Joey's mother impressed us with a fey quality that expressed her insecurity, her detachment from the world and her low physical vitality. We were struck especially by her total indifference as she talked about Joey. This seemed much more remarkable than the actual mistakes she made in handling him. Certainly he was left to cry for hours when hungry, because she fed him on a rigid schedule; he was toilet-trained with great rigidity so that he would give no trouble. These things happen to many children. But Joey's existence never registered with his mother. In her recollections he was fused at one moment with one event or person; at another, with something or somebody else. When she told us about his birth and infancy, it was as if she were talking about some vague acquaintance, and soon her thoughts would wander off to another person or to herself.

12   When Joey was not yet four, his nursery school suggested that he enter a special school for disturbed children. At the new school his autism was immediately recognized. During his three years there he experienced a slow improvement. Unfortunately a subsequent two years in a parochial school destroyed this progress. He began to develop compulsive defenses, which he called his "preventions." He could not drink, for example, except through elaborate piping systems built of straws. Liquids had to be "pumped" into him, in his fantasy, or he could not suck. Eventually his behavior became so upsetting that he could not be kept in the parochial school. At home things did not improve. Three months before entering the Orthogenic School he made a serious attempt at suicide.

13   To us Joey's pathological behavior seemed the external expression of an

overwhelming effort to remain almost nonexistent as a person. For weeks Joey's only reply when addressed was "Bam." Unless he thus neutralized whatever we said, there would be an explosion, for Joey plainly wished to close off every form of contact not mediated by machinery. Even when he was bathed he rocked back and forth with mute, engine-like regularity, flooding the bathroom. If he stopped rocking, he did this like a machine too; suddenly he went completely rigid. Only once, after months of being lifted from his bath and carried to bed, did a small expression of puzzled pleasure appear on his face as he said very softly: "They even carry you to your bed here."

14   For a long time after he began to talk he would never refer to anyone by name, but only as "that person" or "the little person" or "the big person." He was unable to designate by its true name anything to which he attached feelings. Nor could he name his anxieties except through neologisms or word contaminations. For a long time he spoke about "master paintings" and "a master painting room" (*i.e.,* masturbating and masturbating room). One of his machines, the "criticizer," prevented him from "saying words which have unpleasant feelings." Yet he gave personal names to the tubes and motors in his collection of machinery. Moreover, these dead things had feelings; the tubes bled when hurt and sometimes got sick. He consistently maintained this reversal between animate and inanimate objects.

15   In Joey's machine world everything, on pain of instant destruction, obeyed inhibitory laws much more stringent than those of physics. When we came to know him better, it was plain that in his moments of silent withdrawal, with his machine switched off, Joey was absorbed in pondering the compulsive laws of his private universe. His preoccupation with machinery made it difficult to establish even practical contacts with him. If he wanted to do something with a counselor, such as play with a toy that had caught his vague attention, he could not do so: "I'd like this very much, but first I have to turn off the machine." But by the time he had fulfilled all the requirements of his preventions, he had lost interest. When a toy was offered to him, he could not touch it because his motors and his tubes did not leave him a hand free. Even certain colors were dangerous and had to be strictly avoided in toys and clothing, because "some colors turn off the current, and I can't touch them because I can't live without the current."

16   Joey was convinced that machines were better than people. Once when he bumped into one of the pipes on our jungle gym he kicked it so violently that his teacher had to restrain him to keep him from injuring himself. When she explained that the pipe was much harder than his foot, Joey replied: "That proves it. Machines are better than the body. They don't break; they're much harder and stronger." If he lost or forgot something, it merely proved that his brain ought to be thrown away and replaced by machinery. If he spilled something, his arm should be broken and twisted off because it did not work properly. When his head or arm failed to work as it should, he tried to punish it by hitting it. Even Joey's feelings were mechanical. Much later in his therapy, when he had formed a timid attachment to another child and had been rebuffed, Joey cried: "He broke my feelings."

17   Gradually we began to understand what had seemed to be contradictory in Joey's behavior—why he held on to the motors and tubes, then suddenly

destroyed them in a fury, then set out immediately and urgently to equip himself with new and larger tubes. Joey had created these machines to run his body and mind because it was too painful to be human. But again and again he became dissatisfied with their failure to meet his need and rebellious at the way they frustrated his will. In a recurrent frenzy he "exploded" his light bulbs and tubes, and for a moment became a human being—for one crowning instant he came alive. But as soon as he had asserted his dominance through the self-created explosion, he felt his life ebbing away. To keep on existing he had immediately to restore his machines and replenish the electricity that supplied his life energy.

18   What deep-seated fears and needs underlay Joey's delusional system? We were long in finding out. Joey's preventions effectively concealed the problems one by one.

19   During his first year with us Joey's most trying problem was toilet behavior. This surprised us, for Joey's personality was not "anal" in the Freudian sense; his original personality damage had antedated the period of his toilet-training. Rigid and early toilet-training, however, had certainly contributed to his anxieties. It was our effort to help Joey with this problem that led to his first recognition of us as human beings.

20   Going to the toilet, like everything else in Joey's life, was surrounded by elaborate preventions. We had to accompany him; he had to take off all his clothes; he could only squat, not sit, on the toilet seat; he had to touch the wall with one hand, in which he also clutched frantically the vacuum tubes that powered his elimination. He was terrified lest his whole body be sucked down.

21   To counteract this fear we gave him a metal wastebasket in lieu of a toilet. Eventually, when eliminating into the wastebasket, he no longer needed to take off all his clothes, nor to hold on to the wall. He still needed the tubes and motors which, he believed, moved his bowels for him. But here again the all-important machinery was itself a source of new terrors. In Joey's world the gadgets had to move their bowels, too. He was terribly concerned that they should, but since they were so much more powerful than men, he was also terrified that if his tubes moved their bowels, their feces would fill all of space and leave him no room to live. He was thus always caught in some fearful contradiction.

22   Our readiness to accept his toilet habits, which obviously entailed some hardship for his counselors, gave Joey the confidence to express his obsessions in drawings. Drawing these fantasies was a first step toward letting us in, however distantly, to what concerned him most deeply. It was the first step in a year-long process of externalizing his anal preoccupations. As a result he began seeing feces everywhere; the whole world became to him a mire of excrement. At the same time he began to eliminate freely wherever he happened to be. But with this release from his infantile imprisonment in compulsive rules, the toilet and the whole process of elimination became less dangerous. Thus far it had been beyond Joey's comprehension that anybody could possibly move his bowels without mechanical aid. Now Joey took a further step forward; defecation became the first physiological process he could perform without the help of vacuum tubes. It must not be thought that he was proud of this ability. Taking pride in an achievement presupposes that one accomplishes it of one's own free will.

He still did not feel himself an autonomous person who could do things on his own. To Joey defecation still seemed enslaved to some incomprehensible but utterly binding cosmic law, perhaps the law his parents had imposed on him when he was being toilet-trained.

23   It was not simply that his parents had subjected him to rigid, early training. Many children are so trained. But in most cases the parents have a deep emotional investment in the child's performance. The child's response in turn makes training an occasion for interaction between them and for the building of genuine relationships. Joey's parents had no emotional investment in him. His obedience gave them no satisfaction and won him no affection or approval. As a toilet-trained child he saved his mother labor, just as household machines saved her labor. As a machine he was not loved for his performance, nor could he love himself.

24   So it had been with all other aspects of Joey's existence with his parents. Their reactions to his eating or noneating, sleeping or wakening, urinating or defecating, being dressed or undressed, washed or bathed did not flow from any unitary interest in him, deeply embedded in their personalities. By treating him mechanically his parents made him a machine. The various functions of life—even the parts of his body—bore no integrating relationship to one another or to any sense of self that was acknowledged and confirmed by others. Though he had acquired mastery over some functions, such as toilet-training and speech, he had acquired them separately and kept them isolated from each other. Toilet-training had thus not gained him a pleasant feeling of body mastery; speech had not led to communication of thought or feeling. On the contrary, each achievement only steered him away from self-mastery and integration. Toilet-training had enslaved him. Speech left him talking in neologisms that obstructed his and our ability to relate to each other. In Joey's development the normal process of growth had been made to run backward. Whatever he had learned put him not at the end of his infantile development toward integration but, on the contrary, farther behind than he was at its very beginning. Had we understood this sooner, his first years with us would have been less baffling.

25   It is unlikely that Joey's calamity could befall a child in any time and culture but our own. He suffered no physical deprivation; he starved for human contact. Just to be taken care of is not enough for relating. It is a necessary but not a sufficient condition. At the extreme where utter scarcity reigns, the forming of relationships is certainly hampered. But our society of mechanized plenty often makes for equal difficulties in a child's learning to relate. Where parents can provide the simple creature-comforts for their children only at the cost of significant effort, it is likely that they will feel pleasure in being able to provide for them; it is this, the parents' pleasure, that gives children a sense of personal worth and sets the process of relating in motion. But if comfort is so readily available that the parents feel no particular pleasure in winning it for their children, then the children cannot develop the feeling of being worthwhile around the satisfaction of their basic needs. Of course parents and children can and do develop relationships around other situations. But matters are then no longer so simple and direct. The child must be on the receiving end of care and concern given with pleasure and without the exaction of return if he is to feel loved and worthy of respect and consideration. This feeling gives him the ability to trust; he

can entrust his well-being to persons to whom he is so important. Out of such trust the child learns to form close and stable relationships.

26 For Joey relationship with his parents was empty of pleasure in comfort-giving as in all other situations. His was an extreme instance of a plight that sends many schizophrenic children to our clinics and hospitals. Many months passed before he could relate to us; his despair that anybody could like him made contact impossible.

27 When Joey could finally trust us enough to let himself become more infantile, he began to play at being a papoose. There was a corresponding change in his fantasies. He drew endless pictures of himself as an electrical papoose. Totally enclosed, suspended in empty space, he is run by unknown, unseen powers through wireless electricity.

28 As we eventually came to understand, the heart of Joey's delusional system was the artificial, mechanical womb he had created and into which he had locked himself. In his papoose fantasies lay the wish to be entirely reborn in a womb. His new experiences in the school suggested that life, after all, might be worth living. Now he was searching for a way to be reborn in a better way. Since machines were better than men, what was more natural than to try rebirth through them? This was the deeper meaning of his electrical papoose.

29 As Joey made progress, his pictures of himself became more dominant in his drawings. Though still machine-operated, he has grown in self-importance. Now he has acquired hands that do something, and he has had the courage to make a picture of the machine that runs him. Later still the papoose became a person, rather than a robot encased in glass.

30 Eventually Joey began to create an imaginary family at the school: the "Carr" family. Why the Carr family? In the car he was enclosed as he had been in his papoose, but at least the car was not stationary; it could move. More important, in a car one was not only driven but also could drive. The Carr family was Joey's way of exploring the possibility of leaving the school, of living with a good family in a safe, protecting car.

31 Joey at last broke through his prison. In this brief account it has not been possible to trace the painfully slow process of his first true relations with other human beings. Suffice it to say that he ceased to be a mechanical boy and became a human child. This newborn child was, however, nearly 12 years old. To recover the lost time is a tremendous task. That work has occupied Joey and us ever since. Sometimes he sets to it with a will; at other times the difficulty of real life makes him regret that he ever came out of his shell. But he has never wanted to return to his mechanical life.

32 One last detail and this fragment of Joey's story has been told. When Joey was 12, he made a float for our Memorial Day parade. It carried the slogan: "Feelings are more important than anything under the sun." Feelings, Joey had learned, are what make for humanity; their absence, for a mechanical existence. With this knowledge Joey entered the human condition.

"Joey: A 'Mechanical Boy'" is a particularly helpful sample of narration because it is clearly more than a simple story. Specifically, Bettelheim's essay (1) tells us who Joey is and what he was like (descriptive sections); (2) explains how Joey became a "mechanical boy" (narrative/

process); and (3) explains how Bettelheim and others brought Joey to the point where he could "enter the human condition" (narrative/process). Bettelheim not only tells us what happened, but he shows us how in terms of causes and effects. It is this transmission of a sense of significant action—of dynamic process—that is at the heart of narration. We will return to an examination of "Joey" after the reading of the second selection.

The second essay, written by a student writer, should prove an equally helpful illustration of the narrative mode. Before reading it, review the five basic questions concerning narration that precede the Bettelheim essay.

BORIS

Diane Balmer

1   Anthropology majors are required to take a course entitled Physical Anthropology—a study of human structure and evolution. The laboratory for this course consists of a systematic study of the skeleton. This study involves some serious questions of ethics and philosophy. It also involves a personal confrontation with the fact of human mortality.

2   The first few weeks of the class presented no serious problems. In the beginning, the innocuous bones of the arms, legs, and spine are studied. My classmates and I knew they were human, but it is easy to disregard this fact for a vertebra or femur. However, sooner or later the ultimate confrontation occurs: the skull. It is impossible to imagine a human skull as anything but what it is—the residue of a life, the last remains of a thing which once walked and talked and laughed and cried and enjoyed life as much as you ever did. The empty eye sockets, the delicate, paper-thin nasal bones, and the channels where blood vessels once ran reminded me how quickly a life can be reduced to a few lumps of calcified tissue.

3   I managed to survive this first encounter with the dead, but my next was more profound. In some sudden flush of enthusiasm I undertook as an independent study project the analysis of a skeleton. The aim was to determine the age and sex and any other available information about the individual.

4   I went into the lab that first afternoon and faced the most difficult part of the entire project—selecting my subject out of the twenty or so skeletons sitting in boxes under the table at one side of the room. I started pulling out boxes at random and inspected their contents. And I began considering whether I ought to drop the course.

5   For these were not the clean, sterile, sanitized bones of the beginning labs. Most of these skeletons were greasy to the touch and yellow-brown in color. Bits of dried flesh or nerve could be found in some of the cracks. Some of the vertebral columns were loosely strung on wires which allowed them to slip around into weird positions. Little boxes with grease-soaked paper linings held the bones of a hand or foot. And perhaps the most distinctive quality was the smell of these dirty old relics of past humanity.

6   I finally ended up selecting a skeleton labelled 97, partly because of an

unusual bone fusion but primarily because it was about the cleanest specimen I could find. For some reason of which I'm not completely sure, I then christened my subject Boris. I don't know whether it was a perverse joke stemming from my need to add some humor to a morbid situation or a compulsion to recognize the humanity and individuality of this box of artifacts. At any rate, Boris and I were companions one afternoon a week for the next three months.

7   I learned a lot from Boris. He sent me off to the library many times as I tried to determine what he was like. I concluded that he was indeed a Boris and not a Brunhilda, that he stood about 5 feet 2 inches tall, suffered from arthritis, and was missing the tip of one of his thumbs. I found that he had lived a full life, dying sometime after age 55, and that by that time he, typical American, had lost several of his teeth. His heavy bones indicated that, though he was short, he probably was stoutly built, but there's no way of telling how much he weighed. Bits and pieces of his life could be dredged up, but the vital essence was lost forever. His medical records had also been lost, so I have no way of knowing how near the truth any of my speculations were. Whether his friends, children, brothers and sisters are still living somewhere, whether they ever think of him, how he treated them—these were things I wondered about after I left the lab at night, but didn't mention in my write-up at the end of the project. Scientific reports allow very little margin for such subjective confrontations with life, and death.

8   Mortality is a fact which must somehow be faced by everyone. But none of my close friends or relatives has died within my memory, so I had not come face to face with this problem until I met Boris and his associates in the basement of East Hall. I still do not understand the mystery of mortality. Sometimes, though, I think of sitting in the lab holding Boris's head in my lap with the smell of the skeletons all around me, and the thought of death means a little more than it once did.

Notice that "Boris" is a *story* of "what happened" to the author when she took physical anthropology, an account of certain *processes* followed in the laboratory, and an analytical statement of *cause and effect*—on how taking a course altered Balmer's perspective on life (more specifically, on the cause of her heightened consciousness of human mortality). That is, "Boris" illustrates in its own way the three types of narration involved in Bettelheim's account of Joey, three of the most common types of narration seen and written from day to day.

PREWRITING: CHOOSING A TOPIC, ESTABLISHING A NARRATOR, DETERMINING FOCUS AND SCOPE

Among the basic questions writers most frequently ask about narration are the following:

1. What stories, processes, or combinations of causes and effects make good topics?

2. What is my relation to the subject matter and the reader?
3. Since most narration is, inherently, only a part of a longer or on-going narration, how do I determine how much of the whole story to write about?

These questions are crucial to any writer's success in producing successful narration. We can begin to answer each by confronting, in terms of the reading you have just done, the pervasive question of all writing, the question of aim. Narration, like the other modes, is always used for a particular purpose (or purposes), and that purpose always determines the nature of any given narrative—its subject matter, length, complexity, and style.

Choosing a Topic for Narration

Bruno Bettelheim's article was written to inform us of the existence of Joey (and of children like him) and of the work being done at the Shankman Orthogenic School—and to persuade us that both are of more than passing significance. These aims are served through a presentation of the key elements of Joey's life and of a few of the procedures (processes) used in the school. Bettelheim wants to show us that Joey is a boy and not a machine, and he wants to show this in terms of the changes in Joey's behavior. Joey's story makes a good topic for narration because it informs us of and focuses on a significant change—or more precisely, a series of specific changes—in Joey's life as brought about by his relationships with others.

Diane Balmer also chose a good topic, and for the same reason. Her purpose was apparently to make a personal statement, a statement of self-expression concerning an unexpected insight in a course—and to persuade us that her experience (like Boris's and ours) has been significant. Balmer fulfills her aims by telling us something of the process that led to her insight—the physical and emotional steps that led to her perception of what mortality means. She tells us who "Boris" was and something of what happened to him; she tells us what happened in her own mind because of what she learned about Boris. Balmer's essay makes the point that we are significant precisely because things happen to us—and we change.

Two other types of significant change are often the focus of writing based on narrative principles: writing that either reports or explains a process and writing that explains causes and effects. Both the Bettelheim and Balmer essays explain process and cause and effect, though these seem not to have been their primary concern. More typical examples of process writing could be a report on the eruption of a volcano and an article telling us how to buy an appropriate microwave oven. Typical examples of cause-and-effect narration usually stress either the key causes of a given effect or the key effects of a given cause: "Why I will never take another math course," "How getting a full-time job at the age of 14 affected my life," and so on.

Narration should convey to your reader a significant sense of change (cause-effect, process, story) in the course of time; any topic that fulfills this requirement can serve as the focus for your writing.

Exercises on Choosing a Topic for Narration

In doing the following exercises, keep in mind that a topic is a specific focus on a general subject.
1. **Develop topics appropriate for 750-word *personal narratives* on three of the following subjects:**
   a. **Dogs or cats**
   b. **Fraternity or sorority rush**
   c. **Academic scheduling after the first week of classes**
   d. **The day before final exams**
   e. **A used car**
   f. **An extended illness or major handicap**
   g. **A specific course you have taken**
   h. **Recovery from an athletic injury**
   i. **Summer employment**
   j. **One or more siblings**
2. **Develop topics appropriate for 750-word *process themes* on three of the subjects listed in the preceding exercise.**
3. **Develop topics appropriate for 750-word *cause-effect themes* on three of the subjects listed in the first exercise.**

Establishing a Narrator

The dictionary tells us that the verb *to narrate*—"to give an account or description"—comes from the Latin *narrare*, "knowing." For us, the central question is "who knows?" and beyond that, "who writes?" Who is the narrator behind the narration? The answers to these questions (which in practice are really one question) can, like the questions related to subject matter, be found in an analysis of the aims of writings as they relate to the narrative mode.

In *expressive narration* the narrator is the self that expresses. This means that in any situation in which the writer makes no attempt to alter or mask his or her true voice, we can equate the two terms *narrator* and *writer*. But in actuality, we do not see much pure expressive writing. Diaries and journals, for example, are often intentionally withheld from the eyes of outside readers (everyone but the selves who write them), and we only read them under extraordinary circumstances. As for candor, many a "candid" interview or personal account has later been found to have been inhibited or modified by a need to make a good impression, withhold a few embarrassing facts, make reality a bit lighter or darker than it was, or otherwise alter the statements of the expressing self.

In *persuasive narration*, intended to alter the attitudes and actions of the reader or audience, the narrator is significant as an identifiable person, personality, or voice only to the extent that he or she helps to persuade. In some instances, it might actually undermine or prove irrelevant to the persuasive aim to tell the reader who the narrator is. For example, witnesses who lack authority or credibility are better left unnamed and unknown, and sources of information whose names, identities, or personalities might distract from the persuasive point itself often remain anonymous. By the same token, the actual writers of advertisements in the media (many ads are the creations of groups of writers) almost always remain anonymous. Who they are may be important to their firms and families, but not to the potential consumers of the products.

At other times, however, such as those in which eyewitness reports are used to persuade, it is crucial that the reader know who narrates and what the narrator's relationship to the subject is. If, in an effort to persuade us that the typical pet owner is ill-informed, a veterinarian tells us a story of animal mistreatment, it is significant that we know the testimony comes from a professional in the field. Similarly, our acceptance of Diane Balmer's account of her experience in physical anthropology is dependent in part on our knowledge that she is a student, that she had not had much prior concern with the concept of death, and that it is in fact her personal experience being reported.

Thus, narration used for persuasive purposes is conveyed to us by a carefully created narrator—a *persona* who changes, conceals, or misrepresents his or her actual relationship to the whole truth of the subject at hand. For example, when a group of ad writers in New York use a public figure (a famous athlete, for example) to speak the words they have written in order to sell a product, they adopt a persona. And if that athlete projects to us an enthusiasm for the product that he or she may not actually possess, the athlete is also adopting a persona.

In *informative, scientific, and exploratory narration*, the narrator typically presents a low profile in deference to the subject matter itself. Since the end of these aims is to convey, explain, prove, and discover the facts and logical relationships among aspects of a given subject, it is not the author or narrator but his or her handling of the subject that is crucial. Thus it might well prove self-defeating for a researcher, for example, to let his personality intrude on the narration of his lab procedures and findings. Scientists and technical writers especially, because they need to present their work as impartially as possible, normally adopt as purely objective and impersonal a voice as possible. We might assume that Bruno Bettelheim had a much closer and warmer relationship to Joey than the tone and style of his prose reflect. But since his overriding aim is to show us that autism can in fact be systematically analyzed and treated, it is important to him that his writing actually reflects that system and control—even at the expense of certain real and otherwise important aspects of his personality. Bettelheim adopts the role of the objective scientific narrator because that is the type of narration that best helps him meet his primary aims. (But note that because Bettelheim lets Joey speak for himself about human feelings—particularly in the final paragraph—we are ultimately convinced that this particular scientist is a sensitive person and does care deeply about his subject.)

Another example of essentially objective narration is news reporting. Journalists, whose primary responsibility is to report the news without bias and only in terms of verified facts, are expected to narrate as if they have no personal opinion concerning their subjects. Even human interest and feature articles, which are usually less formal than straight reporting, are acceptable forms of journalism only if they are based on accurately transcribed interviews and established facts. The narrator of such a piece may have a personal interest in the subject, and may even show it, but this interest cannot be allowed to detract from the basic credibility required of the narration.

There are, of course, variations to the basic objective pattern just discussed: some highly respected historians, biologists, psychologists, and others have managed to narrate material responsibly without totally doing away with their personalities. One of these is Lewis Thomas, whose books on natural phenomena reflect the personality of a writer who cares about his subject but has never been accused of being scientifically inaccurate. Even some cookbooks, which usually contain "how to" narration in its blandest form, are written with a bit of flair or wit to reflect a narrator who actually enjoys cooking. But neither Eiseley nor the lively cook nor (for that matter) Bettelheim ultimately writes in such a way as to undermine his effectiveness in achieving his primary aim—to convey to us the truth, in a logical and systematic manner.

Since informative, explanatory, and scientific narration are among the types you are likely to be required to do on a regular basis, the following observation is worth remembering: in writing meant to inform, prove, or explore, narrative credibility must be both earned and sustained through the responsible gathering, organization, and presentation of factual information.

Narration and narrators in literary discourse are more complex than those created for any of the aims discussed in the preceding paragraphs. This is because literary (most commonly, fictional) narrators may narrate for any or all of the other aims discussed in this book, as is the case with Huckleberry Finn. Huck is, of course, the narrative persona of Mark Twain (who was really Samuel Clemens). In addition, Huck takes on various personae within the *Adventures of Huckleberry Finn* itself; he adopts, among others, the roles of two girls and Tom Sawyer. And in the various roles he plays, Huck expresses, persuades, informs, explains, and explores. In short, the business of literary narration is a subject in its own right. An introduction to it is provided in Chapter 7.

Exercises on Establishing a Narrator

1. **Write one-paragraph descriptions of the narrative personae projected in television ads for each of two different products.**
2. **Write a one-paragraph description of the most effective type of narrator for one of the following topics:**
   a. **How to select an appropriate pet for your living situation**
   b. **Causes for the recent shift in the public's attitude toward women in (traditionally) male-dominated professions**
   c. **What being a varsity athlete is like**
   d. **How to train for a marathon**
   e. **Effects on retired citizens of the rise in the cost of living**
   f. **How to resolve a conflict with your supervisor or boss**
3. **Compare in class your descriptions of the narrators in the preceding exercise. Explain the reasons for differences in descriptions and the effects different narrators would have on themes written on the three topics.**

Determining Focus and Scope

How much of a potentially long story actually belongs in a relatively short piece of narrative writing? Of course, both Balmer and Bettelheim had to confront this question before writing their respective essays.

Bettelheim helps us focus on the principles of narrative selection by specifically making some comments on it in paragraphs 3 and 32. He tells us that "This time I shall concentrate upon the illness, rather than the treatment." For this reason, and though the article does contain some information about Joey's treatment, Bettelheim's essay is clearly more about Joey, his "family," and the causes of his mechanical behavior than about other autistic children, the clinic, the professional staff, or Bettelheim himself. In addition, Bettelheim consciously chose to end "this fragment of Joey's story" when Joey was twelve. There is no follow-up or elaboration on what Joey was like after having "entered the human condition" simply because that would not have been relevant to the author's chosen aim and focus, as stated in paragraph 3. Bettelheim *satisfies his aims*—to show that Joey is indeed a boy and that autistic behavior can be cured—by focusing on the causes and consequences of various peoples' treatment of him and by focusing on the points in Joey's story when significant changes occurred.

In Balmer's case there was actually much more to her physical anthropology course than the special lab project and her encounter with Boris. There were, for example, selecting and registering for physical anthropology in the first place; the lecture part of the course, with its professor, fellow students, lectures, quizzes, exams, grades, and so on; and the lab as a whole, with its assignments, procedures, and reports. Why and how did she decide what to leave out and what to put in?

Balmer focused her efforts on that specific part of the total story (her physical anthropology experience as a whole) that related significantly to the moment of change she wanted to express her feelings about and convince us was important. The change—in Balmer's attitude toward human mortality—took place in connection with the lab and particularly in connection with "Boris," her special project, so that was what she emphasized. The rest (lectures, exams, and so on) was all true to the total experience of the course, but not really *relevant to the aims* behind the writing.

Thus the narrative mode, like the descriptive, requires that we make judicious selections from the totality of any given subject in order to efficiently convey its significance to an audience.

Finally, of course, a narration is successful to the extent that it is both interesting and credible—to the extent that it gets the reader's attention, holds that attention, and leaves the reader convinced of the importance of what's been told. Readers are interested whenever they are curious, intrigued, enlightened, entertained, confided in, and taught; they are interested in a narration when any of their typical human needs are satisfied by an account of something that happened. A narrative is credible when it provides the reader with a sufficient explanation for how and why something happened in the first place. Explanation involves whatever description, dialogue, facts, and examples are necessary to reflect experience as a process of change and to justify any changes that occur. In assessing the focus and scope of a piece of writing, you must ask whether you have included enough of the kind of material a reader is likely to find both interesting and credible.

Exercises on Determining Narrative Focus and Scope

1. Select one of the topics developed for the exercise on choosing a topic for narration and
   a. identify and describe in one or two sentences its focal point—its turning point or moment of significant change
   b. identify and explain in a paragraph your determination of the beginning and end points for a theme on this topic. Where would you begin and end, and why?

2. **Write a detailed outline (provide specific, relevant material and concrete evidence) of the focal or turning-point section of a theme on either the topic selected for the preceding exercise or one of the other narrative topics developed earlier.**

ORGANIZATION AND DEVELOPMENT OF NARRATION

Organization of material is dependent upon the selection of material relevant to your aim and audience. You can't organize effectively what hasn't been consciously chosen, and it is a waste of time to organize material that will later be cut out because it isn't central to your purpose.

In observing that Bruno Bettelheim's essay was descriptive as well as narrative, you also perceived that the descriptive material had to be taken into account in the development of the writing. In fact, a condensed outline of Bettelheim's article reveals an alternating pattern of narrative and descriptive sections (paragraph numbers are in parentheses):

    I.   Introduction (1–3)

    II.   *Description* of Joey's condition and behavior (4–7)

    III.   *Narration* of how Joey became a "mechanical boy" (8–12)

    IV.   Further *description* and analysis of Joey's behavior (13–17)

    V.   *Narration* of response and treatment (18–23)

    VI.   Further *description* and analysis (24–26)

    VII.   *Narration* of the changes in Joey and conclusion (27–32)

Note that the basic story of Bettelheim's essay—the *basic sequence* of his association with Joey—is contained in the narrative episodes. Section III tells us how Joey became autistic, section V tells us how he was treated at the clinic (with the response to Joey's toilet behavior serving as a key example), and section VII tells us of some of the later changes that took place in Joey's personality. That is, a shorter, strictly narrative essay could have been written using only these sections. But note also that in the end Bettelheim's success as a narrator is partly dependent upon his success as a describer (and, to a lesser extent, a definer). Descriptions give texture and weight to narration, so we should not be surprised that Bettelheim gives us a concrete and spatial, as well as sequential, sense of his relationship to

Joey. The essay as written, with description complementing narration, is more interesting and convincing than a "pure" narration might have been. After all, Bettelheim wants Joey to come across as human and significant, and it is the descriptive sections of his writing that offer visual proof that this is so.

We can also see that the basic organizational pattern of narration involves *causes* and *consequences* arranged in sequence. Since any narration can be seen as a kind of story, narration is at base a matter of organizing in terms of a beginning, a middle, and an end. The beginning involves the causes and the conditions of the change that occurs, and the end involves the consequences or results. The middle is the point or points at which the dynamic process takes place, in which the reader sees causes become consequences.

Of course various types of narrative writing involve different types of beginnings, middles, and ends. These respective parts of the whole are often referred to in various ways—often as determined by subject matter, aim, or audience. The accompanying table, delineating the narrative organization in terms of various types of narrative, is meant to show (1) subsections of the basic parts of narrative, (2) alternate terms for parallel concepts, and (3) that while the terminology may differ with the type of narrative written, the basic pattern remains the same.

Note that while the beginning or end of a narration might well involve statements *about* the action—a statement in which the narrator tells the reader what happened—this should not be the case with the middle. In conveying to the reader the middle section of a narrative event, the writer must take special care *to show how* the occurrence took (or should take) place. The narrator should use description, dialogue, tone, and delineation of character(s) to satisfy this end. For example, it is in part Bettelheim's willingness to let Joey talk to us ("He broke my feelings") that convinces us of the boy's importance. It is the middle of a narration that makes the beginning relevant and the ending credible and significant.

Exercises on Organizing and Developing Narration

1. Refer to the table of types of narrative organization, and make a model outline for each of the types of narrative writing represented. Bring your outlines to class for discussion and modification.
2. Use one of the outline models developed in the previous exercise and outline a story-based, process, or cause-effect theme on a topic of your choice. (Consult the previous exercises in this chapter for suggestions of possible topics.)
3. List sequentially (chronologically) the steps in a specific process with

ORGANIZATION AND TERMINOLOGY FOR VARIOUS TYPES OF NARRATIVE PROSE

	SECTION OF THE NARRATION		
TYPE OF NARRATION	Beginning (action is potential) Causes of change	Middle (action is actual, dynamic) The change itself; sequence	End (action brought to close) Consequences of change
Story or short story	Exposition (or "setting the stage") Statement of situation and motives	Development of plot Disturbance of status quo Complication and conflict Crisis and climax	"Denouement" or impact Consequences
Incident or personal experience essay	Statement of situation before or as action begins	Report of the key aspects of the incident or experience, as they occurred Focus on crisis or turning point	Outcome or consequences of the incident or experience
Process or "how-to" essay	Statement of task List of ingredients or parts Naming of tools	The process itself, in specified order of steps (often numbered in the interest of clarity and accuracy)	Finished product Results
Cause-and-effect essay	Statement of context or conditions Identification of causative factors or forces before they act or interact	Interaction of causes and conditions Causes usually listed in increasing order of importance or necessity	Effect or effects of the action Implications of the effect(s)

which you are familiar but that most others would need instructions to complete. Besides "tasks" such as "stringing a barbed-wire fence" or "how to buy a good used car," consider skills connected with sports ("how to serve a tennis ball," "how to pole vault successfully"), gardening ("how to grow tomatoes on your balcony"), personal relationships ("how to survive an 'obligatory' date"), and other areas in which you have some expertise.

4. Outline or diagram the multiple causes of a single effect or the multiple effects of a single cause with which you are personally familiar. Be sure to

indicate which causes and effects are major ones and which are minor ones.

STYLE IN NARRATION

The style of a narration is the result of many choices made by the writer, but especially choices concerning length, sequence (chronology), tense, and tone. These choices, in turn, are affected by the relationship among the aim, the audience, the writer, and the subject matter in a given discourse. Given such a large number of constantly interacting factors, it is impossible to set forth a single set of practical instructions for narrative style. But a brief discussion of the basic uses and effects of the stylistic elements themselves, in relation to several familiar types of writing, should prove helpful.

In reading the remaining sections of this chapter, keep in mind that consistency is the basis of successful style. Your stylistic choices—whether with regard to length, tense, sequence, or tone—must always be consistent with the aims of a given piece of writing and in relation to each other.

LENGTH. In determining the length of a given piece of narration, keep in mind the primary aim of the writing. Literary narration is, in a sense, written for its own sake, so we find that it can be as long or as short as other considerations (supplementary aims, for example) will allow. Thus narration of the type we see in Aesop's fables is quite short, whereas Tolstoy's *Anna Karenina* is a particularly long novel. Expressive narration is, of course, written for the narrator's sake, so it too can be as long or as short as other factors (such as the reader's patience) allow. Most of the writing we do from day to day, however, is expository (informative, explanatory, exploratory) or persuasive in aim; it is seldom written in and for itself. When this is the case, it is important that you consider in advance of actual composition just how much narration is necessary to make the necessary point(s), and to narrate only what you need.

Expository narration involves as accurate and complete a rendering of a particular episode as is necessary to serve as evidence or supporting material. This was the case in the writing of Balmer's essay on Boris. By contrast, narration used in persuasive discourse is sometimes incompletely and misleadingly limited. Persuasive writing based on logical appeals to the reader will, of course, make some attempt to convey a sense of complete coverage of an event to the reader. But persuasive writing based on an emotional appeal might well involve an artificially shortened (and thus misleading) account. For example, a report on the causes of urban crime that discussed alcohol and drugs but ignored poverty and unemployment would mislead the reader into thinking the problem is simpler than it is.

In the end, narrative length is a matter of determining how much of the whole story is actually useful in fulfilling the writer's particular aim(s).

SEQUENCE OR CHRONOLOGY.   Since an action is a sequence of events in time, an obvious and effective way to narrate it is in chronological terms. For example, an essay in which you lead a reader step by step through a process—putting together a piece of equipment, for example— can only be successful if you tell the reader how to do it in terms of a strict sequence of events. Similarly, scientific reports are normally written in terms of a sequence of established procedures. Given the burden of proof that weighs on a researcher's shoulders, this has to be the basic strategy for performing the work and having it mean anything significant. Of course, in writing that explains processes and in reports, it is common to begin by telling the reader what the basic results or findings are or will be, but the necessary proof of such statements is in the orderly progression of information in the course of the essay or article. Note that Balmer tells us in her first paragraph that her experience with physical anthropology (and eventually with Boris himself) involved "a personal confrontation with the fact of human mortality" and that the rest of the essay bears out this opening assertion.

Similarly, cause-effect writing is based upon our recognition that one or more effects can be the logical result of one or more causes and that their relationship is most clearly conveyed in terms of a chronological sequence. Again, it may well be that both the writer and the reader know from the beginning what the basic causes and effects are, but this does not eliminate a need to clearly explain their relationship in terms of time, that is, in chronological order.

In short, most exposition is written along basically chronological lines of thought and development.

In persuasive writing, style is a means to a particular end—the manipulation of the reader. Thus many variations in the handling of chronology, as well as narrative length, are seen every day. For example, we are all familiar with television ads in which we are not told until the end what product is being sold to us; the effect of such ads is to create curiosity and attention and to leave the name of the product in our minds as a kind of last word, no matter what we remember (or have been told) about its actual merits. By contrast, an ad written to sell us a given product on the basis of logical appeal might actually begin by telling us what it will try to prove: that aspirin A is better than aspirins B and C, for example, or that automobile X gets better mileage than all others in its field. In persuasive narration, the use (or nonuse) of sequential development is typically a function of the amount of information given and the type of appeal being made to the reader—logical, emotional, or ethical. If the appeal is basically logical, then the persuasive narrator has little to gain from withholding either the end of the story or any part of it from the reader. If the appeal is essentially emotional, the narrator might well manipulate the story—its content or its chronology or both—in order to create the desired responses. If the appeal is essentially based on the authority or personal appeal of the narrator, as when celebrities endorse products, the story itself is normally short and straightforward in style, since the personality of the speaker may well be more influential than anything actually being said.

Literary narration might or might not develop chronologically, depending on any of a number of secondary considerations. For example, a typical anthology of narrative literature will contain both stories that hold the reader in suspense by sticking to a strict chronology of events, thus saving the ending until the very last, and stories that begin by telling us of the ending or outcome of the action and develop in terms of an exposition of how that ending was reached. Mystery novels and many detective stories are examples of the first type; an autobiography of a famous person is an example of the second. In one type there is a strong appeal to the reader's sense of curiosity, and in the other an appeal to our need for a noteworthy experience to be explained in interesting and credible terms.

Yet a third kind of story makes liberal use of flashbacks, interpretive asides, and other interruptions of the strictly chronological flow of the narrative. Narration of this type, however, is rare in nonfictional prose.

Finally, in expressive writing, narration might be chronological or not, depending on the narrator's other needs. By definition, however, the subject matter and the order of presentation in expressive writing are of less significance than the narrator's (expresser's) simple need to tell the story in the first place. In short, style itself is often the last thing an expressive narrator has consciously in mind in telling a story.

TENSE.   The most frequently used tenses are past and present. The present tense is most commonly used when the narrator wishes to give to the action a sense of immediacy and eyewitness accuracy. For this reason, present tense is often used in expressive narration, in stories (fictional or nonfictional) conveyed to us in the first person, and in narration that instructs us in a process. The present tense is obviously the tense in which events actually occur, so when conveying the vitality of such events is a primary goal of the writing, the present tense is the one narrators choose.

The past tense, on the other hand, is often used in prose that informs or explains completed action; again, both "Joey" and "Boris" are relevant examples. Biographies and autobiographies, which convey a kind of history, are others. The reason for the use of the past tense in most exposition is simple: there is a sense of accomplished fact—of confirmed truth—inherent in the past tense.

Readers usually consider exposition more credible when it clearly reports and explains the way something *was*; the past holds still for careful examination, analysis, and proof in a way the present does not.

Exploratory narration is a special type of expository prose; it involves an explanation of what has happened, a statement of what is happening, and perhaps even inferences concerning what might happen in the future. Exploratory narration is narration of an event or experience that began in the past but is still in progress. For this reason, both the past and the present tense are often used. The past tense is used with the understanding between writer and reader that the experience being explored in a specific portion of the writing is complete only to a point, and that what is happening or will occur is also part of the whole story and as significant as what has already taken place. The present and future tenses are used in exploratory narration to carefully designate action at specific points in the dynamic exploratory process. It is, of course, this complex relationship among past, present, and future that can make exploration both intriguing in its own right and difficult to convey in writing.

TONE.   Tone, like the other aspects of narrative style, must be clearly established and carefully sustained. Tone is the result of the narrator's relationship to the subject matter and the story he or she is telling. If the narrator's role is essentially objective, as in the case of Bruno Bettelheim reporting on Joey, the tone should also be objective. In practice, this means that the diction and style of the sentences should avoid slanting the story in such a way as to reflect (in the writer) or evoke (in the reader) a particular attitude toward the subject. Bettelheim's professional "report" is not without some sense of Joey's significance as a human being and of the narrator's awareness of this. But this feeling is conveyed to us without casting doubt on either Bettelheim's expertise or the accuracy of what he says. In fact, Bettelheim's essay serves as evidence that an expository essay can be basically objective without being monotonous, unfeeling, and dry.

If the narrator's relationship to a subject or story is subjective—that is, if the narrator wishes to be explicit about his or her relation to, feelings about, or position on a subject—the tone should be consistently subjective. The diction and style of individual sentences and paragraphs should reflect the humor, irony, criticism, praise, or other attitude the narrator wishes to convey.

Exercises on Style in Narration

1. Assign the entire class to watch one or two specific TV programs and to take notes on them. After the viewing(s), discuss the narrative structure(s) of the show(s). In the case of a program that is part of a continuing series, can you identify a narrative pattern that underlies the programs from week to week?
2. For two of the following narrative topics, determine and describe the most effective handling of length, chronology, tense, and tone. For

example, tell which tense you would use in writing a theme on the topic and explain why.

   a. An individual conference with my _____ instructor

   b. A report to the ABC Insurance Company on an accident in which the car you were driving (and which is insured through ABC) incurred $2,000.00 in damages

   c. A lab report on an analytical assignment in your chemistry, biology, or physics course

   d. A news account of a 30-car accident on the _____ Freeway

3. Discuss in class the differences in stylistic choices for the preceding exercise as determined by various members of the class, despite similarity of topics.

4. Write the first two paragraphs of a narrative theme on one of the topics you considered in Exercise 2.

Further Writing Assignments: Narration

1. Write a paper, following the lead of Diane Balmer, in which you narrate your progress (or lack of it) in a recent course or an effort to learn a particular skill (typing, racquetball, and so on).

2. In the style of an Aesop fable, write a 750-word narrative concerning an incident through which you or someone you know learned a useful lesson. Be sure to attach a moral to your fable.

3. Write a 750-word narrative concerning a personal experience that took no more than 10 minutes to occur. (Avoid the clichéd topic of the traffic accident or "near miss.")

4. Write a narrative paper on a topic cited in one of the preceding exercises. Be sure to give special emphasis to the stage(s) of your narration that you consider most important, given your subject matter, audience, and aim.

FURTHER READING AND DISCUSSION

For more practice in reading and analyzing narratives, read the following two narrative discourses and then answer the questions about each of them. Also note the aim of each discourse.

LEARNING TO STALK MUSKRATS

Annie Dillard

1 Learning to stalk muskrats took me several years.

2   I've always known there were muskrats in the creek. Sometimes when I drove late at night my headlights' beam on the water would catch the broad

lines of ripples made by a swimming muskrat, a bow wave, converging across the water at the raised dark vee of its head. I would stop the car and get out: nothing. They eat corn and tomatoes from my neighbors' gardens, too, by night, so that my neighbors were always telling me that the creek was full of them. Around here, people call them "mushrats"; Thoreau called them "Musquashes." They are not of course rats at all (let alone squashes). They are more like diminutive beavers, and, like beavers, they exude a scented oil from musk glands under the base of the tail—hence the name. I had read in several respectable sources that muskrats are so wary they are almost impossible to observe. One expert who made a full-time study of large populations, mainly by examining "sign" and performing autopsies on corpses, said he often went for weeks at a time without seeing a single living muskrat.

3   One hot evening three years ago, I was standing more or less *in* a bush. I was stock-still, looking deep into Tinker Creek from a spot on the bank opposite the house, watching a group of bluegills stare and hang motionless near the bottom of a deep, sunlit pool. I was focused for depth. I had long since lost myself, lost the creek, the day, lost everything but still amber depth. All at once I couldn't see. And then I could: a young muskrat had appeared on top of the water, floating on its back. Its forelegs were folded langorously across its chest; the sun shone on its upturned belly. Its youthfulness and rodent grin, coupled with its ridiculous method of locomotion, which consisted of a lazy wag of the tail assisted by an occasional dabble of a webbed hind foot, made it an enchanting picture of decadence, dissipation, and summer sloth. I forgot all about the fish.

4   But in my surprise at having the light come on so suddenly, and at having my consciousness returned to me all at once and bearing an inverted muskrat, I must have moved and betrayed myself. The kit—for I know now it was just a young kit—righted itself so that only its head was visible above water, and swam downstream, away from me. I extricated myself from the bush and foolishly pursued it. It dove sleekly, reemerged, and glided for the opposite bank. I ran along the bankside brush, trying to keep it in sight. It kept casting an alarmed look over its shoulder at me. Once again it dove, under a floating mat of brush lodged in the bank, and disappeared. I never saw it again. (Nor have I ever, despite all the muskrats I have seen, again seen a muskrat floating on its back.) But I did not know muskrats then; I waited panting, and watched the shadowed bank. Now I know that I cannot outwait a muskrat who knows I am there. The most I can do is get "there" quietly, while it is still in its hole, so that it never knows, and wait there until it emerges. But then all I knew was that I wanted to see more muskrats.

5   I began to look for them day and night. Sometimes I would see ripples suddenly start beating from the creek's side, but as I crouched to watch, the ripples would die. Now I know what this means, and have learned to stand perfectly still to make out the muskrat's small, pointed face hidden under overhanging bank vegetation, watching me. That summer I haunted the bridges, I walked up creeks and down, but no muskrats ever appeared. You must just have to be there, I thought. You must have to spend the rest of your life standing in bushes. It was a once-in-a-lifetime thing, and you've had your once.

6　　　Then one night I saw another, and my life changed. After that I knew where they were in numbers, and I knew when to look. It was late dusk; I was driving home from a visit with friends. Just on the off chance I parked quietly by the creek, walked out on the narrow bridge over the shallows, and looked upstream. Someday, I had been telling myself for weeks, someday a muskrat is going to swim right through that channel in the cattails, and I am going to see it. That is precisely what happened. I looked up into the channel for a muskrat, and there it came, swimming right toward me. Knock; seek; ask. It seemed to swim with a side-to-side, sculling motion of its vertically flattened tail. It looked bigger than the upside-down muskrat, and its face more reddish. In its mouth it clasped a twig of tulip tree. One thing amazed me: it swam right down the middle of the creek. I thought it would hide in the brush along the edge; instead, it plied the waters as obviously as an aquaplane. I could just look and look.

7　　　But I was standing on the bridge, not sitting, and it saw me. It changed its course, veered towards the bank, and disappeared behind an indentation in the rushy shoreline. I felt a rush of such pure energy I thought I would not need to breathe for days.

Exercises on "Learning to Stalk Muskrats"

1. What is the point of view of this example of narration? How is this point of view conveyed in the writing?
2. What are the chronological steps of Dillard's stalking experience?
3. Where does Dillard incorporate definition and description into her narration?
4. How is this essay an account of a process? What makes it more of a story than a process essay?
5. How or why is Dillard's essay on muskrat stalking important?

Exercises on "How to Write a Resume" (pages 316–317)

1. What is the point of view of this reading? How is this point of view conveyed in the writing?
2. According to Simon, what chronological steps and key pieces of information are required in a good resume?
3. How is this selection like a story? How is the selection a process essay?
4. Simon's piece is an advertisement—that is, persuasive in aim. What is it selling and how does it try to persuade us?
5. Describe the style of this reading.

How to write a resume

by Jerrold G. Simon, Ed.D.
Harvard Business School

International Paper asked Jerrold G. Simon, Ed.D., psychologist and career development specialist at Harvard Business School, who has counseled over a thousand people in their search for jobs, to tell you how to go after the job you really want.

If you are about to launch a search for a job, the suggestions I offer here can help you whether or not you have a high school or college diploma, whether you are just starting out or changing your job or career in midstream.

"What do I want to do?"

Before you try to find a job opening, you have to answer the hardest question of your working life: "What do I want to do?" Here's a good way.

Sit down with a piece of paper and don't get up till you've listed all the things you're proud to have accomplished. Your list might include being head of a fund-raising campaign, or acting a juicy role in the senior play.

Study the list. You'll see a pattern emerge of the things you do best and like to do best. You might discover that you're happiest working with people, or maybe with numbers, or words, or well, you'll see it.

Once you've decided what job area to go after, read

"'Who am I? What do I want to do?' Writing your resume forces you to think about yourself."

more about it in the reference section of your library. "Talk shop" with any people you know in that field. Then start to get your resume together.

There are many good books that offer sample resumes and describe widely used formats. The one that is still most popular, the *reverse chronological*, emphasizes where you worked and when, and the jobs and titles you held.

How to organize it

Your name and address go at the top. Also phone number.

What job do you want? That's what a prospective employer looks for first. If you know exactly, list that next under *Job Objective*. Otherwise, save it for your cover letter (I describe that later), when you're writing for a specific job to a specific person. In any case, make sure your resume focuses on the kind of work you can do and want to do.

Now comes *Work Experience*. Here's where you list your qualifications. <u>Lead with your most important credentials</u>. If you've had a distinguished work history in an area related to the job you're seeking, lead

off with that. If your education will impress the prospective employer more, start with that.

Begin with your most recent experience first and work backwards. Include your titles or positions held. And list the years.

Figures don't brag

The most qualified people don't always get the job. It goes to the person who presents himself most persuasively in person and on paper.

So don't just list where you were and what you did. This is your chance to tell *how well you did*. Were you the best salesman? Did you cut operating costs? Give numbers, statistics, percentages, increases in sales or profits.

No job experience?

In that case, list your summer jobs, extracurricular school activities, honors, awards. Choose the activities that will enhance your qualifications for the job.

Next list your *Education*— unless you chose to start with that. This should also be in reverse chronological order. List your high school only if you didn't go on to college. Include college degree, postgraduate degrees, dates conferred, major and minor courses you took that help qualify you for the job you want.

Also, did you pay your own way? Earn scholarships or fellowships? Those are impressive accomplishments.

No diplomas or degrees?

Then tell about your education: special training programs or courses that can qualify you. Describe outside activities that reveal your talents and abilities. Did you sell the most tickets to the annual charity musical? Did you take your motorcycle engine apart and put it back together so it works? These can help you.

Next, list any *Military Service*. This could lead off your resume if it is your only work experience. Stress skills learned, promotions earned, leadership shown.

Now comes *Personal Data*. This is your chance to let the reader get a glimpse of the personal you, and to further the image you've worked to project in the preceding sections. For example, if you're after a job in computer programming, and you enjoy playing chess, mention it.

"Talk about a hobby if it'll help get the job. Want to be an automotive engineer? Tell how you built your own hot rod."

Chess playing requires the ability to think through a problem.

Include foreign languages spoken, extensive travel, particular interests or professional memberships, *if* they advance your cause.

Keep your writing style simple. Be brief. Start sentences with impressive action verbs: "Created," "Designed," "Achieved," "Caused."

No typos, please

Make sure your grammar and spelling are correct. And no typos! Use 8½" x 11" bond paper–white or off-white for easy reading. Don't cram things together. Make sure your original is clean and readable. Then have it professionally duplicated. No carbons.

Get it into the right hands

Now that your resume is ready, start to track down job openings. How? Look up business friends, personal friends, neighbors, your minister, your college alumni association, professional services. Keep up with trade publications, and read help-wanted ads.

And start your own "direct mail" campaign. First, find out about the companies you are interested in–their size, location, what they make, their competition, their advertising, their prospects. Get their annual report–and read it.

No "Dear Sir" letters

Send your resume, along with a cover letter, to a specific person in the company, not to "Gentlemen" or "Dear Sir." The person should be the top person in the area where you want to work. Spell his name properly! The cover letter should appeal to your reader's own needs. What's in it for him?

Quickly explain why you are approaching *his* company (their product line, their superior training program) and what you can bring to the party. Back up your claims with facts. Then refer him to your enclosed resume and ask for an interview.

Oh, boy! An interview!

And now you've got an interview! Be sure to call the day before to confirm it. Meantime, *prepare yourself*. Research the company and the job by reading books and business journals in the library.

On the big day, arrive 15 minutes early. Act calm, even though, if you're normal, you're trembling inside at 6.5 on the Richter scale. At every chance, let your interviewer see that your personal skills and qualifications relate to the job at hand. If it's a sales position, for example, go all out to show how articulate and persuasive you are.

Afterwards, follow through with a brief thank-you note. This is a fine opportunity to restate your qualifications and add any important points you didn't get a chance to bring up during the interview.

Keep good records

Keep a list of prospects. List the dates you contacted them, when they replied, what was said.

And remember, someone out there is looking for someone *just like you*. It takes hard work and sometimes luck to find that person. Keep at it and you'll succeed.

Jerrold Simon

Defining and Dividing

THE IMPORTANCE OF DEFINING AND DIVIDING

The Greek philosopher Plato maintained that the ability to define and divide was at the heart of thinking and writing. Since that time many others have agreed. Even if Plato's position is an overstatement, the very fact that many notable people feel so strongly about it should at least urge you to consider it.

If there is one chapter that is common to nearly all books on expository and technical writing, it is the chapter on definitions. Thus, the authors of these texts agree with Plato. Another belief shared by most writing instructors is that one of the functions of composition courses is to teach students to *analyze*. Now *analysis* is one of those words that nearly all of us use, but to which few of us have given much systematic thought. We haven't, in fact, analyzed our notion of analysis.

Unlike some words whose origins are now unrelated to present use, *analysis* has an etymology that tells us something significant about the current concept. The word comes from two Greek roots, *lysis* meaning "loosening," and *ana* meaning "up"; thus *to analyze* means "to loosen up something," "to resolve something complex into its elements." We do this preeminently when we describe and when we classify, that is, define and divide. For when we describe, we break up a whole into its parts and see their interrelationships; and when we define and divide, we break down a complicated class into its component elements or subclasses and try to understand their connections. Thus when we learn to describe and to classify, we also learn to analyze.

This chapter is an attempt to introduce you to some of the rudiments of thinking and writing about classifications. It may prove to be one of the most useful chapters in the entire book. Without classifications, doctors would be helpless against an undifferentiated mass of diseases, biologists could not write intelligently of the rich complexity of animal life, and auto mechanics could not adapt from one motor to another. No matter what your major area of study is, you are likely to write papers that call for defining and dividing.

SOME EXAMPLES OF DEFINING AND DIVIDING

You are asked in this chapter to consider two quite. different processes. One is the process of recognizing that different individual beings have common characteristics that enable us to consider them as members of the same class. Determining one or more common characteristics is the process of defining; and placing the members with the same characteristics in the same group is often called classifying. Actually, the very process of defining implicitly determines a class; and, conversely, the very process of classifying (placing the members together) implicitly defines a class. In the first essay, Martin Luther King, Jr., attempts to define "nonviolent resistance"; that is, he tries to isolate the characteristics common to the class of acts that opposes racism by nonviolent means. The essay is an extended definition of nonviolent resistance.

The second process studied in this chapter is the reverse of defining and classifying. Instead of grouping similar objects together into one common class, dividing starts with the common class and breaks up the component members into smaller classes. This is the aspect of the chapter that is analytical. The student essay on houseplants is an illustration of this process of dividing—he takes the large class of houseplants and breaks it down successively into smaller subclasses. Dividing, however, like classifying, implies defining. As we shall see, the student continually justifies his dividing process by means of definitions of the subclasses.

Both extended definition and dividing assist us in analysis, for both break up complex notions into their elements, and, as we have seen, that is what analysis means. But defining and dividing break up complex wholes differently.

Prereading Activities for "Pilgrimage to Nonviolence," by Dr. Martin Luther King, Jr.

VOCABULARY. The diction of Dr. King's essay is really quite simple. The only words that might cause some trouble are the following (the paragraph in which the word occurs is given in parentheses):

pilgrimage (title)—a journey to a shrine or holy place
nonviolence—the essay is an extended definition of this word
Gandhi (1,3,6,7)—an Indian nationalist leader who used passive resistance
    and civil disobedience to achieve reform; he was assassinated in 1948;
    Gandhian is the adjective used to describe his theories
boycott (4)—a refusal to use, sell, or buy a product in order to force the maker
    to change a position
eros (9)—romantic love (Greek)
philia (9)—a reciprocal love between personal friends (Greek)
agape (9–14)—an understanding, redeeming goodwill for all men (Greek)

STUDY QUESTIONS.   While reading the selection keep in mind the
questions below. They lead directly to the principles of classifying and
defining to be discussed in the next section.

1. At the end of the essay, is the notion of *nonviolence* quite clear to you?
2. What different techniques of defining *nonviolence* has King used?
3. What are the six basic elements of the notion of *nonviolence*?
4. What are the components of the notion of *agape*?

ORGANIZATION.   If you can answer study questions 3 and 4, you
probably have a fair notion of the structure of the selection. There are two
brief paragraphs of introduction; the remainder of the structure of the
essay can be graphically presented as in Figure 11.1 (the numbers refer to
the paragraphs).

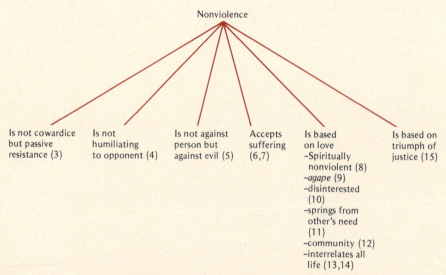

FIGURE 11.1.   Aspects of nonviolence.

PILGRIMAGE TO NONVIOLENCE

Martin Luther King, Jr.

1   When I went to Montgomery as a pastor, I had not the slightest idea that I would later become involved in a crisis in which nonviolent resistance would be applicable. I neither started the protest nor suggested it. I simply responded to the call of the people for a spokesman. When the protest began, my mind, consciously or unconsciously, was driven back to the Sermon on the Mount, with its sublime teachings on love, and the Gandhian method of nonviolent resistance. As the days unfolded, I came to see the power of nonviolence more and more. Living through the actual experience of the protest, nonviolence became more than a method to which I gave intellectual assent; it became a commitment to a way of life. Many of the things that I had not cleared up intellectually concerning nonviolence were now solved in the sphere of practical action.

2   Since the philosophy of nonviolence played such a positive role in the Montgomery Movement, it may be wise to turn to a brief discussion of some basic aspects of this philosophy.

3   First, it must be emphasized that nonviolent resistance is not a method for cowards; it does resist. If one uses this method because he is afraid or merely because he lacks the instruments of violence, he is not truly nonviolent. This is why Gandhi often said that if cowardice is the only alternative to violence, it is better to fight. He made this statement conscious of the fact that there is always another alternative: no individual or group need submit to any wrong, nor need they use violence to right the wrong; there is the way of nonviolent resistance. This is ultimately the way of the strong man. It is not a method of stagnant passivity. The phrase "passive resistance" often gives the false impression that this is a sort of "do-nothing method" in which the resister quietly and passively accepts evil. But nothing is further from the truth. For while the nonviolent resister is passive in the sense that he is not physically aggressive toward his opponent, his mind and emotions are always active, constantly seeking to persuade his opponent that he is wrong. The method is passive physically, but strongly active spiritually. It is not passive nonresistance to evil, it is active nonviolent resistance to evil.

4   A second basic fact that characterizes nonviolence is that it does not seek to defeat or humiliate the opponent, but to win his friendship and understanding. The nonviolent resister must often express his protest through noncooperation or boycotts, but he realizes that these are not ends themselves; they are merely means to awaken a sense of moral shame in the opponent. The end is redemption and reconciliation. The aftermath of nonviolence is the creation of the beloved community, while the aftermath of violence is tragic bitterness.

5   A third characteristic of this method is that the attack is directed against forces of evil rather than against persons who happen to be doing the evil. It is evil that the nonviolent resister seeks to defeat, not the persons victimized by evil. If he is opposing racial injustice, the nonviolent resister has the vision

to see that the basic tension is not between races. As I like to say to the people in Montgomery: "The tension in this city is not between white people and Negro people. The tension is, at bottom, between justice and injustice, between the forces of light and the forces of darkness. And if there is a victory, it will be a victory not merely for fifty thousand Negroes, but a victory for justice and the forces of light. We are out to defeat injustice and not white persons who may be unjust."

6   A fourth point that characterizes nonviolent resistance is a willingness to accept suffering without retaliation, to accept blows from the opponent without striking back. "Rivers of blood may have to flow before we gain our freedom, but it must be our blood," Gandhi said to his countrymen. The nonviolent resister is willing to accept violence if necessary, but never to inflict it. He does not seek to dodge jail. If going to jail is necessary, he enters it "as a bridegroom enters the bride's chamber."

7   One may well ask: "What is the nonviolent resister's justification for this ordeal to which he invites men, for this mass political application of the ancient doctrine of turning the other cheek?" The answer is found in the realization that unearned suffering is redemptive. Suffering, the nonviolent resister realizes, has tremendous educational and transforming possibilities. "Things of fundamental importance to people are not secured by reason alone, but have to be purchased with their suffering," said Gandhi. He continues: "Suffering is infinitely more powerful than the law of the jungle for converting the opponent and opening his ears which are otherwise shut to the voice of reason."

8   A fifth point concerning nonviolent resistance is that it avoids not only external physical violence but also internal violence of spirit. The nonviolent resister not only refuses to shoot his opponent but he also refuses to hate him. At the center of nonviolence stands the principle of love. The nonviolent resister would contend that in the struggle for human dignity, the oppressed people of the world must not succumb to the temptation of becoming bitter or indulging in hate campaigns. To retaliate in kind would do nothing but intensify the existence of hate in the universe. Along the way of life, someone must have sense enough and morality enough to cut off the chain of hate. This can only be done by projecting the ethic of love to the center of our lives.

9   In speaking of love at this point, we are not referring to some sentimental or affectionate emotion. It would be nonsense to urge men to love their oppressors in an affectionate sense. Love in this connection means understanding, redemptive good will. Here the Greek language comes to our aid. There are three words for love in the Greek New Testament. First, there is *eros*. In Platonic philosophy *eros* meant the yearning of the soul for the realm of the divine. It has come now to mean a sort of aesthetic or romantic love. Second, there is *philia* which means intimate affection between personal friends. *Philia* denotes a sort of reciprocal love; the person loves because he is loved. When we speak of loving those who oppose us, we refer to neither *eros* nor *philia*; we speak of a love which is expressed in the Greek word *agape*. *Agape* means understanding, redeeming good will for all men. It is an overflowing love which is purely spontaneous, unmotivated, groundless, and creative. It is not set in motion by any quality or function of its object. It is the love of God operating in the human heart.

10   *Agape* is disinterested love. It is a love in which the individual seeks not his own good, but the good of his neighbor (I Cor. 10:24). *Agape* does not begin by discriminating between worthy and unworthy people, or any qualities people possess. It begins by loving others *for their sakes*. It is an entirely "neighbor-regarding concern for others," which discovers the neighbor in every man it meets. Therefore, *agape* makes no distinction between friend and enemy; it is directed toward both. If one loves an individual merely on account of his friendliness, he loves him for the sake of the benefits to be gained from the friendship, rather than for the friend's own sake. Consequently, the best way to assure one-self that Love is disinterested is to have love for the enemy-neighbor from whom you can expect no good in return, but only hostility and persecution.

11   Another basic point about *agape* is that it springs from the *need* of the other person—his need for belonging to the best in the human family. The Samaritan who helped the Jew on the Jericho Road was "good" because he responded to the human need that he was presented with. God's love is eternal and fails not because man needs his love. St. Paul assures us that the loving act of redemption was done "while we were yet sinners"—that is, at the point of our greatest need for love. Since the white man's personality is greatly distorted by segregation, and his soul is greatly scarred, he needs the love of the Negro. The Negro must love the white man, because the white man needs his love to remove his tensions, insecurities, and fears.

12   *Agape* is not a weak, passive love. It is love in action. *Agape* is love seeking to preserve and create community. It is insistence on community even when one seeks to break it. *Agape* is a willingness to sacrifice in the interest of mutuality. *Agape* is a willingness to go to any length to restore community. It doesn't stop at the first mile, but it goes the second mile to restore community. It is a willingness to forgive, not seven times, but seventy times seven to restore community. The cross is the eternal expression of the length to which God will go in order to restore broken community. The resurrection is a symbol of God's triumph over all the forces that seek to block community. The Holy Spirit is the continuing community creating reality that moves through history. He who works against community is working against the whole of creation. Therefore, if I respond to hate with a reciprocal hate I do nothing but intensify the cleavage in broken community. I can only close the gap in broken community by meeting hate with love. If I meet hate with hate, I become depersonalized, because creation is so designed that my personality can only be fulfilled in the context of community. Booker T. Washington was right: "Let no man pull you so low as to make you hate him." When he pulls you that low he brings you to the point of working against community; he drags you to the point of defying creation, and thereby becoming depersonalized.

13   In the final analysis, *agape* means a recognition of the fact that all life is interrelated. All humanity is involved in a single process, and all men are brothers. To the degree that I harm my brother, no matter what he is doing to me, to that extent I am harming myself. For example, white men often refuse federal aid to education in order to avoid giving the Negro his rights; but because all men are brothers they cannot deny Negro children without harming their own. They end, all efforts to the contrary, by hurting them-

selves. Why is this? Because men are brothers. If you harm me, you harm yourself.

14   Love, *agape*, is the only cement that can hold this broken community together. When I am commanded to love, I am commanded to restore community, to resist injustice, and to meet the needs of my brothers.

15   A sixth basic fact about nonviolent resistance is that it is based on the conviction that the universe is on the side of justice. Consequently, the believer in nonviolence has deep faith in the future. This faith is another reason why the nonviolent resister can accept suffering without retaliation. For he knows that in his struggle for justice he has cosmic companionship. It is true that there are devout believers in nonviolence who find it difficult to believe in a personal God. But even these persons believe in the existence of some creative force that works for universal wholeness. Whether we call it an unconscious process, or impersonal Brahman, or a Personal Being of matchless power and infinite love, there is a creative force in this universe that works to bring the disconnected aspects of reality into a harmonious whole.

Prereading Activities for "Common Houseplants"

"Common Houseplants" is an attempt at dividing by a student in a college composition class. The essay isn't perfect, but it does illustrate well some of the processes of dividing classes into subclasses.

VOCABULARY.   The piece presents a few words that you may not know, particularly the names of some species of houseplants. You will observe, however, that each is carefully defined in the text. In addition, some common words are given technical meanings in the text; these also are carefully defined. You might be on the lookout for the following: *tropical*, *semitropical*, *arid*, *nonarid*, and *striations*.

STUDY QUESTIONS.   You should be able to answer the following questions after reading the selection.

1. What are the two major categories of houseplants?
2. What are the three techniques of defining that the author usually employs to classify his different types of houseplants?
3. Do his divisions seem to overlap?
4. Can you think of other types of houseplants that he has not included in his basic divisions?

ORGANIZATION.   The organization of this paper, like that of nearly all division papers, can be graphically presented in the form of an inverted tree, as Figure 11.2 illustrates. The numbers of the paragraphs corresponding to the branching of the tree are given after the topic of the

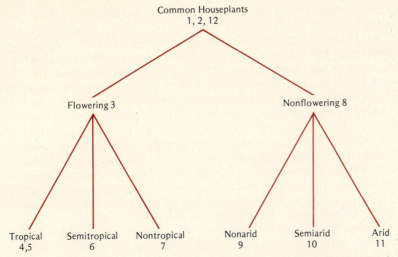

FIGURE 11.2.   The tree structure of "Common Houseplants."

section. Paragraphs 1 and 2, in this case, are introductory, and the last paragraph is a concluding paragraph.

COMMON HOUSEPLANTS

Robert Larry Ackridge

1 In the past few years there has occurred a surge of interest in houseplants as a hobby. Houseplants are living organisms of the vegetable kingdom that grow by the synthesis of materials from soil, water, and air; they are raised almost totally indoors. Houseplants are relatively easy to care for, requiring little care and maintenance, and in return offer their attractiveness and fascination to both the gardener and the casual observer.

2   Numerous varieties of plants are suitable for indoor growth. The ones that are discussed in this theme are the most popular among many American houseplant enthusiasts. They are well-known for their easy care and beauty.

3   This paper classifies these common houseplants into two main categories: flowering and nonflowering houseplants. Flowering houseplants are so entitled because they produce a blossom. They require ample light, either sunlight or artificial. Most varieties are extremely sun-loving.

4   The tropical varieties are among the most beautiful types of flowering plants. The richness of green hues found in their leaves and the vivid exotic colors of their blossoms make them among the most highly prized of houseplants. Tropical plants are those that require a high water content in

their soil to satisfy their desire for high humidity. They also require richly fertilized soil.

5   Two of the most beautiful of the tropicals are the zebra plant and the African violet. The first is so designated because of the fine white striations found upon its dark green leaves; striations are striped markings. The zebra plant puts forth a large yellow blossom that has a light scent. African violets are fuzzy-leafed plants with small purple, pink, or white flowers. They are somewhat difficult to grow, and their soil must never be allowed to dry out.

6   Semitropical plants are those which require average growing conditions with only moderate amounts of light, fertilizer, and water needed. The soil need not be as rich or moist as that for the tropicals. Semitropicals include such plants as begonia and wandering Jew. The begonia is characterized by brightly colored leaves and irregular, ornate flowers. The wandering Jew is a trailing plant with small white blossoms and striped green leaves.

7   Nontropical houseplants are those which thrive in an arid environment with little water. Examples of nontropicals are the century plants, the pincushion cactus, the Thanksgiving cactus, and the Christmas cactus. The century plant is a succulent or juicy plant which blooms once in twenty to thirty years before dying. The pincushion cactus resembles a small green pincushion full of long pins. It has a brilliant blossom. Thanksgiving and Christmas cacti blossom once a year around Thanksgiving and Christmas respectively. Their blossoms are pink or red and give off a pleasant scent.

8   Nonflowering houseplants are those with the absence of blossoms during their lifetime. The beauty of these plants is in their foliage. They are for the most part shade-loving plants with an aversion to direct light. Foliage plants are of basically three humidity types: nonarid, semiarid, and arid.

9   The nonarid type is a houseplant which thrives in humid, moist, cool places. Nonarid houseplants burn easily in direct lighting and must be kept highly watered and fertilized. There is an extreme range of green hues among the nonarids from light grass green to dark forest green. Nonarids include ferns, palms, and philodendrons. Ferns such as Boston fern and asparagus fern have large feathery fronds. Palms are tropical evergreens with unbranched trunks crowned by large, showy pinnate or feathery leaves. Philodendrons are climbing plants with thick, glossy, green leaves.

10   Semiarids require little humidity and don't like excessive water. They are somewhat hardy plants needing little care. Semiarids include house-plants such as the India rubberplant and the fiddle-leaf fig. India rubber plants have large, glossy leaves that are leathery in texture. They are a favorite houseplant due to their beauty and hardiness. The fiddle-leaf fig has large, glossy, thick leaves. It is also a very hardy houseplant.

11   The third type of nonflowering houseplant is the arid group. Such plants need little water and thrive in a sandy soil mixture. They usually require little care. One of the most common in this group is aloe vera, the miracle plant. It is light green with finger-like extensions coming from one root and is called the miracle plant because of the relief the juice of the plant brings to burns and cuts.

12   When choosing a houseplant one should know something about the two basic varieties—flowering and nonflowering. Time should be taken and

careful thought given to choosing among the flowering and nonflowering varieties. One should choose a plant that calls for the amount of time and care the grower wishes to invest. Raising houseplants is a good way to bring nature into your home and to satisfy your esthetic tastes.

PREWRITING: SOME PRINCIPLES OF DEFINING AND DIVIDING

Choosing a Topic for a Definition Paper

Martin Luther King, Jr., and the student who wrote "Common Houseplants" had one attribute in common as writers: both were personally interested in the subject they chose to write about. Although the student did the paper in a composition class, he was not just fulfilling an assignment; he was passing on some useful information to the rest of the class. And, of course, Martin Luther King, Jr., made nonviolent resistance the center of his whole religious and political life. If you look at your academic, political, religious, or leisure activities, you should certainly come up with some concept, notion, group of people, or class of things that holds a strong attraction or repulsion to you and that you strongly suspect is misunderstood by or not even known to some readers.

But not just any concept or class will do. For an extended definition paper, the notion or class must have some measure of complexity. If the notion is so neat and simple that it can be disposed of in a straightforward three-line definition, then it does not call for a paper of extended definition, unless you are attempting a humorous paper, for instance. One type of complexity that often calls for extended definition treatments is the sort of notion that many would call controversial. Such concepts as pornography, democracy, and equality often have to be explained at some length because different people have different conceptions of the same word. For instance, Russians and Americans have quite different notions of the concept of democracy. And the "Moral Majority" and typical readers of *Playboy* magazine have radically different ideas of what *pornography* means and of its importance in our society. Controversial notions, therefore, are a wonderful source for papers of extended definition. The fact that people care enough about them to get riled and ruffled lends a probable interest level to them. And the inherent ambiguity in many controversial notions also makes them amenable to treatment in careful definitional terms.

But a notion need not be controversial in the sense of the preceding paragraph to be considered complex enough to be handled in an extended definition. A "black hole" in astronomy, while conceivably controversial in very esoteric scientific circles, is already complex and yet intriguing enough to the educated common reader to lend itself to an extended definition.

The readers should also be considered in the choice of a topic. You ought to be able to carve out a determinate audience for your paper. If you can't visualize a distinct audience that would be interested in the subject, then you probably ought to look for another topic. Martin Luther King, Jr., felt that there was a vast audience of sympathetic listeners in America for his message about nonviolence. And the student in English 308 thought that he might convert some of the class to his interest in common houseplants in his paper.

Exercises on Choosing a Topic for an Extended Definition

1. Try your academic area for a topic about which you are knowledgeable and in which you are interested. Thus if you are in the physical sciences you might consider topics similar to the following: X rays, radioactivity, electromagnetism, gravity, ions, equilibrium, galaxy, white dwarf, black hole, meteor, comet, computer, and so on. If you are in one of the social sciences, you might consider some of the topics with which some of the best minds of history have wrestled; try to define a democracy, a constitution, government itself, progress, wealth, revolution, and so on. If you have philosophical inclinations try your hand at defining one of the following: virtue, wisdom, time, soul, nature, duty, or freedom. If you have artistic interests try to define one of these notions: art, beauty, music, sonnet, symphony, or a sonata; or you might try to distill the essence of a period in literature, music, or painting—baroque, romantic, classical, neoclassical, abstract expressionistic, or primitive.

   Any student might try an extended definition of his or her own field: astronomy, physics, chemistry, business, marketing, English, government, physical education, secondary education.

2. An extended definition will necessarily be rather complex. Try to foresee, in the choice of a topic, what the elements of the complex notion will be. Martin Luther King, Jr., obviously had a clear idea of the complexity of the notion of nonviolence.

3. Do not be hesitant to call on previous attempts to define your topic. Nearly every area has a dictionary in the field. Consult *The Dictionary of Geology, Crispin's Dictionary of Scientific and Technical Terms*, the *Dictionary of the Social Sciences, A Dictionary of the Natural Environment*, and others, for some help in getting ideas.

Techniques of Definition

Martin Luther King, Jr., in his persuasive piece about nonviolent resistance, illustrated a good number of the techniques of definition, that students are called upon to use in typical college assignments.

First, let us see what the result of a good definition is. What are we trying to do when we define? King was obviously worried that misunderstandings about the relation of nonviolent resistance to segregation would hinder the movement. Consequently, he felt the need to give a careful definition of nonviolence in order that the actions of those in the movement would be properly classified and interpreted. Many inappropriate classifications are mentioned in the text: cowardly, inactive, person-directed, retaliatory, and others. But nonviolence, King says, is none of these. And because people had misclassified, he felt, the nonviolence movement had been hurt. So in this piece King attempts to define and reclassify.

How did King go about it? In writing this essay, King used four of the most frequently used techniques of definition: the logical definition, definition by example, the operational definition, and the stipulative definition. The student author also used three of these methods. Let us examine these four techniques.

LOGICAL DEFINITION.   In paragraph 10, after having mentioned three kinds of love, King proceeds to define the third type, *agape*, more carefully. He begins by saying that it is "disinterested love." In other words, it belongs to the general category of "love," but is different from the other two types of love in being disinterested. In fact, the next five paragraphs are devoted to making clear the differences between *agape* and *philia* and *eros*. Thus King defines *agape* by first placing it in a large class and then by placing it in a subclass of this larger class and by showing how it differs from the other subclasses. We can illustrate this by using the same tree structure used to illustrate the organizational pattern of "Common Houseplants" (see Figure 11.3).

As the diagram makes clear, *agape* is love that does not seek a selfish return from the act of loving, whereas both *eros* and *philia* do. More formally, the large class, love, is called the *genus*, and the three subclasses are called the *species*. And since the difference between *agape* and the other two species is its disinterestedness, this characteristic is called the

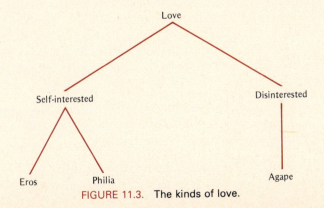

FIGURE 11.3.   The kinds of love.

specific differentia. Consequently, logical definition is often said to be a definition by genus and specific differentia.

The student essay frequently uses this technique of definition. For example, having a blossom is the specific differentia between flowering and nonflowering. Heavily watered rich soils are the specific differentia for the writer's definition of tropical (paragraph 4). In fact, the logical definition is the most frequently used type of definition.

Note that since the logical definition achieves its effect by separating one species from another, that is, by excluding one species from the other, part of the technique of logical definition is negative. Indeed, of the six aspects of nonviolence that Dr. King uses in his definitions, three are negative (see paragraphs 3, 4, and 5). The student paper also uses this technique throughout; indeed, some major classifications are achieved by negation—nontropical, nonarid, and so on. Negative definitions, as the two sample papers illustrate, can be an efficient technique of defining.

DEFINITION BY EXAMPLE.   The second frequently used kind of definition is the definition by example. Children use this type of definition to learn the nature of the things they encounter before they are verbally capable of other kinds of definition. For example, many of us learned what a hippopotamus was by having one pointed out to us at a zoo. That is also how we learned to recognize a chair, a table, a brother, and so on. By using examples, we can often immediately clarify the meaning of a complex definition. We thus use definition by example in conjunction with other kinds of definition.

Both King and the student use examples quite effectively in their essays. In paragraph 3, after having defined nonviolence as *not* being cowardly, King immediately gives an example of brave nonviolence by referring to Gandhi. He also uses the nonviolence in Montgomery to illustrate the nonpersonal nature of his philosophy; in paragraph 11 he uses three examples to illustrate the love based on the need of the beloved, the Samaritan, God, and St. Paul. You can find further evidences of this use of definition by example throughout King's essay.

The student writer systematically illustrates each of his major categories by giving one or more examples of the subclass. Thus the zebra and African violet are examples of the tropicals; the begonia and wandering Jew are examples of the semitropicals; and so on. In addition, the student makes his examples more concrete by describing the particular plant in almost every instance.

The begonia is characterized by brightly colored leaves and irregular, ornate flowers. Wandering Jew is a trailing plant with small white blossoms and striped green leaves. (paragraph 6)

Such definitions are sometimes called *descriptive definitions*.

Defining by examples is usually used in conjunction with other techniques of defining, as can be seen in both King's and the student's writing. There is a simple reason for this. If, for example, a Martian were only shown a brown, four-legged wooden table in an effort to explain what a table is, he might conclude that tables are four-legged creatures, or that all tables are wooden things, or that all tables are brown, and so on. Other types of defining—and perhaps more examples—would be necessary to provide a reasonably complete and useful sense of what a table is. Consequently, defining by example is usually a supportive type of definition.

OPERATIONAL DEFINITION. A particularly important kind of definition in many disciplines is the operational definition. In psychology, education, physics, and chemistry—in general, in many of the so-called hard sciences—the student may be required to define operationally.

What does this mean? An operational definition is usually a logical definition, that is, one using a genus and a specific differentia. But the defining terms of the operational definition must be terms that refer to observable or empirical procedures or operations. Thus, it is possible to define *length* by saying it is "that characteristic of a body that manifests a specific number of units of a measuring rod (such as a meter or a yardstick)." However, a definition like the following would not be an operational definition: "God is a being whose essence is to exist." The terms *God*, *being*, and *essence* are not empirical.

Much of King's essay deals with the nonempirical; as a result some of his definitions and subdefinitions are not operational. "Passive," "cowardice," "justice," and "*agape*," for instance, are difficult to define in terms that refer to the immediately observable. However, nearly all of the student's definitions in "Common Houseplants" are operational. A definition like "African violets are fuzzy-leafed plants with small purple, pink or white flowers" can be empirically checked.

STIPULATIVE DEFINITION. Both King and the author of the student paper take the implicit stand that the definitions they propose correspond somewhat faithfully to the real world: there is something like *agape* in the real world, and something like *justice*, and something like *cowardice*. And certainly there are African violets, begonias, and Christmas cacti.

Sometimes, however, for the purposes of a given paper or speech or experiment, the careful correspondence of reality and the class defined is not critical. And, to stave off unnecessary opposition from readers who may have somewhat different notions of a class, the writer may simply say that he or she is posing a definition of a class that is provisionally being used only in the paper and that makes no overriding claim to correspond with reality. Thus in geometry a line is defined as that which has length, but no width nor height. Actually, in the real world there is nothing like this;

but it is a useful definition in the context. Such a definition is called a *stipulative* or *context* definition. In polemical writing, a stipulative definition is often used precisely to show that the object does not exist in reality. Thus, an opponent of the Christian concept of a god might argue: If there were a Christian God, he would have to be a perfect creature who could not allow evil to come into existence. He might then argue that since evil does exist, a Christian God cannot be postulated.

In specific areas of study, you may encounter other types of definitions, appropriate and useful in particular situations. But at least these four basic types ought to be available to all writers. And all of them can be used for different purposes of discourse: in exposition, in persuasion, in literature, and in self-expression.

In expository writing, some time-honored rules can help you make your definitions clear, useful, and accurate.

Rule 1: The class determined by the defining terms should have the same membership as the class understood by the term to be defined. Thus, although a noun is traditionally defined as a word that refers to a person, place, or thing, such a definition breaks the first rule because *any* word refers to a person, place, or thing. Thus the word *climb* refers to the action of ascending laboriously, and an action is a type of thing. But *climb* is usually a verb and verbs are supposed to be distinguished from nouns. In other words, the membership of the class *noun* is smaller than the membership of the class defined by the defining terms "a word that refers to a person, place, or thing." The definition is potentially confusing.

This particular definition illustrates one of the most frequent faults of definitions—they are too broad. Here, it is quite true that all nouns do refer to persons, places, or things—but so do many other words.

Rule 2: A definition must not be circular, that is, the defining terms must not contain the critical term being defined. Thus, to define a *rational* person as a person who uses his reason is to violate this rule, because *rational* and *reason* are basically the same term, though in slightly different garb. Notice, however, that the repetition of the term *person* in both the term to be defined and in the definition proper is not a violation of this rule, since *rational*, not *person*, is the term in question.

Rule 3: A definition should not be expressed in obscure or figurative language. Generally this means that a definition should be given in the operating vocabulary of the reader, since usually it is presumed that the reader does not know the precise meaning of the new term but will be able to translate it into the meanings of words already known. Thus, Samuel Johnson's notorious definition of a *network* as a "thing reticulated or decussated, at equal distances, with interstices between the intersections"[*]

---

[*]E. L. McAdam, Jr., and George Milne, *Johnson's Dictionary: Modern Selection* (New York: Random House, 1963), p. 263.

breaks this rule. Most people who know the meaning of Johnson's defining terms would already know what a network is.

Exercises on Defining

Assuming you have already chosen a topic and are going to write a paper of extended definition, these exercises should help you in the process. If you are just interested in exercises in definition as such, the exercises at the end of the chapter will be more the sort of general practice you might be looking for.

1. Examine the definitions given of your topic in the dictionaries and encyclopedias for their use of the four different kinds of definitions: logical, operational, stipulative, and by example. If your sources use all of these techniques, see if you can adapt them to your paper. If some of the techniques are not used, try to create definitions that illustrate the types. Sometimes, particularly in the humanities, you might not be able to find a suitable operational definition. Often, in fact, you may have to use a definition by purpose. Some technical definitions are also of this type. Thus, a *watch* is frequently defined as an instrument for telling time.

2. Check each of your definitions by the three rules given for expository definitions, if you are doing that type of paper. The main definition especially should meet these criteria. Your example may not always meet the criteria, but the main logical and operational definitions should. Even if you are not doing an expository paper, the rules can help you sharpen your meanings, at least in the preparatory stage of your writing.

Dividing

As mentioned earlier, defining and dividing are complementary processes, in a manner of speaking. In defining, one takes individual things or groups of things and brings them together under the umbrella of one or more shared characteristics. In dividing, one takes a unified class and separates it into subclasses or into the members of the class. Defining is a process of synthesis and dividing is a process of analysis.

Martin Luther King, Jr., drew together some basic characteristics, shared by different groups of people, and combined them into a unity that he called the concept of nonviolent resistance. The student, on the other hand, took a complex class, common houseplants, and systematically broke it down into various subclasses, each of which he then defined. Both processes are techniques that the college writer must be able to use when the occasion calls for them.

Choosing a Topic for a Paper on Dividing

Choose a class with subclasses, not an object with parts. Possibly the most frequent mistake made by students given an assignment on division is to take an object and divide it up into its parts. This is an understandable error, because *division* in ordinary language can mean division of a class into subclasses or division of a whole into its component parts. But division in a logical and rhetorical sense has the first meaning. To divide *houses* in the rhetorical sense is to end up with different kinds of houses, and each subclass and each subsubclass will always be a kind of house. But to break a *house* down into rooms, closets, a pantry, a kitchen, bathrooms, and so on is not to engage in the rhetorical sense of division in this chapter.

Consequently, check your topic and its subdivisions to see if the subdivisions are really subclasses of the original class.

There ought to be some point to the dividing process. If the division is only viewed as an academic exercise, try to find another topic that is rhetorically meaningful. In effect this means that the reader should see some importance to the distinctions among the divisions and subdivisions. The division of love by King was very important to his thinking, and a failure by his audience to see the distinctions could lead to serious misunderstandings of the concept of nonviolent resistance.

So check your projected distinctions and ask yourself if there is some point or purpose to the breakdown.

Choose a class that is relatively complex. This parallels the advice previously given in discussing the paper on definition. If the breakdown only yields two divisions, you will probably not learn very much from writing a paper on dividing. If the topic you choose is controversial, this is not likely to be the case, since controversial topics are typically more rather than less complex.

Check the resulting subclasses to see if they can be adequately defined. Definition always enters into a substantive dividing paper. That is why definition is considered first in this chapter.

Exercises on Choosing a Topic for Dividing

1. Possibly the best exercise at this stage of your paper is to erect a division tree similar to the tree given for the paper on "Common Houseplants" on page 325.
2. Test your tree by means of the four points given with regard to choosing a topic.
   a. Is the tree really a logical system of classes and not just a breaking up of a whole into its parts?
   b. Is there a rhetorical point to the set of classes and their distinctions?

c. **Is the tree more than a one-level branching?**
d. **Can you provisionally define each of the resulting subclasses?**

The Rules of Division

Let us examine how the writer of "Common Houseplants" goes about the process of dividing. In his theme, he exemplifies most of the basic rules of dividing. Just as with the rules of defining previously explained, these rules are normally applicable only to expository writing, but they can be extended, when useful, to other aims of discourse. The reasons for the rules are given, in each case, with the individual rule.

Rule 1: When possible, a division should be exhaustive; that is, all of the members of the genus class should be allotted to one or another of the subclasses. The student writer's first division of common houseplants into flowering and nonflowering is exhaustive; all common houseplants are accounted for in these two subclasses. But, in a discussion of ethnic minority rights in San Francisco, a "basic" division of minorities into Blacks and Chicanos would be strenuously objected to because it is not exhaustive; in San Francisco the substantial presence of Asians must also be seriously considered, and indeed, still other minorities might object. They might be accounted for with a stipulative definitional category of "miscellaneous."

Sometimes, it is not possible to be exhaustive because all of the subclasses are not known, or because the constraints of time or space do not allow all of them to be considered. If major categories are being passed over, the reader should be advised as to why they are being ignored.

Rule 2: There should be a consistent principle of division at each level of the division process. The student writer was very careful to observe this rule. In Figure 11.2, the tree structure of "Common Houseplants" (p. 325), the first branching of houseplants into flowering and nonflowering uses the principle of the presence or absence of blossoms to separate the subclasses. At the next level, two principles are used concurrently: high-versus low-water content and heavy or light fertilization in the soil.

Note, for example, that a division of athletes into Black, Chicano, and professional violates this rule: racial background is used for the first two subclasses, but not for the last. The result of ignoring the second rule, as this case illustrates, is that the division is usually not exhaustive, different and maybe unrelated issues are raised, and awkward overlappings occur (many Black and Chicano athletes are also professionals).

Observing the principle of division will stave off all of these problems. Sometimes, of course, there may not be an obvious principle of division separating important classes, but the classes still must be considered. The classes must then be divided on an *ad hoc* basis. Often this will happen at the bottom of a tree. Thus, the student's choice of the zebra and the

African violet as examples of the tropical category is *ad hoc* because while there is no basic principle of division, the examples are not without reason; in this case they are both chosen for their beauty.

Rule 3: Unless there is a good reason, the divisions should not overlap. The student's theme illustrates this rule quite consistently. The tropical and the nontropical subclasses do not overlap; in general, none of his subclasses overlap—mainly, it might be pointed out, because he applies a careful principle of division at each level.

The danger of overlap is that it defeats the very purpose for making divisions—to separate one class from another. When classes overlap, they obviously are not carefully separated. There are some situations when overlapping of classes must be considered. But first let's take a more careful look at the various relationships classes have with one another.

Systematizing Classes

In planning a paper involving classes that are subdivisions of a larger class, one of the most important considerations concerns the relationships these various classes have with one another in the system. Indeed, both in defining and in dividing, these relationships operate continually. Nearly all of the basic relationships, as we shall see, occur in either the King or the student theme.

There really are only five major ways in which classes can be connected with one another, and in ordinary language we use all of these nearly every day: (1) a class can be combined with another class to make a sort of superclass; (2) a class can overlap with another class; (3) a class can include a subclass; (4) a class can be equivalent to another class; and (5) a class can exclude another class.

CLASS UNION.   In Figure 11.2 you can see that the class of flowering houseplants is made up of the smaller classes of tropical, semitropical, and nontropical houseplants. The process of combining two or more classes into a larger class is called *class union*.

CLASS INCLUSION.   In the student theme, the class of aloe vera is a subclass of arid houseplants; in fact, all of the examples the student gives are instances of class inclusion. The notion of class inclusion is almost always present in composition, partly because it is the basis of many of the most common of our logical inferences. Whatever can be said of the general class of arid plants can also be said to be true of the subclass of aloe vera. This application of the general class to the subclass and to each member of the class or subclass is one of the major foundations of deductive reasoning.

CLASS EXCLUSION.   The opposite of class inclusion is class exclusion. In the student theme, the arid houseplants exclude the members of the nonarid houseplants.

The use of class inclusion and exclusion enables the student to erect the tree structure that is the basis for the organization of the entire theme on houseplants. The classes on the same level in Figure 11.2 are the classes that are mutually exclusive, and those that branch out from these are the classes that are included in the larger class. In such a tree, the classes at the same level are called *coordinate classes* and those included in a larger class are called *subordinate classes*.

CLASS INTERSECTION.   If the student had chosen to divide his flowering plants into only tropical and nontropical, there would be an area of overlap of the two classes—the class constituting of what he ended up calling semitropical. Such an overlap constitutes class intersection.

Interestingly enough, although one of the traditional rules of expository division warns against overlapping classes (see Rule 3), the rule is systematically violated in much research work. Thus a medical study, investigating the effects of smoking upon people who are cancer victims, is interested in the overlap of cancerous people with smoking people. Notice that such an overlap also calls for a different principle of division. In such cases, certain exclusive subclasses will be established in order to follow up a careful research design, but the fact remains that class intersection will be at the heart of the study.

CLASS EQUIVALENCE.   Another look at Figure 11.2, the student's tree structure for the theme on houseplants, will show some obvious cases of class equivalence. Thus the class of flowering houseplants is made up of the union of its three subclasses. Or, in geometry, the class of equiangular triangles is equivalent to the class of equilateral triangles, at least insofar as class membership is concerned.

COMPARISON AND CONTRAST OF CLASSES AND MEMBERS OF CLASSES.   Once the notions of class exclusion, intersection, and equivalence are understood, it is possible to see what happens when two classes are compared and contrasted or when two members of a class are compared and contrasted. Complete similarity between the two classes would allow one only to compare—in effect the two classes would be equivalent. And complete similarity between two objects would really dissolve the two objects into one. However, complete contrast between two classes would be possible with only mutually exclusive classes.

But if classes or members of classes share some characteristics and not others—in other words belong to some common classes and not to others—then comparison *and* contrast are possible. Thus Generals Grant and Lee share some common characteristics; that is, they belong to some of the same classes (graduates of West Point, generals, Civil War veterans, Mexican War veterans, men offered control of military forces, successful generals in major battles, and so on). They also differ, that is, belong to different classes (Grant was a U.S. president, a politician who left a record of scandal and bribery, a fighter who won battles by means of massive manpower and resources; Lee was an educator, an innovative strategist and tactician, and so on). Comparison and contrast thus usually involve both intersecting and exclusive classes. (Note that when comparison and contrast involve individual members of classes, they are very close to description.)

Exercises on Dividing and Systematizing Classes

For isolated exercises on these issues, which are not incorporated into the writing of an extended paper on dividing, see the exercises at the end of the chapter. The following exercises assume that you have been working your way forward by choosing a topic and have gone through the preliminary exercises on pages 334–335.

1. Check the tentative tree structure for your paper by seeing if all of the resulting divisions and subdivisions follow the three rules of division.

    a. At each branching, are the following subdivisions exhaustive? For example, if you have divided professional athletes into football and baseball players, you have ignored hockey players, soccer players, basketball players, and others. Your division is not exhaustive. If it is not convenient to make an exhaustive division, either include a miscellaneous group that will catch all of the remaining groups or let the reader know why you have not been exhaustive.

    b. Is there a consistent principle of division at each branching? Across each level of your tree you may not have used the same principle, but at each branching you must use the same principle. If you did not, tell the reader why you chose not to.

    c. Do any of your branchings overlap? Check them for overlap. If you insist on overlap—and at the bottom of the tree you may find it necessary to do so—let the reader know why you have broken this third rule.

2. Check your tentative tree structure for inclusion, exclusion, and the other ways of joining classes. This will be a way of ascertaining if your divisions are justifiable. At this stage of the paper, you might ask yourself if you have gotten into too mechanical a way of breaking down the classes, with the result that the system seems almost trivial in its structure. Sometimes you can get a much more meaningful tree structure by introducing a principle of division earlier in a system, depending on what point you are trying to make in the paper. Thus if you are interested in racial discrimination among athletes, it might be more effective to

introduce the racial principle of division at the top or near the top of the tree.

ORGANIZING PAPERS THAT DEFINE AND DIVIDE

The two samples given at the beginning of the chapter illustrate very faithfully the two normal organizational patterns that definition and classification papers embody. "Pilgrimage to Nonviolence" is a typical theme of extended definition and "Common Houseplants" is a typical classification theme.

Extended Definitions

Martin Luther King, Jr., at the end of two paragraphs introducing his topic, tells his listeners what the organizational pattern of his speech will be when he says, "It may be wise to turn to a brief discussion of some basic aspects of this philosophy." He then discusses six of these basic aspects, and he enumerates each new aspect when he finishes the preceding one. The philosophy is a whole made up of six basic parts; and the treatment of each of the parts in turn gives King's listeners a picture of the whole. Indeed, the terms *aspect* and *whole* are returned to in the final clause of the speech: "There is a creative force in this universe that works to bring the disconnected aspects of reality into a harmonious whole."

Such an organizational pattern is usually followed when a paper involves an extended definition of a fairly complex object. The whole of the definition is arrived at by enumerating the parts. Sometimes the whole may be announced at the beginning and repeated at the end; at other times, as in this instance, the parts are handled separately and thus the whole is seen as a sort of climactic surprise.

Note that some smaller organizational patterns operate within this large whole/part structure in "Pilgrimage to Nonviolence." As the diagram on page 320 shows, the first parts of the definition are negative exclusions: in paragraph 3, cowardice is excluded; in paragraph 4, humiliation of the opposition is excluded; and in paragraph 5, attacks against persons are excluded. The remainder of the essay details the three positive aspects of the philosophy of nonviolence: nonviolence accepts suffering (paragraphs 6 and 7), is based on love (paragraphs 8–14), and believes in the final triumph of justice (paragraph 15).

Within the paragraphs devoted to the negative exclusions, there is a further structure of contrast. In paragraph 3, after repudiating cowardice, King insists that his philosophy includes the notion of an active spiritual resistance to evil. And he gives a good example of such resistance, the person who had served as his inspiration and source, Gandhi. The same contrasting structure is used in paragraphs 4 and 5, complete with an example in 5.

The positive section of the essay, paragraphs 6–15, also has some clear organizational subpatterns. It is obvious that the most important of the six aspects of the philosophy is the idea that nonviolence must be based on love. And the treatment of this section is a second illustration of the whole/part technique of ordering paragraphs. Within the individual paragraphs, King uses contrast and examples to expand each of his subparts.

In short, a large whole/part structure organizes the entire speech. And within each of the two major sections of the essay there are repeated uses of contrast and examples. We could say that there is a macrostructure of whole/part and that there are microstructures of contrast and examples within the macrostructure. The macrostructure of whole/part is, as we saw in the chapter on describing, the usual pattern for that mode of writing. But it is frequently used in other modes of discourse, as we see here.

Classification or Divisions

In contrast to King's speech, which is an extended definition, the paper on houseplants is an extended division or classification. The student theme exemplifies the typical macrostructure seen in such writing. Figure 11.2 shows this structure, the tree structure, as it is usually called. Each branching of the tree is treated in succession, so that the ordering structure of the essay is a series of branchings and subbranchings. This is possibly the most common structure of all compositions, as indeed it is one of the most common structures in all nature: rivers show this pattern, glass breaks in this pattern, our veins and arteries feed our bodies by channels and subchannels that branch out in this fashion, and so on.

The microstructures that the student uses to develop his paragraphs are similar to those of Dr. King. He usually gives a definition of the subclass he is considering, then illustrates it with an example.

EXERCISES ON ORGANIZATION

By now most of the material that you are going to put into your essay should be assembled. In fact, you have probably done a good deal of writing on important sections of the essay. The following questions and suggestions should help you organize your essay for your first full draft. The first set of questions relates to the defining theme and the second to the dividing theme.

1. Defining
   a. Have you impressed your reader with the importance of the forth-

coming definitions in your introduction? Does your reader need any necessary background to understand the importance?

   b. Isolate the parts of your definition in a small chart. Ask yourself what order you have been assuming they would follow in the theme. Is there a better order, such as the one King used—the climactic order? Is one part of the definition necessary to understand before another element can be introduced?

   c. Does the point of your paper come through at the end of the presentation? Or has it been lost in the development?

   d. If comparison and contrast are useful in your development, have you exploited their use in the organization of your paragraphs and sentences?

   e. Is there a visible organizing principle to your paragraphs?

2. **Dividing**

   a. Have you impressed your reader with the importance of the division procedure you are about to subject him or her to? Has your reader been provided with any necessary background information?

   b. Construct a definitive tree structure for the essay you are writing. Ask yourself if any of the division principles should be introduced earlier than they have been. Would such a restructuring make the essay easier for you to write or easier for your readers to read? Are some distinctions presupposed by others and therefore must come earlier?

   c. Check the classes in the tree structure and the definitions of each. What types of definitions have you used? Have you used examples whenever possible?

   d. Check the tree structure by the rules of division.

   e. Have you used comparison and contrast if they are called for?

   f. What is the visible structure of your paragraphs?

STYLE IN DEFINING AND DIVIDING

The most important features of the style of a composition will be determined by the aim or purpose of the piece, the audience to which this aim is directed, and the situation in which the audience and writer find themselves. In earlier chapters we have seen some of the stylistic differences among different aims.

But some important features of style derive from the particular way in which we have to look at the world when we define and classify. These features persist regardless of the aim of the discourse. In general, they reflect the fact that in defining and dividing we are always considering characteristics common to some objects and mentally separating these objects from others that do not share the same characteristics. That is, the words we use to detail these collections and separations will in some sense have to be words that bring things together as well as set them apart. Nor will the style simply be limited to the choice of words; it will also include the selection of sentence structure, figures of speech, image clusters, and even the major symbols of the piece.

We see all of these elements vividly in "Pilgrimage to Nonviolence." Because of King's persuasive aim, some of the stylistic features are more highlighted than are the rather neutral traits of the student's theme, which is largely informative in aim. Consequently, it will be more worthwhile for us to examine King's style. (You can profitably compare King's style to that of the poet William Blake in "The Clod and the Pebble," used in the exercises at the end of this chapter as a piece of literary classification and definition.)

We can see the class relations of exclusion and intersection immediately in two clusters of terms, one cluster built around violence and the other built around nonviolence. In the violence cluster are the following: *strong*, *physical*, *unearned*, *defeat*, *humiliate*, and *active*. In the nonviolence cluster are the following: *passive, quiet, stagnant, spiritual, weak, purchased*, and *redeem*. Other terms might be added to each cluster. Note that clusters must not be forced into an interpretation in which all of the nonviolent terms are viewed as having positive connotations, and all of the violent terms are viewed negatively. King doesn't intend that at all. And he has a very clear reason for not drawing such a polar distinction: in each cluster there are words that are *nearly* synonymous with others, but it is precisely the nearness that creates the misunderstanding that he is attacking. Thus it is clear that many would tend to align *strong* and *active* with *violent* and to align *weak*, *passive*, and *stagnant* with *nonviolent*. But King wants his listeners to see that there is a nonviolence that is indeed weak, passive, and stagnant, and that there is also a nonviolence that can be strong, active, and productive.

Consequently, we can see that in King's piece it is necessary to see obvious opposites (antonyms) and obvious similarities (synonyms) in terminology, but we must also be able to see double connotations of words (ambiguities) and even seeming contradictions in words (paradoxes). In the nonviolent person's seeming weakness (he is not physically active) there may be a spiritual strength, and the apparent strength of the physical attacker may in fact be a sign of spiritual weakness.

Besides using kinds of terms—antonyms, synonyms, near synonyms, ambiguities—having to do with interrelationships among classes, classifying themes also involve the use and contrast of abstract and concrete terms.

Both of the selections illustrate this stylistic feature. In the student's theme, as he moves from the largest class down to the specific example, passing through the intermediate subclasses, his choice of terms necessarily moves from the relatively abstract down to the concrete. Notice the movement from houseplant to flowering houseplant to tropical flowering to zebra and African violet to the specific descriptions of each of these (paragraphs 3, 4, and 5). And the diction throughout the entire essay moves in this direction. Thus, as will often happen, the logical process of dividing dictates the organization of the entire piece as well as the organization of the individual paragraphs. The same process dictates the progress of the style—in this case from abstract to concrete, with the concrete terms being used in the definitions by example.

King's essay also deals heavily in both abstract and concrete terms. The abstract terms have to do with the ideals and concepts that are the basis of his philosophy—justice, love, redemption, friendship, and understanding—or their opposites—injustice, hate, evil, enmity, and misunderstanding. In this sense, the essay is quite abstract. Even the three kinds of love are abstract. But, like the student, King also uses concrete terms when he illustrates his definitions by means of examples. Thus Gandhi, Christ, the Sermon on the Mount, Montgomery, rivers of blood, the Samaritan on the road to Jericho, the cross, and others are all terms that refer to concrete realities. They create or re-create pictures or images in the mind of the listener or reader.

When clusters of such images are used, the effect is imagery. And, despite the abstract concepts and terms that King uses, he is also adept at creating clusters of images in his style. Usually, in persuasion and literature, imagery performs a double function. In addition to creating mental pictures that usually are arresting in their own right and give a distinct texture to a style, imagery takes on a favorable or unfavorable association. The images become symbols.

Let us examine a few of these in King's speech. He says, in paragraph 8, "Along the way of life, someone must have sense enough and morality enough to cut off *the chain of hate*." A term like *chain* creates images of prisoners or slaves, and when it is linked to *hate*, the unfavorable connotations that surround *hate* are reenforced by the unfavorable connotations that accompany the images connected with *chain*. "Love, *agape*, is the *only cement that can hold this broken community together*." The first sentence in paragraph 14, uses a different set of images (cement, hold together, broken) to reenforce the favorable connotations of the term *love*. In fact, in most of his paragraphs dealing with abstractions, King manages to find a concrete image to enhance the style.

Besides producing images and acting as symbols, expressions such as "chain of hate" and "cement that can hold a broken community together" also join sets of concepts that have common relationships. In the expression "chain of hate," there is an implicit proportion: chain is to slaves as hate is to races. A similar proportion can be seen in the comparison of love to cement. Such comparisons of common relationships between sets of objects are called *metaphors*, and metaphors are clearly a natural option in language to use when dealing with similar classes. King's style is heavily metaphorical, as our reading has shown.

Thus the process of defining and dividing tends to force the writer to use particular types of words and particular types of figures of speech. Paradox and metaphor are traditionally called *figures of speech*, because in them the ordinary, literal meanings of expressions are given secondary, figurative meanings. The *chain* in "chain of hate" is not a literal one, nor is the *cement* in King's second comparison.

The process of defining and dividing can also affect the structure of sentences. A careful look at the sentence structure in paragraph 5 of "Pilgrimage to Nonviolence" will show how the process of defining is carried out in sentence patterns. In the first sentence, notice the balance of "*against forces of evil* rather than *against persons who happen to be doing the evil.*" Sentence 2 contains a similar juxtaposition: "It is *evil . . . not the persons victimized by evil.*" And notice the verbal oppositions within the same phrase structure of the following sentence: "The tension is, at bottom, between *justice* and *injustice*, between the *forces of light* and the *forces of darkness.*" You can compare the sentence structure throughout the paragraph and indeed in many other parts of the essay.

Much of the opposition within sentences is carried by coordinate conjunctions such as *not only . . . but also*, *not . . . but*, *either . . . or*, and *neither . . . nor*. Sometimes subordinate conjunctions can convey this kind of opposition: "The aftermath of nonviolence is the creation of the beloved community, *while* the aftermath of violence is tragic bitterness" (paragraph 4). Adverbs such as *nevertheless*, *however*, and *nonetheless* have a similar effect.

Finally, as we have already seen, the process of defining and dividing carries on stylistically into the structure of the paragraph, and even into the macrostructure of the entire essay.

Exercises on Style

1. Is your projected audience clear from your first draft? Check your explicit and then your distinct implicit references to the audience. Have a classmate whom you consider somewhat typical of your audience read your paper and ask if he or she agrees with the projections reflected in your references.
2. Will your audience understand your style? Have you explained any necessary technical terms?
3. Has your purpose been carried by your style? Ask this question of a first-draft reader also. Does your style fit the desired medium in which it would be published?
4. Examine your own style, as we did Dr. King's, for antonyms (reflecting class exclusions), synonyms (reflecting class equivalences), paradoxes (reflecting overlaps), and ambiguities (also reflecting overlaps and possibly misunderstood overlaps). If your style has few or none of these features, you might try some of them at points where they would clarify your position.
5. Check your style for image clusters. If your paper lacks imagery, it may

be that you have not used enough concrete examples to illustrate your definitions.

Exercises on Defining and Dividing

1. Chapter 1 of this book is essentially an exercise in defining and dividing. Discuss and then write about the aims of writing as classes of writing. What is the principle of division for the different aims of writing as they are presented in Figure 1.2 (p. 10)? Are medium of publication, situational context, and other criteria also used in the establishment of the differences among the four pieces given on pages 7–13?
   a. What kinds of definitions are given for each of the aims of writing? Do the initial samples of each aim constitute a type of definition by example?
   b. What kinds of definitions are given for each of the modes of writing in Chapter 8, "Introduction to the Modes of Writing"? Do the different samples given constitute instances of definition by example?
2. Draw your own tree of "Kinds of Writing," based upon distinctions of aims of writing and modes of writing. Write a short paragraph indicating the principle of division used for the aims of writing in Chapter 1. Then write a short paragraph indicating the principle of division used at different sections of the modes of writing treatment in Chapter 8.
3. Has the structure of the divisions of aims and modes been the organizational framework for Chapter 1 and Chapter 8? Look at the Contents and see if the organizations of Chapters 1 and 8 have been transferred to the entire textbook.

The preceding questions have been concerned with chapters in a textbook, a book with an informative purpose. The following poem is also an exercise in definition and classification, but, although it contains information, its purpose is also to delight the reader. Read the poem and look for definitions, types of definitions, and contrasts of definitions.

THE CLOD AND THE PEBBLE

William Blake

"Love seeketh not Itself to please,
Nor for itself hath any care;
But for another gives its ease,
And builds a Heaven in Hell's despair."

5   So sung a little Clod of Clay,
    Trodden with the cattle's feet;
    But a Pebble of the brook,
    Warbled out these metres meet:

    "Love seeketh only Self to please,
10 To bind another to its delight;
    Joys in another's loss of ease,
    And builds a Hell in Heaven's despite."

Exercises on "The Clod and the Pebble"

1. What are the two things defined in this poem? Is there a division set up between them? Do the divisions overlap? What are the principles of the division? Do the divisions establish the organizational principle of the poem?
2. What types of definition, using the types given in the preceding parts of the chapter, are used to define love in the poem? Do you believe that the clod and the pebble are giving definitions of different kinds of love or are they giving different aspects of love that coexist?
3. Who are the different speakers in the poem? Who is the speaker for the first stanza? Who is the speaker for the last stanza? Who is the speaker for the middle stanza? Does the speaker of the middle stanza take a stand to agree or disagree with either of the other two speakers?
4. Why does the clod speak first and the pebble last? Would the meaning of the poem have changed substantially if the third stanza had been exchanged with the first and the middle stanza adapted accordingly?
5. Write a paper using definition and division as an approach to this poem. In the paper, you may incorporate the answers to any of the preceding questions. In addition, you should pay close attention to the symmetry of the two parts of the poem, especially the symmetry of the different lines of stanza 1 with stanza 3, although they express diametrically opposite meanings. Finally, you might pay attention to some of the stylistic symmetries and opposites in diction and rhythm. For example, you might want to compare/contrast "despair" with "despite."

Writing Definition and Division Papers

1. In the early part of the chapter we talked about different attitudes to classifying. What are some of the dangers you see in classifying?
   a. Do you know what is meant by a *stereotype*? If you don't, look it up in the dictionary and then ask yourself if you have some stereotypes of your own, or if some of your acquaintances have some. Have you met people who have stereotypes of blacks, Chicanos, Jews, South-

erners, Russians, teachers, politicians, Republicans, and others?

b. Write a short paper on a stereotype you have encountered. If possible, take an example of a member of that class (or several members) and see if he or she corresponds to the characteristics of the stereotype. In the paper, first define the stereotype by outlining the characteristics of the class, then check the stereotype characteristics against the corresponding characteristics of your acquaintance(s).

2. Pick a person of your acquaintance. Then list as many of the groups to which he or she belongs as you can think of. Also list his or her traits that are completely unique, as far as you can ascertain. As a conclusion, write a statement about the role of classifying in knowing people.

3. Write a persuasive essay about drug use. In the essay, make some distinctions among drugs and drug users, and clarify the distinctions by some clear definitions, backed up by examples.

4. Take some concepts in your major field of study that are important to you at this stage of your college career and attempt to define them. In this paper, view your instructor of that field as your audience and assume he or she is trying to check your knowledge of the concepts in an examination. If these definitions are somewhat technical and if you think that your English instructor might not understand them, try to define them in language that he or she would understand. Thus you may end up with a technical and a popular definition of the concept.

5. Take your college newspaper or your city or town newspaper and classify the different articles, ads, comics, editorials, and other sections in it according to aim. Attempt to arrive at a rough percentage of the different aims in the newspaper. You may have to make allowances for overlap of aim (thus an ad may be persuasive and yet contain some information, for instance). Write a short paper on the findings about aims of discourse in your sample newspaper. You may wish also to compare the college to the city newspaper.

6. Take the field in which you are majoring and write a short essay on its main subdivisions. Define each subdivision as accurately as you can. Write this paper with your English instructor as the audience. If possible, erect a tree to structure your presentation. If there are major areas that you do not present, let the reader know this fact.

7. Write a personal essay explaining why you want to be a chemical engineer, a professional violinist, an English instructor, a social worker, a lawyer, or a member of any other profession. In the paper try to define the characteristics of the professional ideal you would like to be. In other words, what are the characteristics of the professional accountant, the professional manager of a business firm, the professional coach, the professional athlete, the professional lawyer, the professional politician, and so on? Try to use definitions by example to reenforce the abstract characteristics you outline.

8. Write an informative essay that classifies the types of governments of countries. Document your sources.

9. Write an informative or persuasive essay that classifies the kinds of pollution caused by your fellow students. Define each type carefully with different types of definitions.

10. Classify the different colleges and universities of your state by different criteria. Make this essay comprehensive in the sense that you account for all of the institutions of higher education in your state. Your divisions may not be comprehensive, but try to create three levels in the tree you erect to classify the colleges. At each level, attempt a careful definition for each division. Write this paper with an acquaintance of yours in high school as the audience.

Evaluating

THE IMPORTANCE OF EVALUATING

In encountering a chapter on evaluation in a book on composition you may be troubled by a curious paradox, a paradox that may be only half conscious. The authors of many composition texts and many teachers who use them frown on "value judgments" and relegate them to some kind of linguistic hell to which other concepts like *opinion* and *subjectivity* have also been consigned. Most composition books, high school or college, do not have chapters on evaluation to parallel those on narration, description, and exposition. Nor is the derogatory treatment of evaluation limited to teachers of composition. Whole disciplines in universities often rule out evaluations as valid types of rational statements. There is a very influential school of academic philosophers who have dismissed all value judgments as meaningless and nonsensical.

What makes these positions seem paradoxical is that the students who become aware of these pejorative attitudes toward value judgments are also vividly aware that they are systematically evaluated by these same teachers, and routinely by their parent(s), their clergy, peers, the police, hiring agencies, the universities or colleges that admitted them, as well as others. In many universities, the students are even asked to evaluate their instructors. Students are also aware that logicians, mechanical engineers, literary critics, physicians, and sports writers *evaluate*, respectively, logical arguments, building materials, novels, new drugs, and football teams; and their evaluations are reported regularly in scientific journals or newspapers. The astute student may even discern that the instructor who condemns "value judgments" is actually making one. Finally, many modern students revolt against a system that has no place for value and many other students repudiate the values of the establishment.

In any case, whether some academics think that they are respectable or not, value judgments surround us at every turn. Family life, politics, business, religion, sex, entertainment, careers, and hobbies all involve values—and are important only because they do.

In studying composition, you encounter values implicitly at every stage. Most notably, each aim of discourse embodies values: for example, scientific discourse seeks truth and literature incorporates beauty. And we try to persuade others to read a book, go to a play, eat at a restaurant, or join a church because we believe that there is a value in such a pursuit.

In the final analysis, the student of composition ought to be able to distinguish a good deduction from an invalid one, a good generalization from an illicit one, a good exploratory procedure from a poor one, good literature from bad literature, effective persuasion from ineffective persuasion, and healthy self-expression from harmful self-expression. Also, evaluations should not be limited to uses of language. By the end of a college career, hopefully a student will have evaluated his or her entire range of value systems, whether religious, political, educational, economic, or whatever. If this is not part of the educational heritage, then the education itself must be judged a failure (and the preceding clause is another value judgment).

SOME EXAMPLES OF EVALUATION

In order to focus our study of evaluating on some particular issues, it will be useful to take a careful look at three different types of evaluations. The first two examples are by professional writers and the third is by a student. We can learn profitably from a careful reading of the three samples.

The first is an evaluation of some of the zoos in a few of the large cities of Texas. Don't be taken in by the tone of such subheadings as "An absolutely arbitrary, subjective, and unscientific rating of Texas zoos." Stephen Harrigan poses some of the most important issues of writing evaluations in this interesting piece.

Prereading Activities

At first glance "Life Behind Bars" may strike you as difficult reading because of the fairly large number of strange words. Most of them, however, are names of animals that we do not ordinarily encounter; as we shall see, the author uses them for a purpose. In any case, you might look up in a dictionary or an encyclopedia some of the following animal terms: monitor lizard, skink, lemur, tamarin, binturong, gecko, hyrax, dik-dik, klipspringer, guan, curassow, gibbon, nylghai, nyala, gaboon viper. Most of the time, however, the meaning will be clear from the text.

But there are quite a few other words in the article that may give you some difficulty. Many college students may have trouble with the following (the paragraph in which a word occurs is given in parentheses):

primate (1)—a member of the most highly developed order of animals
reverberant (1)—re-echoing
veld (2)—open grassy country in South Africa
kopje **(2)**—small hill in South Africa
flaccid (5)—soft, flabby
diorama (8)—a partially three-dimensional setting
viability (14)—ability to live and develop under normal conditions
resaca **(4a)**—lake (Spanish, used in the Southwest)
malevolently (12a)—wishing evil, malicious
anthropomorphic (12a)—characteristic of human beings
rapacious (16)—plundering, greedy
defecate (18)—to excrete waste matter; *feces* is the waste matter itself and *fecal* is the adjective.
totem (20)—an animal or object considered by a clan or family as its symbol and relative
traipse (24)—walk or wander idly
mammalian (30)—of a mammal (an animal having milk-secreting glands)
wattled (36)—built with twigs
aviculturist (39)—a person who raises and cares for birds

As you read the selection ask yourself these questions: (1) What criteria does the author use to evaluate zoos? (2) What attitude does the author take toward the visitors to the zoo? (3) What is the attitude taken toward the animals? (4) Why is the sequence of the piece partly determined by the sequence of the caretakers in the zoo? (5) Is there a pattern in the sequence of the caretakers?

LIFE BEHIND BARS

Stephen Harrigan

What are nice animals like you doing in a zoo like this?

1 When he makes his rounds of the zoo at night Dick Bonko often stops his electric cart in front of the primate house and sits there eavesdropping on the inhabitants. He says that the noise the primates make at night is very different from the madhouse racket—the shrieks and whoops and strange reverberant moans—with which they express themselves during the day. It is instead a low-pitched, mumbling sound, like human beings muttering

nonsense syllables in their sleep. Long after dark, with only Bonko there to hear them, the monkeys speak in tongues.

2   One night I made the rounds with him. We sat in the cart and listened for a long time, but no sound at all came from the primate house, nor from the rest of the Houston Zoo. There was no moon that night, and it was so dark that I could not be sure if the movement inside the cages was something I really perceived or only imagined. I pictured all the zoo animals stretched out on the ground with their heads resting on their forelimbs, like bored, disconsolate dogs. They were sleeping, or merely waiting out the night, complying with their natural cycles in the constricted environment of the zoo. Few of them had ever seen the velds or kopjes or rain forests they had been designed to inhabit. They had no idea where on earth they were or what their presence here meant to the constant human swarm that passed by their cages every day. But it was impossible to imagine that all those animals— Asiatic bears and scimitar-horned oryx, tapir and tigers and fennec foxes— lay there unaware, empty of sensation, soulless. They knew something. What was it?

3   "Naw, they're not going to say anything," Bonko said, driving away from the primate house. He stopped at the alligator pond and cocked his head, listening again.

4   "Sometimes at night you'll hear 'em growlin'," he whispered. "They'll make a funny sound with their bodies—a vibration sound—and then that tail'll slap the water. You hear that sound and you don't know what it is but you're ready to leave the zoo. Then sometimes you'll see 'em bouncin' back and forth in the water. They get to quiverin', like, and that's when they give you the spook."

5   But the alligators did not oblige. They lay there by the pond, great flaccid shapes a shade lighter than the darkness around them. Bonko headed up to the reptile house, reminiscing along the way about the times when, making his nocturnal rounds, he'd been scared half to death by a stray house cat unexpectedly brushing up against his leg.

6   Bonko is the night watchman at the Houston Zoo. Like all employees there, he is a civil servant, since the zoo is fundamentally a municipal enterprise. He is a quiet old man who seems comfortable with his routine, which involves making a circuit of the zoo every two hours, checking on the temperature of the buildings and noting any obvious distress on the part of the animals. Occasionally he might have to roust a group of drunk medical students off the grounds, or put in an emergency call to the vet, or keep an escaped mental-patient from nearby Ben Taub hospital from committing suicide in the bear pits.

7   Before he became a night watchman Bonko worked as a keeper, at Houston and at a zoo in Clovis, New Mexico. Way before that, back in 1936, he worked on the National Bison range in Montana. "I don't know what decided me on this kind of work," he said. "I guess it was really decided for me before I even knew there was such a thing as a zoo. My dad was a cowboy and my mother's family were all stock raisers. I worked considerable with feedin' stock and my granddad gave me a Shetland pony when I was four or five. I grew up with animals. I have respect for them."

8   At the reptile house Bonko got out of the cart and went inside to read the thermostats. The lights were still on in the exhibits, and I could see the Houston Zoo's famous display of the effects of a venomous snakebite—a model of a human arm covered with ghastly black sores that looked like some sort of carnivorous fungus. The snakes and monitor lizards and thick-bodied skinks—glistening and moving by patient degrees in their little dioramas—gave Bonko the creeps. He was more comfortable in the small-mammal house, where we went next. It contained a large assortment of furtive, dreamlike creatures: miniature lemurs that hopped about like crickets, tufted tamarins with faces like those plastic shrunken heads sold in joke shops, a flying fox bat that hung upside down and held her newborn against her breast with her wing.

9   We went back behind the displays, into a perimeter area where off-exhibit animals were kept in plain metal cages. In a little kitchen Bonko read the thermostat and noted the temperature on a clipboard. On the way out he stopped at the cage of a red-fronted lemur and let it play tug-of-war with his ball-point pen. The lemur moved about in a disturbingly human way, as if it were in reality a miniature man who had put on some weird, bug-eyed costume.

10   "I guess my favorite animals to work with when I was a keeper were the big cats," Bonko told me as we continued on his rounds. "The cats aren't afraid of you—they'll come after you if they want to. It keeps you alert. You work with the other animals, you get lax. You don't stay as sharp in your mind as you do workin' with the big cats.

11   "I like the birds pretty well. If I was comin' in the gate lookin' for a job and knowin' what I know today about the zoo, the big cats would be the one's I'd ask for, and next would be the birds. I don't care about workin' monkeys at all. They're too dirty, for one thing. You never know when one of em's gonna hit you alongside the head with a load of crap."

12   The Houston Zoo, a more or less typical big-city zoo, is in the process of evolving from a haphazard, exploitative menagerie to a center for wildlife husbandry. "We want to become producers, not consumers, of wildlife," John Werler told me. Werler is the zoo director. His office, in the reptile building, is not quite as large as the adjoining exhibit area for the endangered Houston toad.

13   We had a long, thoughtful conversation about zoos, during which the phone on Werler's desk rang with regularity. The calls were from people who wanted to know the zoo's operating hours or who wanted advice on such matters as inducing box turtles to mate. There was a call from some disco demento type who had acquired a Bengal tiger to supplement his ego and was now eager to sell the creature to the zoo. On April Fools' Day, Werler said, it is impossible to conduct any business on the phone. Secretaries all over town leave message slips on their bosses' desks advising them to call "Mr. Fox" or "Mr. Bear" at the zoo's phone number.

14   "We no longer want what we call a 'postage stamp' collection," Werler explained between phone calls. "We want fewer species and more natural groupings of those that we have. This also gives us more of a genetic viability. Almost every major zoo is gearing up in this area."

ZOOS WHO

An absolutely arbitrary, subjective, and unscientific rating of Texas zoos.

1a   Our reactions to zoos are based largely upon notions of decor that may be irrelevant to the zoo's inhabitants. A given animal may be as content in a steel cage with a doggy dish as he would be in a vast stage set depicting his native pampas. Simulated waterfalls, concrete baobab trees, and decorative Watusi shields are not necessarily a guarantee of the animal's well-being.

2a   What we must assume an animal needs from a zoo environment are the same things we would need if we were held captive there: room to move, shelter, cleanliness, an appropriate diet, company, and privacy. Few zoos provide all of these things for all of their animals, and so one's reaction toward a particular zoo may vary from exhibit to exhibit.

3a   The following assessments of the state's major zoos are admittedly subjective, based on my own reactions as a casual visitor. The zoos are listed more or less in order of preference.

Islands of Sanity

4a   Brownsville's Gladys Porter Zoo is the most acceptable zoo in Texas. Built in 1973, it is also the newest zoo in the state and the only one designed with a clear vision of what a zoo should be. Despite the outdoor Muzak and the preponderance of fake rock works that make it look like a gigantic electric train layout, the zoo impresses you immediately with its thoughtfulness and restraint. In the best latter-day fashion, there are no cages or bars. Instead there are islands and expansive enclosures, separated from the visitor's walkway by the waters of a resaca. The happy effect of all this is that none of the animals seem particularly neurotic. Even the great burly chimp who, after a spectacular windup, throws feces at visitors, seems to do so only out of a sense of sport. Don't miss the northern leaftailed gecko and the pygmy hedgehog.

5a   Located at 500 Ringgold/ (512) 546-7187/ Open daily 10 a.m.–dusk/ Adults $3, students $2, children $1.

Elephant Walk

6a   The San Antonio Zoo is a very large one, built mostly into an old quarry site that provides spacious habitats for some of the larger mammals. Portions of the zoo, such as the African plains exhibit, are striking and well conceived. Unfortunately, most of the big cats and primates are housed in small, ugly cages only a few feet removed from the zoo clientele, which on a typical summer weekend consists of raucous adolescents and crying, overheated babies. The elephants are put to work giving rides to a dozen children at a time on platforms set upon the apexes of their backbones. When the ride concession is closed, the elephants are chained by a hind foot and a sign out in front proclaims "Elephant's Day Off." San Antonio is for the most part an unrepentant, WPA-era zoo, with Mold-A-Rama machines and shacks selling watered-down soft drinks at every turn of the trail, the kind of place where kids can drop cotton candy into the open mouth of a pygmy hippopotamus and no one seems to mind. A grand institution but a disturbing zoo.

7a   Located at 3903 N. St. Mary's/ (512) 734-7183/ Open daily 9:30 a.m.–5 p.m./ Adults $2, children 75 cents.

Gone Fishing

8a   The newer sections of the Forth Worth Zoo are exceptional, with large outdoor exhibits that seem designed to blend in with the natural features of Forest Park. Fort Worth also has the best signs of any zoo in the state. In the excellent aquarium, I measured four square feet of posted information on the electric eel. But just past the aquarium the slums begin, rows of cinder-block or chain-link cages that, one assumes, are even more dispiriting to the animals than they are to the visitors. The children's zoo, which is soon to be replaced, looks like an abandoned miniature golf course whose fanciful hazards—giant pumpkins and miniature castles—have been taken over by guinea pigs and hyraxes.

9a   Located at 2727 Zoological Park Drive, off S. University/ (817) 870-7050/ Open daily 9 a.m.–5 p.m./ Adults $1, children free.

For the Birds

10a   The Houston Zoo is discussed at length in the adjoining article.

11a   Located at Hermann Park, 1612 Zoo Circle/ (713) 523-0149/ Children's zoo, tropical bird house, and gorilla house open Monday through Saturday 10 a.m.–4 p.m., Sunday 10-5/ Other areas open daily 9:30–6/ Free.

Backyard Zoo

12a   One of the first animals I saw at the Dallas Zoo was a gorilla sitting in a yoga position and staring malevolently through the fogged window that separated us. My assessment of his foul mood was, no doubt, an anthropomorphic one, but it colored the rest of my visit. The Dallas Zoo is well laid out, with numbered exhibits, so that you feel a sense of forward progression as you stroll about. I liked the combined reptile and bird house and found some amusement in the fact that one corner of the zoo abutted a residential neighborhood, affording residents a view of dik-diks and klipspringers and giant red kangaroos from their living room windows. Most of the rest of the zoo I found either unexceptional or unacceptable. The grizzly bear, for instance, whose range in the wild covers several hundred square miles, was housed in a pit about the size of my bedroom. Scattered through the zoo are sentimental sculptures— five little children riding on the back of a rhinoceros, a girl swinging from the neck of a giraffe—meant to demonstrate the benign affection of the animal world for the human species. It doesn't wash.

13a   Located at Marsalis Park, 621 E. Clarendon/ (214) 946-5154/ Open daily 9 a.m.–5 p.m./ Adults $1, children 50 cents/ Parking $1 on weekends and holidays.

S.H.

15   Werler leaned forward as he talked, his elbows on his knees. He seemed to have a sense of mission, which is appropriate, since zoos today are likely the final hope for the survival of a great number of wild species.

16   Werler said he could not remember the last time the Houston Zoo had bought an animal. Most of the new residents had either been born here or were on breeding loan from other zoos. The enlightened posture among zoo people these days is to regard the institution primarily as a way of holding endangered species in trust. While their wild counterparts are stripped of their habitat or poached into extinction, the zoo animals will be reproducing, keeping the species alive for the day when they might be reintroduced into a less rapacious world.

17   Everyone wants to believe this, but among even the most optimistic zoo people a secret, disturbing voice keeps whispering that the wild populations of the earth are doomed. Soon the zoos will be filled with living examples of creatures the planet can no longer support. There is already a term for them—"cage relics."

18   The Houston Zoo's progress toward its mission is impeded by the usual shortage of funds and by its own past, which lives on in the form of crowded and outmoded facilities. Houston's reptile and bird collections are among the finest in the country; it has a new if rather eccentric-looking gorilla habitat; an aquarium and administration complex is already under construction; and there are plans for a new cat habitat and clinic. But many of the zoo's animals continue to live out their lives in featureless kennels, left over from the days when the term "zoological garden" gave off no hint of irony, as if all those drooling, defecating, cage-crazy beasts were no more cognizant, or disturbing to their human observers, than an exhibition of exotic orchids.

19   I have from time to time thought of myself as being "against" zoos, but it is perhaps closer to the truth to say that I have always been troubled by my own fascination with them. The zoo was the nexus of my childhood. It was not only the animals that were on display there but also the possibility they suggested that all life did not disappear beyond the rim of human awareness. I thought of the animals as spirit guides, willing to point the way to this new dimension. I felt secure among them and managed to interpret their numbed awareness as some exotic concern for my own well-being.

20   But of course the zoo animals were not the benevolent totems I had invented for myself. They were misplaced creatures, kidnapped from their environments and displayed for human amusement and human profit. As an adult, I don't feel that connection I felt as a child. I remember only the polar bear, pacing in his stainless steel cage with a fluid, waltzlike motion that did not vary in the slightest particular for all the years of his life, or a gorilla—with that same metronomic regularity—endlessly regurgitating and eating his own vomit. Such behavior is not necessarily neurotic; it could be merely an extension of natural activities. But even viewing the best behaved animals in the zoo, one senses a loss, a kind of spoilage. It is a distressingly neutral feeling to stand there in front of a Malaysian binturong or an Indian elephant and realize that nothing is happening, that no information is being transmitted, that you are both bored.

21   But I keep visiting zoos; I am a "zoogoer." It's a habit, I suppose, and it has its provocative moments. I came to the Houston Zoo thinking that if I was

not able to form a firm opinion about zoos, I could at least learn something about what goes on inside them.

22   The basic thing that goes on in a zoo is what is referred to politely as "removing the fecal." During a week at the zoo I heard it referred to politely only once. There is a lot of the fecal around. Its raw materials are hay, fruit, vegetables, various sizes of dog biscuits, white mice, hard-boiled eggs, Zu-Preem protein compound, insects, and—for the vampire bats—blood from local slaughterhouses.

23   A young woman named Carmen Beard, a big-cat keeper, was kneeling beside a small clump of grass in the tiger pit. It was evident that one of the tigers had taken his ease at this spot a few days back. Beard picked through the grass with a look of professional distaste and then, seeing that it was beyond salvation, simply uprooted it, and tossed it into her garbage bag.

24   The tiger habitat consists of an island surrounded by a deep dry moat, the whole thing made out of some sort of spray-on concrete that is meant to suggest solid rock but feels brittle and hollow beneath the feet. While I glanced back across the moat to be sure the tigers were still locked up in their holding pens, Beard traipsed across the island and then down into the moat carrying her shovel and trash bag. She sang a John Denver song to herself as she shoveled the scat.

25   "What gets me," she said, interrupting her song, "is you'll be in this pit cleaning it out and the people will just stand up there and stare at you. I don't know why they're so fascinated. Do they think these animals clean up after themselves?

26   "I was talking to these people the other night. When I told them where I worked, the girl says, 'Can you believe that? She has to shovel lion shit and she *likes* it!' Well, I don't like that part of it, but it's not that big a deal. It's like having a child and having to change its diaper."

27   Down in the moat her voice bounced off the textured walls. "I'm not real wild about this moat at all," she said. "It's beautiful and everything but it only has this one tiny drain. Those cats they put in there have got really big feces that just won't go down the drain. Then there's this echo. When there are a lot of kids up there screaming it sounds like an insane asylum. It's really eerie. I can imagine how those poor cats must feel."

28   After she was through with the moat Beard walked back inside the building. The interior of the cat house consists of a wide corridor with cages on both sides, each one of which has an outside compartment that serves as the display area. I had been advised to walk in the center of the corridor, since the cats have been known to take swipes at passersby. At this time of the morning—eight o'clock, an hour before the zoo opens to the public—they were alert and curious. I was aware of their eyes, which were as hard and brilliant as minerals, and of their languid, soaring grace when they jumped up and down off their wooden platforms. The tigers and lions and leopards tracked me with their eyes as I walked down the hallway, and their keen scrutiny made me realize that I was no longer in the zoo; I was in their home.

29   "Albert!" Beard called to one of the Bengal tigers, who had laid his great head up against the bars and was staring off into space in a masterful feline way. "That's my boy! You're my favorite kitty, yes, you are!"

30   Beard is a slight woman in her early twenties, with a forthright mammalian love for the great cats and bears that are in her charge. The way she spoke to the tigers and scratched their big tabby ears made me think she saw herself as their defender; someone who, if the battle lines were ever drawn, would stand on the side of the animals.

31   She started out working in the children's zoo, but after her husband died a year ago she didn't feel like meeting and dealing with the public every day. She wanted quiet and privacy, the mute solace of pacing beasts. The management assigned her to the bears and cats. It's the most dangerous job in the zoo, since it is assumed that a Kodiak bear or a Bengal tiger would not think twice about eating its beloved keeper if it should find itself suddenly in the same pit with her.

32   While I stood in the center of the corridor and stared at the cats, Beard and another woman keeper named Pat O'Connor hosed out the interior cages, every once in a while giving the occupants a friendly squirt.

33   "Are zoos good or are zoos bad?" O'Connor mused as she yanked a kink out of her hose. "I don't know. You can weigh the pros and cons forever; it's like a balance scale. All of us sit around and talk about zoos all the time, trying to decide."

34   As the cats slunk and leaped all about them and growled for their Zu-Preem, the two women showed me snapshots of a snow leopard cub that had been born in the zoo in the spring and had died at the age of ten weeks from causes that were still undetermined. They commented on the photographs in a wistful, detached manner. Since the snow leopard is an endangered species, the cub's body had been donated to the Houston Museum of Natural Science instead of being hauled to the dump, which is where most of the animals that die at the zoo go.

35   "They're going to mount him," Beard said. "I'm going to go over there when they're through, I guess. I know it's going to upset me, but I just want to know if they did a good job."

36   I spent some time in the bird area, admiring the zoo's collection of Central and South American guans and curassows, which are varieties of wild ornamental fowl, wattled and tufted, with radiant plumage. Certain species of guans, I had read in my animal encyclopedia, are "irresistibly attracted to fire" and are lured to their capture by small fires set in the branches of trees.

37   The guans and curassows were all housed in a string of outdoor cages known as the pheasant run. This was a specialized collection with only one anomaly, an apparition called the great hornbill. The hornbill's beak, like the toucan's, looks like an oversized wax banana, but the beak has an extra component above it, a kind of air scoop that makes the entire bird look—as we used to say of eccentric, otherworldly automobiles—"customized."

38   The bird house itself was closed to the public because of an outbreak of Newcastle disease in the city. The curator, Robert Berry, took me through anyway. It's an intriguing building, with large exhibit windows and an open "rain forest" where the birds fly about more or less freely.

39   Berry is a dry, unsentimental man who put himself through college working as a professional dancer. Before he came to work at the zoo he was a private aviculturist. "I don't have any emotional attachment to birds at all,"

he said as we stood in the rain forest. "I respect them as living creatures, but I don't like to scratch them on the head and all that. I appreciate the beauty and the behavior of them."

40   Berry recently earned international attention for the Houston Zoo when he bred, for the first time in captivity, a scarlet cock-of-the-rock chick. Cocks-of-the-rock come from the Amazon valley and have huge puffball crests on their heads that make the males, with their bright orange plumage, look like pieces of fruit.

41   After the first chick was born Berry and his associates fretted about its diet until they discovered that the benign-looking cock-of-the-rock was in fact a latent bird of prey. The mother passed up the fruit she was offered in favor of a mouse that she caught herself. The keepers, who had been setting out rodent poison, took the mouse away from her, but then Berry brought a lizard from the reptile house and held it up in the air. The female immediately swooped down from her perch, plucked the lizard out of Berry's fingers, crushed it in her beak, and poked it down the chick's throat.

42   Although the chick died soon after this breakthrough, two more were born the next year. Berry took them home with him, nursing them 24 hours a day for six weeks, peeling their grapes for them, feeding them chopped newborn mice and blueberries, and monitoring—as Berry wrote in an article for a zoo magazine—"the character of the bowels." One of the birds died; the other, named Geronimo, survived, although Berry had a few tense moments in transporting him to the zoo. "The bird became carsick and regurgitated all of its food," he wrote. "Not only did I go into shock, I also became suicidal."

43   On my way out of the building I stopped for a while at the exhibit featuring a male cock-of-the-rock. The bird sat on a limb, placid and undemanding. It and the rest of the birds elicited curiosity and occasional amazement, but one could view them without that emotional disturbance that the more sentient and slovenly creatures of the zoo provoke.

44   The birds are living ornaments, elements in a design, but there are some animals that no human design can truly accommodate. I went into the primate house, pausing to dip the soles of my shoes into a chemical bath so that I would not track in the diseases of the outside world. Inside, the primate house had the red brick construction and wide corridors of an elementary school. One of the keepers was eating a piece of lemon pie for breakfast, and another was heating a frozen sweet roll on a pice of aluminum foil that was placed on the burner of a stove.

45   The siamang gibbons had started their morning hooting, and it was difficult to hear anyone speak. The gibbons had a big cage at one end of the house, and as they yelled they swung about on their grapevines, moving through the air with an astonishing, fluid velocity. In the wild they are capable of grabbing birds in flight.

46   I strolled down the corridor with an old-time keeper named Oscar Mendieta. He was rubbing with a rag at a dark spot on his shirt where a chimpanzee named Kamaka had just scored a hit with his own by-products. "In the morning he'll throw carrots or biscuits at me," Mendieta said, sounding hurt, "but shit he seldom throws anymore."

47   When we passed Kamaka's cage he beat furiously against the walls and bared his fangs but threw nothing. An agile gibbon across the hall casually

shoved her posterior up against the bars. "She's in estrus right now," Mendieta said, "She's presenting to me. She always does that."

47a   Mendieta has been at the zoo since 1957. Today the Houston Zoo requires of its employees some kind of formal animal care experience, which can be acquired by a kind of apprenticeship set up through the children's zoo. But in 1957 there were no particular qualifications. Mendieta had been working for an oil drum company, washing out barrels. One day he and his wife visited the zoo. "You know what, honey?" he said, "I think I'd like to work here." He took the city civil service test and found there were openings in water, sewer, and zoo.

48   "When I retire I plan to raise chickens or something," he told me. "I don't think I can ever get way from working with animals."

49   For most of the morning the staff cleaned out the cages and washed the floors with a chemical solution. I watched as a woman named Beryl Fisher, a former circus elephant trainer, entered the orangutan cage carrying two grocery bags filled with Purina Monkey Chow and fruit. The orangs liked to open the bags themselves and compare the contents.

50   While Fisher sat in the center of the cage they soared overhead on the grapevines and dropped, unannounced, into her lap. Then they stalked about on the sides of their feet with their arms wrapped about their torsos, staring at me through the bars. I could not help reading the gazes of the other primates as sober and accusing, but the orangutans emanated an unsettling mildness. These two had been born and bred in zoos, but in the forests of Borneo and Sumatra, where their species is being harassed into extinction, the word "orangutan" suggests a shadowy human nature—it means "man of the woods."

51   The Houston Zoo has one gorilla. It used to have two, but now a sign at the entrance of the habitat informs visitors: "Due to the untimely death of 'Je-Je,' our male gorilla, from colitis with secondary kidney failure, only the female is on display."

52   The female's name is Vanilla. She lives by herself in a large circular building that looks from the outside like the stump of a giant tree. The exhibit area is contained indoors, a great swath of stage scenery with sculptured terraces and dead trees and a tiny waterfall that cascades through a series of pools. Off the exhibit area are small cages where Vanilla prefers to spend her time. When the keeper leaves in the afternoon he turns on a television and Vanilla takes her food into one of these cages and watches cartoons.

53   When I dropped by one morning Bill Grissom, Vanilla's keeper, had locked her out in the exhibit area and was waiting for her to urinate so he could get a sample of her urine and run it through the contents of a box labeled "Subhuman Primate Pregnancy Test." In great apes, the test works not only for discovering pregnancy but for determining ovulation. Once they have Vanilla's ovulation pattern figured out, they'll try to inseminate her.

54   "The problem is the males," Grissom told me. "A guy at Baylor has electroejaculated five different gorillas and they've all been infertile."

55   Grissom let Vanilla in and gave her a cup of an orange juice, milk, and wheat-germ oil mixture, along with a raw egg. She cracked the egg in one hand and sucked out the contents, then looked at me and stuck her tongue out.

56   "That's a greeting," Grissom said. "She expects you to return it."

57   I did, but it seemed to communicate nothing to her. She held out her hand, wanting me to touch it. I had been warned not to, since one or the other of us could transmit TB. I just looked at the hand, feeling uncertain and flustered. The nails were black and very thick, and the palm and fingers looked upholstered. She kept withdrawing her hand and offering it again distractedly, as if it was a matter of indifference to her whether I touched it or not.

58   "Sometimes she's just like us," Grissom said. "She gets off in her own little world. Since Je-Je died she's kind of a crybaby at times. When I leave her out in the morning to pee she'll scream at me, like she's saying, 'Come back! Don't leave me out here!'

59   "Je-Je was probably the biggest draw of the whole zoo. Sometimes you try to forget about him, but the public won't let you. They come in and say they remember how he used to do something or other and it'll bring it all back."

60   Grissom lives in fear that Vanilla will contract TB or some other disease from the visitors. He or another keeper usually sits on a folding chair out in front of the habitat, to make sure no one throws anything inside it. Vanilla can see him out there while she is on display; in that constant stream of twittering, gaping, guffawing creatures about whom she knows nothing, there is at least one steady, familiar face.

61   During most of my time at the zoo I was part of that crowd, drifting along with them from cage to habitat in an aimless fashion, roving past a whole section of animals and barely seeing them at all. I kept making the same circuit of the zoo over and over, pacing, wanting to cover ground. Eventually certain animals began to stand out. In the children's zoo I watched a group of alligator snapping turtles through a window in the side of their pool. They lay on the bottom, and every now and then a single perfect bubble would emerge from one of their bony nostrils. They had pale, parchment-colored eyes overlaid with a design that reminded me of an old-fashioned television test pattern. When it was time for them to come up for air they had to fight their way off the bottom, clawing for the surface in a heavy, ungainly manner.

62   In that same part of the zoo there were two Galapagos tortoises mating, the male propped up against the female's back as if some fortuitous natural event like an earthquake had placed him there. He made a deep lowing noise with each thrust and moved against her back like a jeep stuck in high gear at the bottom of a hill.

63   Early in the morning, before the Houston miasma had had a chance to assert itself and cause the animals to wheeze and pant and lollygag around, before the smell of stale popcorn began to infest the air, it was possible to believe that the zoo was an innocent pleasure. That was when you would see Kodiak bears, as large as bison, perform backward somersaults, when the keepers led skittish camels around the grounds for their morning walk. At that hour the most mysterious, compelling animals in the zoo turned out to be the antelope and deer I routinely passed by, giving them hardly a look as I trailed my fingers along their chain-link corrals. Every movement of the small fallow deer seemed involuntary, hinged on some ancient evolutionary

lesson. But the great horse-headed antelopes, the nylghais, the nyalas, were more aware of themselves. Their bodies were disjointed and misproportioned; they seemed to have turned out that way not in fulfillment of the genetic code but by an act of will on the part of the animal.

64   In the reptile house every creature had that air of deliberate presence, of having been created for a reason that human beings were somehow specifically proscribed from understanding.

65   In the hallways and warrens behind the exhibit cages, the reptile keepers, who as a rule were bearded and cerebral, spent a good deal of time cleaning the glass in terrariums, transferring torpid snakes from one to the other as if they were coils of stout wire.

66   "Most of the animals back here," a keeper named John McLain told me, "are juveniles being raised to maturity or separated for breeding purposes. This one, for instance, is a male, and this one over here is a female. When they finally meet each other we hope there'll be more than a handshake going on."

67   The snakes he was referring to were Bismarck ringed pythons. There were other pythons around: Angolans, reticulateds (which the staff called retics), and a baby green tree python, which was brilliant yellow in its immaturity and which, coiled upon a twig, managed to suggest a sea horse.

68   Placed at intervals throughout the reptile house were wall units labeled "Snakebite Alarm Box." If a keeper should get bitten by a venomous snake—an event that has not happened here for years—the alarm is sounded in the reptile house. The zoo keeps antivenin on hand—"If we can't get the antivenin," McLain said, "we won't stock the snake"—and has frequent snakebite drills to keep reaction time to a minimum.

69   While McLain cleaned the terrariums I wandered about a little, inspecting various exotic tree frogs, a washtub full of three-week-old Chinese alligators, a pair of deadly gaboon vipers as thick as my arm that made a loud snoring sound I could hear twenty yards away. There was another noise, an incessant squeaking that I realized I had been hearing all along. It came from a small cage full of newborn mice, pink and hairless, crowded together like packing material. There was another cage next to it, equally crowded with baby mice in the next stage of development, with new pelts of white fur.

70   I could not take my eyes off them. All those mewling infant mice, as insignificant as the sawdust that covered the bottoms of the cages in which they would be ingested by a finicky snake. They reminded me of the term used by fishermen to describe the unwelcome, inedible species that occasionally take the hook: "trash fish."

71   From the reptile house it was perhaps fifty yards and several rungs up the evolutionary ladder to the elephant compound. The keeper there is a woman named Lucille Sweeney, and when I walked up she was putting her two Indian elephants through a low-key circus routine that involved having them stand up on a stool and raise their forelimbs. Sweeney works the elephants this way not to please the visitors but to keep the elephants in control and used to her presence. That way she can groom them with no trouble, scraping off dead skin with a stiff wire brush and maintaining their feet, which are subject to a variety of diseases.

72   When the male elephant—Thai—reared up on the stool, he used the

opportunity to unload a prodigious amount of the fecal. There was a first-grade class there watching him, and they were properly grossed out and agog at the evidence of his subsequent sexual arousal. The teachers tried to divert the kids' attention to Indu, the female who was considerably more discreet.

73   "Get that trunk up, Indu!" Sweeney was calling. "Get it up. Oh, look at that girl stand."

74   Lucille Sweeney first came to work at the zoo more than ten years ago after she had finished her honors thesis on William Faulkner. She thought she would give herself a year to "get animals out of my system," but it became her life's work.

75   "The first elephant I ever saw was at the circus. They let us little ones come up close and sit on the floor. So there I was, watching these huge animals go by. I was awestruck. That these creatures would actually work for a human being when they had so much power to hurt was beautiful to me."

76   She used to visit the Houston Zoo a lot when she was a little girl. Her favorite animal was the bull elephant, Hans, who was already getting along in years and who died in 1979 at the age of 62. It was Sweeney who was with him when they put him to sleep by injecting a combination of barbiturates through a vein in his ear. She had grown up to be his keeper.

77   "I had three years with Hans," she said. "That's all I had. I would have loved to have been with him for his last twenty or thirty years."

78   Before Sweeney took over as his keeper Hans had been in chains day and night throughout the first half of his long life at the zoo. He was skittish about people, but she got him gentled down enough to trust her. By that time he had severe arthritis from the chains, and the pad of one of his feet was beginning to rot. Finally there was just nothing left to support him, and he collapsed. They hauled his body out of the elephant enclosure with a low truck, and buried it on the grounds.

79   Sweeney related all this soberly. Her attention was focused on Thai and Indu now, who were eating a load of roughage, sweeping it up dexterously in their trunks. Thai came over and flopped his trunk over the rail that separated us. I touched it, as he seemed to want, and he coiled it around my arm and nearly yanked me into the pen with him. His bulk, his power, his knowledge were inexpressible. I had that old sentimental boyhood dream: that we understood each other, that my mind converged with his in all the crucial particulars. But I am an adult, and I realized if that fantasy were true I would not have been at the zoo in the first place, staring dumbly at those eyes and at the wide trackless brow between them.

80   That is perhaps one of the things a human being can finally learn at the zoo. We dominate the animals there, we have their attention, we are in fact their salvation. But we should not expect this to matter to them. On those nights that Dick Bonko talks about, when the monkeys settle down and begin to babble in their wordless speech, they are talking to each other and not to us.

The second sample is also a professional piece, a routine entry on spot removers from *Consumer Reports 1979 Buying Guide Issue*. Unlike the first piece, which is an interesting overlap of informative, persuasive, and literary aims, this piece is almost a pure example of informative discourse as to aim and of evaluation as to mode (although classification and description are used to achieve the evaluation).

You should have no vocabulary problems with this piece at all, since the authors knew they were writing for a popular audience and chose their words with this in mind. But the following guiding questions may help you read the selection. (1) What criteria are used to evaluate the spot removers? (2) Does there seem to be a hierarchy in the importance of the criteria? (3) What characteristics differentiate the three levels in the ranking? (4) Is there any noticeable organizing principle in the presentation of the information in this brief selection?

SPOT REMOVERS

Try to remove a spot right after you get it. Often, a quick application of cold water will do the job. If it takes more than that, or if water will damage the fabric, you may want to use a spot remover. Before you try anything, make sure that removing the spot won't leave the fabric permanently marked. If a garment's care label states "professionally dry-clean only," don't try to remove a stain yourself. Take the garment to the cleaners and tell them what caused the stain. If the label indicates the garment should *not* be dry-cleaned, don't use spot removers; their solvents may damage the fibers. Before using a spot remover, test it on an inconspicuous part of the garment. Manipulate the fabric as you would in cleaning a real spot. Even though the fibers may be undamaged, the appearance of a fabric can be spoiled by rings, running dyes, or a marred fabric finish. TEST SPOT MIXTURES, developed to simulate the sort of spots that might be caused by food, were: a coffee-cream-and-sugar mix, a mustard-mayonnaise-catsup-and-gravy mix, and a mix of several red wines. We also prepared a mix of grease, soot, and road dust—the kind of stain you might get when working around a car. We applied those mixtures uniformly to fabric squares of cotton, polyester, and nylon. We applied each spot remover as its label directs and compared results with those we got from a five-minute soak and rinse in plain water, and from spotting with heavy-duty liquid detergent followed by machine-washing in warm water with the detergent. Only *Whoosh!* consistently outdid the washing regimen, but note that it requires the use of water.

Hazards.

Many spot removers are flammable and all those in common use are poisonous. The Federal Hazardous Substances Act has set down regulations for fire hazards. Under those regulations three of the products we bought should have bee labeled "Flammable," and all of them were. We rated all three Not Acceptable because much safer products are available to do the same job. All the Acceptable liquid products contain chlorinated hydrocarbons, petroleum distillates, or both. Such chemicals, or their vapors, may irritate skin, eyes, and lungs and may be harmful or fatal if swallowed.

Packaging and Application.

The removers come in a variety of cans, glass bottles, and other containers (see Ratings). The container is usually tall and narrow-based—be careful not to knock over and splash the dangerous contents on a table, floor, or yourself. Dropping and breaking a glass container presents the same kind of hazard. With some samples of *Whoosh!*, the paste dried in the tube and was hard to squeeze out. The *Brush Top* bottle has a useful, built-in applicator; it would hold spills to a trickle if you accidently overturned the bottle. But removing a cap liner before we used the applicator, and replacing the liner afterwards, was a nuisance.

Ratings.

Consumer Reports, June 1977. Listed by groups in order of estimated overall quality; within groups, listed alphabetically. All were judged reasonably effective in removing simple clear-grease stains, but not *CU*'s test stains except as noted. All have a container closure judged insufficiently child-resistant. Except as noted, each is packaged in a screw-cap container and lacks an applicator.

The following was judged effective on CU's *test spots. Because it requires the use of water, the product was judged suitable for use only on fabrics that water will not harm.*

WHOOSH! SPOT REMOVER. Paste in tube. Labeled as eye irritant and combustible.

The following were judged much less effective on CU's *test spots than the preceding. Because they contain solvents, the products were judged suitable for use only on fabrics that solvents will not harm.*

BRUSH TOP HANDY APPLICATOR SUPER SPOT REMOVER. Liquid in applicator bottle. Labeled as combustible, harmful or fatal if swallowed, and having a harmful vapor.
CARBONA CLEANING FLUID. Liquid in bottle. Labeled as combustible, harmful or fatal if swallowed, and having a harmful vapor.
ENERGINE CLEANING FLUID FIREPROOF. Liquid in can. Label fails to warn contents may be harmful if inhaled or swallowed and that careful use requires adequate ventilation.
SUNNYSIDE CARBO-CHLOR NON-FLAMMABLE CLEANING SOLVENT AND SPOT REMOVER. Liquid in can. Labeled as having potentially harmful vapor.
WALGREEN'S FIREPROOF SPOT & FABRIC CLEANER. Liquid in can. Labeled as potentially harmful if inhaled or swallowed.

Not Acceptable

The following were judged Not Acceptable for home use because they are labeled to contain trichloroethylene, which the National Cancer Institute

*judged potentially hazardous to human health on the basis of its tests that
indicated cancer-causing activity by the chemical in laboratory mice.*

AERO NON-COMBUSTIBLE SPOT REMOVER. Liquid in applicator bottle.
AFTA CLEANING FLUID. Liquid in can.

*The following were judged Not Acceptable for home use because they
posed excessive fire hazards. All were appropriately labeled "Flammable."*

GODDARD'S DRY CLEAN SPOT REMOVER. Aerosol spray.
TEXIZE K2r SPOT LIFTER. Paste in tube.
WALGREEN'S FLAMMABLE SPOT & FABRIC CLEANER. Liquid in can.

The third example of evaluating is a speech written by a high school
student at the end of his senior year. Danny Orange had spent his first
three years in high school at Anderson High School in affluent northwest
Austin, Texas. Anderson High School was a modern plant, recently
constructed, and equipped with the best resources and teachers that money
could buy. It was attended by white students from professional, upper-
and middle-class families. Then, because of a court decision, which had
been contested for years at every level of appeal, massive busing was
ordered for all years of the junior and senior high school systems in the
Austin Independent School District. White students from northwest and
southwest Austin were bused to Johnston High School in the eastern part
of the city, an area largely populated by blacks and Chicanos. Some of the
blacks and Chicanos were bused to high schools in other parts of the city.
As a result of the court decision, Danny Orange found himself finishing his
high school career in a totally different situation from that of his first three
years.

This speech was his evaluation of the decision of the court. He
delivered it at the commencement exercises in May, 1981. There has been
no attempt to edit out the oral flavor of the speech.

SALUTATORIAN SPEECH

Johnston High School, 26 May 1981

Danny Orange

1   At the outset, let me say that as salutatorian of Johnston High School, I
    represent many people, not just myself. This class of 1981 is a unique one.
    We're unique in that we are the first bused class of Johnston. This group of
    people consists of a diversified selection of Austinites:

        some are from South Austin
        some are from East Austin
        some are from North Austin

How the class got this way and what busing's done to us are the themes of my remarks today.

2   Before I get into that, there is credit due to many people whom I would like to recognize. First, I'd like to congratulate the members of the class of '81 for making this year a great year and a helluva lot of fun. Secondly, I feel that the parents of these kids deserve to be mentioned, for, if anything, the mere fact that they've survived eighteen years. And last, thanks ought to be given to the faculty and administration for giving seniors special treatment and striving to make us happy.

3   But first let me say that this speech is not designed to convince you of the merits or drawbacks of busing and desegregation. More than likely, all of you have formed a definite opinion on busing. Until now, virtually all opinions and viewpoints on the subject have been presented by people who will never know what it's like to be bused. This speech will present the opinion of one who has been bused—my opinion—and I'm sure this view is not held by everybody.

4   Before we concern ourselves with details, let's ask ourselves: What is an education? An education is not merely books, classrooms, and memorizations. You probably learn more from people than you do from books. High school is not just a preparation for college, it's a preparation for life, and in life you have to deal with people. We learned how to in school, our school, Johnston.

5   And now that the year is over, we can look back and see that desegregation went very smoothly, but the question is, *did we accomplish anything*?

6   Before we can determine this we have to investigate the history of desegregation in Austin. In the beginning, busing in Austin was limited for a long time to just minority students. Nobody ever dreamed that large scale desegregation was ever going to come about.

7   But when it did happen, it took us all by surprise. All I remember is that suddenly there was a public uproar about busing. There was even the possibility mentioned that we would be switching schools on January 23, in the middle of the year. We went to rallies, made bumper stickers, and chanted, "Hell no, we won't go!"

8   And through it all I wondered why people didn't want their kids to go to Johnston.

Was it the expense?
The Blacks and the Chicanos?
Was it the losing football team?
Was it the fact that the kids had already established a loyalty to a school?
Was it the lack of academic quality or the long bus ride?

9   If you look at these closely, only one of them is really a valid argument against busing; and that is the long bus ride. Many new Johnstonites say they like Johnston better than their old school, but they despise the long bus ride. [Authors' note: Some of the students were bused 44 miles a day, 22 miles each way.]

10   But there is one other point I mentioned that could be used to justify integration—and that is the supposed lack of academic quality. The fact that Johnston long held the reputation of being a vocational school vividly points out why we need desegregation. For example, Johnston has never had a real

calculus class before this year. During first semester we had *one* original Johnston student in our calculus class. It's true that all of the others were from Anderson or Crockett, but the fact that a Johnston student had the *opportunity* to take calculus means something. It means that from now on, kids will be able to take classes that didn't even exist here before.

11   The examples go on and on, but what this comes down to is an opinion, whether these examples justify integration. I happen to feel that they do. And the courts have ruled that, in order to implement integration, students will be bused.

My scholastic education hasn't really been hurt by the move to Johnston. But it may not have been helped either. The courses I would've taken at Anderson I took at Johnston. But what counts is the teacher. I believe that the quality of the class depends on the quality of the teacher, and the teachers at Johnston are generally pretty good. The shortcoming that they do have is that they haven't had many opportunities to teach advanced classes—and this will change with time.

12   On the other hand, my *real* education has been vastly improved by my move to Johnston. I learned a lot about different lifestyles and different parts of town, and I learned how to get along with people who were from an entirely different slice of life than I was. But, most importantly, I had a great time doing it.

13   So what have we accomplished?

We have succeeded in what some people thought was impossible.
We brought three very different groups together, and they now function as one community.
We have created a powerful campus that derives its strength from diversity. And
We have survived as friends.

14   There's another point I feel I need to bring up, and that concerns the people who avoided busing. I don't know how prevalent this was in South Austin, but I know of several people who did it in North Austin. They did this by any of a number of methods, both legal and illegal:

they moved
they changed their addresses
they went to private schools
they bought apartments

The list goes on.

15   What they did is place themselves *above* the law and consider themselves immune to a federal court order. I would have to say to these people that they've made a mistake, for in missing out on Johnston High School, they've missed a very valuable learning experience, as well as one of the best times of their lives.

16   So, in conclusion, I would have to say that this year at Johnston has been a valuable experience for me, as well as one of the best years of my life.

17   In my somewhat more deranged moments I thank God that I was bused, for if I wasn't, I would not have met all you wonderful people. Thank you. Good night. And good luck to the Johnston High School Class of 81.

PREWRITING: PROCESSES INVOLVED IN PREPARING AN EVALUATION

The Dimensions of a Value System: The Communication Triangle Again

These three examples can serve us in sorting out some of the sometimes complex issues of evaluation. Writers on evaluation often call these various issues the different dimensions of a value system. For our purposes it may be convenient to organize them around a model that we have used at several stages in this text, the communication triangle. As we saw in Chapter 1, the communication triangle involves a writer, a reader, a subject matter, and the language used to unite these three into a process of communication. In the case of evaluation, the subject matter involves the object that is being evaluated and the language constitutes the essay or theme.

Issues relating to the object concern the types of objects that can be evaluated and where exactly the *value* of an object is located (the *locus* of the value). Issues relating to the writer have to do with the particular faculty or faculties of the writer involved in making the evaluation, the method by which the evaluation is carried out, and the writer's hierarchy of values. Issues relating to the reader have to do with the reader's hierarchy of values, especially if it differs from that of the writer and with the acceptance of the norm of evaluation posed by the writer. Issues having to do with the theme itself have to do with organization and style.

Thus the dimensions of the value system can be represented graphically, as in Figure 12.1, by clustering them around the components of the communication triangle. Such a diagram does not at all attempt to present all of the dimensions of a value system but it does attempt to isolate some of the important issues that the writer must consider in evaluating. And, although the diagram has a reasonable reliability, it also simplifies some of the issues for graphic purposes. Indeed, as has been the case with the communication triangle throughout the textbook, we must look upon it here as a teaching tool of some usefulness but not as a dogma that must be totally adhered to. All of the triangle parts interact with all the other parts.

Object Issues

The three evaluation samples assess very different types of objects: zoos, spot removers, and a Supreme Court decision. As we saw, anything can be evaluated and from many points of view. Further, evaluating is as extensive a mental operation as describing, classifying, or narrating, and

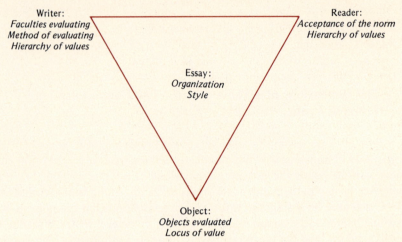

FIGURE 12.1.   The dimensions of a value system.

the process of evaluation is often more complex than that of the other modes. Let us look at some of these complexities.

LOCUS OF VALUE.   Whenever we make a value judgment about some object, we are saying that the object has value or that it lacks value. But we might ask the obvious question: Do objects really have value or do we just impute or assign values to them? Are values in the object or only in the subject who evaluates?

Some values seem to be only subjective. My taste in music may not at all be your taste. In what sense are any values objective or are they all like musical taste? There is no doubt that the editors of *Consumer Reports* believe that Texize K2r Spot-Lifter is not an acceptable spot remover because it poses "excessive fire hazards," and they further believe that this judgment is not simply a whimsical or subjective feeling that they, the editors, have about this product. They believe that research has furnished objective evidence that such a fire hazard exists with this spot remover and that other researchers and users would confirm such a danger if they tested the product in question.

In the same fashion, Stephen Harrigan believes that he is not the only individual who will find the deficiencies that he finds in the San Antonio Zoo. Now, it might be objected that some of the observers of this zoo might not consider the adolescents "raucous," or might not think the drinks were watered-down "at every turn of the trail," and some will not object to putting the elephants to work—these seem to be personal and subjective values.

Harrigan is aware of this. In fact, the subhead under the inset "Zoos Who" reads "An absolutely arbitrary, subjective, and unscientific rating of

Texas zoos." But Harrigan is being ironic here; he really feels that *the audience to whom he is writing* will object to the same aspects of the zoo he objects to. He also believes that they can also detect the level of noise, the ubiquitous sale of drinks, and the fact that animals are put to work. These characteristics are observable; some find them objectionable and others don't. For those who agree with Harrigan that such characteristics are undesirable in a zoo, the zoo will be viewed as a poor one. Since these characteristics can be observed, they can be called objective.

The article on zoos, however, raises a quite different issue of objectivity if we focus, not on the inset that ranks the five main Texas zoos, but on the major portion of the article in which Harrigan takes the reader through the Houston zoo, talks about the different sections, and introduces the reader to the caretakers and the favorite animals. This part of the essay is undoubtedly more *subjective*, personal, and emotional than is the evaluative inset.

And yet a curious inversion takes place in this segment of the article. The inversion is signaled by the first subheading of the article, "What are nice animals like you doing in a zoo like this?" Normally, in a piece about animals and people, the animals would be the *objects* and the people would be the *subjects*. But this subheading hints at a reversal of the roles. And the first paragraph makes clear that the subheading is to be taken seriously. At night the animals make a "low-pitched, mumbling sound, *like human beings* muttering nonsense syllables in their sleep. Long after dark . . . *the monkeys speak in tongues.*" The suggestion continues in the second paragraph; the animals know something and they are contrasted to "the constant human swarm that passed by their cages every day."

This contrast is sustained throughout the essay. The villains of the story are the visitors to the zoo, the "constant human swarm," "the drunk medical students," the "raucous adolescents" and "overheated babies," the kids who "can drop cotton candy into the open mouth of a pygmy hippopotamus and no one seems to mind," and others. The heroes and heroines of the piece are the caretakers and the animals. Both are portrayed as beings with feelings and sensitivities and often they resent and isolate themselves from the visitors. Frequently the caretaker and the pet animal are paired in intimate twosomes: Beryl and Je-Je, Grissom and Vanilla, Sweeney and Hans the elephant, Beard and Albert the tiger, Mendieta and Kamaka the chimpanzee.

There is a message about objectivity in this inverted world. Harrigan is making the point that we humans have dehumanized ourselves by our total lack of feeling and sensitivity for the animals in most of our zoos. We end up putting innocent animals in prisons, hence the title "Life Behind Bars." Our own notions of subjectivity and objectivity about animals ought to be reexamined. The main theme of this section of the essay throws further light on the subheading of the "Zoos Who" inset, to which we referred earlier, "An absolutely arbitrary, subjective, and unscientific rating of Texas zoos.'' By the end of the article, it is distressingly clear that Harrigan's attitude is not absolutely arbitrary, nor subjective, nor unscientific.

Many evaluations end up doing something like this to our values and hierarchies of values; our values will be upside down and we will be forced to reassess our unexamined assumptions.

CHOOSING A TOPIC.   Nearly everything we have said about the object of value can be of some assistance in helping to find a topic for an evaluation theme.

In one sense, it is easier to find a topic for evaluation than for any of the other modes. Although evaluating has been placed last in our study of modes of discourse, evaluation is not a late arrival on the scene of human thought. We only pay attention to something because it interests us, because it has value. We may have had to search for events to narrate, objects to describe, or concepts to define; but we shouldn't have to look very hard to find something we value. It may be that the values we have are so ingrained in us that they are not usually subjected to reflective analysis on our part, but they are there dictating the whole rhythm of our lives.

One of the easiest set of values to write about, at least in the sense of being conscious, is the set that is undergoing change at a given time. If you are departing from a set of values you acquired at home in the direction of another set that seems to be undermining the first, you might consider such a topic for an evaluation theme. The values could be academic, career oriented, political, or religious. They need not be so fundamental; you may simply be changing allegiances to sports idols or teams, movie actors or actresses, or clothes fashions. Or the pattern of your friends, your music, or your reading may be changing. Any of these changes is symptomatic of a change of values. And because you are moving from one value to another, you can involve both in a comparison or contrast of values.

The locus of value should be taken into account in view of the aim of discourse you are writing. If your paper is to be an expository piece that will explain or prove something with solid evidence, or explore a subject seriously, or pass on verifiable and factual information, you will stress the objective loci of value—the type that can be validated by the reader, should he or she choose to do so. But if your piece is personally expressive, literary, or even persuasive, then you can draw more on subjective loci of value.

It is not enough that the writer be convinced of the importance of the issue; the reader is the one who must be sold on the evaluation you are presenting. Consequently, you must choose a topic that interests you and that has the potential of interesting your reader. Even the norms of evaluation that you will use must be agreed upon by your reader. Let us look at some questions and exercises that can help you select a topic in light of these considerations.

Exercises on Selecting a Topic

1. If no immediate topic jumps to your mind when you are told to write an evaluation theme, then make a rapid inventory of your own value system by asking yourself some searching questions.
   a. What do I spend most of my free time doing?
   b. What have I spent most of my own money on, after necessities have been taken care of?
   c. If I weren't constrained by schedules and obligations dictated by others, what would I be doing? If my formal education were finished, what would I be doing?
2. Given a topic, the next major concern should be establishing the purpose of the paper that you are going to write. Is it going to be expository (explaining, proving, informing, exploring), persuasive, literary, or expressive?
3. Who is the audience for the paper? Can you visualize a typical reader, or better still, can you find a typical reader who would be willing to read and react to your earlier drafts?
4. What point do you intend to make with the paper? This is a narrower question than the aim of the discourse, which was discussed in question 2. You could prove many things in an evaluation paper; this question asks you to specify.
5. What particular object are you going to evaluate? What particular aspect?

Writer Issues

Nearly all of the preceding questions focused on the topic itself, but they could not help also focusing on the writer since the writer was choosing the topic. Let us look at some of these writer issues a bit more closely.

As we noted, there are three issues having to do with the writer that are important here: the method of evaluating, the faculties of evaluation, and the hierarchy of the writer's values.

METHOD OF EVALUATING. All three readings display the typical method of evaluating, which many writers use in arriving at their final assessments. Let us examine this technique.

The evaluation of spot removers is given in the rankings at the end of the article. But the section that precedes it makes very clear to the reader the norms to be used in the rankings. The four paragraphs preceding the rankings explain the criteria quite specifically. A good spot remover must not spoil the fabric of the garment, must not cause the dye to run, must not leave water rings, and must not mar the finish; all of these are spelled out in the first paragraph. In the next paragraph the reader is acquainted with the more obstinate type of spots used for the tests of the removers. In the third paragraph the health and fire hazards of some removers are outlined. Finally the packaging assets and liabilities of the various removers are given. By the end of the brief introduction, the reader has a clear conception of the norms that the authors are using in the evaluations of the products under consideration. The application of these norms to the products is almost a formula. If a product meets the norms, the product is acceptable; if it doesn't the product is not acceptable.

The same technique is used in both of the other two pieces. At the beginning of the inset (p. 354), Harrigan sets up the criteria he will use to evaluate the five zoos:

> What we must assume an animal needs from a zoo environment are the same things we would need if we were held captive there: room to move, shelter, cleanliness, an appropriate diet, company, and privacy. Few zoos provide all of these things for all of their animals, and so one's reaction toward a particular zoo may vary from exhibit to exhibit.

Harrigan applies these criteria consistently throughout the inset and indeed throughout the entire article. If we agree with his criteria, we should agree with his conclusions, assuming his factual findings are accurate.

Danny Orange, the salutatorian, also sets up his criteria when he asks about the nature of education, its academic goals, and its life goals. Since Johnston met both of these goals, he pronounces favorably upon his senior year there and upon the court decision that decreed it.

In each of these three cases, the method of evaluation can be reduced to a principle similar to the following: *If the object achieves a desired end, then it is valuable; it can be demonstrated that the object does achieve this end; therefore it is valuable.* And, of course, if it does not achieve the desired end or, in so doing, achieves other undesirable ends, then the object is not valuable or is harmful.

The first part of the italicized principle is the *conditional norm*—if the object meets this norm, it will be judged valuable. The second part *applies* the norm to the object to be evaluated—usually there is an empirical testing or tryout of the object. The third part of the principle draws the inference that is implicit in the other two parts: the object is either valuable or not depending on whether it meets or does not meet the norm. In summary, we might say that the method of evaluation consists of three steps: stating the *norm*, *applying* the norm to the object, and *evaluating*.

Each example makes an evaluation in terms of an end to be achieved. But there is another type of evaluation that judges value in terms of meeting the specifications of a rule or law, regardless of the end that is achieved—in a sense the end is to meet the rule. For example, many

Christians accept the Ten Commandments that were given to Moses and judge many moral situations in terms of compliance or noncompliance with one of these Commandments. Sometimes such decisions are made *regardless of the consequences*. In these cases we have simple *rule* evaluation, not *purpose* evaluation. Thus a person who applies the Fifth Commandment, "Thou shalt not kill," indiscriminately in all situations even to the forbidding of abortions necessary to save the life of the mother, is applying the rule strictly, regardless of the consequences.

Purpose evaluations and rule evaluations, however, make up nearly all evaluations, as far as methods of evaluating are concerned. In both cases, there is a norm (a purpose or a rule), an application of the norm to the object, and a consequent evaluation. These methods apply to all aims of discourse. Even literary evaluations in poetry or fiction or expressive evaluations of the most subjective and whimsical sort follow these methods.

HIERARCHY OF VALUES. In the case of even the same individual, two different norms, whether purposes or rules, may conflict with each other. A person may have to choose between lying or killing in the case where a lie could save a life. Which norm takes precedence? To solve such conflicts, most of us have arranged our norms in a certain scale of importance. Thus many people would choose to tell a lie if it could save a life, everything else being equal. Such a scale of values is usually called a *hierarchy of values*.

In the writing of evaluations, hierarchies of values become critical when the hierarchy of values of the writer comes into conflict with the hierarchy of values of the reader. We will return to this concern when we examine the reader issue. First, one other important issue concerned with the writer, and related closely to subjective evaluations, must be given brief consideration.

FACULTIES OF EVALUATION. In the report on spot removers, some of the removers were judged to be irritating to the eyes or to have a harmful vapor. Clearly, not only the reasoning ability of the evaluator, but also his or her senses must be a part of these evaluations. Similarly, in an evaluation of teas in the same issue, "Woody, musty, strawlike, or perfumy traces weren't acceptable," whereas moderate bitterness and moderate tartness were acceptable.* And in these cases, evaluators must be called in whose senses of taste and smell can be trusted. These reports from the senses are then incorporated into the final evaluation. In fact, they are a part of the second stage of the evaluation: applying the norm to the object.

---

*"Tea," *Consumer Reports Buying Guide Issue* (Mount Vernon, New York, 1978), p. 85.

Besides reason and sensations, other faculties are used in many evaluations. It is obvious to all of us that emotions play a substantial role in many of our evaluations in family life, in love, in national issues, in religion, and so on. This is so overwhelmingly true that some philosophers have maintained that all evaluations are, at bottom, emotive.

Again, particularly in the area of ethics, certain evaluations seem necessarily to incorporate aspects of the will. The law courts and some, if not all, moral theorists, insist that the element of *intent*, of wanting to do something, is an essential element in some types of actions. Plagiarism, for instance, in most states, is a crime that incorporates the element of intent; and in most schools and colleges, cheating, collusion, and plagiarism require the element of intent to be *evaluated* as breaking the rules of the institution. Similarly, courts distinguish between voluntary and involuntary manslaughter.

All of these various cases illustrate a further complexity involved in the process of evaluating. Many different human faculties are involved in value judgments of different types.

What all of this tells the writer is that evaluation is not a purely rational act. It often involves all the intensity of which some senses may be capable; it often involves emotions of quite different kinds and degrees; and it may involve an exercise of will power or the perception of such an exercise on the part of someone else. You can find these complexities in the evaluation of the zoos and in the student's evaluation of the experiment in desegregation. They are even evident in the expository piece from *Consumer Reports*.

Audience Issues

Let us now look at two of the major issues that the writer must consider, which relate directly to his audience. Although all three samples are instructive, the most fascinating of the three from this standpoint is Harrigan's study of the zoos. It is interesting for our purposes because Harrigan had to solve both of the two major issues evaluators face with audiences that are not immediately receptive to the evaluation they are asked to accept. The first issue, you will recall, had to do with acceptance of the norm that will be applied to the object to arrive at the ultimate evaluation (see pages 373–375). The second issue had to do with the conflict of the hierarchy of values of the writer with that of the reader.

Because Harrigan realizes that the norms of evaluation he will ask the reader to accept are based on a hierarchy of values that the reader may not initially accept, Harrigan first works on the hierarchy of values. Notice that the actual bald statement of norms is given at the beginning of "Zoos Who" (page 354). These norms are then applied, almost in formulaic fashion, to the five zoos in the rest of the inset. But "Zoos Who" is not encountered until after the reader has gone through a substantial part of the first section of the article. In fact, if a reader follows the narrative sequence, he or she will first read all of the section about the Houston zoo before returning to the inset.

The treatment of the reader in the inset differs from the treatment in the main body of the article. The main body of the article, the tour through the Houston zoo, does not directly address the reader until the final paragraph. The last paragraph, repeating a motif sounded in the first, says that the monkeys are not talking to us, but to each other. The isolation of the reader from the world of the zoo has been the careful work of the entire article. As we saw in discussing the *subjects* and *objects* in the article, there is an inversion of value systems: the animals and the caretakers become the humanlike creatures with feelings and sensitivities and a sense of each others' languages, whereas the visiting people are the real brutes who should be behind bars. But this glaring reversal of ordinary values has happened slowly and unobtrusively. The readers have not been called upon at all to change their values. They haven't even been addressed directly at all. In a sense they have been silent spectators to the travelogue. They witness the author and the caretakers address each other and occasionally address the animals. But they haven't been involved in any of the dialogue. This friendly, sensitive, and beautiful (in its own way) world of the zoo has been screened off. But it has been even more violently screened off from the visitors. The screaming kids, the raucous adolescents, the overheated babies—notice the emphasis on youth—are deliberately excluded from the world of the zoo. The readers obviously cannot side with them. Ultimately the readers must realize that such a crowd will never understand the zoo:

In the reptile house every creature had that air of deliberate presence, of having been created for a reason that human beings were somehow specifically proscribed from understanding. (paragraph 62)

Those who understand the animals, respect them, know their language, and feel for them include the caretakers and the author—and, hopefully, the readers, *after making the tour*. The tour introduces them to 10 caretakers, all of whom respect and love the animals under them. Harrigan goes to great lengths to establish this point and you, the reader, can check it out for yourself (see paragraphs 7, Bonko; 12, Werler; 29, Beard; 36, Berry; and other examples). By the end of the tour we are ready to accept Harrigan's position that the animals are "cognizant" (paragraph 18); that the way we treat them should be "disturbing to human observers" (paragraph 18); that they are misplaced creatures, "kidnapped from their environment and displayed for human profit" (paragraph 20); and that we should keep them "alive for the day when they might be reintroduced into a less rapacious world" (paragraph 16).

The readers have been slowly moved away from the stereotyped manner of looking at a zoo and at animals and are ready for the norms that they will be asked to use in reading "Zoos Who."

Harrigan's technique teaches us two critical lessons about audience-author relationships. A writer who senses a conflict in hierarchy of values must first address this problem, although he or she may not choose an open confrontation. Then the author may be ready to propose his or her norms (purpose or rule) to the reader. In this case, as we have seen, Harrigan's norm is a purpose: Zoos ought to exist for a purpose and we have dehumanized ourselves by subverting the purpose and substituting entertainment and profit.

Harrigan's inversion of the reader's value system was accomplished only through an adroit sequence of vignettes, miniature sketches of caretakers and animals in the different sections of the zoo. This sequencing is a matter of organization, to which we should now turn.

Exercises on the Method of Evaluation and the Audience

1. **At this stage of your preparation can you articulate your norms of evaluation clearly to yourself? Draw up a precise list of these norms, even if you do not intend to express them explicitly in the paper (for instance, if you are doing an expressive, or literary, or persuasive paper).**
   a. **Are these norms clear enough to be understood by the reader?**
   b. **Is your reader likely to grant you these norms? If not, you must establish their validity, either by deriving them from some principles your reader would grant you or by establishing them on independent evidence.**
2. **Is the application of the norms to the object being evaluated clear to the reader?**
   a. **Is the object itself adequately described so that the reader can align the object and the norms?**
   b. **You might try this alignment on a reader.**
3. **Do the norms of evaluation ask the reader to readjust his or her hierarchy of values? If so, do you want this done explicitly or implicitly?**
4. **If this paper is a paper that requires objective proof, have you given careful attention to the deductive or inductive techniques of proof?**
   a. **Ordinarily in an evaluative theme, deductive proof will be used to derive or apply the norms of evaluation.**
   b. **Inductive evidence in an evaluative theme nearly always involves the generalizations made about the object to see if it conforms or does not conform to the norm.**
   c. **In either case, you might want to refer back to Chapter 5, "Explaining and Proving," to refresh your memory on these matters. This stage of your paper preparation could require considerable field, library, or personal analytic work.**

ORGANIZATION OF EVALUATION THEMES

With organization we come to the *essay* section of the communication triangle, the fourth set of issues that we outlined in Figure 12.1 at the beginning of the chapter.

In an overall sense, all three of the essays have a similar organizational format and all three derive from the basic principles of all evaluation: the positing of the norm, the application of the norm to the object, and the resulting evaluation. The spot remover article first posits the norms in the introductory paragraphs and then applies them to the objects in turn, evaluating each as the norms are applied. The student, after a brief introduction, posits his norms for education in paragraph 4, and then presents the object in juxtaposition with the norms, and the evaluation follows as naturally as the conclusion of a syllogism follows from the first two premises. We have already examined the two large structures of the article about the Texas zoos, but it might be useful to take a more careful look at the smaller structures operating within these two frameworks.

To explain the organization of "Life Behind Bars," it might be useful to present an outline of the sections, with paragraphs listed at the ends of the lines (see next page).

We examined the relationship between the main body of the article and "Zoos Who" when we talked about the reader issues of adjusting a hierarchy of values and acceptance of the norms. Now let us take a brief look at the interior structure of the two macrostructures.

The interior structure of the inset is indicated by the author: "The zoos are listed more or less in order of preference" (paragraph 3a). This is the same order as in the second part of the spot-remover article, when the editors moved from the most preferred to the least preferred.

The interior structure of the main body of the essay, however, is more complex. The introduction and the conclusion (both of which take place at night, in contrast to the body, which takes place in the mornings), establish the tone and the theme. The theoretical statement of the theme comes when Harrigan talks to Werler, the director of the zoo. But the practical justification of this statement occurs in the body of the essay, the detailed tour through the five main sections of the zoo and, more importantly, the acquaintance with the caretakers and their favorites.

The interior organization of the main body seems to be framed by the two most sympathetic caretakers, Beard and Sweeney, and their favorites, Albert the tiger and Hans the elephant. There is little doubt that Sweeney is the most sympathetically treated of all the caretakers. In a sense she is the climax of the story and her handling of Hans is beautifully told. After Sweeney and Hans, we are again ready for night and the restatement of the theme.

Structure of "Life Behind Bars"

    I.   Introduction (1–21)
        A. The mini-tour—Bonko, the night watchman (1–11)
        B. Werler, the administrator (12–21)

```
┌─────────────────────────────────┐
│          Zoos Who               │
│                                 │
│     Norms (1a–3a)               │
│     Brownsville (4a–5a)         │
│     San Antonio (6a–7a)         │
│     Fort Worth (8a–9a)          │
│     Houston (10a–11a)           │
│     Dallas (12a–13a)            │
└─────────────────────────────────┘
```

    II.   Body (22–79)
        A. Cats
            1. Beard and Albert the Tiger (22–35)
            2. Conner and the snow leopard (34–35)
        B. Birds: Berry and the cock-of-the-rock chick (36–43)
        C. Primates
            1. Mendieta and Kamaka (44–48)
            2. Fisher and the orangs (49–50)
            3. Grissom and Vanilla (51–60)
        D. Reptile house (preceded by another small tour): McLain and the pythons (61–70)
        E. Elephants: Sweeney and Hans (71–79)

    III.   Conclusion (80)

Exercises on Organizing the Theme

    There really are only two basic issues in organizing the ordinary theme of evaluation. One concerns the introduction and the other the body of the material.

1. Does the introduction make clear the importance of the evaluation to be presented? Has necessary background material been omitted?
2. Are the three major elements of the body clear to the reader?
    a. Is the *object* presented at the most advantageous time in the essay? If a sort of dramatic method of presentation is desired, it might be presented before the norms.
    b. Are the norms clear to the audience? Sometimes, especially in expository papers, they must be presented first and even justified before proceeding with the presentation of the object and the

evaluation itself. At other times, norms are best left implicit, so that the reader can supply them.

c. Is the application of the norms to the object clear to the reader? Sometimes, of course, the presentation of the norms and the presentation of the object allow the reader to draw his or her own conclusions. Such strategy is often effective with quite intelligent and informed readers. At other times, however, the opposite is the case: the evaluation must be presented at the outset in most precise terms, repeated in the body of the essay, and reiterated in the conclusion. This strategy is needed if the material is quite difficult or if the readers are not too informed on the issue.

THE STYLE OF EVALUATING

Much has been written about the style of evaluative writing, mostly focusing on the presence of "loaded" words, words that indicate a bias or subjective position. The assumption behind much of this analysis is that ordinary prose shouldn't evaluate and that, consequently, when "value" words do make their way into writing, something underhanded, even immoral, is taking place. Hopefully, this entire chapter has given you a different attitude toward evaluation and expository themes that evaluate.

It is true, though, that evaluating does call on some language resources that are not conspicuous in other types of prose. There have to be some loaded words, even in the most neutral scientific and informative prose when evaluation is going on. The spot remover article certainly should not be labeled flaming oratory or yellow journalism. Yet it says of the best spot remover found in the experiments: "Labeled as eye irritant and combustible." And the second ranked remover, Brush Top Handy Applicator Super Spot Remover, is labeled as "combustible, harmful or fatal if swallowed, and having a harmful vapor." These are not nice words; and the product was judged "suitable for use only on fabrics that solvents will not harm." Most likely, the manufacturers of this product felt that this is not neutral prose.

Let us look at some of the characteristics of evaluative pieces. The first, and probably the major factor determining the style of any evaluation, is the aim of the discourse. Scientific and expository evaluations tend to be similar to the tone and style of the article on the spot remover; it is restrained, precise, and informative. Expressive, literary, and persuasive evaluations can be emotional, however, sometimes even intense and passionate.

Harrigan's article is an interesting combination of the informative and the persuasive, with even a strand of the expressive. Consequently, it might be worthwhile to look at some of the rather arresting features of his style.

Anthologized in a textbook like this, Harrigan's article may strike you as unusual, even mildly bizarre. But it is characteristic of the type of journalism in the magazine in which it originally occurred. The writing is mildly sophisticated—notice the large number of vocabulary items listed in the prereading activity. Not only is the diction somewhat discriminating, so also is the theme of value-system inversion that is worked out. In other words, although the essay may initially strike you as unconventional, it is really conventional *for the magazine and the audience it addresses*. The other two samples, in their own ways, are also conventional. The salutatorian address follows the conventions of high school graduations but still manages to be effective. And the spot remover assessment adheres carefully to the conventions of publications of this sort.

The style of "Life Behind Bars," which comes across so effectively, is closely bound up with the method of evaluation and with the organizational pace of the article. As was pointed out earlier, the hierarchy of values of the reader is challenged slowly but relentlessly in the movement of the main body of the essay. The world of the caretaker and the animals (and the author) is vividly and consistently contrasted to the world of visitors of the zoo. The confrontation of the two worlds allows Harrigan to muster a number of different stylistic devices to reenforce the evaluation. Place, time, nature, characters, miniplots, personification and depersonification, symbols, and other elements are combined to construct each world.

The two worlds occupy different settings. One is the *natural* and original habitations of the animals, the velds, kopjes, rain forests, islands, expansive enclosures, and ranges of hundreds of miles. The other is *artificial*, sprayed concrete fake rock, sentimental sculptures, Muzak, constricted environments, rows of cinder-block or chain-link cages, oil drums, stage scenery, and so on.

The two worlds, nature and artifice, move in different time dimensions. The real world is the world of the night and the early morning, the time of the caretakers and the cared-for animals, and the time of the author's tours. The artificial, consuming world of the visitors to the zoo is the hot noon and afternoon.

We have already referred to the cast of characters of the worlds. They make up the ultimate inverted subject and object actors and patients in the overturned hierarchy of values that Harrigan is constructing. And these characters act out miniplots that symbolize the themes of the essay; they illustrate the love and respect of the caretakers for the animals. And the animals are the *people* in the minidramas.

At the end all of these elements of the two worlds have become symbols of Harrigan's theme. Possibly the most dominant and recurring symbol of the inversion of the two worlds is the continual reference to "removing the fecal," as the caretakers call it. It is repulsive to the visitors; but there is a distinct progression in the attitudes of the caretakers. Bonko, the night watchman, doesn't "care about working with the monkeys at all. They're too dirty, for one thing. You never know when one of em's gonna hit you alongside the head with a load of crap" (paragraph 11). Harrigan sees "removing the fecal" as the "basic thing that goes on in a zoo" (paragraph 22). Beard, in charge of the tigers, compares the job to changing the diaper of a child (paragraph 26). And Mendieta almost completely reverses the attitude of Bonko and of the visitors to the zoo. Harrigan tells us:

> He was rubbing with a rag at a dark spot on his shirt where a chimpanzee named Kamaka had just scored a hit with his own by-products. "In the morning he'll throw carrots or biscuits at me," Mendieta said, sounding hurt, "but shit he seldom throws anymore." (paragraph 46)

Perhaps nothing more dramatically symbolizes the differences between two worlds. It is in the style finally that the opposition can most clearly be seen. But the logic of the evaluation, the organization of the entire piece, in fact all of the elements of the essay support each other in carrying out the contrast.

Exercises on the Style of an Evaluative Theme

Many of the exercises and questions on style of the previous chapters, especially in the chapters on the aims of writing, will be applicable here. Depending on your purpose, you might refer to these exercises. But some questions about style usually recur in evaluation themes. Let us focus on a few of the most important.

1. *Loaded words.* We distinguished between two types of loaded words in the text. There are the emotionally loaded words that apply to the evaluation and there are the words that are used in the description of the object, which themselves might have emotional connotations. The examples given of the latter include "combustible," "fatal if swallowed," and "having a harmful vapor." These words can be defended, even in an expository paper, because they are verifiable by the reader. To use the term we used in Chapter 11, they are *operationally definable.* The emotionally loaded words that accompany the evaluation are justifiable if the evaluation has been carried out according to the terms of the writer-reader contract, given the type of paper being written. Check for both types of loaded words in your paper, and draw up lists of the two types of words.

2. *Purpose.* These two types of loaded words will be handled quite differently, depending on the purpose of the paper.

   a. If the paper is an expository paper, the descriptive terms ought to be carefully defined initially. The loaded terms ought to accompany the evaluation only at the time of the evaluation.

   b. If the paper is literary, expressive, or persuasive, the loaded terms ought to be exploited for the aim of the paper. If the paper is persuasive, has the loaded language of the ethical and the pathetic arguments been exploited? (On these terms, see Chapter 3 if you have forgotten their stylistic implications.) Two of the three samples analyzed in the chapter are exemplary in this respect.

3. *Graphics.* Have you given any thought to the use of graphics in your paper? Pictures of the object, charts, sketches, and other tools often enhance an evaluation theme.

Exercises on Evaluating

1. Turn back to page 245 and reread the review of the play that appeared on Broadway in 1972. As you read it, try to isolate the evaluative elements in it from the descriptive or narrative or even classificatory elements. Then answer the following questions.

   a. Would you say that all readers of this review (originally intended for a New York audience) would look upon the play with the same reactions the author had? Would you characterize this as a *subjective* or an *objective* assessment? Or would you rather go with a view that it might be *intersubjective*, that is, a healthy segment of the readers of a New York daily might be inclined to accept the assumptions on which the author relied for his inferences and would find the play unacceptable on these grounds?

   b. What assumptions has the author made in his derogatory evaluations? Go through the piece and attempt to isolate the assumptions that the author expects his readers to grant him. For example, it seems obvious that he expects a program printer to give the audience an accurate listing of scenes and songs; that "some sort of meaningful entertainment" must emerge from the "narrative segments" the author indicates; that he clearly finds a "homosexual enthusiasm" in performance and in text a "tasteless" element (at least in this play); and others. Which of these assumptions would you be prepared to grant the author?

     Which of the evaluations seem to be made on the basis of assumptions not made clear (at least implicitly) in the article? Has the author told the reader why the musical disaster was *drab* or *pallid*? Why is *Heathen* the "ugliest production of many seasons," why is it "scenically misdesigned," and why is it "ludicrously costumed"? Is it possible that the author expects the reader to have general norms for drabness, for pallidness, and for the ugly, the scenically misdesigned, and ludicrous costuming? Do you think the average reader has such norms? Would these norms agree with those of the author, generally speaking?

   c. What do you think of the style of this piece? Make a list of the loaded words that might not appear in a news story about the same item.

    d. What do you think is the purpose or what are the purposes of this piece? Do you think some persuasion is involved? In other words, do you think the author is trying to deter some potential customers from wasting their money on *Heathen*? Is the author also trying to entertain? Would some readers find this review amusing? Does the amusement contribute to making other purposes more palatable? If you feel there is a persuasiveness to the piece, is it assisted by the entertaining devices, particularly of the style?

    e. What is the organizational structure of the piece? The middle paragraphs do not follow an obvious sequence. Would the effect of the review change if paragraph 2 were to be placed after the next two paragraphs? Or if paragraphs 6, 7, and 8 were to be placed before 4 and 5?

    The first and last paragraphs seem to frame the rest of the material, in the sense of giving a view of the whole before presenting the parts. Could this be viewed as an organization drawing from the descriptive nature of the presentation, that is, the whole-part relationship? Explain.

    f. Write a paper based on some of the preceding considerations. The paper would be a *descriptive* analysis of an evaluative review. Write it for your fellow students as audience.

2. Write a paper analyzing some of your own value judgments. Consider the object being evaluated (or at least the aspect of the object under consideration), the locus of the value (subjective or objective), the faculty you use in making the evaluation, and the assumptions you use as the norms for evaluation. Ask yourself if your assumption uses a purpose or a rule as norm. You can apply this paper to your moral judgments, your political judgments, your assessments of friends, or your evaluations of automobiles, football teams, and so on.

3. Analyze the Ten Commandments from the following perspectives: range of audience, source of obligation, rule or purpose, norm, hierarchy of values, faculty of evaluation.

4. Analyze the value system implicit in your college's grading system. Consider some of the following points: range of audience (people expected to accept the evaluations), the kind of norm involved (rule or purpose), the method by which the norm is applied to the particular instance (theme, test, or performance), and hierarchy of values.

5. Analyze the evaluations present in the descriptive passage by Solzhenitsyn in Chapter 9. Consider the same points we have been suggesting in the preceding questions: range of audience, possible antagonistic audiences, kinds of norms involved (rule or purpose), methods by which the norms are applied to the particular instances under consideration (the Czarist and the Soviet prison systems), and the hierarchy of values implicit in the piece.

6. Analyze the value system of a local politician (campus, city, state, nation) from the same perspectives suggested in the preceding question.

Writing Evaluations

PROBLEMS WITH EVALUATION THEMES.   Most themes that attempt to evaluate something are an interesting combination of inductive and deductive themes—two types considered in the chapter on "Proving and Explaining." Even when the theme is not an expository theme with explicit logical patterns, the logic of deduction and induction will be implied. The reason for this is simple: evaluation always implies the application of a general norm (purpose or rule) to a particular object. The application of the general norm to the particular case is a matter of a deductive sequence in logic. But the matter of proving that the general principle applies to the particular case quite frequently involves the making of some statements about the particular object; frequently this involves making generalizations from particulars, and this is an inductive procedure.

You therefore usually face two processes. First, you must get your audience to accept the norm you will use. Second, you must apply that norm to the individual case in point. This frequently involves a careful inspection of the object to be evaluated, and often this inspection takes up the major portion of the essay. Thus, Harrigan's statement of his norms for evaluating zoos is a fairly short part of the essay. Most of the essay consists in applying the norms to the five zoos (see pages 356–363).

CAMPUS TOPICS.   You could evaluate many aspects of your college life: your instructors, the available programs, the cultural activities, the social facilities, the food, the dormitory facilities, the guidance procedures, the counseling facilities, the library, the athletic teams, and so on. You might want to evaluate the usefulness of fraternities or of intercollegiate athletic events; or the effectiveness of the student assembly, the administrative officers, the janitorial staff, the board of regents, or others.

One very useful approach in evaluations is the contrastive approach: contrast one professor with another, one team with another, one library with another, or one institution with another.

1. If you decide to do a "proof" evaluation, that is, a thesis paper that will incorporate convincing evidence of your evaluation(s), then the aim of the evaluation paper is to prove by logical procedures. This may involve the careful inductive or deductive (or both) procedures of these types of themes as they were presented in the chapter on "Proving and Explaining."
2. If you decide to do a persuasive evaluation, then all the evaluative material should be incorporated into the machinery of the persuasive techniques examined in Chapter 3. And, of course, more stylistic options are available in persuasion than in the restrained language of expository writing.
3. Your instructor may allow you to do an expressive evaluation, one in which the

evaluations are much more personal and subjective and the language changes considerably (as in a journal).

CITY AND STATE TOPICS. In the city in which you live, or in your college town, many objects are simply begging to be evaluated. Indeed, you may evaluate them informally in oral language with your friends every day. The day-care, hospital, transportation, recreation, and other types of facilities might be evaluated. Local restaurants might be evaluated or local night life or local cultural activities. Current politicians, police, the school system, the town-gown relationships, job possibilities for summer and winter, ethnic relationships in the city, hiring practices in the town—all of these and many other facets of local life can be looked into. On a larger scale, most of these can be transferred to the state perspective and evaluated.

It is important to note that the same *problems* considered before any of the writing topics are still relevant here. And the same types of themes (expository, persuasive, expressive, even literary) suggested in (1), (2), and (3) above are also possible here.

DISCOURSE TOPICS. At the beginning of this chapter, we used three particular evaluation themes, which we examined for examples of the principles of evaluation. But, instead of objects for *classificatory* analysis, as they were then, the same three themes might be objects of *evaluation*. Using your own norms of what you think would be successful evaluations, you might assess these three pieces as successful (or not, or partially successful) evaluations.

Other types of evaluations are possible. You might evaluate your local newspaper (possibly by using a comparison-contrast technique again). You might evaluate a novel or a short story you recently read (or you might evaluate one of the short fiction pieces used in the chapter on narration). You might evaluate a weekly periodical you use regularly (maybe compare *Newsweek* and *Time*—but the comparison must incorporate evaluative elements). You might evaluate your college newspaper. You might evaluate one of the textbooks you are using. Since this is the last chapter in this textbook you might evaluate this text as a book that is supposed to help you learn to write intelligent prose.

Index

The Issues and Strategies in the Aims and Modes

	Writer Issue	Reader Issue	Subject-Matter Issue
AIMS			
Self-Expression	The self	Others	The world
Persuading	Ethical proof	Pathetic proof	Logical proof
Informing	Factuality	Surprise value	Comprehensiveness
Explaining and Proving	Definitions	Rules of interpretation	Evidence
Exploring	Searching for a new answer	Raising questions	Testing the new answer
Writing Poems and Stories	Creativity and craft	Esthetic pleasure and interpretation	Plot: Complication, conflict, resolution
MODES			
Description	Point of view	Selectivity principle	Object to be described
Narration	Persona of author and narrator	Purpose of the narration	Event or sequence to be narrated
Defining and Dividing	Choice of techniques for defining and dividing	Purpose of the definition-division	Class(es) to be defined or divided
Evaluation	Faculties evaluating Method of evaluation Hierarchy of values	Acceptance of the norm Hierarchy of values	Object(s) to be evaluated Locus of value